THE CLAY SANSKRIT LIBRARY
FOUNDED BY JOHN & JENNIFER CLAY

EDITED BY

RICHARD GOMBRICH

WWW.CLAYSANSKRITLIBRARY.COM
WWW.NYUPRESS.ORG

First Edition 2005.

The Clay Sanskrit Library is co-published by
New York University Press
and the JJC Foundation.

Further information about this volume
and the rest of the Clay Sanskrit Library
is available on the following websites:
www.claysanskritlibrary.com
www.nyupress.org

ISBN 0-8147-8288-4

Artwork by Robert Beer.
Cover design by Isabelle Onians.
Layout & typesettting by Somadeva Vasudeva.
Printed in Great Britain by St Edmundsbury Press Ltd,
Bury St Edmunds, Suffolk, on acid-free paper.
Bound by Hunter & Foulis, Edinburgh, Scotland.

THE HEAVENLY EXPLOITS

BUDDHIST BIOGRAPHIES FROM THE DIVYĀVADĀNA

VOLUME ONE

EDITED AND TRANSLATED BY
JOEL TATELMAN

NEW YORK UNIVERSITY PRESS
JJC FOUNDATION
2005

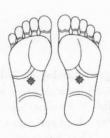

Library of Congress Cataloging-in-Publication Data
Tripiṭaka. Sūtrapiṭaka. Avadāna. Divyāvadāna.
English & Sanskrit. Selections.
The heavenly exploits / edited and translated by Joel Tatelman.
p. cm. – (The Clay Sanskrit library)
Includes bibliographical references and index.
ISBN 0-8147-8288-4 (cloth : alk. paper)
I. Tatelman, Joel.
II. Title. III. Series.
BQ1562.E5T38 2005
294.3'823–dc22 2004018035

CONTENTS

A *sandhi* grid is printed on the inside of the back cover

SANSKRIT ALPHABETICAL ORDER

Vowels:	*a ā i ī u ū ṛ ṝ ḷ ḹ e ai o au ṃ ḥ*
Gutturals:	*k kh g gh ṅ*
Palatals:	*c ch j jh ñ*
Retroflex:	*ṭ ṭh ḍ ḍh ṇ*
Labials:	*p ph b bh m*
Semivowels:	*y r l v*
Spirants:	*ś ṣ s h*

GUIDE TO SANSKRIT PRONUNCIATION

a	b*u*t
ā, â	r*a*ther
i	s*i*t
ī, î	f*ee*
u	p*u*t
ū, û	b*oo*
ṛ	vocalic *r*, American p*ur*dy or English p*re*tty
ṝ	lengthened *ṛ*
ḷ	vocalic *l*, ab*le*
e, ê, ē	m*a*de, esp. in Welsh pronunciation
ai	b*i*te
o, ô, ō	r*o*pe, esp. Welsh pronunciation; Italian s*o*lo
au	s*ou*nd
ṃ	*anusvāra* nasalizes the preceding vowel
ḥ	*visarga*, a voiceless aspiration (resembling English *h*), or like Scottish lo*ch*, or an aspiration with a faint echoing of the preceding vowel so that *taiḥ* is pronounced *taih*^{i}

k	lu*ck*
kh	blo*ckh*ead
g	*g*o
gh	bi*gh*ead
ṅ	a*n*ger
c	*ch*ill
ch	mat*chh*ead
j	*j*og
jh	aspirated *j*, he*dgeh*og
ñ	ca*ny*on
ṭ	retroflex *t*, *t*ry (with the tip of tongue turned up to touch the hard palate)
ṭh	same as the preceding but aspirated
ḍ	retroflex *d* (with the tip of tongue turned up to touch the hard palate)
ḍh	same as the preceding but aspirated
ṇ	retroflex *n* (with the tip of tongue turned up to touch the hard palate)
t	French *t*out
th	ten*t h*ook

d	*d*inner
dh	guil*dh*all
n	*n*ow
p	*p*ill
ph	u*ph*eaval
b	*b*efore
bh	a*bh*orrent
m	*m*ind
y	*y*es
r	trilled, resembling the Italian pronunciation of *r*
l	*l*inger
v	*w*ord
ś	*sh*ore
ṣ	retroflex *sh* (with the tip of the tongue turned up to touch the hard palate)
s	hi*ss*
h	*h*ood

CSL PUNCTUATION OF ENGLISH

The acute accent on Sanskrit words when they occur outside of the Sanskrit text itself, marks stress, e.g. Ramáyana. It is not part of traditional Sanskrit orthography, transliteration or transcription, but we supply it here to guide readers in the pronunciation of these unfamiliar words. Since no Sanskrit word is accented on the last syllable it is not necessary to accent disyllables, e.g. Rama.

The second CSL innovation designed to assist the reader in the pronunciation of lengthy unfamiliar words is to insert an unobtrusive middle dot between semantic word breaks in compound names (provided the word break does not fall on a vowel resulting from the fusion of two vowels), e.g. Maha·bhárata, but Ramáyana (not Rama·áyana). Our dot echoes the punctuating middle dot (·) found in the oldest surviving samples of written Sanskrit, the Ashokan inscriptions of the third century BCE.

The deep layering of Sanskrit narrative has also dictated that we use quotation marks only to announce the beginning and end of every direct speech, and not at the beginning of every paragraph.

CSL PUNCTUATION OF SANSKRIT

The Sanskrit text is also punctuated, in accordance with the punctuation of the English translation. In mid-verse, the punctuation will not alter the *sandhi* or the scansion. Proper names are capitalized, as are the initial words of verses (or paragraphs in prose texts). Most Sanskrit metres have four "feet" *(pāda):* where possible we print the common *śloka* metre on two lines. The capitalization of verse beginnings makes it easy for the reader to recognize longer metres where it is necessary to print the four metrical feet over four or eight lines. In the Sanskrit text, we use French *Guillemets* (e.g. *«kva saṃcicīrṣuḥ?»*) instead of English quotation marks (e.g. "Where are you off to?") to avoid confusion with the apostrophes used for vowel elision in *sandhi*.

Sanskrit presents the learner with a challenge: *sandhi* ("euphonic combination"). *Sandhi* means that when two words are joined in connected speech or writing (which in Sanskrit reflects speech), the last letter (or even letters) of the first word often changes; compare the way we pronounce "the" in "the beginning" and "the end."

In Sanskrit the first letter of the second word may also change; and if both the last letter of the first word and the first letter of the second are vowels, they may fuse. This has a parallel in English when a nasal consonant is inserted between two vowels that would otherwise coalesce: "a pear" and "an apple." Sanskrit vowel fusion may produce ambiguity. The chart at the back of each book gives the full *sandhi* system.

Fortunately it is not necessary to know these changes in order to start reading Sanskrit. For that, what is important is to know the form of the second word without *sandhi* (pre-*sandhi*), so that it can be recognized or looked up in a dictionary. Therefore we are printing Sanskrit with a system of punctuation that will indicate, unambiguously, the original form of the second word, i.e., the form without *sandhi*. Such *sandhi* mostly concerns the fusion of two vowels.

In Sanskrit, vowels may be short or long and are written differently accordingly. We follow the general convention that a vowel with no mark above it is short. Other books mark a long vowel either with a bar called a macron (*ā*) or with a circumflex (*â*). Our system uses the macron, except that for initial vowels in *sandhi* we use a circumflex to indicate that originally the vowel was short, or the shorter of two possibilities (*e* rather than *ai*, *o* rather than *au*).

When we print initial *â*,	before *sandhi* that vowel was *a*
î or *ê*,	*i*
û or *ô*,	*u*
âi,	*e*

âu,	*o*
ā,	*ā* (i.e., the same)
ī,	*ī* (i.e., the same)
ū,	*ū* (i.e., the same)
ē,	*ī*
ō,	*ū*
āi,	*ai*
āu,	*au*

’, before *sandhi* there was a vowel *a*

FURTHER HELP WITH VOWEL SANDHI

When a final short vowel (*a*, *i* or *u*) has merged into a following vowel, we print ’ at the end of the word, and when a final long vowel (*ā*, *ī* or *ū*) has merged into a following vowel we print ” at the end of the word. The vast majority of these cases will concern a final *a* or *ā*.

Examples:

What before *sandhi* was *atra asti* is represented as *atr’ âsti*

atra āste	*atr’ āste*
kanyā asti	*kany” âsti*
kanyā āste	*kany” āste*
atra iti	*atr’ êti*
kanyā iti	*kany” êti*
kanyā īpsitā	*kany” ēpsitā*

Finally, three other points concerning the initial letter of the second word:

(1) A word that before *sandhi* begins with *ṛ* (vowel), after *sandhi* begins with *r* followed by a consonant: *yatha” rtu* represents pre-*sandhi* *yathā ṛtu*.

(2) When before *sandhi* the previous word ends in *t* and the following word begins with *ś*, after *sandhi* the last letter of the previous word is *c* and the following word begins with *ch*: *syāc chāstravit* represents pre-*sandhi syāt śāstravit*.

(3) Where a word begins with *h* and the previous word ends with a double consonant, this is our simplified spelling to show the pre-*sandhi*

form: *tad hasati* is commonly written as *tad dhasati*, but we write *tadd hasati* so that the original initial letter is obvious.

COMPOUNDS

We also punctuate the division of compounds (*samāsa*), simply by inserting a thin vertical line between words. There are words where the decision whether to regard them as compounds is arbitrary. Our principle has been to try to guide readers to the correct dictionary entries.

EXAMPLE

Where the Deva·nágari script reads:

कुम्भस्थली रक्षतु वो विकीर्णसिन्दूररेणुर्द्विरदाननस्य।
प्रशान्तये विघ्नतमश्छटानां निष्ठ्यूतबालातपपल्लवेव॥

Others would print:

kumbhasthalī rakṣatu vo vikīrṇasindūrareṇur dviradānanasya /
praśāntaye vighnatamaśchaṭānāṃ niṣṭhyūtabālātapapallaveva //

We print:

Kumbha|sthalī rakṣatu vo vikīrṇa|sindūra|reṇur dvirad'|ānanasya
praśāntaye vighna|tamaś|chaṭānāṃ niṣṭhyūta|bāl'|ātapa|pallav" êva.

And in English:

May Ganésha's domed forehead protect you! Streaked with vermilion dust, it seems to be emitting the spreading rays of the rising sun to pacify the teeming darkness of obstructions.

Padma·gupta's "Nava·sáhasanka and the Serpent Princess" I.3

INTRODUCTION

"THE HEAVENLY EXPLOITS" *(Divy'/âvadāna)*, is a collection of thirty-eight Buddhist biographical stories. These saints' legends authenticated local Buddhist traditions and dramatized the importance of moral discipline, karma, religious giving and especially the power of faith and devotion.

As a genre of Buddhist literature, the Sanskrit term *avadāna* denotes a narrative of an individual's religiously significant deeds. Often these constitute full-fledged religious biographies, sometimes of eminent monks, sometimes of ordinary lay disciples, sometimes of several members of a single family. Avadánas ("Exploits") portray, frequently with thematic, narrative and poetic sophistication, human actions that embody the truths propounded in Buddhist doctrine (Dharma) and discipline (Vínaya).

They also offer tantalizing glimpses, more or less transformed by imagination, of Indian Buddhism "on the ground": social customs, economic practices, political conditions, family life, relations between the sexes, and religious practices, both Buddhist and non-Buddhist. Avadánas range from formulaic tales that rather mechanically dramatize the workings of karma and the efficacy of faith and devotion, to fantastic adventure stories, to the erudite art of virtuoso poets. As do our modern novels and short stories, these narratives offer something for every taste.

The literature draws on diverse sources: actual lives (though we can only infer this), the numerous accounts of the life of the Buddha, including tales of his former births, biographical accounts in the canonical literature, and a vast pan-Indian store of secular story-literature.

Indian Buddhists composed "Exploits" from about the second century BCE. to at least the thirteenth century CE. Thereafter Buddhists elsewhere in Asia continued the tradition in both classical and vernacular languages. In particular, from the fourteenth century to the seventeenth century the Newars of Nepal produced an extensive Avadána literature in Sanskrit that adapted earlier Indian works. In India and beyond, "Exploits" also inspired important bodies of narrative painting. In Nepal, Sri Lanka and Southeast Asia, even now these narratives and their like contribute to the vernacular literatures. Indeed, in some traditional contexts, such stories carried the force of legal precedent.

A tripartite narrative structure, inherited from the earliest Játakas and common to all Avadánas, reflects the always present concern to portray the "effects of deeds" from one birth to another. First a "story of the present," then a "story of the past" and finally a "juncture," or key, where the narrator at last identifies characters in the story of the past as former births of characters in the story of the present. For the story of the past, some versions substitute a "prediction": typically, at the conclusion of the story, the protagonist vows to attain Awakening, and the Buddha confirms the fulfillment of the vow and reveals the name by which that Awakened individual will be known. Clearly, then, an Avadána requires a special kind of "omniscient" narrator, one whose awareness penetrates aeons into the past and future. Thus only the Buddha or an arhat, a disciple who has attained Awakening, can act as narrator. It is enough, though, to affirm that the story has been handed down by a succession of Awakened teachers. The precursors and models for all this are two: the Játakas and the stories of others' past births which the Buddha tells in various canonical Sutras.

The earliest Avadánas, like the Thera·vadin *Apadāna* and the Mula·sarvásti·vadin *Sthavir'/âvadāna*, are brief autobiographical verse narratives attributed to individual monks and nuns. As in most Játakas, the story of the present functions principally as a narrative frame within which to tell the story of the past. These collections represent a late stage in the old pan-Indian tradition of "ascetic poetry." The legends that grew up around the figure of the great Mauryan emperor Ashóka (mid-third century B.C.E), the earliest of which also predate the Common Era, provided another narrative model for the growing "Exploits" literature. The literary form here is prose mixed with verse, but in contrast to the early verse *avadāna*s, while these legends do not ignore Ashóka's previous births, they devote far more attention to his present life, particularly to his exercise of power, his family problems, his relations with the monk Upagúpta and his religious activities.

The anonymous stories included in the first to second century, extra-canonical anthologies like the *Avadāna/śataka* and *Karma/śataka* as well as many in the *Divy'/âvadāna*, are similarly composed in prose interspersed with verses. The prose passages in turn are of two broad types: a "canonical" or "religious" style that frequently incorporates or imitates the hieratic, oral, repetitive style of the early canonical works, and a "folktale" or "secular" style distinctive for its short, matter-of-fact descriptions and terse, often evocative dialogue. Over all, the stories of the *Avadāna/śataka* are the shortest, most fomulaic and "mechanical," those of the *Karma/śataka* less so and those of the *Divy'/âvadāna* the most developed and diverse.

Many *Avadāna/śataka* stories retain the emphasis on past-life narratives, fewer *Karma/śataka* stories, until, in many *Divy'/âvadāna* narratives, the proportion is quite reversed. This is certainly true of the stories presented in the present volume. The Avadánas of Koti·karna, Purna and Makándika reduce the story of the past almost to nothing, while the story of the present becomes the *raison d'être* of the tale. Attention has shifted away from deeds in previous births to actions in the here and now. As in all "Exploits", doctrinally, the story of the past still represents the morally significant deed (karma) and the story of the present its consequences (karma·vipáka). At the same time, concentrating on the protagonist's life in the present enabled the authors to draw more freely upon the rich tradition of popular literature—and, we must assume, on characteristic circumstances in the lives of actual men and women.

Since it is a Játaka, or story of one of the Buddha's previous births—also called a Bodhi·sáttvavadána, or "Exploits of the future Buddha"—the *Sudhana/kumār'/âvadāna* reverses this structure, with a very brief "tale of the present" introducing, and a rapid "identification of the characters" concluding, the Buddha's narrative of his life as Prince Súdhana of Hástina·pura, and with the bulk of the story set in an ancient, though very recognizable, epoch.

While the *Divy'/âvadāna* as we have it may have been compiled as late as the eighth century, many of the stories may date back to the beginning of the Common Era. These narratives derive largely from the monastic codes of the Mula·sarvásti·vadins (21 stories) and other Buddhist ordination traditions (nine stories), but also adapt or incorporate canonical Sutras (chapters 2, 3, 17, 34) and passages from the works of classical Sanskrit poets (chapters 26–29, 36, 38).

The *Divy'|âvadāna* portrays the adventures, both realistic and fantastical, of wealthy merchants who became Buddhist monks (chapters 1, 2, 8, 35), recounts the familial, religious and political conflicts in the lives of Indian kings (chapters 3, 26–29, 37) and describes the origins of the "Wheel of Life," now well known in the West from Tibetan paintings (chapter 21). We also find the conversion of Mara, the Buddhist personification of death and desire (chapter 26), and two versions of the history of Súdhana and Mano·hara, one of the few true love stories in Buddhist literature (chapters 30, 31), and we learn both what happens when a Brahman wanderer offers his daughter to the Buddha (chapter 36) and when an outcaste woman falls in love with an eminent monk (chapter 33). We encounter, too, women who study Buddhist scripture in their own homes and others who, out of love or jealousy, cast spells, blind their own sons or commit mass murder (chapters 27, 33, 36).

The early Avadánas offer many tales of adventurous seafaring merchants who later achieve eminence as Buddhist monks. The first two *Divy'|âvadāna* stories, "The Exploits of Purna" (*Pūrṇ'|âvadāna*) and "The Exploits of Koti·karna" (*Koṭīkarṇ'|âvadāna*)—which are also the first two stories in the present volume—are fine examples of this type of story. While the several *Divy'|âvadāna* manuscripts diverge widely from one another, these are the only two of the thirty-eight stories that appear in all the manuscripts and always in the same place, as the first and second story respectively.

The *Pūrṇ'|âvadāna*, *Divy'|âvadāna* 2, is a folktale of a type widespread in India and indeed throughout the world, which chronicles a clever young man's rise from despised illegitimate "son of a slave girl" to merchant prince and favorite of the king. It is also a Buddhist religious biography that dramatizes the momentous choice between a worldly and a spiritual career and that chronicles how the "apostle of Shrona·parántaka" brought both the Buddha's teaching and the Buddha himself to his native land. We learn about sibling rivalry, about attitudes toward women, about mercantile rivalries and the guild system, about religious practices among both laity and ordained and about how the Buddha's teaching spread throughout the Indian subcontinent.

The very structure of the story combines canonical and commentarial sources to create a narrative that unites the doctrinal detail and authority of the latter with the human dimension and religious practical detail of the former. We learn what scriptures were popular and of the diverse psychic powers attributed to Awakened individuals. And of course we learn of the enormous impact, for good and ill, of morally significant human actions. And so long as we remember that "Exploits" deal not with historical fact but with religious and narrative meaning we can come away from our reading with a profound appreciation for a literary genre that has played an essential part in Buddhist self-understanding for more than two thousand years.

We find many of the same features in the first *Divy'|âvadāna* story, the *Koṭikarṇāvadāna*, though orchestrated and apportioned differently. Here we accompany Koti·karna on the overseas trading voyage where he encounters those from his own city, now reborn as hungry ghosts, who recount to him their own *avadānas* and induce him to intercede on their behalf with the family members they had wronged. We also witness conflicts between the hero's religious avocation and his filial piety on the one hand, and between the healthy piety of the common man and woman and the self-serving skepticism of greedy government officials on the other. And, lest any reader get the wrong idea, as in all this literature, we see again and again that moral virtue and religious observance lead to material wealth.

In the third story, the *Sudhana/kumār'/âvadāna*, we have a Buddhist version of the heroic quest. We meet the wise and virtuous prince, his father, the ignorant and corruptible king, the monarch's evil, ambitious minister, and the exotic, beautiful woman who becomes the prince's wife and, in the end, after many trials, his queen. And of course there is the prince's long and dangerous quest, a film version of which would tax the special-effects technologies of even the wealthiest modern studios. That the principal action takes place in a past life—in contrast to the other stories in this first volume—makes it doctrinally permissible to narrate not only a "Buddhist love story" but one with a happy ending, for such a conclusion does not affect the overarching doctrine that the true goals are renunciation, overcoming the passions, and Awakening.

Our fourth story, *Divy'/âvadāna* 36, the *Mākandik'/âvadāna*, expands a terse account in the canonical literature into a full-fledged narrative by splicing the story of the

Brahmanical ascetic who offers his nubile daughter to the Buddha onto a version of the pan-Indian legend of King Rudráyana, famous for his political intrigues and amorous entanglements, which is then continued in *Divy'|âvadāna* 37. As in the Purna and Koti·karna stories, family relationships are very much part of the drama. And as in the Purna story, but to a much greater degree, we cannot escape the theme of female wickedness. There the petty jealousies of Purna's aunts deprive him of his patrimony; here the malignant jealousy of a co-wife leads to mass murder. Nor must we omit to mention the man-eating sirens of Sri Lanka! Yet for all that, the Buddhist ethos does not accommodate tragedy in the Greek or Shakespearean sense.

But I wish to introduce, not analyze, these stories. For that, the reader can follow up leads in the bibliography and on the Clay Sanskrit Library website (www.claysanskritlibrary.org). In sum and in conclusion, I invite you to read the stories, in Sanskrit, in English, in both. And may four lead to many others.

The Sanskrit Texts of the Stories

The editions of these stories are based on the following sources.

Koṭikarṇ' | âvadāna (*Divy' | âvadāna 1*): Cowell-Neil 1886:1–24; Dutt-Shastri 1942–50:III, 4, 159–193; Bailey 1950:167–173; Vaidya 1–14.

Pūrṇ'|âvadāna (*Divy'|âvadāna* 2): Cowell-Neil 24–55, Bailey 1950: 174–183, Vaidya 15–33.

Sudhana|kumār'|âvadāna (*Divyāvadāna 30*): Cowell-Neil 435-461; Dutt-Shastri 122–159; Bailey 1951: 93–99; Speyer 1902: 355–356.

Mākandik'|âvadāna (*Divy'|âvadāna* 36): Cowell-Neil 515–544, Vaidya 446–464.

Reference Works

Edgerton, Franklin. 1953. [BHSG & BHSD] *Buddhist Hybrid Sanskrit Grammar and Dictionary.* Vol. I: Grammar. Vol. II: Dictionary. London: Yale University Press. Reprint, Kyoto: Rinsen Book Co., 1985. [Essential reference, especially the dictionary, for Buddhist Sanskrit.]

Bagchi, S., ed. 1967–70. [MSV] *Mūlasarvāstivāda-vinayavastu.* 2 vols. Buddhist Sanskrit Texts 16. Darbhanga, Bihar: The Mithila Institute. [Reprint, without critical apparatus, of Dutt-Shastri 1942–50.]

Bailey, D.R. Shackleton. 1951. "Notes on the *Divyāvadāna* Part II", *Journal of the Royal Asiatic Society,* new series, vol. 83, pp. 82–102. [Textcritical notes on *Divyāvadāna* 3–7, 9-10, 17, 23–25, 30–31.]

— 1950. "Notes on the *Divyāvadāna* Part I", *Journal of the Royal Asiatic Society,* new series, vol. 82, pp. 166–184. [Textcritical notes on *Divyāvadāna* 1–2.]

Cowell, E.B. & Neil, R.A., ed. 1886. [CN] *The Divyāvadāna: A Collection of Early Buddhist Legends.* Cambridge: Cambridge University Press. Reprint, Delhi & Vārāṇasī: Indological Book House, 1987. [The *editio princeps;* reprinted in Vaidya 1959a without critical apparatus and with various corrections, omissions and errors, but with new versions of Dívyavadána 26–29 and 33, based on the critical editions of Mukhopadhyaya 1954, 1963.]

Dutt, Nalinaksha & Shastri, Shiv Nath, ed. 1942–50. *The Gilgit Manuscripts,* vol. III, parts 1–4 (Mūlasarvāstivāda-vinayavastu). Shrinagar and Calcutta. [Contains less than scrupulous editions of *Divyāvadāna* 1 and 30, and other narratives, based on a sixth century Sanskrit manuscript and the Tibetan translation.]

Huber, Édouard, 1906. "Études de littérature bouddhique V: Les sources du *Divyāvadāna*", *Bulletin de l'École Française d'Extrême-Orient 6,* pp. 1–43, 335–340.

Speyer, Jacob Samuel, 1902. "Critical Remarks on the Text of the *Divyāvadāna*", *Wiener Zeitschrift für die Kunde des Morgenlandes 16,* pp. 103–130, 340–361.

VAIDYA, P.L., ed. 1959a. [V] *Divyāvadānam.* Buddhist Sanskrit Texts 20. Darbhanga, Bihar: The Mithila Institute. [Deva·nágari reprint, without critical apparatus, and with small omissions in many chapters, of COWELL & NEIL's original edition, with chapters 26–29 and 33 based on the critical editions of MUKHOPADHYAYA 1954 and 1963.]

1
THE STORY OF SHRONA KOTI·KARNA

Oṃ namaḥ
sarva|buddha|bodhi|sattvebhyaḥ!

Buddho bhagavāñ Śrāvastyāṃ viharati sma Jeta|vane 'nāthapiṇḍadasy' ārāme. tasmin samaye 'śm'|âparāntake Vāsava|grāmake Balaseno nāma gṛha|patiḥ prativasaty āḍhyo mahā|dhano mahā|bhogo vistīrṇa|viśāla|parigraho Vaiśravaṇa|dhana|pratispardhī.

Tena sādṛśāt kulāt kalatram ānītam. sa tayā sārdhaṃ krīḍati ramate paricārayati. tasya krīḍato ramamāṇasya paricārayato na putro na duhitā. so 'putraḥ putr'|âbhinandī Śiva|Varuṇa|Kubera|Śakra|Brahm'|ādīn āyācate. ārāma|devatāṃ vana|devatāṃ śṛṅgāṭaka|devatāṃ bali|pratigrāhikāṃ devatām. saha|jāṃ saha|dharmikāṃ nity'|ânubaddhām api devatām āyācate.

Asti c' âiṣa loka|pravādo yad āyācana|hetoḥ putrā jāyante duhitaraś c' êti. tac ca n' âivam. yady evam abhaviṣyad ek'|âikasya putra|sahasram abhaviṣyat tad|yathā rājñaś cakra|vartinaḥ. api tu trayāṇāṃ sthānānāṃ saṃmukhī|bhāvāt putrā jāyante duhitaraś ca. katameṣāṃ trayāṇām? mātā|pitarau raktau bhavataḥ saṃnipatitau, mātā kalyā bhavati' rtumatī, gandharvaś ca pratyupasthito bhavati. eṣāṃ trayāṇāṃ sthānānāṃ saṃmukhī|bhāvāt putrā jāyante duhitaraś ca. sa c' âivam āyācana|paras tiṣṭhati.

Om! Homage
to all the Buddhas and Bodhi·sattvas!

THE LORD BUDDHA was staying at Shravásti, in Prince Jeta's Grove in Anátha·píndada's park. At that time, in Ashma·parántaka,* in the village of Vásava,* there lived a householder named Bala·sena. He was wealthy, having a great deal of money and other possessions. His properties were extensive. Indeed his wealth rivalled that of the God of Wealth, Vaishrávana himself.

Bala·sena took a wife from a family similar to his own. He enjoyed himself with her, made love to her and otherwise dallied with her. Although he enjoyed himself, made love and otherwise dallied with her, neither son nor daughter was born. Having no son and being enthusiastic about sons, he entreated Shiva, Váruna, Kubéra, Shakra, Brahma and the other gods as well as the garden deity, the forest deity, the deity who dwells at the crossroads and the deity who accepts offerings. He entreated, too, his hereditary tutelary deity, who shared his traditions.

It is popularly said that as a result of such entreaties sons are born and daughters, too. But this is not so. If it were, every man would have a thousand sons, just like a universal monarch. Rather, it is due to a conjunction of three conditions that sons are born and daughters, too. What three? The father and mother, full of passion, unite; the mother is healthy and in her fertile period; and a being in the intermediate stage between births is at hand. These are the three conditions through the conjunction of which sons are born

Anyatamaś ca sattvaś carama|bhavikaḥ, carit'|âiṣī, gṛhīta|mokṣa|mārgo 'bhimukho nirvāṇe, bahir|mukhaḥ saṃsārāt, anarthikaḥ sarva|bhava|gati|cyuty|upapattiṣu, antima|deha|dhārī, anyatamasmād deva|nikāyāc cyutvā, tasyāḥ prajā|patyāḥ kukṣim avakrāntaḥ.

1.5 Pañc' āveṇikā dharmā ekatye paṇḍita|jātīye mātṛ|grāme. katame pañca? raktaṃ puruṣaṃ jānāti, viraktaṃ jānāti. kālaṃ jānāti' rtuṃ jānāti. garbham avakrāntaṃ jānāti. yasya sakāśād garbho 'vakrāmati, taṃ jānāti. dārakaṃ jānāti, dārikāṃ jānāti. saced dārako bhavati, dakṣiṇaṃ kukṣiṃ niśritya tiṣṭhati. saced dārikā bhavati, vāmaṃ kukṣiṃ niśritya tiṣṭhati.

S" ātta|man'|ātta|manāḥ svāmina ārocayati, «diṣṭy" ārya|putra vardhasva! āpanna|satv" âsmi saṃvṛttā! yathā ca me dakṣiṇaṃ kukṣiṃ niśritya tiṣṭhati, niyataṃ dārako bhaviṣyati!»

So 'py ātta|man'|ātta|manā udānam udānayati: «apy ev' âhaṃ cira|kāl'|âbhilaṣitaṃ putra|mukhaṃ paśyeyam. jāto me syān n' âvajātaḥ. kṛtyāni me kurvīta. bhṛtaḥ pratibibhṛyāt. dāyādyaṃ pratipadyeta. kula|vaṃśo me cira|sthitiko

and daughters too.* Nevertheless, Bala·sena continued to devote himself to entreating the gods.

Now, there was a certain being who was about to take up his last existence, who desired to follow a spiritual career, who had grasped the way to liberation, who had turned toward nirvana and away from the cycle of birth and death. With no desire for any state of existence, for any realm of rebirth, for any falling from higher to lower life-forms, or for any form of rebirth, and who would be bearing his last body, descended from a certain company of deities to enter that fertile womb.

A woman born with intelligence possesses five special 1.5
qualities. What are these five? She recognizes a man who is impassioned and one who is not. She recognizes the right time for lovemaking, that is to say, when she is fertile. She recognizes when the new life has entered her womb, and from whose presence. She knows whether the child will be a boy or a girl: if a boy, it attaches itself to the right side of the womb; if a girl, to the left.

Bala·sena's wife, her mind transported by delight, declared to her husband, "Thanks be to heaven, noble one! You have cause for congratulation! I am with child—and since it has attached itself to the right side of my womb, it will certainly be a boy!"

Bala·sena, also transported by delight, made this solemn, joyous declaration: "With luck I shall look upon the face of the son for whom I have yearned for such a long time! May the son born to me not be misbegotten! May he carry on my business! When I have supported him may he in turn support me. May he inherit from me. My family's lineage

bhaviṣyati. asmākaṃ c' âpy atīta|kāla|gatānām alpaṃ vā prabhūtaṃ vā dānāni dattvā puṇyāni kṛtv" âsmākaṃ nāmnā dakṣiṇām ādekṣyati. ‹idaṃ tayor yatra yatr' ôpapannayor gacchator anugacchatv iti.›»

Āpanna|sattvāṃ ca tāṃ viditv" ôpari|prāsāda|tala|gatām ayantritāṃ dhārayati śīte śīt'|ôpakaraṇair uṣṇa uṣṇ'|ôpakaraṇair* vaidya|prajñaptair āhārair n' âtitiktair n' âtyamlair n' âtilavaṇair n' âtimadhurair n' âtikaṭukair n' âtikaṣāyais tikt'|âmla|lavaṇa|madhura|kaṭuka|kaṣāya|vivarjitair āhāraiḥ, hār'|ârdha|hāra|vibhūṣita|gātrīm apsarasam iva nandana|vana|vicāriṇīṃ mañcān mañcaṃ pīṭhāt pīṭhaṃ carantīm anavatarantīm adhar imāṃ* bhūmim.

Na c' âsyāḥ kiṃ|cid amanojña|śabda|śravaṇaṃ yāvad eva garbhasya paripākāya. s" âṣṭānāṃ vā navānāṃ vā māsānām atyayāt prasūtā. dārako jāto abhirūpo darśanīyaḥ prāsādiko gauraḥ kanaka|varṇaś chattr'|ākāra|śirāḥ pralamba|bāhur vistīrṇa|viśāla|lalāṭaḥ saṃgata|bhrūr uttuṅga|nāso ratna|pratyuptikayā karṇikayā āmuktay" âlaṃkṛtaḥ.

1.10 Balasenena gṛha|patinā ratna|parīkṣakā āhūy' ôktāḥ, «bhavantaḥ, ratnasya mūlyaṃ kuruta» iti. «na śakyate ratnasya mūlyaṃ kartum» iti. dharmatā khalu yasya ratnasya na śakyate mūlyaṃ kartuṃ tasya koṭī|mūlyaṃ kriyate. te kathayanti, «gṛha|pate, asya ratnasya koṭī mūlyam» iti.

will endure for a long time! Moreover, when I have become a has-been, he shall give gifts, great or small, perform meritorious deeds and make over to me the benefit of having done so, saying, 'Wherever my parents are reborn, may this merit follow them.'"

On learning that she was with child, Bala·sena maintained his wife—now ensconced at her ease on the flat roof of their mansion—with everything needed* in cold or heat, with foods, recommended by a physician, that were neither too bitter, too sour, too salty, too sweet, too pungent nor too astringent, with a diet free from all those flavors. Adorned with pearl necklaces of sixty-four and one hundred and eight strings, she was like a nymph wandering in the Garden of Delight in Indra's heaven who makes her way from one couch to another and from one seat to another without descending to this earth below.

Nor did Bala·sena's wife hear a single displeasing sound during the entire course of her pregnancy. After the passage of eight or nine months, she gave birth. It was a boy. He was well formed, good-looking, handsome, with a pale golden complexion, a large, round head, long arms, a broad brow, eyebrows that joined and a prominent nose. In addition, he was adorned with an earring, set with a jewel, fastened on him.

The householder Bala·sena summoned assayers of gem- 1.10
stones, whom he instructed, "Gentlemen, assess the value of this jewel." They said they were unable to assess the jewel's value. It was customary, for a jewel the value of which was impossible to assess, to assign a worth of ten million.

Tasya jñātayaḥ saṃgamya samāgamya trīṇi saptakāny ekaviṃśati|divasāni vistareṇa jātasya jāti|mahaṃ kṛtvā nāma|dheyaṃ vyavasthāpayanti. «kiṃ bhavatu dārakasya nāma?» iti.

Jñātaya ūcuḥ, «ayaṃ dārakaḥ koṭī|mūlyayā ratna|pratyuptikay" āmuktayā jātaḥ Śravaṇeṣu ca nakṣatreṣu. bhavatu dārakasya Śroṇaḥ Koṭīkarṇa iti nāma.»

Yasminn eva divase Śroṇaḥ Koṭīkarṇo jātas tasminn eva divase Balasenasya gṛha|pater dvau preṣya|dārakau jātau. ten' âikasya «Dāsaka iti» nāma|dheyaṃ vyavasthāpitam aparasya «Pālaka iti.»

Śroṇaḥ Koṭīkarṇo 'ṣṭābhyo dhātrībhyo 'nupradatto dvābhyām aṃśa|dhātrībhyāṃ dvābhyāṃ krīḍanikābhyāṃ dvābhyāṃ mala|dhātrībhyāṃ dvābhyāṃ kṣīra|dhātrībhyām. so 'ṣṭābhir dhātrībhir unnīyate vardhyate kṣīreṇa dadhnā nava|nītena sarpiṣā sarpir|maṇḍen' ânyaiś c' ôttapt'|ôttaptair upakaraṇa|viśeṣaiḥ. āśu vardhate hrada|stham iva paṅkajam.

1.15 Sa yadā mahān saṃvṛttas tadā lipyām upanyastaḥ saṃkhyāyāṃ gaṇanāyāṃ mudrāyām uddhāre nyāse nikṣepe vastra|parīkṣāyāṃ vāstu|parīkṣāyāṃ dāru|parīkṣāyāṃ ratna|parīkṣāyāṃ hasti|parīkṣāyām aśva|parīkṣāyāṃ kumāra|parīkṣāyāṃ kumārikā|parīkṣāyām. so 'ṣṭāsu parīkṣās' ûdghāṭako vācakaḥ paṇḍitaḥ paṭu|pracāraḥ saṃvṛttaḥ.

So the assayers declared, "Householder, this jewel is worth ten million."

Bala·sena's relatives arrived and assembled and for three weeks, that is twenty-one days, they celebrated the newborn's birth festivities, after which they were settling on him a name: "What shall this boy be named?"

The relatives declared, "This boy was born wearing an earring set with a gemstone worth ten million and under the stars of the constellation of Shrávana—let his name, therefore, be Shrona Koti·karna."*

And on the very day that Shrona Koti·karna was born, two sons were born to servants of the householder Bala·sena. To one he gave the name Dásaka, "Servitor," to the other the name Pálaka, "Protector."

Shrona Koti·karna was handed over to eight nurses—two to carry him about, two to play with him, two to keep him clean and two wet nurses. Raised by these eight nurses, who nourished him with milk, yoghurt, fresh butter, clarified butter and its by-products, and other pure and choice foods, Shrona Koti·karna grew rapidly, like a lotus in a lake.

When he grew older, Shrona was tutored in letters, count- 1.15
ing, arithmetic, hand-calculation, accounting and ways of solving mathematical problems. He also learned to inspect and assess textiles, real estate, lumber, jewels, elephants, horses and young men and women. Shrona became an expounder, an explainer, a scholar, an expert in the evaluation of these eight.*

Tasya pitrā trīṇi vāsa|gṛhāṇi māpitāni, haimantikaṃ graiṣmikaṃ vārṣikam. trīṇy udyānāni māpitāni, haimantikaṃ graiṣmikaṃ vārṣikam. trīṇy antaḥ|purāṇi pratyupasthāpitāni jyeṣṭhakaṃ madhyamaṃ kanīyasam. sa upari|prāsāda|tala|gato niṣpuruṣeṇa tūryeṇa krīḍati ramate paricārayati.

Balaseno gṛha|patir nityam eva kṛṣi|karm'|ânta udyuktaḥ. sa Koṭīkarṇas taṃ pitaraṃ paśyati nityaṃ kṛṣi|karm'|ânta udyuktam. sa kathayati, «tāta, kasy' ârthe tvaṃ nityam eva kṛṣi|karm'|ânte udyuktaḥ.»

Sa kathayati, «putra, yathā tvam upari|prāsāda|tala|gato niṣpuruṣeṇa tūryeṇa krīḍasi ramasi paricārayasi, yady aham apy evam eva krīḍeyaṃ rameyaṃ paricārayeyam, na cirād ev' âsmākaṃ bhogās tanutvaṃ parikṣayaṃ paryādānaṃ gaccheyuḥ.»

Sa saṃlakṣayati, «mam' âiv' êyaṃ codanā kriyate.» sa kathayati, «tāta, yady evam, paṇyam ādāya deś'|ântaraṃ gacchāmi. mahā|samudram avatarāmi.»

1.20 Pitā kathayati, «putra, tāvantaṃ me ratna|jātam asti, yadi tvaṃ tila|taṇḍula|kola|kulattha|nyāyena ratnāni paribhokṣyase, tath" âpi me ratnānāṃ parikṣayo na syāt.»

Sa kathayati, «tāta, anujānīhi mām, paṇyam ādāya mahā|samudram avatarāmi» iti. Balasenena tasy' âvaśyaṃ nirbandhaṃ jñātv" ânujñātaḥ. Balasenena gṛha|patinā Vāsava|grāmake ghaṇṭ" âvaghoṣaṇaṃ kāritam. «yo yuṣmākam

Shrona's father had three mansions constructed, one for each season: winter, summer and monsoon. He also had three parks constructed, one for each season. And he established three harems to wait upon Shrona, Senior, Intermediate and Junior. Ensconced on the flat roof of his mansion, with music played only by women, the youth enjoyed himself with, made love to and dallied with them.*

As for the householder Bala·sena, he applied himself constantly to farming. Koti·karna, observing this, asked him why.

Bala·sena replied, "Son, you ensconce yourself on the flat roof of your mansion, with music played only by women, enjoying yourself with, making love to and otherwise dallying with them—if I, too, were to enjoy myself, in just the same way, soon our wealth would dwindle, shrink and finally be exhausted."

Shrona Koti·karna reflected, "This reproof is made for my benefit." Then he said, "Father, if that is so, I shall take trade-goods and leave for foreign lands. I shall cross the great ocean."

His father replied, "Son, so extensive are the riches I 1.20
possess that if you were to use them as you would sesame seeds, rice grains, jujube berries or lentils, even then would they not be exhausted."

Said Shrona Koti·karna, "Father, grant me permission to take trade-goods and cross the great ocean." The householder Bala·sena, realizing his son's intractable insistence, granted his permission. Bala·sena then had the proclamation bell rung in the village of Vásava and announced: "He

utsahate Śroṇena Koṭīkarṇena sārtha|vāhena sārdham aśulken' âgulmen' âtara|paṇyena mahā|samudram avatartuṃ, sa mahā|samudra|gamanīyaṃ paṇyaṃ samudānayatu.» pañcabhir vaṇik|śatair mahā|samudra|gamanīyaṃ paṇyaṃ samudānītam.

Balaseno nāma gṛha|patiḥ saṃlakṣayati, «kīdṛśena yānena Śroṇaḥ Koṭīkarṇo yāsyati?» sa saṃlakṣayati, «sacedd hastibhiḥ, hastinaḥ su|dū|rakṣyā dur|bharāś ca. aśvā api su|dū|rakṣyā dur|bharāś ca. gardabhāḥ su|poṣāḥ smṛtimantaś ca. gardabha|yānena gacchatu.» iti.

Sa pitr" āhūy' ôktaḥ, «putra, na tvayā sārthasya purastād gantavyaṃ n' âpi pṛṣṭhataḥ. yadi balavān cauro bhavati sārthasya purastān nipatati. dur|balo bhavati pṛṣṭhato nipatati. tvayā sārthasya madhye gantavyaṃ na ca te sārthikebhyaḥ so 'rtho vaktavyaḥ.»

Dāsaka|Pālakāv apy abhihitau, «putrau, yuvābhyāṃ na kena|cit prakāreṇa Śroṇaḥ Koṭīkarṇo moktavyaḥ» iti.

1.25 Ath' âpareṇa samayena Śroṇaḥ Koṭīkarṇaḥ kṛta|kautuka|maṅgala|svasty|ayano mātuḥ sakāśam upasaṃkramya pādayor nipatya kathayati, «amba, gacchāmi. avalokitā bhava, mahā|samudram avatarāmi.» sā ruditum ārabdhā. sa kathayati, «amba, kasmād rodiṣi?»

among you who has the will to accompany the caravan-leader Shrona Koti·karna across the ocean, free from customs duties, escort charges and freight fees, let him gather together trade-goods for transport across the great ocean." Five hundred merchants gathered together trade-goods for transport across the great ocean.

The householder Bala·sena reflected, "On what sort of vehicle should Shrona Koti·karna travel?" He reflected further. "If on elephants, elephants are very difficult to guard and difficult to maintain. Horses too are very difficult to guard and difficult to maintain. Donkeys are easy to feed and have good memories. Let him travel by donkey-cart."

Calling Shrona Koti·karna, he said, "Son, travel neither at the head of the caravan nor at the rear. If a thief is strong, he will attack the front of the caravan; if he is weak, he will attack the rear. So travel in the middle of the caravan and do not reveal to the other merchants your reason for doing so."

Bala·sena also spoke to Dásaka and Pálaka: "My sons, under no circumstances are you two to let Shrona Koti·karna go off on his own."

Some time later Shrona Koti·karna, having performed 1.25
the rituals to ensure a lucky and successful journey, went to see his mother. He threw himself at her feet and said, "Mama, I'm leaving. Watch over me—I'm crossing the great ocean." She began to cry. Koti·karna said, "Mama, why are you crying?"

Mātā s'|âśru|durdina|vadanā kathayati, «putra, kadā|cid ahaṃ putrakaṃ punar api jīvantaṃ drakṣyāmi?» iti. sa saṃlakṣayati, «ahaṃ maṅgalaiḥ saṃprasthitaḥ. iyam īdṛśam amaṅgalam abhidhatte.» sa ruṣitaḥ kathayati, «amba, ahaṃ kṛta|kautūhala|maṅgala|svasty|ayano mahā|samudraṃ saṃprasthitaḥ. tvaṃ c' ēdṛśāny amaṅgalāni karoṣi. apāyān kiṃ na paśyasi?» iti.

Sā kathayati, «putra, kharaṃ te vāk|karma niścāritam. atyayam atyayato deśaya. apy ev' âitat karma tanutvaṃ parikṣayaṃ paryādānaṃ gacchet.» sā ten' âtyayam atyayataḥ kṣamāpitā.

Atha Śroṇaḥ Koṭīkarṇaḥ kṛta|kautūhala|maṅgala|svasty|ayanaḥ śakaṭair bhārair moṭaiḥ piṭakair uṣṭrair gobhir gardabhaiḥ prabhūtaṃ samudra|gamanīyaṃ paṇyam āropya mahā|samudraṃ saṃprasthitaḥ. so 'nupūrveṇa grāma|nagara|nigama|pallī|pattaneṣu cañcūryamāṇo mahā|samudra|taṭam anuprāptaḥ. nipuṇataḥ sāmudraṃ yāna|pātraṃ pratipādya mahā|samudram avatīrṇo dhana|hārakaḥ. so 'nuguṇena vāyunā ratna|dvīpam anuprāptaḥ. tena tatr' ôpaparīkṣy' ôpaparīkṣya ratnānāṃ tad vahanaṃ pūritaṃ tadyathā tila|taṇḍula|kola|kulatthānām. so 'nuguṇena vāyunā saṃsiddha|yāna|pātro Jambudvīpam anuprāptaḥ. sa sārthas tasminn eva samudra|tīre āvāsitaḥ.

His mother, her face gloomy and tearful, replied, "Son, when shall I again see my little boy alive?" Koti·karna reflected, "I am setting out with efforts to ensure good luck. She says such unlucky things!" He then spoke in anger, "Mama, I have performed the rituals to ensure a lucky and successful journey and am about to set out—and you are creating such bad luck! Do you not see the misfortunes that will result?"

She replied, "Son, you have committed the offense of harsh speech. Confess the transgression so that the karma may dwindle, shrink and finally be exhausted." Shrona Koti·karna then asked her to pardon his transgression.

Then, having again performed the rituals to ensure a lucky and successful journey, Shrona Koti·karna employed carts, bales, bundles, baskets, camels, cattle and donkeys to load the abundant trade-goods for transport across the ocean. Then he set out for the great ocean. Passing through villages, cities, towns and hamlets, in due course he reached the seashore. There he had an ocean vessel skillfully fitted out, then embarked on the great ocean to acquire wealth. A favorable wind brought Shrona to Ratna·dvipa, "Island of Jewels." After fully investigating the island, Shrona filled the ship with jewels as if they were sesame seeds, rice grains, jujube berries or lentils. Then a favorable wind brought him back to India, his ship safe and sound. The caravan disembarked on the very stretch of seashore from which it had embarked.

Asau Śroṇaḥ Koṭīkarṇo 'pi sārtha|vāho Dāsaka|Pālakāv ādāya sārtha|madhyād ekānte 'pakramya āyaṃ vyayaṃ ca tulayitum ārabdhaḥ. paścāt ten' âsau Dāsako 'bhihitaḥ, «Dāsaka, paśya, sārthaḥ kiṃ karoti» iti. sa gato yāvat paśyati sārthaṃ suptaṃ so 'pi tatr' âiva suptaḥ.

1.30 Dāsakaś cirāyat' îti kṛtvā, Pālako 'bhihitaḥ. «Pālaka, paśya, sārthaḥ kiṃ karoti» iti. sa gato yāvat paśyati sthorāṃ lardayantaṃ sārthaṃ so 'pi sthorāṃ lardayitum ārabdhaḥ.

Dāsakaḥ saṃlakṣayati, «Pālakaḥ sārtha|vāhaṃ śabdāpayiṣyati.» Pālako 'pi saṃlakṣayati, «Dāsakaḥ sārtha|vāhaṃ śabdāpayiṣyati» iti. sa sārthaḥ sarātrim eva sthorāṃ lardayitvā saṃprasthitaḥ. so 'pi gāḍha|nidr"|âvaṣṭabdhaḥ śayitaḥ.

Sa sārthas tāvad gato yāvat prabhātam. te kathayanti, «bhavantaḥ, kva sārtha|vāhaḥ?»

«Purastād gacchati.» purastād gatvā pṛcchanti, «kva sārtha|vāhaḥ?»

«Pṛṣṭhata āgacchati.» pṛṣṭhato gatvā pṛcchanti, «kva sārtha|vāhaḥ?»

1.35 «Madhye gacchati.» madhye gatvā pṛcchanti, «yāvat tatr' âpi n' âsti?»

Dāsakaḥ kathayati, «mama buddhir utpannā, Pālakaḥ sārtha|vāhaṃ śabdāpayiṣyati.»

Pālako 'pi kathayati, «mama buddhir utpannā, Dāsakaḥ sārtha|vāhaṃ śabdāpayiṣyati» iti.

The caravan-leader Shrona Koti·karna took Dásaka and Pálaka, went off some distance from the middle of the caravan and began to tally income and expenditure. After some time, Shrona told Dásaka, "Dásaka, go see what the caravan is doing." Dásaka went and, when he saw that the caravaners were sleeping, right then and there he too went to sleep.

Shrona, noticing that Dásaka was taking a long time, told 1.30
Pálaka, "Pálaka, go see what the caravan is doing." Pálaka went and, when he saw that the company was unloading cargo, he too began to unload cargo.

Dásaka thought, "Pálaka will call the caravan-leader." Pálaka, for his part, thought, "Dásaka will call the caravan-leader." That very night the company finished unloading the cargo and departed. As for Shrona Koti·karna, a great drowsiness overcame him and he fell fast asleep.

The company travelled on until daybreak. Then the merchants asked, "Sirs, where is the caravan-leader?"

"He's travelling up at the front." They went to the front and asked, "Where is the caravan-leader?"

"He's bringing up the rear." They went to the rear and asked, "Where is the caravan-leader?"

"He's travelling in the middle." They went to the middle 1.35
and asked, "Is the caravan-leader not here either?"

Dásaka replied, "I thought that Pálaka was going to call the caravan-leader."

As for Pálaka, he declared, "I thought that Dásaka was going to call the caravan-leader."

«Bhavantaḥ, na śobhanaṃ kṛtaṃ yad asmābhiḥ sārtha|vāhaś choritaḥ. āgacchata nivartāmaḥ»

Te kathayanti, «bhavantaḥ, yadi vayaṃ nivartiṣyāmaḥ, sarva ev' ânayena vyasanam āpatsyāmaḥ. āgacchata, kriyā|kāraṃ tāvat kurmaḥ. tāvan na kenacic Chroṇasya Koṭīkarṇasya mātā|pitṛbhyām ārocayitavyaṃ yāvad bhāṇḍaṃ pratiśāmitaṃ bhavati» iti. te kriyā|kāraṃ kṛtvā gatāḥ.

1.40 Śroṇasya Koṭīkarṇasya mātā|pitṛbhyāṃ śrutam, «Śroṇaḥ Koṭīkarṇo 'bhyāgataḥ» iti. tau pratyudgatau. «kva sārtha|vāhaḥ?»

«Madhya āgacchati.» madhye gatvā pṛcchataḥ, «kva sārtha|vāhaḥ?» iti.

Te kathayanti, «pṛṣṭhata āgacchati.» pṛṣṭhato gatvā pṛcchataḥ, «kva sārtha|vāhaḥ?»

«Purastād gacchati» iti. tais tāvad ākulī|kṛtau yāvad bhāṇḍaṃ pratiśāmitam. tataḥ paścāt te kathayanti, «amba, tāta, vismṛto 'smābhiḥ sārtha|vāhaḥ» iti.

Tābhyām eka āgatya kathayati, «ayaṃ Śroṇaḥ Koṭīkarṇo 'bhyāgataḥ» iti. tasya tāv abhisāraṃ dattvā pratyudgatau na paśyataḥ. apara āgatya kathayati, «amba, tāta, diṣṭyā vardhasv' âyaṃ Śroṇaḥ Koṭīkarṇo 'bhyāgataḥ» iti. tasya tāv abhisāraṃ dattvā pratyudgatau na paśyataḥ. tau yāvan na kasya cit punar api śraddadhātum ārabdhau.

1.45 Tābhyām udyāneṣu deva|kuleṣu chattrāṇi ghaṇṭā vyajanāni sthāpitāni yeṣv akṣarāṇi likhitāni, «yadi tāvac Chroṇaḥ Koṭīkarṇo jīvati, laghv āgamaya. atha cyutaḥ kāla|gatas tasy' âiva gaty|upapatti|sthānāt sthān'|ântara|viśeṣatāyai.» tau śokena rudantāv andhī|bhūtau.

"Sirs, it is no fine thing we have done, abandoning the caravan-leader. Come! Let us turn back!"

They replied, "Sirs, if we turn back, through this imprudence we shall all suffer calamity. Come! Let us make an agreement: No one is to inform Shrona Koti·karna's parents until the merchandise has been stored away." All accepted the agreement and went on.

Shrona Koti·karna's parents heard that he had arrived. 1.40
They went to meet him. "Where is the caravan-leader?"

"He's travelling in the middle of the caravan." They went to the middle and asked, "Where is the caravan-leader?"

The men replied, "He's travelling at the rear." They went to the rear and asked, "Where is the caravan-leader?"

"He's travelling at the front." The men confused the two until the merchandise was stored away. Then, however, they told them, "Mother, father—we forgot the caravan-leader."

Then one man came and told them, "Shrona Koti·karna has arrived." They rewarded him, went to meet their son, but did not see him. Another fellow came and said, "Mother, father! Thanks be to heaven! You have cause for congratulations—Shrona Koti·karna has arrived!" The couple rewarded him, went to meet their son, but did not see him. After that, they began to believe no one.

In parks and temples, they placed parasols, bells and fans 1.45
on which they had inscribed the words "If Shrona Koti·karna is only alive, bring him back quickly! If he has departed this life, bring him from his present realm and mode of rebirth* to another, better one." Weeping with grief, the couple went blind.

Śroṇaḥ Koṭīkarṇaḥ sārtha|vāho 'pi sūry'|âṃśubhiḥ spṛṣṭa ātāpitaḥ prativibuddho yāvat sārthaṃ na paśyati. n' ânyatra gardabha|yānam eva. sa taṃ gardabha|yānam abhiruhya saṃprasthitaḥ rātrau ca vātena pravāyatā vālukayā mārgo vyapoḍhaḥ pihitaḥ. te ca gardabhāḥ smṛtimanto mārgam āghrāy' āghrāya śanair manda|mandaṃ saṃprasthitāḥ. sārtha|vāhaḥ saṃlakṣayati, «kasmād ete śanair manda|mandaṃ gacchanti?» iti kṛtvā pratoda|yaṣṭyā tāḍitāḥ. te saṃbhrāntā ākulī|bhūtāḥ smṛti|bhraṣṭā unmārgeṇa saṃprasthitā yāvad anyatamāṃ śāl'|âṭavīṃ praviṣṭāḥ.

Te tṛṣ"|ārtā vihvala|vadanā jihvāṃ nirṇāmayya gacchanti. tān dṛṣṭvā tasya kāruṇyam utpannam. sa saṃlakṣayati, «yady etān n' ôtsrakṣyāmi, anayena vyasanam āpatsye. ko 'sau nirghṛṇa|hṛdayas tyakta|para|lokaś ca ya eṣāṃ pratoda|yaṣṭiṃ kāye nipātayiṣyati?» tena ta utsṛṣṭāḥ: «ady'|âgreṇa acchinn'|âgrāṇi tṛṇāni bhakṣayata anavamarditāni, pānīyāni pibata anāvilāni, catur|diśaṃ ca śītalā vāyavo vāntu!» iti.

Sa tān utsṛjya padbhyāṃ saṃprasthito yāvat paśyaty āyasaṃ nagaram uccaṃ ca pragṛhītaṃ ca. tatra dvāre puruṣas tiṣṭhati, kālo raudraś caṇḍo lohit'|âkṣa udviddha|piṇḍo loha|laguḍa|vyagra|hastaḥ. sa tasya sakāśam upasaṃkrāntaḥ. upasaṃkramya taṃ puruṣaṃ pṛcchati, «asty atra bhoḥ puruṣa pānīyam» iti. sa tūṣṇīm avasthitaḥ. bhūyas tena pṛṣṭaḥ «asty atra nagare pānīyam» iti. bhūyo 'pi sa tūṣṇīm avasthitaḥ. tena sārtha|vāhena tatra praviśya «pānīyaṃ pānīyam» iti śabdo niścāritaḥ.

Meanwhile, the caravan-leader Shrona Koti·karna, touched and warmed by the sun's rays, awoke, but, except for his donkey-cart, saw no caravan. So he mounted the donkey-cart and set out, but during the night a sandstorm covered and effaced the path. The donkeys, remembering the way, smelled the air constantly and proceeded very slowly and cautiously. The caravan-leader reflected, "Why are these donkeys moving so slowly and hesitantly?" So thinking, he began to beat them with his goad. The donkeys, agitated, became confused, forgot where they were going and proceeded along the wrong path until they entered a forest of Shala trees.

Afflicted by thirst, showing their distress on their faces, tongues hanging out, the donkeys carried on. Seeing them, Koti·karna felt sorry for them. He reflected, "If I do not set these animals free, that unwise course will lead to disaster. What cruel-hearted man would forsake the next world by causing the goad to fall on these animals' bodies?" So Koti·karna set the donkeys free, saying, "From now on eat fresh, uncut, untrampled grass, drink from clear waters and let the cool winds blow on you from all around!"*

After setting the donkeys free, Koti·karna continued until he saw a high and lofty city made of iron. There at the gate stood a man, swarthy, fierce, red-eyed, tall in stature and holding an iron club in his hands. Koti·karna approached him and, having approached, asked, "My good man, is there any water in this place?" The man remained silent. Again he questioned him, "Is there water in this city?" Again the man remained silent. The caravan-leader then entered the place, crying out, "Water! water!"

Yāvat pañca|mātraiḥ preta|sahasrair dagdha|sthūṇā|sadṛśair asthi|yantravad ucchritaiḥ sva|keśa|roma|praticchannaiḥ parvata|saṃnibh'|ôdaraiḥ sūcī|chidr'|ôpama|mukhair anuparivāritaḥ Śroṇaḥ Koṭīkarṇaḥ. te kathayanti, «sārtha|vāha, kāruṇikas tvam. asmākaṃ tṛṣ"|ârtānāṃ pānīyam anuprayaccha.»

1.50 Sa kathayati, «bhavanto 'ham api pānīyam eva mṛgayāmi. kuto 'haṃ yuṣmākaṃ pānīyam anuprayacchāmi?» iti.

Te kathayanti, «sārtha|vāha, preta|nagaram idam. kutaḥ khalv atra pānīyam? ady' âsmābhir dvādaśabhir varṣais tvat|sakāśāt ‹pānīyaṃ pānīyam› iti śabdaḥ śrutaḥ.»

Sa kathayati, «ke yūyaṃ bhavantaḥ kena vā karmaṇ" êh' ôpapannāḥ?»

Ta ūcuḥ, «Śroṇa, duṣ|kuhakā Jāmbudvīpakā manuṣyāḥ. n' âbhiśraddadhāsyasi.»

«Aham, bhavantaḥ, pratyakṣa|darśī. kasmān n' âbhiśraddadhāsye?» te gāthāṃ bhāṣante:

1.55 Ākrośakā roṣakā vayaṃ
matsariṇaḥ kuṭukuñcakā vayam.
dānaṃ ca na dattam aṇv api
yena vayaṃ preta|lokam āgatāḥ.

«Śroṇa, gaccha! puṇya|maheś'|ākhyas tvam. asti kaś cit tvayā dṛṣṭaḥ preta|nagaraṃ praviṣṭaḥ svasti|kṣemābhyāṃ nirgacchan?»

At that moment, five thousand hungry ghosts, resembling scorched pillars and towering skeletons, covered in hair from head to toe, with bellies like mountains and mouths like the eyes of needles, expectantly surrounded Shrona Koti·karna. They said, "Caravan-leader, you are a compassionate man. We are tormented by thirst! Give us water!"

He replied, "Sirs, I, too, am hunting for water. Where 1.50
can I find water to give you?"

Said they, "Caravan-leader, this is a city of hungry ghosts. How could there be water in this place? Just now, for the first time in twelve years, in your presence, we heard the word 'water'."

Koti·karna said, "Who are you, sirs? And what deed led you to be reborn here?"

They replied, "Shrona, the men of India are a skeptical lot. You won't believe us."

"I can see what's before my own eyes. Why shouldn't I believe you?" The hungry ghosts recited this stanza:

Abusive and wrathful were we, 1.55
Envious and stingy were we.
We gave not the smallest gifts:
That's why we have come to the realm of hungry
ghosts.

"Leave this place, Shrona! You are great due to merit acquired in previous births. Have you seen anyone enter a city of hungry ghosts whose good fortune and forbearance enabled him to depart?"

Sa saṃprasthito yāvat ten' âsau puruṣo dṛṣṭaḥ. sa ten' ôktaḥ: «bhadra|mukha, aho bata! yadi tvayā mam' ārocitaṃ syāt, ‹yath" êdaṃ preta|nagaram› iti, n' âham atra praviṣṭaḥ syām.»

Sa ten' ôktaḥ: «Śroṇa, gaccha! puṇya|maheś'|ākhyas tvaṃ yena tvaṃ preta|nagaraṃ praviśya svasti|kṣemābhyāṃ nirgataḥ.»

Sa saṃprasthito yāvad aparaṃ paśyaty āyasaṃ nagaram uccaṃ ca pragṛhītaṃ ca. tatr' âpi dvāre puruṣas tiṣṭhati, kālaś caṇḍo lohit'|âkṣa udviddha|piṇḍo loha|laguḍa|vyagra|hastaḥ. sa tasya sakāśam upasaṃkrāntaḥ. upasaṃkramy' âivam āha, «bhoḥ puruṣa! asty atra nagare pānīyam.» sa tūṣṇīṃ vyavasthitaḥ. bhūyas tena pṛṣṭaḥ, «bhoḥ puruṣa! asty atra nagare pānīyam?» sa tūṣṇīṃ vyavasthitaḥ. tena tatra praviśya «pānīyaṃ pānīyam» iti śabdaḥ kṛtaḥ. anekaiḥ preta|sahasrair dagdha|sthūṇ"|ākṛtibhir asthi|yantravad ucchritaiḥ sva|keśa|roma|praticchannaiḥ parvat'|ôdara|saṃnibh'|ôdaraiḥ sūcī|chidr'ôpama|mukhair anuparivāritaḥ.

1.60 Te kathayanti, «Śroṇa, kāruṇikas tvam. asmākaṃ tṛṣ'|ârtānāṃ pānīyam anuprayaccha.»

Sa kathayati, «aham api bhavantaḥ pānīyam eva mṛgayāmi. kuto 'haṃ yuṣmākaṃ pānīyaṃ dadāmi?» iti.

Te kathayanti, «Śroṇa, preta|nagaram idam. kuto 'tra pānīyam? ady' âsmābhir dvā|daśabhir varṣais tvat|sakāśāt ‹pānīyaṃ pānīyam› iti śabdaḥ śrutaḥ.»

Shrona Koti·karna continued until he came across a man. He said to him, "Alas, good sir! If you tell me, 'This is a city of hungry ghosts,' I will not enter the place."

The man replied, "Go, Shrona! You are great due to merit acquired in previous births. This enabled you to enter a city of hungry ghosts while your good fortune and forbearance enabled you to depart."

Koti·karna continued until he saw another high and lofty city made of iron. There, too, stationed at the gates was a man, swarthy, wild, fierce, red-eyed, tall in stature and holding an iron club in his hands. Koti·karna approached him and having approached, spoke thus: "My good man, is there, in this city, any water?" The man remained silent. Again he questioned him. "My good man, is there, in this city, any water?" The man remained silent. Koti·karna entered the city, calling out, "Water! water!" Many thousands of hungry ghosts, resembling burned pillars and towering skeletons, covered in hair from head to toe, with bellies like mountains and mouths like the eyes of needles, expectantly surrounded him.

They said, "Shrona, you are a compassionate man. We 1.60
are tormented by thirst. Give us water!"

He replied, "Sirs, I, too, am hunting for water. Where do I find water to give to you?"

Said they, "Shrona, this is a city of hungry ghosts. How could there be water in this place? Just now, for the first time in twelve years, in your presence, we heard the word 'water.'"

Sa c' āha, «ke yūyaṃ bhavantaḥ kena vā karmaṇ" êh' ôpapannāḥ?»

Ta ūcuḥ, «Śroṇa, duṣ|kuhakā Jāmbudvīpakā manuṣyāḥ. n' âbhiśraddadhāsyasi.»

1.65 Sa c' āha, «ahaṃ bhavantaḥ pratyakṣa|darśī. kasmān n' âbhiśraddadhāsye.» te gāthāṃ bhāṣante:

Ārogya|madena mattakā
  yauvana|bhoga|madena mattakāḥ.
dānaṃ ca na dattam aṇv api
  yena vayaṃ preta|lokam āgatāḥ.

«Śroṇa, gaccha! puṇya|maheś'|ākhyas tvam. asti kaś cit tvayā dṛṣṭaḥ śruto vā preta|nagaraṃ praviśya svasti|kṣemābhyāṃ jīvan nirgacchan?»

Sa saṃprasthito yāvat ten' âsau puruṣo dṛṣṭaḥ. sa ten' ôktaḥ: «bhadra|mukha, aho bata! yadi tvayā mam' ārocitaṃ syāt, yath" êdaṃ preta|nagaram iti, n' âiv' âham atra praviṣṭaḥ syām.»

Sa kathayati, «Śroṇa, gaccha! puṇya|maheś'|ākhyas tvam. asti kaś cit tvayā dṛṣṭaḥ śruto vā preta|nagaraṃ praviśya svasti|kṣemābhyāṃ jīvan nirgacchan?»

1.70 Sa saṃprasthito yāvat paśyati sūryasy' âsta|gamana|kāle vimānam. tatra catasro 'psaraso 'bhirūpāḥ prāsādikā darśanīyāḥ. ekaś ca puruṣo 'bhirūpo darśanīyaḥ prāsādiko 'ṅgada|kuṇḍala|vicitra|mäly'|ābharaṇ'|ânulepanas tābhiḥ sārdhaṃ

He said, "Who are you, sirs? And what deed led you to be reborn here?"

They replied, "Shrona, the men of India are a skeptical lot. You won't believe us."

Said Shrona, "I can see what is before my own eyes. 1.65
Why shouldn't I believe you?" The hungry ghosts recited this stanza:

Drunk with the intoxication of good health,
Drunk with the intoxication of the pleasures of youth;
We gave not the smallest gifts:
That's why we have come to the realm of hungry ghosts.

"Go, Shrona! You are great due to merit acquired in previous births. Have you ever seen or heard of anyone who entered a city of hungry ghosts and whose good fortune and forbearance enabled him to depart alive?"

Shrona Koti·karna continued until he saw a man. To him he said, "Alas, good sir, if you tell me, 'This is a city of hungry ghosts,' I will certainly not enter the place."

Replied the man, "Go, Shrona! You are great due to merit acquired in previous births. Have you ever seen or heard of anyone who entered a city of hungry ghosts and whose good fortune and forbearance enabled him to depart alive?"

Shrona Koti·karna carried on until, just as the sun was 1.70
setting behind the western mountain, he saw an airborne palace. In it were four heavenly nymphs, shapely, beautiful and gracious, and a single man, well formed, handsome and gracious, wearing bracelets, earrings and colorful gar-

krīḍati ramate paricārayati. sa tair dūrata eva dṛṣṭaḥ. te taṃ pratyavabhāṣitum ārabdhāḥ, «svāgatam, Śrona! m" âsi tṛṣito bubhukṣito vā?»

Sa saṃlakṣayati, «nūnaṃ devo 'yaṃ vā nāgo vā yakṣo vā bhaviṣyati.» āha ca, «ārya, tṛṣito 'smi bubhukṣito 'smi.» sa taiḥ snāpito bhojitaḥ. sa tasmin vimāne tāvat sthito yāvat sūryasy' âbhyudgamana|kāla|samayaḥ. sa tair uktaḥ, «Śroṇa, avatara! ādīnavo 'tra bhaviṣyati.»

So 'vatīrya ek'|ânte prakramy' âvasthitaḥ. tataḥ paścāt sūryasy' âbhyudgamana|kāla|samaye tad vimānam antarhitam. tā apy apsaraso 'ntarhitāḥ. catvāraḥ śyāma|śabalāḥ kurkurāḥ prādur|bhūtāḥ. tais taṃ puruṣam avamūrdhakaṃ pātayitvā tāvat pṛṣṭha|māṃśān utpāṭy' ôtpāṭya bhakṣito yāvat sūryasy' âsta|gamana|kāla|samayaḥ. tataḥ paścāt punar api tad vimānaṃ prādur|bhūtam, tā apsarasaḥ prādur|bhūtāḥ. sa ca puruṣo 'bhirūpo darśanīyaḥ prāsādiko 'ṅgada|kuṇḍala|vicitra|māly'|ābharaṇ'|ânulepanas tābhiḥ sārdhaṃ krīḍati ramate paricārayati.

Sa teṣāṃ sakāśam upasaṃkramya kathayati, «ke yūyaṃ kena ca karmaṇ" êh' ôpapannāḥ?»

Te procuḥ, «Śroṇa, duṣ|kuhakā Jāmbudvīpakā manuṣyāḥ. n' âbhiśraddadhāsyasi.»

1.75 Sa c' āha, «ahaṃ pratyakṣa|darśī. kathaṃ n' âbhiśraddadhāsye?»

lands and anointed with fragrant oils, who was enjoying himself with, making love to and otherwise dallying with them. Catching sight of Koti·karna when he was still a good distance away, they began to call out to him, "Welcome, Shrona! Are you not thirsty or hungry?"

He reflected, "Surely this is a god or a divine serpent or a demigod!" And he replied, "Noble sir, I am indeed thirsty and hungry!" They bathed and fed him, and Koti·karna tarried in that palace until the time the sun was about to rise. Then they told him, "Shrona, descend! This place is about to become a scene of misery!"

Koti·karna descended, stepped off to one side and waited. Then, at the moment the sun rose, the palace vanished. The heavenly nymphs, too, vanished. A quartet of black, spotted hounds appeared. Hanging the man up by his feet, they continually tore off and devoured the flesh from his back until the sun was again setting behind the western mountain. Then the palace again materialized, as did the heavenly nymphs. The man, well formed, handsome and gracious, wearing bracelets, earrings and colorful garlands and anointed with fragrant oils, then resumed enjoying himself with, making love to and otherwise dallying with them.

Approaching them, Shrona Koti·karna said, "Who are you and what deeds led you to be reborn in this place?"

They replied, "Shrona, the men of India are a skeptical lot. You won't believe us."

Said he, "I can see what is before my own eyes! How can 1.75
I not believe you?"

«Śroṇa, ahaṃ Vāsava|grāmaka aurabhrika āsī.* urabhrān praghātya praghātya māṃsaṃ vikrīya jīvikāṃ kalpayāmi. Āryaś ca Mahākātyāyano mam'|ânukampay" āgatya kathayati, ‹bhadra|mukha, aniṣṭo 'sya karmaṇaḥ phala|vipākaḥ. virama tvam asmāt pāpakād asad|dharmāt.›

N' âhaṃ tasya vacanena viramāmi. bhūyo bhūyaḥ sa māṃ vicchandayati, ‹bhadra|mukha, aniṣṭo 'sya karmaṇaḥ phala|vipākaḥ. virama tvam asmāt pāpakād asad|dharmāt! tath" âpy ahaṃ na prativiramāmi.›

Sa māṃ pṛcchati, ‹bhadra|mukha, kiṃ tvam etān urabhrān divā praghātayasy āhosvid rātrau?›

May" ôktaḥ, ‹Ārya, divā praghātayāmi› iti.

1.80 Sa kathayati, ‹bhadra|mukha, rātrau śīla|samādānaṃ kiṃ na gṛhṇāsi?› mayā tasy' ântikād rātrau śīla|samādānaṃ gṛhītam. yat tad rātrau śīla|samādānaṃ gṛhītam, tasya karmaṇo vipākena rātrāv evaṃ|vidhaṃ divyaṃ sukhaṃ pratyanubhavāmi. yan mayā div" ôrabhrāḥ praghātitāḥ, tasya karmaṇo vipākena div" âivaṃ|vidhaṃ duḥkhaṃ pratyanubhavāmi.» gāthāṃ ca bhāṣate:

Divasaṃ para|prāṇa|pīḍakaḥ
    rātrau śīla|guṇaiḥ samanvitaḥ.
tasy' âitat karmaṇaḥ phalaṃ hy
    anubhavāmi kalyāṇa|pāpakam.

"Shrona, I was a shepherd in the village of Vásava. I routinely slaughtered sheep, sold their flesh and thereby earned a living. One day, out of compassion, the Holy Maha·katyáyana came to see me and said, 'My dear fellow, most undesirable will be the ripening of the fruit of your actions. Desist from this wickedness which violates the True Doctrine!'

But I did not stop on account of his exhortation. Again and again Maha·katyáyana sought to dissuade me, saying, 'My dear fellow, most undesirable will be the ripening of the fruit of your actions. Desist from this wickedness which violates the True Doctrine!' Even so, I did not stop.

[On another occasion,] Maha·katyáyana asked me, 'My dear fellow, do you slaughter these sheep during the day or at night?'

Said I, 'Holy One, I slaughter during the day.'

He told me, 'My dear fellow, at night, why not take upon 1.80
yourself the moral precepts?' Then, at night I undertook to observe the moral precepts at his prompting. And since at night I took the moral precepts, the result of that action is that at night, as you have seen, I enjoy heavenly bliss. But since during the day I continued to slaughter sheep, the result of that action is that by day, as you have also seen, I endure pain and suffering." And he recited this verse:

By day, crushing others' lives,
By night endowed with the virtues of the moral precepts:
The fruit of this karma is indeed
That I experience good and evil.

«Śroṇa, gamiṣyasi tvaṃ Vāsava|grāmakam?»

«Gamiṣyāmi.»

«Tatra mama putraḥ prativasati. sa urabhrān praghātya praghātya jīvikāṃ kalpayati. sa tvayā vaktavyaḥ: «dṛṣṭas te mayā pitā. sa kathayati, aniṣṭo 'sya karmaṇaḥ phala|vipākaḥ. viram' âsmāt pāpakād asad|dharmāt.»

1.85 «Bhoḥ puruṣa, yat tvam evaṃ kathayasi, ‹duṣ|kuhakā Jāmbudvīpakā manuṣyāḥ› iti n' âbhiśraddadhāsyati.»

«Śroṇa, yadi na śraddadhāsyati, vaktavyaḥ: ‹tava pitā kathayati, asi|sthān'|âdhastāt suvarṇasya kalaśaḥ pūrayitvā sthāpitaḥ. tam uddhṛty' ātmānaṃ samyak|sukhena prīṇaya. Āryaṃ ca Mahākātyāyanaṃ kālena kālaṃ piṇḍakena pratipāday' âsmākaṃ ca nāmnā dakṣiṇām ādeśaya. apy ev' âitat karma tanutvaṃ parikṣayaṃ paryādānaṃ gacchet.›»

Sa saṃprasthito yāvat sūryasy' âbhyudgamana|kāla|samaye paśyaty aparaṃ vimānam. tatra ek" âpsar" âbhirūpā darśanīyā prāsādikā, ekaś ca puruṣo 'bhirūpo darśanīyaḥ prāsādiko 'ṅgada|kuṇḍala|vicitra|māly'|ābharaṇ'|ânulepanas tayā sārdhaṃ krīḍati ramate paricārayati. sa taṃ dūrata eva dṛṣṭvā pratyavabhāṣitum ārabdhaḥ, «svāgatam, Śroṇa! mā tṛṣito 'si, mā bubhukṣito 'si vā?»

"Shrona, will you go to Vásava village?"

"I will."

"My son lives there. By regularly slaughtering sheep he earns his livelihood. Please tell him that you saw his father, who says, 'Most undesirable will be the ripening of the fruit of your actions. Desist from this wickedness which violates the True Doctrine.'"

"My good fellow, you have already told me that the men 1.85
of India are a skeptical lot. Your son won't believe me."

"Shrona, if he doesn't believe you, tell him that his father says, 'Underneath the slaughtering pen I buried a jar full of gold. Dig it up and enjoy yourself in perfect felicity. And from time to time provide the Holy Maha·katyáyana with alms and assign the merit of those offerings to me. Then maybe this evil karma of mine will diminish, wane and finally exhaust itself.'"

Shrona Koti·karna proceeded until, just at the time when the sun was going to rise, he saw another aerial palace. In it was a heavenly nymph, shapely, beautiful and gracious. There was also a man, similarly well formed, handsome and gracious, wearing bracelets, earrings and colorful garlands and anointed with fragrant oils, who was enjoying himself with, making love to and otherwise dallying with her. Seeing Koti·karna when he was still quite a distance away, he began to call out, "Welcome, Shrona! Are you not thirsty? Are you not hungry?"

Sa saṃlakṣayati, «nūnam ayaṃ devo vā nāgo vā yakṣo vā bhaviṣyati.» sa kathayati, «tṛṣito 'smi bubhukṣitaś ca.» sa tābhyāṃ snāpito bhojitaḥ. sa tasmin vimāne tāvat sthito yāvat sūryasy' âstaṃ|gamana|kāla|samayaḥ. sa tābhyām uktaḥ, «Śroṇa, avatarasva! ādīnavo 'tra bhaviṣyati.» sa dṛṣṭ'|ādīnavo 'vatīry' âik'|ânte 'vasthitaḥ.

Tataḥ paścāt sūryasy' âstaṃ|gamana|kāla|samaye tad vimānam antarhitam. s" âpy apsar" ântarhitā. mahatī śata|padī prādur|bhūtā. tayā tasya puruṣasya kāyena kāyaṃ sapta|kṛtvo veṣṭayitvā tāvad upari|ṣṭhān mastakaṃ bhakṣitaṃ yāvat sa eva sūryasy'| âbhyudgamana|kāla|samayaḥ. tataḥ paścāt punar api tad vimānaṃ prādur|bhūtam. s" âpy apsarāḥ prādur|bhūtā, sa ca puruṣo 'bhirūpo darśanīyaḥ prāsādiko 'ṅgada|kuṇḍala|vicitra|māly'|ābharaṇ'|ânulepanas tayā sārdhaṃ krīḍati ramate paricārayati.

1.90 Sa tam upasaṃkramya pṛcchati, «ko bhavān, kena karmaṇ" êh' ôpapannaḥ?»

Sa evam āha, «Śroṇa, duṣ|kuhakā Jāmbudvīpakā manuṣyāḥ. n' âbhiśraddadhāsyasi.»

Sa kathayati, «ahaṃ pratyakṣa|darśī. kasmān n' âbhiśraddadhāsye?»

Sa kathayati, «yady evam, ahaṃ Vāsava|grāmake brāhmaṇa āsī* pāradārikaḥ. Āryaś ca Mahākātyāyano mam' ânukampay" āgatya kathayati, ‹bhadra|mukha, aniṣṭo 'sya

Koti·karna reflected, "Surely this one is a god or a divine serpent or a demigod!" And he replied, "I am indeed thirsty and hungry!" The couple had him bathed and fed and Koti·karna tarried in that palace until the time the sun was about to set. Then the man told him, "Shrona, descend! This place is about to become a scene of misery!" Koti·karna, who had already beheld misery, descended and stood off to one side.

Then, just at the moment when the sun was setting behind the western mountain, the palace vanished. The heavenly nymph, too, vanished and an enormous centipede appeared. It wrapped its body seven times around the man's body and devoured his head from above, right up until the moment the sun rose. Then, once again, the palace appeared. The heavenly nymph also appeared and the man, well formed, handsome and gracious, wearing bracelets, earrings and colorful garlands and anointed with fragrant oils, enjoyed himself with, made love to and otherwise dallied with her.

Shrona Koti·karna approached and asked the man, "Who 1.90
are you, sir, and as a result of what deeds were you reborn in this place?"

The man spoke thus: "Shrona, the men of India are a skeptical lot. You wouldn't believe me."

Said he, "I can see what is before my own eyes! Why should I not believe you?"

The man said, "If that is the case, I was a brahmin in Vásava village who consorted with other men's wives. And the Holy Maha·katyáyana, out of compassion, came to see me and said, 'My dear fellow, most undesirable will be the ripen-

karmaṇaḥ phala|vipākaḥ. virama tvam asmāt pāpakād asad|dharmāt.›

Tasya vacanen' âhaṃ na prativiramāmi. bhūyo bhūyaḥ sa māṃ vicchandayati. tath" âpy ahaṃ tasmāt pāpakād asad|dharmān na prativiramāmi.

1.95 Sa māṃ pṛcchati, ‹bhadra|mukha, para|dārān kiṃ tvaṃ divā gacchasy āhosvid rātrau?› sa may" âbhihitaḥ, ‹Ārya, rātrau.›

Sa kathayati, ‹bhadra|mukha, divā kiṃ na śīla|samādānaṃ gṛhṇāsi?› mayā tasy' ântike divā śīla|samādānaṃ gṛhītam. yat tan may" Āryasya Mahākātyāyanasy' ântikād divā śīla|samādānaṃ gṛhītam, tasya karmaṇo vipākena div" âivaṃ|vidhaṃ divyaṃ sukhaṃ pratyanubhavāmi. yat tad rātrau para|dār'|âbhigamanaṃ kṛtam, tasya karmaṇo vipākena rātrāv evaṃ|vidhaṃ duḥkhaṃ pratyanubhavāmi.» gāthāṃ ca bhāṣate:

Rātrau para|dāra|mūrchito
divasaṃ śīla|guṇaiḥ samanvitaḥ:
tasy' âitat karmaṇaḥ phalaṃ hy
anubhavāmi kalyāṇa|pāpakam

Śroṇa, gamiṣyasi tvaṃ Vāsava|grāmakam? tatra mama putro brāhmaṇaḥ pāra|dārikaḥ. sa vaktavyaḥ: ‹dṛṣṭas te mayā pitā. sa kathayati, «aniṣṭo 'sya karmaṇaḥ phala|vipākaḥ. viram' âsmāt pāpakād asad|dharmāt.»›»

ing of the fruit of your actions. Desist from this wickedness which violates the True Doctrine!'

But I did not stop on account of his exhortation. Again and again Maha·katyáyana sought to dissuade me. Even so, from that wickedness which violates the True Doctrine I did not desist.

He asked me, 'My dear fellow, do you consort with others' 1.95
wives during the day or at night?' I told him, 'Holy One, at night.'

He replied, 'My dear fellow, during the day, why not take upon yourself the moral precepts?' Then, in his presence, I undertook to observe the moral precepts during daytime. And since at the Holy Katyáyana's prompting, I undertook to observe the moral precepts by day, the result of that action is that during the day, as you have seen, I enjoy heavenly bliss. But since at night I consort with other men's wives, the result of that action is that at night, as you have also seen, I endure pain and suffering." And he recited this verse:

By night, infatuated with others' wives,
By day endowed with virtues of the moral precepts:
The fruit of that karma is indeed
That I experience good and evil.

Shrona, will you go to Vásava village? I have a son there, a brahmin who consorts with other men's wives. Tell him, 'I have seen your father, who says, "Most undesirable will be the ripening of the fruit of your actions. Desist from this wickedness which violates the True Doctrine."'"

Sa c' āha, «bhoḥ puruṣa! tvam evaṃ kathayasi, ‹duṣ|kuhakā Jāmbudvīpakā manuṣyāḥ› iti. n' âbhiśraddadhāsyati.»

1.100 «Śroṇa, yadi na śraddadhāsyati, vaktavyaḥ: ‹tava pitā kathayati, agni|ṣṭomasy' âdhastāt survarṇa|kalaśaḥ pūrayitvā sthāpitaḥ. tam uddhṛty' ātmānaṃ samyak|sukhena prīṇaya. Āryaṃ ca Mahākātyāyanaṃ kālena kālaṃ piṇḍakena pratipādaya. asmākaṃ ca nāmnā dakṣiṇām ādeśaya. apy ev' âitat karma tanutvaṃ parikṣayaṃ paryādānaṃ gacchet.›»

Sa saṃprasthito yāvat paśyaty aparaṃ vimānam. tatr' âikā strī, abhirūpā darśanīyā prāsādik" âṅgada|kuṇḍala|vicitra|māly'|ābharaṇ'|ânulepanā. tasyāś caturṣu paryaṅka|pādakeṣu catvāraḥ pretā baddhās tiṣṭhanti. sā taṃ dūrata eva dṛṣṭvā, pratyavabhāṣitum ārabdhā, «Śroṇa, svāgatam! mā tṛṣito 'si, mā bubhukṣito 'si vā?»

Sa saṃlakṣayati, «nūnaṃ dev" îyaṃ vā nāgī vā yakṣī vā bhaviṣyati.» sa kathayati, āryе, tṛṣito 'smi bubhukṣito 'smi!»

Tay" âsāv udvartitaḥ snāpita āhāro dattaḥ, uktaṃ ca, «Śroṇa, yady ete kiṃ cin mṛgayanti, ‹mā dāsyasi› ity uktvā, teṣāṃ sattvānāṃ karma|svakatāṃ pratyakṣī|kartu|kāmā vimānaṃ praviśy' âvasthitā.»

But Shrona replied, "My good man, you've already said that the men of India are a skeptical lot! He won't believe me."

"Shrona, if he doesn't believe you, tell him that his fa- 1.100
ther says, 'Beneath the fire-altar I buried a jar full of gold. Dig it up and enjoy yourself in perfect felicity. And from time to time provide the Holy Maha·katyáyana with alms and assign the merit of those offerings to me. Then maybe this evil karma of mine will diminish, wane and finally exhaust itself.'"

Koti·karna proceeded until he saw another aerial palace. In it was a woman, shapely, beautiful and gracious, wearing bracelets, earrings and colorful garlands and anointed with fragrant oils. She had four hungry ghosts tied to four footstools. The woman saw Koti·karna from a long way off and began to call out to him, "Shrona, welcome! Are you not thirsty or hungry?"

He reflected, "Certainly this woman must be a goddess or a divine serpent or a demigod!" And he said, "Noble lady, I am indeed thirsty and hungry!"

She raised him up into the palace, had him bathed and given a meal, and said, "Shrona, if these creatures begin to hunt for something to eat, I shall say: 'Give them nothing,' and, desiring to make apparent that those beings, are responsible for their own karma, I shall enter the aerial palace and stay there."

Te mṛgayitum ārabdhāḥ. «Śroṇa, kāruṇikas tvam. bubhukṣitā vayam. asmākam anuprayaccha.» ten' âikasya kṣiptaṃ busa|plāvī prādur|bhūtā. aparasya kṣiptaṃ, ayo|guḍaṃ bhakṣayitum ārabdhaḥ. aparasya kṣiptaṃ, sva|māṃsaṃ bhakṣayitum ārabdhaḥ. aparasya kṣiptaṃ, pūya|śoṇitaṃ prādur|bhūtam.

1.105 Sā paśyati visra|gandhena nirgatam. «Śroṇa! na nivāritas tvam? kasmāt tvay" âiṣāṃ dattam? kiṃ mama kāruṇikāyās tvam eva kāruṇika|taraḥ?»

Sa kathayati, «bhagini, tav' âite ke bhavanti?»

Sā kathayati, «ayaṃ me svāmī, ayaṃ me putraḥ, iyaṃ me snuṣā, iyaṃ me dāsī.»

Sa āha, «ke yūyaṃ, kena vā karmaṇ" êh' ôpapannāḥ?»

Tay" ôktam, «Śroṇa, duṣ|kuhakā Jāmbudvīpakā manuṣyā iti. n' âbhiśraddadhāsyasi.»

1.110 «Ahaṃ, bhagini, pratyakṣa|darśī. kasmān n' âbhiśraddadhāsye?»

Sā kathayati, «ahaṃ Vāsava|grāmake brāhmaṇy āsīt. mayā nakṣatra|rātryāṃ pratyupasthitāyāṃ praṇītam āhāraṃ sajjī|kṛtam. Āryaś ca Mahākātyāyano mam' ânukampayā Vāsava|grāmake piṇḍāya prāvikṣat. sa mayā dṛṣṭaḥ kāya|prāsādikaś citta|prāsādikaḥ. cittam abhiprasannaṃ dṛṣṭvā sa mayā prasāda|jātayā piṇḍakena pratipāditaḥ. tasyā mama

The hungry ghosts began to hunt for something to eat, saying, "Shrona, you are a compassionate man. We are famished! Give us something to eat!" When he threw a bit of food to one, it turned into a beetle. When he threw some to another, it turned into an iron ball, which the hungry ghost began to devour. When he threw some to another, that hungry ghost began to devour its own flesh. And when he threw food to another, it turned into pus and blood.

The woman saw that Shrona Koti·karna was leaving be- 1.105
cause of the stench of raw meat. "Shrona! Did I not forbid you to feed these creatures? Why did you give food to them? Have you more compassion for these creatures than I do?"

Replied Shrona Koti·karna, "Fair lady, what are these creatures to you?"

Said she, "This one is my husband; this one, my son; this one, my daughter-in-law and this one, my maidservant."

Koti·karna said, "Who are you and what karma led you to be reborn in this place?"

She replied, "Shrona, the men of India, it is said, are a skeptical lot. You wouldn't believe me."

"I can see what's in front of my eyes. Why shouldn't I 1.110
believe you?"

She said, "I was a woman of the priestly class, living in Vásava village. On the night of the moon entering a new constellation I had prepared some choice dishes. Meanwhile, out of compassion for me, the Holy Maha·katyáyana had entered Vásava village for alms. I caught sight of him, brightly serene in body and mind. On realizing that he was

buddhir utpannā, ‹svāminam anumodayāmi, prāmodyam utpādayiṣyati› iti.

Sa snātv" āgato may" ôktaḥ, ‹ārya|putra, anumodasva! may" Āryo Mahākātyāyanaḥ piṇḍakena pratipāditaḥ.› sa ruṣitaḥ, ‹yāvad brāhmaṇānāṃ na dīyate jñātīnāṃ vā jñāti|pūjā na kriyate, tāvat tvayā tasmai muṇḍakāya śramaṇakāy' âgra|piṇḍakaṃ dattam!› so 'marṣa|jātaḥ kathayati, ‹kasmāt sa muṇḍakaḥ śramaṇako busa|plāvīṃ na bhakṣayati?› iti. tasya karmaṇo vipāken' âyaṃ busa|plāvīṃ bhakṣayati.

Mama buddhir utpannā, ‹putraṃ tāvad anumodayāmi. prāmodyam utpādayiṣyati› iti. so 'pi may" ôktaḥ, ‹putra, anumodasva! may" Āryo Mahākātyāyanaḥ piṇḍakena pratipāditaḥ.› so 'pi ruṣitaḥ, ‹yāvad brāhmaṇānāṃ na dīyate jñātīnāṃ vā jñāti|pūjā na kriyate, tāvat tvayā tasmai muṇḍakāya śramaṇakāy' âgra|piṇḍakaṃ dattam.› so 'py amarṣa|jātaḥ kathayati, ‹kasmāt sa muṇḍakaḥ śramaṇako 'yo|guḍaṃ na bhakṣayati?› iti. tasya karmaṇo vipāken' âyam ayo|guḍaṃ bhakṣayati.

Nakṣatra|rātryāṃ pratyupasthitāyāṃ jñātayaḥ praheṇakāni mama preṣayanti. tāny ahaṃ snuṣāyāḥ samarpayāmi. sā praṇītāni praheṇakāni bhakṣayitvā mama lūhāny upanāmayati. ahaṃ teṣāṃ jñātīnāṃ saṃdiśāmi, ‹kiṃ nu yūyaṃ dur|bhikṣe yathā lūhāni praheṇakāni preṣayatha?› iti. te mama saṃdiśanti, ‹na vayaṃ lūhāni preṣayāmo 'pi tu praṇītāny

favorably disposed, serene faith arose in my heart and I presented him with almsfood. I thought: 'I'll share this joy with my husband; I'll have him join me in rejoicing!'

He came in, having just bathed. I said to him, 'Rejoice with me, noble one! I have just presented the Holy One, Maha·katyáyana, with almsfood!' My husband was furious. 'We don't give food to brahmins and we don't honor our kinsmen this way, yet to this wretched, shaven-headed ascetic you give our best food!' In a rage, he continued, 'Why doesn't that wretched, shaven-headed ascetic eat beetles?' The consequence of that deed is that this one now eats beetles.

Then the thought occurred to me, 'In the meantime, I'll share this joy with my son. I'll have him join me in rejoicing!' To him I said, 'Rejoice with me, my son! I have just presented the Holy One, Maha·katyáyana, with almsfood!' He, too, was furious. 'We don't give food to brahmins and we don't honor our kinsmen this way, yet to this wretched, shaven-headed ascetic you give our best food!' And he, too, in a rage, continued, 'Why doesn't that wretched, shaven-headed ascetic eat iron balls?' The consequence of that deed is that this one now eats iron balls.

On the night of the moon entering a new constellation, relatives sent me some delicacies. I entrusted them to my daughter-in-law. She ate those choice delicacies and presented me with coarse stuff. I pointed out the inferior quality of the food to those relatives: 'Are you short of food, that you are sending me this coarse stuff?' They pointed out to me: 'We didn't send coarse stuff! On the contrary, we sent

eva praheṇakāni preṣayāmaḥ.› mayā snuṣ" âbhihitā, ‹vadhūke mā tvaṃ praṇītāni praheṇakāni bhakṣayitv" âsmākaṃ lūhāny upanāmayasi.› sā kathayati, ‹kiṃ na sva|māṃsāni bhakṣayati y" âhaṃ tvadīyāni praheṇakāni bhakṣayāmi?› iti. iyaṃ tasya karmaṇo vipākena sva|māṃsāni bhakṣayati.

1.115 Nakṣatra|rātryāṃ pratyupasthitāyām ahaṃ dārikāyā haste praṇītāni praheṇakāni dattvā jñātīnāṃ preṣayāmi. sā tāni praṇītāni praheṇakāni mārge 'nto bhakṣayitvā teṣāṃ lūhāny upanāmayati. te mama saṃdiśanti, ‹kiṃ nu tvaṃ dur|bhikṣe yathā lūhāny asmākaṃ praheṇakāni preṣayasi?› iti. ahaṃ teṣāṃ saṃdiśāmi, ‹n' âhaṃ lūhāni preṣayāmy api tu praṇītāny ev' âhaṃ preṣayāmi!› iti. mayā dārik" âbhihitā, ‹dārike mā tvaṃ praṇītāni praheṇakāni bhakṣayitvā teṣāṃ lūhāny upanāmayasi.› sā kathayati, ‹kiṃ nu pūya|śoṇitaṃ na bhakṣayati yā tvadīyāni praheṇakāni bhakṣayati?› iti. tasya karmaṇo vipāken' êyaṃ pūya|śoṇitaṃ bhakṣayati.

Mama buddhir utpannā, ‹tatra pratisaṃdhiṃ gṛhṇīyāṃ, yatr' âitān sarvān svakaṃ svakaṃ karma|phalaṃ paribhuñjānān paśyeyam› iti. yayā may" Ārya|Mahākātyāyanaṃ piṇḍakena pratipādya praṇīte trayas|triṃśe deva|nikāya upapattavyaṃ, s" âhaṃ mithyā|praṇidhāna|vaśāt preta|mahar|dhikā saṃvṛttā.

Śroṇa, gamiṣyasi tvaṃ Vāsava|grāmakam. tatra mama duhitā veśyaṃ vāhayati. sā tvayā vaktavyā: ‹dṛṣṭās te mayā pitā mātā bhrātā bhrātur jāyā dāsī. te kathayanti, «aniṣṭo 'sya karmaṇaḥ phala|vipākaḥ. viram' âsmāt pāpakād asad|dharmāt.»››

the very choicest delicacies!' So I said to my daughter-in-law, 'Young woman, you must not eat the choice delicacies and present the rest of us with coarse stuff.' Said she, 'Why don't I eat my own flesh, I who ate your delicacies?' The consequence of that deed is that this girl eats her own flesh.

On the night of the moon entering a new constellation, I 1.115
placed choice delicacies in my maidservant's hands and sent her to our relatives. She ate those choice delicacies on the way and presented them with coarse stuff. They pointed this out to me: 'Are you short of food, that you are sending me this coarse stuff?' I pointed out to them, 'I didn't send coarse stuff! On the contrary, I sent the very choicest delicacies!' I told my maidservant, 'Girl, you must not eat the choice delicacies and present our relatives with coarse stuff.' Said she, 'Why doesn't she eat pus and blood, the one who ate your delicacies?' The consequence of that deed is that this one now eats pus and blood.

Then the thought occurred to me, 'Wherever I can behold each of these experiencing the consequences of their respective actions, there may I take rebirth.' I myself presented the Holy Maha·katyáyana with almsfood in order to take rebirth in the company of thirty-three gods, but due to the power of that improper earnest wish I was reborn as a hungry ghost of great power.

Shrona, will you go to Vásava village? There my daughter plies the trade of a prostitute. Tell her, 'I have seen your father, mother, brother, sister-in-law and maidservant. They say: "Most undesirable will be the ripening of the fruit of your actions. Desist from this wickedness which violates the True Doctrine."'"

«Bhagini, tvam eva kathayasi, ‹duṣ|kuhakā Jāmbudvīpakā manuṣyāḥ. n' âbhiśraddadhāsyanti.›»

«Śroṇa, yadi na śraddadhāsyati, vaktavyā: ‹tava paurāṇe paitṛke vāsa|gṛhe catvāro loha|saṃghāṭāḥ suvarṇasya pūrṇās tiṣṭhanti, madhye ca sauvarṇa|daṇḍa|kamaṇḍaluḥ. te kathayanti, tam uddhṛty' ātmānaṃ samyak|sukhena prīṇaya, Āryaṃ ca Mahākātyāyanaṃ kālena kālaṃ piṇḍakena pratipādaya, asmākaṃ ca nāmnā dakṣiṇām ādeśaya. apy ev' âitat karma tanutvaṃ parikṣayaṃ paryādānaṃ gacchet.›» tena tasyāḥ pratijñātam.

1.120 Evaṃ tasya paribhramato dvā|daśa varṣā atikrāntāḥ. tay" ôktaḥ, «Śroṇa, gamiṣyasi tvaṃ Vāsava|grāmakam?»

«Bhagini, gamiṣyāmi.»

Sa tasminn eva vimāna abhirūḍhaḥ. tayā teṣām eva pretānām ājñā dattā, «bhavantaḥ, gacchata! Śroṇaṃ Koṭīkarṇaṃ suptam eva Vāsava|grāmake paitṛka udyāne sthāpayitvā, āgacchata.» sa tair Vāsava|grāmake paitṛka udyāne sthāpitaḥ. sa prativibuddho yāvat paśyati ghaṇṭāś chattrāṇi vyajanāny akṣarāṇi likhitāni: «yadi tāvac Chroṇaḥ Koṭīkarṇo jīvati, laghv āgamaya kṣipram āgamaya. atha cyutaḥ kāla|gato gaty|upapatti|sthānāt sthān'|ântara|viśeṣatāyai.»

Sa saṃlakṣayati, «yady ahaṃ mātā|pitṛbhyāṃ mṛta eva gṛhītaḥ, kasmād bhūyo 'haṃ gṛhaṃ praviśāmi? gacchāmy Ārya|Mahākātyāyanasy' ântikāt pravrajāmi» iti.

"Sister, it is you who say, 'The men of India are a skeptical lot. They won't believe.'"

"Shrona, if she doesn't believe you, tell her, 'In your late father's house are four copper jars filled with gold, with a golden water pot among them.' The members of your family say, 'Dig it up and enjoy yourself in perfect felicity. And from time to time provide the Holy Maha·katyáyana with alms and assign the merit of those offerings to us. Then maybe this evil karma of ours will diminish, wane and finally exhaust itself.'" Koti·karna promised to do as she asked.

While he wandered in this way, twelve years had passed. 1.120
She said to Koti·karna, "Shrona, will you go to Vásava village?"

"Fair lady, I will."

Koti·karna climbed into that same aerial palace. The lady then gave a command to those same hungry ghosts: "Go now! Place Shrona Koti·karna, asleep, in his father's garden in Vásava village. Then return." They indeed placed him in Vásava village in his father's garden. Koti·karna awoke, and at once beheld bells, parasols and palm-leaf fans, all inscribed with letters, which read, "If Shrona Koti·karna is only alive, bring him back soon, bring him back quickly! If he has departed this life bring him from the circumstances of his present realm and mode of rebirth to another, better one."

He reflected, "If my mother and father take me for dead, why should I return to the household life? I'll go before the Holy Maha·katyáyana and take up the religious life."

Atha Śroṇaḥ Koṭīkarṇo yen' Āyuṣmān Mahākātyāyanas ten' ôpasaṃkrāntaḥ. adrākṣīd Āyuṣmān Mahākātyāyanaḥ Śroṇaṃ Koṭīkarṇaṃ dūrād eva dṛṣṭvā ca punaḥ Śroṇaṃ Koṭīkarṇam idam avocat: «ehi, Śroṇa! svāgataṃ te! dṛṣṭas te, Śroṇa, ayaṃ lokaḥ paraś ca lokaḥ?»

1.125 Sa kathayati, «dṛṣṭo Bhadanta Mahākātyāyana. labhey' âhaṃ, Bhadanta Mahākātyāyana, sv|ākhyāte dharma|vinaye pravrajyām upasaṃpadaṃ bhikṣu|bhāvam. careyam ahaṃ bhagavato 'ntike brahma|caryam.»

Sa āryeṇ' ôktaḥ, «Śroṇa, smaryatāṃ tāvat pūrvikāṃ pratijñāṃ paripūraya. yathā|gṛhītān saṃdeśān samarpaya» iti.

Sa tasy' âurabhrikasya sakāśam upasaṃkrāntaḥ. «bhadra|mukha, dṛṣṭas te pitā mayā. sa kathayati, ‹aniṣṭo 'sya karmaṇaḥ phala|vipākaḥ. viram' âsmāt pāpakād asad|dharmāt.›»

«Bhoḥ puruṣa, adya mama pitur dvā|daśa varṣāṇi kāla|gatasya. asti kaś cid dṛṣṭaḥ para|lokāt punar āgacchan?»

«Bhadra|mukha, eṣo 'ham āgataḥ.» n' âsau śraddadhāti. «bhadra|mukha, yadi na śraddadhāsi, sa tava pitā kathayati, ‹asi|sthān'|âdhastāt suvarṇasya kalaśaḥ pūrṇas tiṣṭhati. tam uddhṛty' ātmānaṃ samyak|sukhena prīṇaya. Āryaṃ ca Mahākātyāyanaṃ kālena kālaṃ piṇḍakena pratipāday' âsmākaṃ ca nāmnā dakṣiṇām ādeśaya. apy ev' âitat karma tanutvaṃ parikṣayaṃ paryādānaṃ gacchet.›»

So Shrona Koti·karna went to see the Venerable Maha·katyáyana. The Venerable Maha·katyáyana saw Shrona Koti·karna from a long way off and, on catching sight of him, called out to Shrona Koti·karna, "Come, Shrona! Welcome! Have you seen, Shrona, this world and the next world too?"

He replied, "I have, Venerable Maha·katyáyana. Vener- 1.125
able Maha·katyáyana, I wish to take the lower and higher ordinations in the Doctrine and Discipline which are so well expounded and to become a monk. I wish to practice the holy life in the presence of the Lord."

Koti·karna was addressed by the Holy One, "Remember, Shrona—fulfill the promise you made. Deliver the messages just as you received them."

Koti·karna went to see the shepherd. "My dear fellow, I have seen your father. He says, 'Most undesirable will be the ripening of the fruit of your actions. Desist from this wickedness which violates the True Doctrine.'"

"My good man, by now it's twelve years since my father died! Is there any one you have seen who has returned from the other world?"

"My dear fellow, I have returned." But the man didn't believe Koti·karna. "My dear fellow, if you don't believe me, this is what your father said: 'Beneath the slaughtering pen there is a water pot filled with gold. Dig it up and enjoy yourself in perfect felicity. And from time to time provide the Holy Maha·katyáyana with alms and assign the merit of those offerings to me. Then maybe this evil karma of mine will diminish, wane and finally exhaust itself.'"

1.130 Sa saṃlakṣayati, «na kadā cid evaṃ mayā śruta|pūrvam. paśyāmi tāvat saced bhūtaṃ bhaviṣyati, sarvam etat satyam.» tena gatvā khanitaṃ yāvat paśyati sarvaṃ tat tath" âiva. ten' âbhiśraddadhātam.

Tataḥ paścāt sa pāra|dārikasya sakāśam upasaṃkrāntaḥ. upasaṃkramya kathayati, «bhadra|mukha, dṛṣṭas te mayā pitā. sa kathayati, ‹aniṣṭo 'sya karmaṇaḥ phala|vipākaḥ. viram' âsmāt pāpakād asad|dharmāt.›»

Sa kathayati, «bhoḥ puruṣa, adya mama pitur dvā|daśa varṣāṇi kālaṃ gatasya. asti kaś cit tvayā dṛṣṭaḥ para|lokaṃ gatvā punar āgacchan?»

«Bhadra|mukha, eṣo 'ham āgataḥ.» n' âsau śraddadhāti. sa c' āha, «bhadra|mukha, sacen n' âbhiśraddadhāsi, tava pitr" âgni|ṣṭomasy' âdhastāt suvarṇasya kalaśaḥ pūrayitvā sthāpitaḥ. sa kathayati, ‹tam uddhṛty' ātmānaṃ samyak|sukhena prīṇaya. Āryaṃ ca Mahākātyāyanaṃ kālena kālaṃ piṇḍakena pratipāday' âsmākaṃ ca nāmnā dakṣiṇām ādeśaya. apy ev' âitat karma tanutvaṃ parikṣayaṃ paryādānaṃ gacchet.›»

Sa saṃlakṣayati, «na kadā cid etan mayā śruta|pūrvam. paśyāmi tāvat saced bhūtaṃ bhaviṣyati, sarvam etat satyam.» tena gatvā khanitaṃ yāvat paśyati sarvaṃ tat tath" âiva. ten' âbhiśraddadhātam.

1.135 Tataḥ Śroṇaḥ Koṭīkarṇas tasyā veśyāyāḥ sakāśam upasaṃkrāntaḥ. upasaṃkramya kathayati, «bhagini, dṛṣṭās te mayā mātā, pitā, bhrātā, bhrātur jāyā, dāsī. te kathayanti,

The shepherd's son reflected, "Never before have I heard such a thing! I'll just see—if the treasure is actually there, then it's all true." He went and began digging until he saw that it all was just as Koti·karna had said. Then he believed. 1.130

Then, after that, Koti·karna approached the man who consorted with others' wives. After approaching him, he said, "My dear fellow, I have seen your father. He says, 'Most undesirable will be the ripening of the fruit of your actions. Desist from this wickedness which violates the True Doctrine!'"

The man replied, "My good man, by now it's twelve years since my father died! Is there anyone you have seen who has gone to the other world and returned?"

"Good sir, I have returned." But he didn't believe Koti·karna. "Good sir, if you don't believe me, you should know that your father filled a water jar with gold and buried it beneath the fire-altar. And he says, 'Dig it up and enjoy yourself in perfect felicity. And from time to time provide the Holy Maha·katyáyana with alms and assign the merit of those offerings to me. Then maybe this evil karma of mine will diminish, wane and finally exhaust itself.'"

The man reflected, "Never before have I heard such a thing! I'll just see—if the treasure is actually there, then it's all true." He went and began digging until he saw that it all was just as Koti·karna had said. Then he believed.

Then Shrona Koti·karna went to see the prostitute. After approaching her, he said, "Sister, I have seen your mother, father, brother, sister-in-law and maidservant. They say, 'Most undesirable will be the ripening of the fruit of your 1.135

‹aniṣṭo 'sya karmaṇaḥ phala|vipākaḥ. viram' âsmāt pāpakād asad|dharmāt.›»

Sā kathayati, «bhoḥ puruṣa, adya mama mātā|pitror dvā|daśa varṣāṇi kāla|gatayoḥ. asti kaś cit tvayā dṛṣṭaḥ para|lokaṃ gatvā punar āgacchan?»

Sa kathayati, «eṣo 'ham āgataḥ.» sā na śraddadhāti. sa kathayati, «bhagini, sacen n' âbhiśraddadhāsi, te kathayanti, ‹tava paurāṇe paitṛke vāsa|gṛhe catasro lohī|saṃghāṭāḥ suvarṇa|pūrṇās tiṣṭhanti, madhye ca sauvarṇa|daṇḍa|kamaṇḍaluḥ. tam uddhṛty' ātmānaṃ samyak|sukhena prīṇaya. Āryaṃ ca Mahākātyāyanaṃ kālena kālaṃ piṇḍakena pratipāday' âsmākaṃ ca nāmnā dakṣiṇām ādeśaya. apy ev' âitat karma tanutvaṃ parikṣayaṃ paryādānaṃ gacchet.›»

Sā saṃlakṣayati, «na kadā cin mayā śruta|pūrvam. paśyāmi tāvat saced bhūtaṃ bhaviṣyati, sarvam etat satyam.» tayā gatvā khanitaṃ yāvat paśyati sarvaṃ tat tath" âiva. tay" âbhiśraddadhītam.

Śroṇaḥ Koṭīkarṇaḥ saṃlakṣayati, «sarvo 'yaṃ lokaḥ suvarṇasya śraddadhāti, na tu kaś cin mama śraddhayā gacchati» iti. tena vaipuṣpitam—tasya śiśutve suvarṇena daśanā baddhāḥ. tay" âsau pratyabhijñātaḥ. «syād āryaḥ Śroṇaḥ Koṭīkarṇaḥ! evaṃ me ‹bhaginī› îti janaḥ saṃjānīte!»

1.140 Tayā gatvā tasya mātā|pitṛbhyām ārocitam: «amba! tāta! Koṭīkarṇo 'bhyāgataḥ» iti. anekais teṣām ārocitam. te na kasya cit śraddhayā gacchanti. te kathayanti, «putri, tvam apy asmākam utprāsayasi.»

actions. Desist from this wickedness which violates the True Doctrine.'"

She replied, "My good man, by now my mother and father have been dead for twelve years. Is there anyone you have seen who has gone to the other world and returned?"

Koti·karna said, "I have returned." But she didn't believe him. He continued, "Sister, if you don't believe me, they said: 'In your late father's house are four copper jars filled with gold, with a golden water pot among them. Dig them up and enjoy yourself in perfect felicity. And from time to time provide the Holy Maha·katyáyana with alms and assign the merit of those offerings to us. Then maybe this evil karma of ours will diminish, wane and finally exhaust itself.'"

The woman reflected, "Never before have I heard such a thing! I'll just see—if the treasure is actually there, then it's all true." She went and began digging until she saw that it all was just as Koti·karna had said. Then she believed.

Shrona Koti·karna reflected, "Everyone believes in gold, but no one believes me!" He smiled—in childhood his teeth had been covered in gold—and she recognized him, crying out, "It must be the noble Shrona Koti·karna! That's why this fellow calls me 'sister'!"

She went and informed his mother and father: "Mother! 1.140
Father! Koti·karna has arrived!" But many others had thus informed them. By now his parents believed no one. They said to her, "Daughter, even you mock us."

Yāvad asau svayam eva gatvā kathayati, «amba! tāta! vande» iti. tena dvāra|koṣṭhake sthitv" ôtkāśana|śabdaḥ kṛtaḥ. hiraṇya|svaro 'sau tābhyāṃ svareṇa pratyabhijñātaḥ. tasya śabdena sarvaṃ gṛham āpūritam. tau tasya kaṇṭhe pariṣvajya ruditum ārabdhau. tayor bāṣpeṇa paṭalāni sphuṭitāni. draṣṭum ārabdhau.

Sa kathayati, «amba, tāta, anujānīdhvam—pravrajiṣyāmi samyag eva śraddhayā agārād anagārikām.»

Tau kathayataḥ, «putra, āvāṃ tvadīyena śokena rudantāv andhī|bhūtau. idānīṃ tvām ev' āgamya cakṣuḥ pratilabdham. yāvad āvāṃ jīvāmas tāvan na pravrajitavyam. yadā kālaṃ kariṣyāmas tadā pravrajiṣyasi.»

Ten' āyuṣmato Mahākātyāyanasy' ântikād dharmaṃ śrutvā, śrota|āpatti|phalaṃ sākṣāt|kṛtaṃ, mātā|pitarau ca śaraṇa|gamana|śikṣā|padeṣu pratiṣṭhāpitau. āgama|catuṣṭayam adhītaṃ sakṛd|āgāmi|phalaṃ sākṣāt|kṛtaṃ, mātā|pitarau satyeṣu pratiṣṭhāpitau.

1.145 Apareṇa samayena tasya mātā|pitarau kāla|gatau. sa taṃ dhana|jātaṃ dīn'|ânātha|kṛpaṇa|vaṇīpakebhyo dattvā, daridrān adaridrān kṛtvā, yen' Āyuṣmān Mahākātyāyanas ten' ôpasaṃkrāntaḥ. upasaṃkramy' Āyuṣmato Mahākātyāyanasya pādau śirasā vanditvā, ek'|ânte 'sthāt. ek'|ânte sthitaḥ, Śroṇaḥ Koṭīkarṇa Āyuṣmantaṃ Mahākātyāyanam idam avocat: «labhey' âham, Ārya|Mahākātyāyana, sv|ākhyāte

Just then, the very man himself came up and said, "O Mother and Father, I pay my respects to you." Then, standing in the entrance hall, he spoke more clearly. That golden voice his parents recognized by its tone. His voice filled the entire house. Koti·karna's parents clasped him around the neck and began to weep. Their tears dissolved the film over their eyes and once again they could see.

Koti·karna said, "Mother, Father, please grant permission—I shall go forth, with right faith, from the home life into homelessness."

They replied, "Son, from weeping out of grief over you, we went blind. Now it is because of you we have regained our sight. For as long as we live, do not take up the religious life. When we die, then you may."

Koti·karna, after listening to the Venerable Maha·katyáyana expound the Dharma, attained the fruit of Entry into the Stream,* while his mother and father were established in Going for Refuge and in the Rules of Training. Koti·karna studied the Four Collections of Scripture and attained the fruit of a Once-Returner. His mother and father were established in the Four Holy Truths.

Some time later, Koti·karna's mother and father passed 1.145
away. He gave away his inheritance to the wretched, to the widows and orphans, to the poor and to beggars. Having thus made the needy prosperous, he went to see the Venerable Maha·katyáyana. Having approached, he prostrated himself at the Venerable Maha·katyáyana's feet, then stood to one side. Standing off to one side, he said this to the Venerable Maha·katyáyana: "Venerable Maha·katyáyana, I

dharma|vinaye pravrajyām upasampadaṃ bhikṣu|bhāvam. carey' âhaṃ bhagavato 'ntike brahma|caryam.» sa Āyuṣmatā Mahākātyāyanena pravrājitaḥ. tena pravrajya Mātṛk"|ādhītā, anāgāmi|phalaṃ sākṣāt|kṛtam.

Aśm'|âpar'|ântakeṣu jana|padeṣv alpa|bhikṣukam. kṛcchreṇa daśa|vargo gaṇaḥ paripūryate. sa trai|māsīṃ śrāmaṇero vidhāritaḥ. dharmatā khalu yathā buddhānāṃ bhagavatāṃ śrāvakāṇāṃ dvau saṃnipātau bhavataḥ. yaś c' Āṣāḍhyāṃ varṣ'|ôpanāyikāyāṃ yaś ca Kārttikyāṃ paurṇa|māsyām.

Tatra ye Āṣāḍhyāṃ varṣ'|ôpanāyikāyāṃ saṃnipatanti, te tāṃs tān uddeśa|yoga|manasi|kāra|viśeṣān udgṛhya paryavāpya tāsu tāsu grāma|nagara|nigama|rāṣṭra|rāja|dhānīṣu varṣām upagacchanti. ye Kārttikyāṃ paurṇa|māsyāṃ saṃnipatanti, te yath"|âdhigatam ārocayanti, uttare ca paripṛcchanti Sūtrasya Vinayasya Mātṛkāyāḥ. evam eva mahā|śrāvakāṇām api.

Atha ye Āyuṣmato Mahākātyāyanasya sārdhaṃ|vihāry|ante|vāsikā bhikṣavas tāṃs tān uddeśa|yoga|manasi|kāra|viśeṣān udgṛhya paryavāpya tāsu tāsu grāma|nagara|nigama|rāṣṭra|rāja|dhānīṣu varṣām upagatāḥ, te trayāṇāṃ vārṣikā-

wish to take the lower and higher ordinations in the Doctrine and Discipline which are so well expounded and to acquire the status of a monk. I wish to practice the holy life in the presence of the Lord." The Venerable Maha·katyáyana then ordained Shrona Koti·karna a novice. After his ordination, he learned the Systematic Doctrine and attained the fruit of a Non-Returner.

Among the people of Ashma·parántaka there were few Buddhist monks. It was exceedingly difficult to fill a quorum of ten. For the three months of the rainy season, Koti·karna carried on as a novice. Now it has been a rule among the Lord Buddhas' disciples to hold two assemblies each year. These take place at the full moon in the month of Ashádha, at the beginning of the rainy season, and at the full moon in the month of Kárttika.

At these, those who assemble in Ashadha at the beginning of the rainy season learn and master various special teachings, yogic practices and techniques of mental concentration, then pass the rainy season in various villages, cities, towns, kingdoms and royal capitals. Those who assemble at the full moon in Karttika describe what they had learned and, toward the end of the assembly, question one another about the Buddha's discourses, the Monastic Code and the Systematic Doctrine. The disciples of the Buddha's chief disciples do the same.

When those monks who had stayed in the Venerable Maha·katyáyana's monastery as his pupils* had learned and mastered the various special teachings, yogic practices and techniques of mental concentration and had passed the rainy season in various villages, cities, towns, kingdoms and

ṇāṃ māsāṇām atyayāt kṛta|cīvarā niṣṭhita|cīvarāḥ samādāya pātra|cīvaraṃ yen' Āyuṣmān Mahākātyāyanas ten' ôpasaṃkrāntāḥ.

Upasaṃkramy' Āyuṣmato Mahā|kātyāyanasya pādau śirasā vanditv" âik'|ânte niṣaṇṇāḥ. ek' ânte niṣadya, yath"|âdhigatam ārocayanti, uttare ca paripṛcchanti. daśa|vargo gaṇaḥ paripūrṇaḥ. sa ten' ôpasaṃpāditaḥ. tena Piṭaka|trayam adhītam. sarva|kleśa|prahāṇād arhattvaṃ sākṣāt|kṛtam. arhan saṃvṛttas trai|dhātuka|vīta|rāgaḥ sama|loṣṭa|kāñcana ākāśa|pāṇi|tala|samacitto vāsī|candana|kalpo vidyā|vidārit'|âṇḍa|kośo vidy"|âbhijñā|pratisaṃvit|prāpto bhava|lābha|lobha|sat|kāra|parāṅ|mukhaḥ s'|êndr'|ôpendrāṇāṃ devānāṃ pūjyo mānyo 'bhivādyaś ca saṃvṛttaḥ.

1.150 Ath' Āyuṣmato Mahākātyāyanasya sārdhaṃ|vihāry|ante|vāsikā Āyuṣmantaṃ Mahākātyāyanaṃ yāvat tāvat paryupāsy' Āyuṣmantaṃ Mahākātyāyanam idam avocan: «dṛṣṭo 'smābhir upādhyāyaḥ paryupāsitaś ca. gacchāmo vayaṃ Bhagavantaṃ paryupāsiṣyāmahe.»

royal capitals, at the end of those three months they, with their new robes made and properly arranged, put on their outer robes, took up their almsbowls and went before the Venerable Maha·katyáyana.

Having approached the Venerable Maha·katyáyana, they honored his head with their feet and sat down to one side. Seated to one side, they described what they had learned and asked one another questions. The quorum of ten was filled and from it Shrona Koti·karna received the higher ordination. He studied the three collections of scriptures and, by abandoning all defilements, attained Arhatship. An Arhat he became, free from passion for anything in the three worlds: to him, a lump of gold and a clod of earth were the same; so, too, the palm of the hand and the open sky; so, too, being cut with a hatchet and being rubbed with sandalwood paste. With knowledge he cracked open the shell of that egg, the mundane world: he realized the Three Knowledges,* the Six Superknowledges and the Four Analytical Knowledges. From conditioned existence, with its gain and greed, fame and honor, he had turned away. He became worthy of the respectful salutation, honor and worship of the gods themselves, not excepting Indra and Upéndra (Vishnu).

Then those monks who had stayed in the Venerable Ma- 1.150
ha·katyáyana's monastery and who had during that time attended and honored the Venerable Maha·katyáyana said this to him: "We have beheld and respectfully attended you, O spiritual preceptor. Now we wish to visit and respectfully attend the Lord."

Sa c' āha, «vatsāḥ, evaṃ kurudhvam. draṣṭavyā eva paryupāsitavyā eva hi Tathāgatā Arhantaḥ samyak|saṃbuddhāḥ.»

Tena khalu punaḥ samayena Śroṇaḥ Koṭīkarṇas tasyām eva parṣadi saṃniṣaṇṇo 'bhūt saṃnipatitaḥ. ath' Āyuṣmāñ Śroṇaḥ Koṭīkarṇa utthāy' âsanād ek'|âṃsam uttarā|saṅgaṃ kṛtvā, dakṣiṇaṃ jānu|maṇḍalaṃ pṛthivyāṃ pratiṣṭhāpya yena Āyuṣmān Mahākātyāyanas ten' âñjaliṃ kṛtvā, praṇamya Āyuṣmantaṃ Mahākātyāyanam idam avocat: «dṛṣṭo may" ôpādhyāyo dṛṣṭaś ca Bhagavān dharma|kāyena no tu rūpa|kāyena. gacchāmi, upādhyāya, rūpa|kāyen' âpi taṃ Bhagavantaṃ drakṣyāmi.»

Sa āha, «evam, vatsa, kuruṣva. durlabha|darśanā hi, vatsa, Tathāgatā Arhantaḥ samyak|saṃbuddhās tad|yath" āudumbara|puṣpam. asmākaṃ ca vacanena Bhagavataḥ pādau śirasā vandasv' âlp'|ābādhatāṃ ca pṛcch' âlp'|ātaṅkatāṃ ca lagh'|ûtthānatāṃ ca yātrāṃ ca balaṃ ca sukhaṃ c' ânavadyatāṃ ca sukha|sparśa|vihāratāṃ ca. pañca praśnāṃś ca pṛccha:

Aśm'|âpar'|ântakeṣu, bhadantaḥ, jana|padeṣu alpa|bhikṣukam. kṛcchreṇa daśa|varga|gaṇaḥ paripūryate. tatr' âsmābhiḥ kathaṃ pratipattavyam? kharā bhūmir go|kaṇṭak'|âdhānāt. Aśm'|âpar'|ântakeṣu jana|padeṣv idam evaṃ|rūpam āstaraṇaṃ pratyāstaraṇaṃ tad|yathā: avi|carma go|carma mṛga|carma chāga|carma. tad|anyeṣu jana|padeṣv idam

Maha·katyáyana said, "Do so, my sons. One should indeed behold, one should indeed respectfully attend the Tathágatas, the Arhats, the Perfectly Awakened Ones."

At that very time, Shrona Koti·karna, who was seated in that very assembly, presented himself. The Venerable Shrona Koti·karna rose from his seat, removed his outer robe from one shoulder, knelt with his right knee on the ground, reverently saluted the Venerable Maha·katyáyana with folded hands and said this to him: "I have beheld you, my spiritual preceptor, and I have beheld the Lord in the body of his doctrines, but never in his physical form. I wish to go, too, O preceptor; I wish to behold the Lord also in his physical form."

Maha·katyáyana replied, "My son, you may do so. It is rare indeed, my son, to obtain sight of the Tathágatas, the Arhats, the Perfectly Awakened Ones—as rare as seeing a flower on the sacred fig tree. On my behalf, prostrate yourself at the Lord's feet and inquire whether he is free from disease and from illness, whether he is in good physical condition, hale, hearty, at ease and in agreeable and comfortable circumstances. Ask him, also in my name, these five questions:*

Among the people of Ashma·parántaka there are few monks. It is exceedingly difficult to fill a quorum of ten. In this matter, how are we to proceed? The ground is rough due to trampling by the hooves of cattle. Among the people of Ashma·parántaka, there are in use such seats and cushions as those made of sheepskin, cowhide, antelope skin and goatskin. Among other peoples, there are in use such seats and cushions as those made of grass, tree bark, silk* and

evaṃ|rūpam āstaraṇaṃ pratyāstaraṇaṃ tad|yathā: erako merako jandurako* mandurakaḥ. evam ev' Âśm'|âpar'|ântakeṣu jana|padeṣv idam evaṃ|rūpam āstaraṇaṃ pratyāstaraṇaṃ tad|yathā: avi|carma pūrva|vat. udaka|śuddhikā manuṣyāḥ snāna|samudācārāḥ. bhikṣur bhikṣoś cīvarakāni preṣayati. itaś|cyutāni tatr'|â|saṃprāptāni. kasy' âitāni naiḥsargikāni?» adhivāsayaty Āyuṣmāñ Śroṇaḥ Koṭīkarṇa Āyuṣmato Mahākātyāyanasya tūṣṇīṃ|bhāvena.

1.155 Ath' Āyuṣmāñ Śroṇaḥ Koṭīkarṇas tasyā eva rātrer atyayāt pūrv'|āhṇe nivāsya, pātra|cīvaram ādāya, Vāsava|grāmakaṃ piṇḍāya prāvikṣat. Vāsava|grāmakaṃ piṇḍāya caritvā, kṛta|bhakta|kṛtyaḥ paścād|bhakta|piṇḍa|pātraḥ pratikrāntaḥ. yathā|paribhukta|śayan'|āsanaṃ pratiśāmayya samādāya pātra|cīvaraṃ yena Śrāvastī tena cārikāṃ carann anupūrveṇa Śrāvastīm anuprāptaḥ.

Ath' Āyuṣmāñ Śroṇaḥ Koṭīkarṇaḥ pātra|cīvaraṃ pratiśāmayya pādau prakṣālya yena Bhagavāṃs ten' ôpasaṃkrāntaḥ. upasaṃkramya vanditv" âik'|ânte niṣaṇṇaḥ. tatra Bhagavān Āyuṣmantam Ānandam āmantrayate sma: «gaccha, Ānanda, Tathāgatasya Śroṇasya ca Koṭīkarṇasy' âika|vihāre mañcaṃ prajñapaya.»

«Evaṃ bhadanta,» ity Āyuṣmān Ānandas Tathāgatasya Śroṇasya ca Koṭīkarṇasy' âika|vihāre mañcaṃ prajñapya yena Bhagavāṃs ten' ôpasaṃkrāntaḥ. upasaṃkramya Bhagavantam idam avocat: «prajñaptaḥ, bhadanta, Tathāgatasya Śroṇasya ca Koṭīkarṇasy' âika|vihāre mañco yasy' êdānīṃ Bhagavān kālaṃ manyate.»

cotton. In the same way among the people of Ashma·parántaka there are in use such seats and cushions as those made of sheepskin and the others mentioned before. Men clean themselves with water; they bathe as their normal practice. A monk sends to another monk robes that are dispatched from one place but fail to reach the other. Who forfeits them?" The Venerable Shrona Koti·karna consented to the Venerable Maha·katyáyana's request by remaining silent.

At the end of that same night, the following morning, 1.155
the Venerable Shrona Koti·karna dressed himself, took up his almsbowl and outer robe and entered Vásava village for alms. He made his alms-round in Vásava village, ate the food he had collected and after eating returned from his alms-round. Then, putting away the bed and seat he had used and again taking up his robe and bowl, he set out for and in due course reached Shravásti.

Then the Venerable Shrona Koti·karna put away his bowl and robe, washed his feet and went to see the Lord. He approached the Lord, reverently saluted him and sat down to one side. At that, the Lord summoned the Venerable Ananda: "Go, Ananda, prepare a sleeping platform in the same hut for the Tathágata and the Venerable Shrona Koti·karna."

Saying, "Very well, Venerable Sir," the Venerable Ananda prepared a sleeping platform in the same hut for the Tathágata and Shrona Koti·karna and then approached the Lord. Having approached, he said this to the Lord: "It is ready, Venerable Sir, a sleeping platform in the same hut for the Tathágata and Shrona Koti·karna, if the Lord thinks now is the right time."

Atha Bhagavāñ Śroṇaś ca Koṭīkarṇo yena vihāras ten' ôpasaṃkrānto yāvad vihāraṃ praviśya niṣaṇṇaḥ. yāvat smṛtiṃ pratimukham upasthāpya. ath' Āyuṣmān api Śroṇaḥ Koṭīkarṇaḥ, bahir vihārasya pādau prakṣālya, vihāraṃ praviśya, niṣaṇṇaḥ, paryaṅkam ābhujya yāvat pratimukhaṃ smṛtim upasthāpya. tāṃ khalu rātriṃ Bhagavān Āyuṣmāṃś ca Śroṇaḥ Koṭīkarṇa āryeṇa tūṣṇī|bhāven' âtināmitavān. atha Bhagavān rātryāḥ pratyūṣa|samaye Āyuṣmantaṃ Śroṇaṃ Koṭīkarṇam āmantrayate sma: «pratibhātu te, Śroṇa, dharmo yo mayā svayam abhijñāy' âbhisaṃbudhy' ākhyātaḥ.»

Ath' Āyuṣmāñ Śroṇo Bhagavatā kṛt'|âvakāśo 'śm'|âpar'|ântikayā svara|guptikay" Ôdānam, Pār'|āyaṇam, Satya|dṛṣṭim, Śaila|gāthāḥ, Muni|gāthāḥ, Sthavira|gāthāḥ, Sthavirī|gāthāḥ, Artha|vargīyāṇi ca Sūtrāṇi vistareṇa svareṇa sv'|âdhyāyaṃ karoti. atha Bhagavāñ Śroṇasya Koṭīkarṇasya kathā|paryavasānaṃ viditvā, Āyuṣmantaṃ Śroṇaṃ Koṭīkarṇam idam avocat: «sādhu! sādhu! Śroṇa. madhuras te dharmo bhāṣitaḥ praṇītaś ca yo mayā svayam abhijñāy' âbhisaṃbudhy' ākhyātaḥ.»

1.160 Ath' Āyuṣmataḥ Śroṇasya Koṭīkarṇasy' âitad abhavat, «ayaṃ me kālo Bhagavata upādhyāyasya vacas" ārādhayitum» iti viditv" ôtthāy' āsanād yāvad Bhagavantaṃ praṇamy' êdam avocat: «Aśm'|âpar'|ântakeṣu jana|padeṣu Vāsava|grāmake, bhadanta, Mahākātyāyanaḥ prativasati, yo ma

Then the Lord and Shrona Koti·karna approached the hut, while the Lord entered, sat down and established himself in mindfulness. As for the Venerable Shrona Koti·karna, he washed his feet outside the hut, entered, sat down, and assumed a cross-legged posture until he, too, had established himself in mindfulness. That entire night the Lord and the Venerable Shrona Koti·karna allowed to pass in holy silence. Then, at the time when night gives way to morning, the Lord addressed the Venerable Shrona Koti·karna: "Let it inspire you to recite, Shrona, the Dharma that I by myself have cognized, perfectly comprehended and made known."

At that, the Venerable Shrona Koti·karna, given the opportunity by the Lord, recited in full, in the accent of Ashma·parántaka, but with the proper intonation, "The Exultations," "The Way to the Further Shore," "Discerning the Truth," "The Mountaineer's Verses," "The Sage's Verses," "Verses of the Elder Monks," "Verses of the Elder Nuns" and "Discourses Concerning the Goal." The Lord, when he knew that Shrona Koti·karna had finished speaking, said to him: "Excellent! Excellent, Shrona! Mellifluous is the Dharma you have spoken and presented, the Dharma that I by myself have cognized, perfectly comprehended and made known."

Then it occurred to the Venerable Shrona Koti·karna, 1.160
"Now is the time for me to employ my preceptor's words to obtain the Lord's favor." So thinking, he rose from his seat, bowed before the Lord and said, "Among the people of Ashma·parántaka, O Venerable sir, in Vásava village dwells the Venerable Maha·katyáyana, who is my spiritual preceptor. He prostrates himself before the Lord and asks whether

upādhyāyaḥ. sa Bhagavataḥ pādau śirasā vandate 'lp'|ābādhatāṃ ca pṛcchaty alp'|ātaṅkatāṃ ca lagh'|ûtthānatāṃ ca yātrāṃ ca balaṃ ca sukhaṃ c' ânavadyatāṃ ca sukha|sparśa|vihāratāṃ ca. pañca ca praśnān pṛcchati.» [vistareṇ' ôccārayitavyāni].

Atha Bhagavāñ Śroṇaṃ Koṭīkarṇam idam avocat: «akālaṃ te, Śroṇa, praśna|vyākaraṇāya. saṃgha|melake praśnaḥ pṛcchyeta. tatra kālo bhaviṣyati praśnasya vyākaraṇāya.»

Atha Bhagavān kālyam ev' ôtthāya purastād bhikṣu|saṃghasya prajñapta ev' āsane niṣaṇṇaḥ. ath' Āyuṣmāñ Śroṇaḥ Koṭīkarṇo yena Bhagavāṃs ten' ôpasaṃkramya bhagavataḥ pādau śirasā vanditv" âik'|ânte 'sthāt. ek'|ânta|sthito Bhagavantam idam avocat: «Aśm'|âpar'|ântakeṣu jana|padeṣu, Vāsava|grāmake, bhadanta, Mahākātyāyanaḥ prativasati, yo ma upādhyāyaḥ. sa Bhagavataḥ pādau śirasā vandate 'lp'|ābādhatāṃ ca pṛcchati yāvat sparśa|vihāratāṃ ca.» [pañca ca praśnāni vistareṇ' ôccārayitavyāni yathā pūrvam uktāni yāvat «kasya naiḥsargikāni»].

Bhagavān āha, «tasmād anujānāmi pratyantimeṣu jana|padeṣu Vinaya|dhara|pañcamena gaṇen' ôpasaṃpadā, sadā snānam, eka|palāśika upānahe dhārayitavye, na dvipuṭe na tri|puṭe. sā cet kṣaya|dharmiṇī bhavati, argalakaṃ dattvā dhārayitavye. carma dhārayitavyam. bhikṣur bhikṣoś cīvarakāni preṣayati itaś cyutāni tatr' â|saṃprāptāni na kasya cin naiḥsargikāni.»

you are free from disease and from illness, whether you are in good physical condition, hale, hearty, at ease and in agreeable and comfortable circumstances. And he asks five questions." [These are to be recited in full.]

Then the Lord said this to Shrona Koti·karna: "This is not the time, Shrona, for the elucidation of your questions. It is during the meeting of the Order that questions should be asked. Then it will be the time to elucidate your questions."

Then, right at daybreak, the Lord rose and sat down before the Order of Monks on the designated seat. The Venerable Shrona Koti·karna approached the Lord, prostrated himself at his feet and stood off to one side. Standing off to one side, he said this to the Lord: "Among the people of Ashma·parántaka, Venerable sir, in the village of Vásava, dwells Maha·katyáyana, who is my spiritual preceptor. He prostrates himself at the Lord's feet and asks whether you are free from disease, . . . and in agreeable and comfortable circumstances." [And here the five questions are to be stated in full, as before, up to "which monk forfeits them."]

The Lord said, "Accordingly, I authorize, for the border lands, conferral of the higher ordination by a quorum of five at least one of whom has mastered the Vinaya, frequent bathing and wearing sandals with single-layered soles, but not with double- or triple-layered soles. If a sandal has a hole in it, it should be patched and the pair should continue to be worn. Leather may be worn. And when a monk sends to another monk robes that are dispatched from one place but fail to reach the other, no one forfeits them."

Āyuṣmān Upālī Buddhaṃ Bhagavantaṃ pṛcchati, «yad uktam, bhadanta, Bhagavatā pratyantimeṣu jana|padeṣu Vinaya|dhara|pañcamena gaṇen' ôpasaṃpadā, tatra katamo 'ntaḥ, katamaḥ pratyantaḥ?»

1.165 «Pūrveṇa, Upālin, Puṇḍravardhanaṃ nāma nagaram, tasya pūrveṇa Puṇḍrakakṣo nāma dāvaḥ. so 'ntaḥ, tataḥ pareṇa pratyantaḥ. dakṣiṇena Śarāvatī nāma nagarī, tasyāḥ pareṇa Śarāvatī nāma nadī. so 'ntaḥ, tataḥ pareṇa pratyantaḥ. paścimena Sthūṇ'|Ôpasthūṇakau brāhmaṇa|grāmakau. so 'ntaḥ, tataḥ pareṇa pratyantaḥ. uttareṇa Uśīra|giriḥ. so 'ntaḥ, tataḥ pareṇa pratyantaḥ.»

Bhikṣavaḥ saṃśaya|jātāḥ sarva|saṃśaya|cchettāraṃ Buddhaṃ Bhagavantaṃ pṛcchanti, «kiṃ, bhadanta, Āyuṣmatā Śroṇena Koṭīkarṇena karma kṛtam, yasya karmaṇo vipāken' āḍhye mahā|dhane mahā|bhoge kule jātaḥ, ratna|pratyuptikayā karṇa āmuktikayā, Bhagavataḥ śāsane pravrajya, sarva|kleśa|prahāṇād arhattvaṃ sākṣāt|kṛtam.»

Bhagavān āha, «bhūta|pūrvam, bhikṣavaḥ, Vārāṇasyāṃ nagaryāṃ Kāśyapo nāma Tathāgato 'rhan samyak|saṃbuddho Bhagavāñ Śāstā loka utpannaḥ. tena khalu samayena Vārāṇasyāṃ dvau jāyā|patikau. tābhyāṃ Kāśyapasya samyak|saṃbuddhasy' ântike śaraṇa|gamana|śikṣā|padāny udgṛhītāni. yadā Kāśyapaḥ samyak|saṃbuddhaḥ sakalaṃ Bu-

The Venerable Upáli asked the Lord, "What the Lord stated—that in the border lands he authorizes higher ordination by a quorum of five at least one of whom has mastered the Vinaya—in such cases, what is within the border, what is beyond it?"

"To the east, Upáli, is the city called Pundra·várdhana; 1.165
to the east of that, the forest called Pundra·kaksha. That forest is within the border; past it is beyond the border. To the south is the city called Sharávati; beyond that, the river also called Sharávati. That river is within the border; past it is beyond the border. To the west are two brahmin villages, Sthuna and Upasthúnaka. Those two villages are within the border; past them is beyond it. To the north is Mount Úshira. It is within the border; past it is beyond."

Their doubts aroused, the monks questioned the Buddha, who resolves all doubts: "Venerable sir, what deed did the Venerable Shrona Koti·karna perform due to the ripening of which he was born, wearing an earring set with jewels, into a wealthy family possessed of great riches and extensive properties and then, going forth into the homeless life under the Lord's Teaching, attained Arhatship as a result of the abandonment of all defilements?"

The Lord replied, "Long ago, monks, there arose in the world, in the city of Varánasi,* a Tathágata named Káshyapa,* an Arhat, a Fully Awakened Buddha, a Lord, a Teacher. There dwelled in Varánasi at that same time a certain couple, husband and wife. In the presence of Káshyapa, the Fully Awakened Buddha, they went for refuge and took upon themselves the lay disciple's rules of training. When the Fully Awakened Buddha Káshyapa completely fulfilled the

ddha|kāryaṃ kṛtvā, nirupadhiśeṣe nirvāṇa|dhātau parinirvṛtaḥ, tasya Rājñā Kṛkinā catū|ratna|mayaṃ caityaṃ kāritaṃ samantād yojanam ardha|yojanam uccatvena. tena tatra khaṇḍa|sphuṭa|pratisaṃskaraṇāya ye pūrva|nagara|dvāre kara|pratyāyā uttiṣṭhante, te tasmin stūpe 'nupradattāḥ.

Yadā Kṛkī Rājā kāla|gataḥ, tasya putra, Sujāto nāmnā, sva|rājye pratiṣṭhāpitaḥ. tasy' âmātyaiḥ stokāḥ kara|pratyāyā upanāmitāḥ. rājā pṛcchati, ‹kiṃ|kāraṇam asmākaṃ bhavadbhiḥ stokāḥ kara|pratyāyā upanāmitāḥ? kim asmākaṃ vijite kara|pratyāyā n' ôttiṣṭhante?›

Te kathayanti, ‹Deva, kutaḥ kara|pratyāyā uttiṣṭhante? ye, Deva, pūrva|dvāre kara|pratyāyāḥ, te vṛddha|rājñā stūpe khaṇḍa|sphuṭa|pratisaṃskaraṇāya prajñaptāḥ. yadi Devo 'nujānīte, vayaṃ tān kara|pratyāyān samucchindāmaḥ.›

1.170 Sa kathayati, ‹bhavantaḥ, yan mama pitrā kṛtaṃ Brahma|kṛtaṃ tat Śakra|kṛtaṃ tat.›

Te saṃlakṣayanti, ‹yadi Devo 'nujānīte, vayaṃ tathā kariṣyāmo yathā svayam eva te kara|pratyāyā n' ôtthāsyanti.› taiḥ sa dvāro baddhvā sthāpitaḥ. na bhūyaḥ kara|pratyāyā uttiṣṭhante.

Tasmin stūpe caṭita|sphuṭitakāni prādur|bhūtāni. tau jāyā|patī vṛddhī|bhūtau tatr' âiva stūpe parikarma kurvāṇau tiṣṭhataḥ.

duties of a Buddha and attained complete emancipation in the state of nirvana that is entirely free from conditioned existence, King Krikin had built for him a relic-mound* made of the four jewels, a league in circumference and half a league in height. In order to provide for the repair of cracks and breaks, the king donated to that relic-mound all tributes and taxes collected at the city's eastern gate.

When King Krikin passed away, his son, Sújata by name, established his own rule. His ministers, however, delivered only small amounts of tax and tribute. The king asked, 'Why is it that you deliver to me only small amounts of tax and tribute? Is tax and tribute not collected in my realm?'

His ministers replied, 'Your majesty, from where could taxes and tributes be collected? Those taxes, your majesty, which are collected at the eastern gate, the late king reserved for the repair of cracks and breaks in the Stupa. If your majesty consents, we will completely cut off the flow of tax and tribute.'

Said the king, 'Gentlemen, what my father did was done 1.170
by Brahma and Shakra.'

The ministers reflected, 'If his majesty consents, we shall make it so that no taxes and tributes are received.' They barred the gate and left it that way. No longer were taxes and tributes received.

On that Stupa cracks and fissures appeared. The elderly husband and wife regularly cleaned and adorned that very Stupa.

Uttarā|pathāc ca sārtha|vāhaḥ paṇyam ādāya Vārāṇasīm anuprāptaḥ. ten' âsau dṛṣṭaḥ stūpaś caṭita|sphuṭitakaiḥ prādur|bhūtaiḥ. sa dṛṣṭvā pṛcchati, ‹amba, tāta, kasy' âiṣa stūpa?› iti.

Tau kathayataḥ, ‹Kāśyapasya samyak|saṃbuddhasya.›

1.175 ‹Kena kāritaḥ?›

‹Kṛkinā Rājñā.›

‹Na tena rājñ" âsmin stūpe khaṇḍa|sphuṭa|pratisaṃkaraṇāya kiṃ cit prajñaptam?›

Tau kathayataḥ, ‹prajñaptam. ye pūrva|nagara|dvāre kara|pratyāyās te 'smin stūpe khaṇḍa|sphuṭa|pratisaṃskaraṇāya niryātitāḥ. Kṛkī Rājā kāla|gataḥ. tasya putraḥ Sujāto nāmna sva|rājye pratiṣṭhitaḥ. tena te kara|pratyāyāḥ samucchinnāḥ. ten' âsmin stūpe caṭita|sphuṭitakāni prādur|bhūtāni.›

Tasya ratna|karṇikā karṇa āmuktikā. tena sā ratna|karṇik" âvatārya tayor dattā. ‹amba, tāta, anayā ratna|karṇikay" âsmin stūpe khaṇḍa|sphuṭa|pratisaṃskāraṃ kurutam iti. yāvad ahaṃ paṇyaṃ visarjayitv" āgacchāmi. tataḥ paścād bhūyo 'pi dāsyāmi.› tais tāṃ vikrīya tasmin stūpe khaṇḍa|sphuṭita|pratisaṃskāraḥ kṛtaḥ. aparam utsarpitam.

1.180 Ath' âpareṇa samayena sārtha|vāhaḥ paṇyaṃ visarjayitv" āgataḥ. tena sa dṛṣṭaḥ stūpo 'secanaka|darśanaḥ. dṛṣṭvā sa ca bhūyasy" âpi mātray" âbhiprasannaḥ. sa prasāda|jātaḥ pṛcchati, ‹amba, tāta, mā yuṣmābhiḥ kiṃ cid uddhārī|kṛtam.›

Then a caravan-leader, bringing trade-goods, arrived in Varánasi from the north country. He saw the Stupa on which cracks and fissures had appeared and, having seen this, he asked, 'Mother, Father, whose Stupa is this?'

They told him, 'It's the Stupa of Káshyapa, the Fully Awakened Buddha.'

'Who had it built?' 1.175

'King Krikin.'

'Did that king not reserve any revenue for the repair of cracks and breaks in that Stupa?'

The couple replied, 'He did. The taxes and tribute received at the city's eastern gate he donated for the repair of cracks and breaks in that Stupa. But King Krikin passed away. His son, Sújata by name, has established his own rule. He has completely cut off the taxes and tribute. And on that Stupa cracks and fissures have appeared.'

The caravan-leader had a jewelled earring fastened on one ear. He took it off and gave it to the old couple. 'Mother, Father, use this to repair the cracks and breaks in the Stupa. I shall just deliver my wares and return. Then, after that, I'll donate even more.' The old couple sold the earring and repaired the cracks and breaks in the Stupa. What was left over they set aside.

Some time later, having delivered his wares, the cara- 1.180
van-leader returned. He saw that the Stupa had a pleasing appearance. And so seeing, he was inspired with serene faith to an even greater degree. Thus inspired, he asked, 'Mother, Father, I hope you didn't incur any debt?'

Tau kathayataḥ, ‹putra, n' âsmābhiḥ kiṃ cid uddhārī|kṛtaṃ kiṃ tv aparam utsarpitaṃ tiṣṭhati.›

Tena prasāda|jātena yat tatr' âvaśiṣṭam aparaṃ ca dattvā, mahatīṃ pūjāṃ kṛtvā, praṇidhānaṃ ca kṛtam: ‹anen' âhaṃ kuśala|mūlen' āḍhye mahā|dhane mahā|bhoge kule jāyeyam. evaṃ|vidhānāṃ ca dharmāṇāṃ lābhī syām. evaṃ|vidham eva śāstāram ārāgayeyaṃ mā virāgayeyam› iti.

Kiṃ manyadhve, bhikṣavaḥ? yo 'sau sārtha|vāha eṣa ev' âsau Śroṇaḥ Koṭīkarṇaḥ. yad anena Kāśyapasya samyak|saṃbuddhasya stūpe kārāṃ kṛtvā, praṇidhānaṃ kṛtam, tasya karmaṇo vipāken' āḍhye mahā|dhane mahā|bhoge kule jātaḥ. mama śāsane pravrajya sarva|kleśa|prahāṇād arhatvaṃ sākṣāt|kṛtam. aham anena Kāśyapena samyak|saṃbuddhena sārdhaṃ sama|javaḥ sama|balaḥ sama|dhuraḥ sama|sāmānya|prāptaḥ śāst" ārāgito na virāgitaḥ.

Iti hi, bhikṣavaḥ, ‹ek'|ânta|kṛṣṇānāṃ karmaṇām ek'|ânta|kṛṣṇo vipākaḥ, ek'|ânta|śuklānāṃ karmaṇām ek'|ânta|śuklo vipākaḥ, vyatimiśrāṇāṃ karmaṇāṃ vyatimiśro vipākaḥ.› tasmāt tarhi, bhikṣavaḥ, ek'|ânta|kṛṣṇāni karmāṇy apāsya vyatimiśrāṇi c' âik'|ânta|śukleṣv eva karmasv ābhogaḥ karaṇīyaḥ. ity evaṃ vaḥ, bhikṣavaḥ, śikṣitavyam.

The couple replied, 'Son, we did not incur any debt; rather, what was left over remains set aside.'

Inspired with serene faith, the caravan-leader donated to the Stupa what was left over from repairing it and more. He then held a splendid devotional ceremony at which he made this earnest wish: 'By this deed, which plants roots of merit, may I take rebirth in a wealthy family possessed of great riches and extensive properites! May I obtain such qualities! And may I gratify and not displease just such a teacher as the Buddha Káshyapa!'

What do you think, monks? He who was that caravan-leader, he is no other than Shrona Koti·karna. Because in worshipping at the Stupa of the Fully Awakened Buddha Káshyapa he made that earnest wish, he was, as a result of that deed, reborn in a wealthy family possessed of great riches and extensive properties, went forth into the homeless life in accordance with my teaching and attained Arhatship. As a teacher, I possess the same fleetness and power as the Fully Awakened Buddha Káshyapa, bear an equal burden, have attained the same universality and am gratified, not displeased by Shrona Koti·karna.

Therefore, monks, it is said, 'The ripening of wholly black deeds is itself wholly black; the ripening of wholly white deeds is itself wholly white; and the ripening of mixed deeds is itself mixed.' Therefore, then, monks, abandon wholly black deeds as well as mixed deeds and direct your earnest efforts to wholly white deeds. In this way, monks, should you train yourselves.

1.185 Bhikṣava ūcuḥ, «kiṃ, bhadanta, Āyuṣmatā Śroṇena Koṭīkarṇena karma kṛtaṃ yasya karmaṇo vipākena dṛṣṭa eva dharme 'pāyā dṛṣṭāḥ.»

Bhagavān āha, «yad anena mātur antike khara|vāk|karma niścāritam—tasya karmaṇo vipākena, dṛṣṭa eva dharmo 'pāyā dṛṣṭāḥ» iti.

Idam avocad Bhagavān. ātta|manasas te bhikṣavo Bhagavato bhāṣitam abhyanandan.

iti Śrī|divy'|âvadāne
Koṭī|karṇ'|âvadānaṃ prathamam.

The monks said, "Venerable sir, what deed did the Venerable Shrona Koti·karna perform due to the ripening of which he witnessed, in this present visible world, wretched states of existence?" 1.185

The Lord replied, "Because he committed the deed of harsh speech in front of his mother—it was due to the ripening of that deed that he witnessed, in this present visible world, wretched states of existence."

Thus spoke the Lord. Their hearts gladdened, the monks rejoiced at the Lord's words.

Thus concludes "The Story of Koti·karna,"
the first narrative in "The Heavenly Exploits."

2
THE STORY OF PURNA

BHAGAVĀÑ ŚRĀVASTYĀṂ VIHARATI sma Jeta|vane 'nātha-piṇḍadasy' ārāme. tena khalu samayena Sūrpārake nagare, Bhavo nāma gṛha|patiḥ prativasati, āḍhyo mahā|dhano mahā|bhogo vistīrṇa|viśāla|parigraho Vaiśravaṇa|dhana|samudito Vaiśravaṇa|dhana|pratispardhī.

Tena sādṛśāt kulāt kalatram ānītam. sa tayā sārdhaṃ krīḍati, ramate, paricārayati. tasya krīḍato ramamāṇasya paricārayataḥ kāl'|ântareṇa patny āpanna|sattvā saṃvṛttā. s" âṣṭānāṃ navānāṃ vā māsānām atyayāt prasūtā. dārako jātaḥ.

Tasya trīṇi saptakāny eka|viṃśati|divasāni vistareṇa jātasya jāti|mahaṃ kṛtvā, nāma|dheyaṃ vyavasthāpyate: «kiṃ bhavatu dārakasya nāma?» iti.

Jñātaya ūcuḥ, «ayaṃ dārako Bhavasya gṛha|pateḥ putraḥ; tasmād bhavatu ‹Bhavilaḥ›» iti nāma|dheyaṃ vyavasthāpitam.

2.5 Bhūyo 'py asya krīḍato ramamāṇasya paricārayataḥ, putro jātaḥ. tasya ‹Bhavatrātā› iti nāma|dheyaṃ vyavasthāpitam. punar apy asya putro jātaḥ. tasya ‹Bhavanandī› iti nāma|dheyaṃ vyavasthāpitam.

Yāvad apareṇa samayena Bhavo gṛha|patir glānaḥ saṃvṛttaḥ. so 'ty|arthaṃ paruṣa|vacana|samudācārī yataḥ patnyā putraiś c' âpy upekṣitaḥ. tasya preṣya|dārikā. sā saṃlakṣayati, «mama svāmin" ânekair upāya|śata|sahasrair bhogāḥ samudānītāḥ. sa idānīṃ glānaḥ saṃvṛttaḥ. sa eṣa patnyā putraiś c'

THE LORD WAS STAYING AT SHRAVÁSTI, in Prince Jeta's Grove in Anátha·píndada's park. At that same time there lived in the city of Surpáraka a householder by the name of Bhava. He was wealthy, having a great deal of money and other possessions. His properties were. Indeed, his wealth rivalled that of the God of Wealth, Vaishrávana himself.

Bhava took a wife from a family similar to his own. He enjoyed himself with her, made love to her and otherwise dallied with her. Some time passed in this way, and his wife became pregnant. After the passage of eight or nine months she gave birth to a son.

Three weeks, that is, twenty-one days later, Bhava performed the child's birth-ceremonies and settled upon a name. "What name should the child be given?"

His relatives said, "This boy is the son of Bhava; let him, therefore, be given the name Bhávila, 'Little Bhava.'" And so his name was settled.

Again Bhava enjoyed himself with his wife, made love 2.5
to her and otherwise dallied with her, and another son was born. He was given the name Bhava·trata, "Bhava's Protector." Some time after that another son was born, and he was named Bhava·nandin, "Bhava's Joy."

Some time later, the householder Bhava fell ill, and because of his exceedingly abusive language his wife and even his sons would have nothing to do with him. He had, however, a slave girl, who thought to herself, "In so many ways my master has accumulated wealth. Now he has fallen ill, and his wife and even his sons will have nothing to do with him. It would not be right for me too to ignore him." So

âpy upekṣitaḥ. na mama pratirūpaṃ syād yad ahaṃ svāminam adhyupekṣeyam» iti. sā vaidya|sakāśaṃ gatvā kathayati, «ārya, jānīṣe tvaṃ Bhavaṃ gṛha|patim?»

«Jāne. kiṃ tasya?»

«Tasy' âivaṃ|vidhaṃ glānyaṃ samupajātam. sa patnyā putraiś c' âpy upekṣitaḥ. tasya bhaiṣajyaṃ vyapadiśa» iti.

Sa kathayati, «dārike, tvam eva kathayasi, ‹sa patnyā putraiś c' âpy upekṣitaḥ› iti. atha kas tasy' ôpasthānaṃ karoti?»

2.10 Sā kathayati, «aham asy' ôpasthānaṃ karomi. kiṃ tv alpa|mūlyāni bhaiṣajyāni vyapadiśa» iti. tena vyapadiṣṭam, «idaṃ tasya bhaiṣajyam» iti.

Tatas tayā kiṃ cit sva|bhaktāt samudānīya, kiṃ cit tasmād eva gṛhād apahṛty' ôpasthānaṃ kṛtam. sa, svasthī|bhūtaḥ, saṃlakṣayati, «ahaṃ patnyā putraiś c' âdhyupekṣitaḥ. yad ahaṃ jīvitaḥ, tad asyā dārikāyāḥ prabhāvāt. tad asyāḥ pratyupakāraḥ kartavyaḥ» iti. sā ten' ôktā, «dārike, ahaṃ patnyā putraiś c' âpy upekṣitaḥ. yat kiṃ cid ahaṃ jīvitaḥ sarvaṃ tava prabhāvāt. vada—kiṃ te varam anuprayacchāmi» iti.

Sā kathayati, «svāmin, yadi me parituṣṭo 'smi, bhavatu me tvayā sārdhaṃ samāgamaḥ» iti.

Sa kathayati, «kiṃ te mayā sārdhaṃ samāgamena? pañca kārṣāpaṇa|śatāny anuprayacchāmi, adāsīṃ c' ôtsṛjāmi» iti.

Sā kathayati, «svāmin, dūram api pāram api gatvā, dāsy ev' âham, yadi tu ārya|putreṇa sārdhaṃ samāgamo bhavati, evam adāsī bhavāmi» iti.

she went to see the doctor and said, “Sir, do you know the householder Bhava?”

“I do. What of him?”

“He is suffering from some kind of illness. His wife and even his sons will have nothing to do with him. Please prescribe some medicine.”

Said the doctor, “Girl, you yourself say that your master is ignored by his wife and even by his sons. Who, then, is taking care of him?”

She replied, “I am taking care of him. In any case, please 2.10
prescribe some inexpensive medicines.” The doctor recommended a certain medicinal herb.

She collected some from her own supplies, took more from the household stores and began treatment. Bhava regained his health. Later he thought, “My wife and even my sons ignored me. That I have recovered is entirely due to this girl. I must therefore reciprocate her kindness.” Bhava addressed her: “Young woman, my wife and even my sons ignored me. That I am alive is entirely due to you. Tell me—what reward can I offer you?”

She replied, “Master, if you are pleased with me, let me have sex with you.”

He rejoined, “What’s the point of your having sex with me? I can offer you five hundred silver coins and send you off as a free woman!”

She said, “Master, whether living far away from here or even in the next life, I shall still be a slave; but if I have sexual relations with a gentleman, I shall thereby become a free woman.”

2.15 Ten' âvaśyaṃ nirbandhaṃ jñātv" âbhihitā, «dārike, yadā kalyā saṃvṛtta" rtumatī, tadā mam' ārocayiṣyasi» iti. s" âpareṇa samayena kalyā saṃvṛtta" rtumatī, tayā tasy' ārocitam. tato Bhavena gṛha|patinā tayā sārdhaṃ paricāritam. s" āpanna|sattvā saṃvṛttā. yam eva divasam āpanna|sattvā saṃvṛttā, tam eva divasam upādāya Bhavasya gṛha|pateḥ sarv'|ârthāḥ sarva|karm'|ântāś ca paripūrṇāḥ.

Sā tv aṣṭānāṃ vā navānāṃ māsānām atyayāt prasūtā. dārako jāto 'bhirūpaḥ, darśanīyaḥ, prāsādikaḥ, gauraḥ, kanaka|varṇaḥ, chatr'|ākāra|śīrṣaḥ, pralamba|bāhuḥ, vistīrṇa|lalāṭaḥ, saṃgata|bhrūḥ, tuṅga|nāsaḥ. yasminn eva divase dārako jātaḥ, tasminn eva divase Bhavasya gṛha|pater bhūyasyā mātrayā sarv'|ârthāḥ sarva|karm'|ântāḥ paripūrṇāḥ.

Tasya jñātayaḥ saṃgamya samāgamya trīṇi saptakāny eka|viṃśati|divasāni vistareṇa jātasya jāti|mahaṃ kṛtvā, nāma|dheyaṃ vyavasthāpyate. «kiṃ bhavatu dārakasya nāma» iti.

Jñātaya ūcuḥ, «yasminn eva divase dārako jātaḥ, tasminn eva divase Bhavasya gṛha|pater bhūyasyā mātrayā sarv'|ârthāḥ sarva|karm'|ântāḥ paripūrṇāḥ. tasmād bhavatu ‹Pūrṇaḥ› iti nāma|dheyaṃ vyavasthāpitam.

Pūrṇo dārako 'ṣṭābhyo dhātrībhyo 'nupradattaḥ: dvābhyām aṃsa|dhātrībhyāṃ, dvābhyāṃ krīḍanikā|dhātrībhyāṃ, dvābhyāṃ mala|dhātrībhyāṃ, dvābhyāṃ kṣīra|dhātrībhyām. so 'ṣṭābhir dhātrībhir unnīyate, vardhyate kṣīreṇa, dadhnā, navanītena, sarpiṣā, sarpi|maṇḍena, anyaiś c' ôttapt'|ôttaptair upakaraṇa|viśeṣaiḥ. āśu vardhate hrada|stham iva paṅka|jam.

Realizing her determined obstinacy, he declared, "Young 2.15
woman, when you are in your fertile period and in good health, let me know." Later, in good health and having reached her fertile period, she informed him. Then she had sexual relations with the householder Bhava and conceived. And the very day on which she conceived marked the fulfillment of all Bhava's goals and all of his undertakings.

After eight or nine months she gave birth. It was a boy. He was well formed, good-looking, handsome, with a pale golden complexion, a large, round head, long arms, a broad brow, eyebrows that joined and a prominent nose. On the very day that boy was born, to an even greater degree than before, all of the householder Bhava's goals and all of his undertakings were fulfilled.

Three weeks, that is, twenty-one days later, Bhava's relatives arrived and assembled, performed the child's birth-ceremonies and settled upon a name. "What name should the child be given?"

The relatives said, "On the very day this boy was born, to an even greater degree than before, all of the householder Bhava's goals and all of his undertakings were fulfilled. Therefore, let him be given the name Purna, 'Fulfilled.'

The infant Purna was given over to the care of eight nurses: two to carry him about, two as wet nurses, two to keep him clean and two to play with him. Raised by these eight nurses, who nourished him with milk, yoghurt, fresh butter, clarified butter and its by-products, and other pure and choice foods, Purna grew rapidly, like a lotus in a lake.

2.20 Yadā mahān saṃvṛttaḥ, tadā lipyām upanyastaḥ, saṃkhyāyāṃ, gaṇanāyāṃ, mudrāyām, uddhāre, nyāse, nikṣepe, vastra|parīkṣāyāṃ, vastu|parīkṣāyāṃ, dāru|parīkṣāyāṃ, ratna|parīkṣāyāṃ, hasti|parīkṣāyām, aśva|parīkṣāyāṃ, kumāra|parīkṣāyāṃ, kumārikā|parīkṣāyām. aṣṭāsu parīkṣās' ûdghaṭakaḥ, vācakaḥ, paṇḍitaḥ, paṭu|pracāraḥ saṃvṛttaḥ.

Tato Bhavena gṛha|patinā Bhavil'|ādīnāṃ putrāṇāṃ yath"|ânupūrvyā niveśāḥ kṛtāḥ. te patnībhiḥ sārdham atīva saṃraktā nirasta|vyāpārā maṇḍana|paramā vyavasthitāḥ. tato Bhavo gṛha|patiḥ kare kapolaṃ dattvā, cintā|paro vyavasthitaḥ. sa putrair dṛṣṭaḥ pṛṣṭaś ca: «tāta, kasmāt tvaṃ kare kapolaṃ dattvā, cintā|paro vyavasthita?» iti.

Sa kathayati, «putrakāḥ, na tāvan mayā niveśaḥ kṛto yāvat suvarṇa|lakṣaḥ samudānīta iti. te yūyaṃ nirasta|vyāpārāḥ patnīṣv aty|arthaṃ saṃraktā maṇḍana|paramā vyavasthitāḥ. mam' âtyayād gṛhaṃ śocanīyaṃ bhaviṣyati. kathaṃ na cintā|paro bhaviṣyāmi?» iti.

Bhavilena ratna|karṇikā pinaddhā. sa tām avatārya, Dārukarṇikāṃ pinahya, pratijñām ārūḍhaḥ: «na tāvat ratna|karṇikāṃ pinahyāmi yāvat suvarṇa|lakṣaḥ samupārjitaḥ» iti. apareṇa Stavakarṇikā. apareṇa Trapukarṇikā. teṣāṃ yās tāḥ saṃjñā ‹Bhavilo›, ‹Bhavatrāto›, ‹Bhavanandī› iti tā antarhitāḥ. ‹Dārukarṇī›, ‹Stavakarṇī›, ‹Trapukarṇī›, iti prādur|bhūtāḥ. te paṇyam ādāya mahā|samudraṃ saṃprasthitāḥ.

When he grew older, Purna was tutored in letters, counting, arithmetic, accounting, finance, debt-collection and commercial law. He also learned to inspect and assess textiles, real estate, lumber, jewels, elephants, horses and young men and women. He became an expounder, an explainer, a scholar, an expert in the evaluation of these eight valuable commodities. 2.20

Then the householder Bhava arranged marriages for his three older sons in order of seniority, beginning with Bhávila. But they and their wives, filled with passion, preoccupied with adorning themselves, neglected their business. As a result of this, the householder Bhava stayed head in his hands, lost in anxious thought. He was thus observed by his sons, who asked him, "Papa, why do you stay with your hand in your hands, lost in anxious thought?"

He replied, "My sons, I did not marry until I had amassed a hundred thousand gold coins. All of you, however, infatuated with your wives, are preoccupied with adorning yourselves and neglect your business. After my death, this will become a pitiful house! How can I not lose myself in anxious thought?"

Bhávila had been wearing a jewelled earring. He removed it, and, having put on a wooden one, made a vow: "I shall not wear a jewelled earring until I, too, have amassed a hundred thousand gold coins." And his two brothers donned a lac and a tin earring respectively. Thereafter their names—Bhávila, Bhava·trata and Bhava·nandin—were forgotten and they became known as "Wood-Earring," "Lac-Earring" and "Tin-Earring." Then those brothers supplied themselves with trade-goods and set out on the great ocean.

Pūrṇaḥ kathayati, «tāta, aham api mahā|samudraṃ gacchāmi» iti. sa kathayati, «putra, bālas tvam. atr' âiva tiṣṭh' āvāryāṃ vyāpāraṃ kuru.» sa tatr' âiv' âvasthitaḥ. te 'pi saṃsiddha|yāna|pātrā āgatāḥ. mārga|śramaṃ prativinodya kathayanti, «tāta, kalyatām asmadīyaṃ paṇyam» iti. tena kalitam. ek'|âikasya suvarṇa|lakṣā saṃvṛttā. Pūrṇen' âpi tatr' âiva dharmeṇa nyāyena vyavahāratā s'|âtirekā suvarṇa|lakṣā samudānītā. Pūrṇo 'pi pituḥ pādayor nipatya kathayati, «tāta, mam' âpi kalyatām āvārī|samutthitaṃ dravyam» iti.

2.25 Sa kathayati, «putra, tvam atr' âiv' âvasthitaḥ. kiṃ tava kalyate?»

Sa kathayati, «tāta, kalyatām. tath" âpi jñātaṃ bhaviṣyati» iti. kalitam. yāvan nyāy'|ôpārjitasya suvarṇasya mūlyaṃ varjayitvā sātiriktā suvarṇa|lakṣā saṃvṛttā. Bhavo gṛha|patiḥ prīti|saumanasya|jātaḥ saṃlakṣayati, «puṇya|maheś'|ākhyo 'yaṃ sattvo yen' êh' âiva sthiten' êyat suvarṇaṃ samupārjitam!» iti.

Yāvad apareṇa samayena Bhavo gṛha|patir glānaḥ saṃvṛttaḥ. sa saṃlakṣayati, «mam' âtyayād ete bhedaṃ gamiṣyanti. upāya|saṃvidhānaṃ kartavyam» iti. tena te 'bhihitāḥ, «putrakāḥ, kāṣṭhāni samudānayata» iti. taiḥ kāṣṭhāni samudānītāni. sa kathayati, «agniṃ prajvālayata» iti. tair agniḥ prajvālitaḥ. Bhavo gṛha|patiḥ kathayati, «ek'|âikam alātam apanayata» iti. tair apanītam. so 'gnir nirvāṇaḥ. sa kathayati, «putrakāḥ, dṛṣṭo vaḥ?» «tāta, dṛṣṭaḥ.»

Purna said, "Father, I, too, shall set out on the great ocean," but his father replied, "Son, you are still a child. Stay here and do business in the shop." And so Purna stayed there at home in Surpáraka. As for the others, they returned, their ship safe and sound. After recovering from the fatigue of travel, they said, "Father, tally our profits." He did so—and each had earned one hundred thousand gold coins. As for Purna, right there in the shop in Surpáraka, he had acquired, through honest trade, more than a hundred thousand gold coins. Purna flung himself at his father's feet and said, "Father, tally the wealth earned in my shop."

Bhava replied, "My son, you have been here all this time. 2.25
What can you have earned?"

Said Purna, "Father, let it be counted. Then its value will be known." When it was counted, leaving aside the capital with which he had started out, there was more than a hundred thousand gold coins honestly acquired. The householder Bhava, pleased and delighted, thought, "Truly he is a being who is great due to merit acquired in previous births to have earned this much money while staying right here!"

After some time the householder Bhava fell ill. He reflected, "After my death, these sons of mine will have a falling-out. Some kind of stratagem for preventing this must be devised." And so he said to them, "My dear sons, collect some sticks of wood." They brought some wood. Then he said, "Light a fire with them." They lit a fire. After a while, the householder Bhava said, "Remove the hot coals, one by one." They removed all of the coals and the fire was extinguished. Bhava asked, "My sons, did you see what happened?" "Father," they replied, "we saw!"

Sa gāthāṃ bhāṣate:

Jvalanti sahit'|âṅgārā
  bhrātaraḥ sahitās tathā.
pravibhaktā niśāmyanti
  yath" âṅgārās tathā narāḥ.

2.30 Putrakāḥ, na yuṣmābhir mam' âtyayāt strīṇāṃ śrotavyam:

Kuṭumbaṃ bhidyate strībhir
  vāgbhir bhidyanti cāturāḥ.
dur|nyasto bhidyate mantraḥ
  prītir bhidyati lobhataḥ.» iti

Te 'nyā niṣkrāntāḥ. Bhavilas tatr' âiv' âvasthitaḥ. sa ten' ôktaḥ, «putra, na kadā cit tvayā Pūrṇo moktavyaḥ. puṇya|maheś'|ākhyo 'yaṃ sattvaḥ» ity uktvā.

Sarve kṣay'|ântā nicayāḥ
  patan'|ântāḥ samucchrayāḥ.
saṃyogā viprayog'|ântā
  maraṇ'|ântaṃ ca jīvitam.

Iti kāla|dharmeṇa saṃyuktaḥ.

2.35 Tair nīla|pīta|lohit'|âvadātair vastraiḥ śivikām alaṃ|kṛtya, mahatā saṃskāreṇa śmaśānaṃ nītvā, dhmāpitaḥ. tatas te śoka|vinodanaṃ kṛtvā kathayanti, «yad" âsmākaṃ pitā jīvati, tadā tad|adhīnāḥ prāṇāḥ. yad idānīṃ nirasta|vyāpārās tiṣṭhāmaḥ, gṛham avasādaṃ gamiṣyati. na śobhanaṃ bhaviṣyati. yan nu vayaṃ paṇyam ādāya deś'|ântaraṃ gacchāmaḥ?» iti.

Bhava recited the following verses:

Brothers, united, glow brightly,
Like a mass of hot coals;
Divided, both men and coals expire.

My sons, after I am gone, do not be swayed by your wives: 2.30

Families are divided by women,
Clever men by words;
A spell, badly recited, has its efficacy destroyed,
Just as greed destroys affection."

The others departed. Bhávila, the eldest, remained. His father told him, "Son, you must never forsake Purna. He is a being who is great by reason of his merit." And so saying, he recited another verse:

All accumulation ends in loss,
All exaltation in decline,
All union in separation,
And all life in death.

After reciting this verse, Bhava submitted to the law of time.

Bhava's sons adorned the funeral bier with cloth of dark 2.35
blue, yellow, red and white, and, in accordance with the solemn rite, bore Bhava to the burning-ground and there cremated him. Later, after recovering from their grief, they said, "When our father was alive, our lives depended on him. If we now neglect business, our family will go into decline. That would be unseemly. Suppose now we take trade-goods and travel to foreign lands?"

Pūrṇaḥ kathayati, «yady evam, aham api gacchāmi» iti.

Te kathayanti, «tvam atr' âiv' āvāryāṃ vyāpāraṃ kuru. vayam eva gacchāmaḥ» iti. te paṇyam ādāya deś'|ântaraṃ gatāḥ. Pūrṇo nyasta|sarva|kāryas tatr' âiv' âvasthitaḥ.

Dharmatā khalv īśvara|gṛheṣu divasa|parivyayo dīyate. tās teṣāṃ patnayo dārikāḥ parivyaya|nimittaṃ preṣayanti. Pūrṇo 'pi dhanibhiḥ śreṣṭhibhiḥ sārtha|vāhair anyaiś c' ājīvibhiḥ parivṛto 'vatiṣṭhate. tās tv avakāśaṃ na labhante. yadā ta utthāya prakrāntā bhavanti, tadā tāsāṃ divasa|parivyayaṃ dadāti. tā dārikāś cira|cirād āgacchant' îty upālabhyante. tā evam arthaṃ vistareṇ' ārocayanti. tāḥ kathayanti, «evaṃ hi teṣāṃ bhavati yeṣāṃ dāsī|putrāḥ kuleṣv aiśvaryaṃ vaśe vartayanti» iti.

Bhavila|patnyā dārik" âbhihitā: «tvayā kālaṃ jñātvā, gantavyam» iti. sā kālaṃ jñātvā, gacchati śīghraṃ labhate. anyāś cirayanti. tābhiḥ sā pṛṣṭā, «tvaṃ kathaṃ śīghraṃ labhase?» tayā sarvaṃ samākhyātam. tā api tayā sārdhaṃ gantum ārabdhāḥ. tā api śīghraṃ pratilabhante. tāḥ svāminībhir uktāḥ. «kim atra kāraṇam idānīṃ śīghram āgacchatha» iti.

Purna spoke up. "In that case, I want to go, too."

His brothers told him, "No, you stay and do business right here in our shop. We'll be the ones to go overseas." And so, taking trade-goods, they set out for foreign parts. Purna, entrusted with all responsibilities, remained behind.

Now, it was the practice among well-to-do families for housekeeping money to be distributed on a daily basis. The brothers' wives sent their maidservants to get their housekeeping money. Purna, however, was surrounded by wealthy men, guildmasters, caravan-leaders and others who lived by commerce, and so the maidservants did not get the opportunity to see him. When the men rose and departed, Purna gave the maidservants the housekeeping money. But when the girls returned after such a long absence, they were reprimanded. They explained to their mistresses the reason for their tardiness, giving all the details, and declared, "Well, that's what happens to those in families where the sons of slave girls control the family wealth!"

Bhávila's wife addressed her maidservant: "You should go to see Purna when you know the time is right." Now that the girl knew just the right time, she set off and quickly obtained the housekeeping money. But the others took a long time. They questioned their fellow servant, saying, "How do you get the housekeeping money so quickly?" She gave them a complete account. And so they began to go with her and to get the housekeeping money without delay. Later, their mistresses questioned them: "How is it that now you return so quickly?"

2.40 Tāḥ kathayanti, «ārogyaṃ jyeṣṭha|bhartṛkāyā bhavatu! yadā tasyā dārikā gatā bhavati, tadā labhyate. vayaṃ tayā sārdhaṃ gacchāmaḥ» iti.

Tāḥ saṃjāt'|âmarṣāḥ kathayanti, «evaṃ hi teṣāṃ bhavati yeṣāṃ dāsī|putrāḥ kuleṣv aiśvaryaṃ vaśe vartayanti» iti.

Yāvad apareṇa samayena Bhavilo Bhavatrāto Bhavanandī ca sahitāḥ samagrāḥ saṃmodamānā mahā|samudrāt saṃsiddha|yāna|pātrā āgatāḥ. Bhavilena patnī pṛṣṭā, «bhadre, śobhanam Pūrṇena pratipālitā tvam?» iti.

Sā kathayati, «yathā bhrātrā putreṇa vā» iti. te 'nye 'pi svāmibhyāṃ pṛṣṭe kathayataḥ, «evaṃ hi teṣāṃ bhavati yeṣāṃ dāsī|putrāḥ kuleṣv aiśvaryaṃ vaśe vartayanti» iti.

Tau saṃlakṣayataḥ, «suhṛd|bhedakāḥ striyo bhavanti» iti.

2.45 Yāvad apareṇa samayena kāśika|vastr'|āvāry udghāṭitā. tat|samanantaraṃ Bhavilasya putro gataḥ. sa Pūrṇena kāśika|vastra|yugen' ācchāditaḥ. anyābhyāṃ dṛṣṭvā sva|putrāḥ preṣitā yāvat kāśika|vastr'|āvārī ghaṭṭitā phuṭṭaka|vastr'|āvāry udghāṭitā. te ca daiva|yogāt saṃprāptāḥ. te Pūrṇena phuṭṭakair vastrair ācchāditāḥ.

Te dṛṣṭvā svāminoḥ kathayataḥ, «dṛṣṭaṃ yuvābhyām apareṣāṃ kāśika|vastrāṇi dīyante, pareṣāṃ phuṭṭakāni» iti. tābhyām anusaṃjñaptir dattā: «kim etad eva bhaviṣyati? nūnaṃ kāśika|vastr'|āvārī ghaṭṭitā phuṭṭaka|vastr'|āvāry udghāṭitā» iti.

The maidservants replied, "May Eldest Brother's wife enjoy good health! When her maidservant goes to see Purna, she receives the housekeeping money without delay. We now go with her." 2.40

The wives of the two younger brothers grew angry and said, "That's what happens to those in families where the sons of slave girls control the family wealth!"

In time, Bhávila, Bhava·trata and Bhava·nandin, all together, united, conversing amiably, returned from across the great ocean, their ship safe and sound. Bhávila asked his wife, "My dear, did Purna take proper care of you?"

She told him, "As if he were my own son or brother." The other two wives were questioned by their husbands, whom they told, "That's what happens to those in families where the sons of slave-girls control the family wealth!"

The two men thought, "Women cause divisions among friends."

On another occasion, Purna was offering for sale Benares 2.45
silk cloth. Just then Bhávila's son arrived. He was clad by Purna in two lengths of fine Benares silk. Seeing this, the wives of the other two brothers sent their own sons, just when Purna had run out of silk and had started to sell coarse cotton cloth. So, as luck would have it, when they arrived, they were clad by Purna in coarse cotton.

The two women, seeing this, said to their husbands, "You see! Some are given fine Benares silk, while some receive only cheap cotton!" The two men offered the following explanation: "What can be done about it? It's just that by the time our sons arrived Purna had run out of silk and was selling coarse cotton."

Yāvad apareṇa samayena śarkar"|āvāry udghāṭitā. Bhavilasya ca putro gataḥ. tena śarkarā|modako labdhaḥ. taṃ dṛṣṭv" ânyābhyāṃ sva|putrāḥ preṣitāḥ. te daiva|yogād guḍ'|āvāryām udghāṭitāyāṃ gatāḥ. tair guḍo labdhaḥ. tābhis taṃ dṛṣṭvā svāminau tathā tathā bhagnau yathā gṛha|vibhāgaṃ kartum ārabdhau.

Tau parasparaṃ saṃjalpaṃ kurutaḥ: «sarvathā vinaṣṭā vayaṃ gṛhaṃ bhājayāmaḥ» iti. ekaḥ kathayati, «jyeṣṭhataraṃ śabdayāmaḥ.» ekaḥ kathayati, «vicārayāmas tāvat kathaṃ bhājayāmaḥ» iti. tau sva|buddhyā vicārayataḥ: «ekasya gṛha|gataṃ kṣetra|gataṃ ca, ekasy' āvārī|gataṃ deś'|ântara|gataṃ c' âikasya Pūrṇakaḥ. yadi jyeṣṭhataro gṛha|gataṃ kṣetra|gataṃ ca grahīṣyati, śaknumo vayam āvārī|gatena deś'|ântara|gatena c' ātmānaṃ saṃdhārayitum. ath' āvārī|gataṃ deś'|ântara|gataṃ ca grahīṣyati, tath" âpi vayaṃ śaknumo gṛha|gatena kṣetra|gatena c' ātmānaṃ saṃdhārayituṃ Pūrṇakasya ca maryādā|bandhaṃ kartum» iti. tāv evaṃ saṃjalpaṃ kṛtvā, Bhavilasya sakāśaṃ gatau. «bhrātaḥ, vinaṣṭā, vayaṃ bhājayāmo gṛham» iti.

Sa kathayati, «suparīkṣitaṃ kartavyam—gṛha|bhedakāḥ striyo bhavanti» iti.

2.50 Tau kathayataḥ, «parīkṣitam asmābhiḥ. bhājayāmaḥ» iti.

Sa kathayati, «yady evam, āhūyantāṃ kulāni» iti.

Tau kathayataḥ, «pūrvam ev' âsmābhir bhājitam. ekasya gṛha|gataṃ kṣetra|gataṃ ca, ekasy' āvārī|gataṃ deś'|ântara|gataṃ ca, ekasya Pūrṇakaḥ.»

On another occasion, Purna was selling sweets. Bhávila's son went to the shop and received a sugar cake. Seeing this, the wives of the other two brothers sent their sons, but, as luck would have it, they arrived when Purna had begun to sell molasses, and so the boys were given molasses. Seeing this, the two women carried on so much that their husbands undertook to divide the joint family.

The two husbands conferred: "We are lost either way. We must divide the family." One said, "We should talk to our elder brother." The other said, "First let us decide how we should divide the family's wealth." The two came up with a plan: "One of us gets the house and the land, one gets the shop and the foreign holdings, and one gets little Purna. If our elder brother takes the house and the land, then we will be able to maintain ourselves with the shop and foreign holdings. And if he takes the shop and the overseas trade, we will still be able to maintain ourselves with the house and land and put a limit on Purna's claims." After conferring in this way, the two paid a visit to Bhávila. "Brother, it's no use; let us divide the family."

Said Bhávila, "We should act only after having thought it over carefully—women cause division in families."

The other two replied, "We have already thought it over. 2.50
Let us make the division."

Bhávila said, "Well, if that is so, let us call the family together."

Said the other two, "We've already decided on what the division should be. One of us gets the house and land, one gets the shop and the overseas trade, and one gets little Purna."

Sa kathayati, «Pūrṇasya pratyaṃśaṃ n' ânuprayacchatha?»

Tau kathayataḥ, «dāsī|putraḥ saḥ! kas tasya pratyaṃśaṃ dadyāt? api tu, sa ev' âsmābhir bhājitaḥ. yadi tav' âbhipretaṃ tam eva gṛhāṇa» iti.

2.55 Sa saṃlakṣayati, «ahaṃ pitr" âbhihitaḥ: ‹sarva|svam api te parityajya, Pūrṇo grahītavyaḥ› iti. gṛhṇāmi Pūrṇam» iti viditvā kathayati, «yady evaṃ bhavatu mama Pūrṇakaḥ» iti.

Yasya gṛha|gataṃ kṣetra|gataṃ ca, sa tvaramāṇo gṛhaṃ gatvā kathayati, «jyeṣṭha|bhrātṛke, nirgaccha!» sā nirgatā. «mā bhūyaḥ pravekṣyasi.»

«Kasy' ârthāya?»

«Asmābhir bhājitaṃ gṛham.»

Yasy' āvārī|gataṃ deś'|ântara|gataṃ ca, so 'pi tvaramāṇa āvārīṃ gatvā kathayati, «Pūrṇaka, avatara» iti. so 'vatīrṇaḥ. «mā bhūyo 'bhirokṣyasi.»

2.60 «Kiṃ|kāraṇam?»

«Asmābhir bhājitaṃ gṛham.»

Yāvad Bhavila|patnī Pūrṇakena sārdhaṃ jñāti|gṛhaṃ saṃprasthitā. dārakā bubhukṣitā roditum ārabdhāḥ. sā kathayati, «Pūrṇa, dārakāṇāṃ pūrva|bhakṣikām anuprayaccha» iti.

Sa kathayati, «kārṣāpaṇaṃ prayaccha.»

Asked Bhávila, "Are you not offering Purna a share?"

"He is the son of a slave girl! Who would give him a share? On the contrary, we have considered him as part of the property that is to be divided. take just him, if that is what you want!"

Bhávila thought, "I was told by our father: 'Even if you 2.55
have to forsake all your worldly possessions, you must take care of Purna.' I will take Purna." And, having decided this, he said, "If that is so, then I shall have little Purna."

Then the brother who received the house and land, making haste, went to the house and called out, "Elder Brother's wife! Come out!" She came out. "You may never again enter this house."

"For what reason?"

"We have divided the family's holdings. This house is mine."

As for the brother who received the shop and the foreign trade, he, making haste, went to the shop and said, "Purna, come down!" He came down. "You may never enter this shop again."

"Why?" 2.60

"We have divided the family's holdings. This shop is mine."

And so Bhávila's wife, accompanied by Purna, set out for the home of her relatives. The children were hungry and began to cry. She said, "Purna, get the children some breakfast."

He said, "Give me a coin."

Sā kathayati, «tvay" êyatībhiḥ suvarṇa|lakṣābhir vyavahṛtam—dārakāṇāṃ pūrva|bhakṣik" âpi n' âsti?»

2.65 Pūrṇaḥ kathayati, «kim ahaṃ jāne yuṣmākaṃ gṛha īdṛś" îyam avasthā bhaviṣyat' îti. yadi mayā jñātam abhaviṣyan, may" ânekāḥ suvarṇa|lakṣāḥ saṃhāritā abhaviṣyan.» dharmat" âiṣā striya ārakūṭa|māṣakān vastr'|ânte badhnanti. tay" ārakūṭa|māṣako dattaḥ. «pūrva|bhakṣikām ānaya!» iti.

Sa tam ādāya, vīthīṃ saṃprasthitaḥ. anyatamaś ca puruṣaḥ, samudra|velā|preritānāṃ kāṣṭhānāṃ bhāram ādāya, śīten' âbhidruto vepamāna āgacchati. sa tena dṛṣṭaḥ pṛṣṭaś ca, «bhoḥ puruṣa! kasmād evaṃ vepase?»

Sa kathayati, «aham api na jāne. mayā c' âyaṃ bhāraka utkṣipto bhavati mama c' ēdṛśī samavasthā.»

Sa dāru|parīkṣāyāṃ kṛtāvī. sa tat kāṣṭhaṃ nirīkṣitum ārabdhaḥ. paśyati tatra go|śīrṣa|candanam. sa ten' âbhihitaḥ, «bhoḥ puruṣa, kiyatā mūlyena dīyate?»

«Pañcabhiḥ kārṣāpaṇa|śataiḥ.»

2.70 Tena taṃ kāṣṭha|bhāraṃ gṛhītvā, tad go|śīrṣa|candanam apanīya, vīthīṃ gatvā, kara|patrikayā catasraḥ khaṇḍikāḥ kṛtāḥ. tac cūrṇakasy' ârthaṃ kārṣāpaṇa|sahasreṇa vikrītaṃ vartate. tatas tasya puruṣasya pañca|kārṣāpaṇa|śatāni dattāny uktaṃ ca, «enaṃ kāṣṭha|bhārakam—amuṣmin gṛhe Bhavila|patnī tiṣṭhati tatra naya—vaktavyā, ‹Pūrṇena preṣitam› iti.»

She replied, "In the course of doing business many hundreds of thousands of gold coins passed through your hands—is there not enough left even for the children's breakfast?"

Said Purna, "How could I have known that your family 2.65
would end up like this? Had I known this would happen, I would have appropriated several hundred thousand." It is, however, the practice for women to tie a few brass coins in the hem of their saris; Bhávila's wife gave Purna a brass coin, saying, "Bring some breakfast!"

Taking the money, Purna set out for the market. A man was approaching carrying a load of sticks that had been washed up on the seashore and trembling with cold. Purna saw him and asked, "Greetings, my good man! Why are you trembling so?"

The man replied, "I don't know. I picked up this load of wood and since then I've been in this condition."

Now, Purna was expert in the assessment of different types of wood. He started to examine the wood and saw that it was yellow sandalwood. He asked the man, "Good fellow, what price would you take for this wood?"

"Five hundred coins."

Purna accepted this price, took the load of yellow san- 2.70
dalwood and carried it off. He proceeded to the market, where, with a saw, he cut off four small pieces. These he sold to be ground into fragrant powder for one thousand coins. He then paid the man his five hundred coins and told him, "This load of wood—take it to the house over there where Bhávila's wife is staying, and tell her, 'Purna sent it.'"

Ten' âsau nīto yathā|vṛttaṃ c' ārocitam. s" ôrasi prahāraṃ dattvā, kathayati, «yady asāv arthāt paribhraṣṭaḥ, kiṃ prajñay" âpi paribhraṣṭaḥ? ‹pakkam ānaya!› iti, pācanaṃ preṣitam! tad eva n' âsti yat paktavyam!» iti.

Pūrṇena śeṣa|katipaya|kārṣāpaṇair dāsa|dāsī|go|mahiṣī|vastrāṇi jīvit'|ôpakaraṇāni pakkam ādāy' āgatya dampatyor upanāmitavān. tena kuṭumbaṃ saṃtoṣitam.

Atr'|ântare Saurpārakīyo rājā dāha|jvareṇa viklavī|bhūtaḥ. tasya vaidyair go|śīrṣa|candanam upādiṣṭam. tato 'mātyā go|śīrṣa|candanaṃ samanveṣayitum ārabdhāḥ. tair vīthyāṃ pāraṃparyeṇa śrutam. te, Pūrṇasya sakāśaṃ gatvā, kathayanti, «tav' âsti go|śīrṣa|candanam?»

Sa āha, «asti.»

2.75 Te ūcuḥ, «kiyatā mūlyena dīyate?»

Sa āha, «kārṣāpaṇa|sahasreṇa.»

Taiḥ kārṣāpaṇa|sahasreṇa gṛhītvā, rājñaḥ pralepo dattaḥ, svasthī|bhūtaḥ. rājā saṃlakṣayati, «kīdṛśo 'sau rājā yasya gṛhe go|śīrṣa|candanaṃ n' âsti?» rājā pṛcchati, «kuta etat?»

«Deva, Pūrṇāt.»

«Āhūyatām Pūrṇakaḥ.»

The man took the wood to the house just as Purna had instructed and recounted all that had happened. Bhávila's wife gave him a blow on the chest and cried, "If Purna has lost his money, has he also lost his sense? 'Bring some cooked food,' I told him, and he sends firewood for cooking! There is nothing to cook!"

With the money that was left over, Purna purchased such necessities of life as a manservant and a maidservant, cattle and water buffaloes andclothes; these he brought back and offered to Bhávila and his wife with the cooked food. This gave the family great satisfaction.

About this time, the King of Surpáraka became ill with a high fever. His physicians prescribed yellow sandalwood and so his ministers undertook a search for some. In the marketplace they talked to one person after another. Then they paid a visit to Purna, whom they asked, "Have you any yellow sandalwood?"

He told them, "I have."

They asked, "For what price will you sell it?" 2.75

Purna replied, "For a thousand coins."

The ministers bought some for a thousand coins. After an ointment prepared from the sandalwood was given to the king, he regained his health. The king considered, "Now, what sort of king is he in whose home there is no yellow sandalwood?" Then he asked, "From whom was this obtained?"

"Your majesty, from Purna."

"Summon this Purna fellow."

2.80 Sa dūtena gatv" ôktaḥ, «Pūrṇa, Devas tvāṃ śabdāpayati» iti.

Sa vicārayitum ārabdhaḥ, «kim|arthaṃ māṃ rājā śabdāpayati?» sa saṃlakṣayati, «go|śīrṣa|candanen' âsau rājā svasthī|bhūtaḥ. tad|arthaṃ māṃ śabdāyati. sarvathā go|śīrṣa|candanam ādāya gantavyam.» sa go|śīrṣa|candanasya tisro gaṇḍikā vastreṇa pidhāya, ekāṃ pāṇinā gṛhītvā, rājñaḥ sakāśaṃ gataḥ.

Rājñā pṛṣṭaḥ, «Pūrṇa, asti kiṃ cid go|śīrṣa|candanam?»

Sa kathayati, «Deva, idam asti.»

«Kim asya mūlyam?»

2.85 «Deva, suvarṇa|lakṣā.»

«Aparam asti?»

«Deva, asti.» tena tās tisro gaṇḍikā darśitāḥ. rājñ" âmātyānām ājñā dattā, «Pūrṇasya catasraḥ suvarṇa|lakṣāḥ prayacchata» iti.

Pūrṇaḥ kathayati, «Deva, tisro dīyantām. eka|gaṇḍikā Devasya prābhṛtam» iti. tatas tasya tisro dattāḥ.

Rājā kathayati, «Pūrṇa, parituṣṭo 'ham. vada, kiṃ te varam anuprayacchāmi?» iti.

2.90 Pūrṇaḥ kathayati, «yadi me Devaḥ parituṣṭaḥ, Devasya vijite 'paribhūto vaseyam» iti. rājñ" âmātyānām ājñā dattā, «bhavanto 'dy' âgreṇa kumārāṇām ājñā deyā, na tv evaṃ Pūrṇasya» iti.

The messenger who had gone to the house where he was 2.80
staying said, "Purna, his majesty summons you."

Purna began to think, "Why does the king summon me?" And then it occurred to him. "It is by using the yellow sandalwood that the king has regained his health. That is why he summons me. Well, I must certainly go and take the yellow sandalwood with me." Having concealed three pieces of the yellow sandalwood in his clothes, and carrying one piece in his hand, Purna went before the king.

The king asked him, "Purna, have you any yellow sandalwood?"

Purna told him, "Your majesty, I have this piece."

"What is the price?"

"Your majesty, a hundred thousand gold coins." 2.85

"Have you any more?"

"Yes, your majesty, I have." And Purna showed the king the other three pieces. The king commanded his ministers, "Give Purna four hundred thousand gold coins."

Said Purna, "Your Majesty, give three hundred thousand. One piece is a gift to Your Majesty." And so Purna received three hundred thousand gold coins.

The king said, "Purna, I am well pleased. Tell me, what boon shall I grant you?"

Purna replied, "If your majesty is pleased with me, may 2.90
I be permitted to live in your majesty's kingdom undisturbed?" The king commanded his ministers, "Sirs, from this day forth, you may give orders even to the crown princes, but not to Purna."

Yāvan mahā|samudrāt pañca|mātrāṇi vaṇik|śatāni saṃsiddha|yāna|pātrāṇi Sūrpārakaṃ nagaram anuprāptāni. vaṇig|grāmeṇa kriyā|kāraḥ kṛtaḥ: «na kena cid asmākaṃ samastānāṃ nirgaty' âikākinā vaṇijāṃ sakāśam upasaṃkramitavyam. gaṇa eva saṃbhūya bhāṇḍaṃ grahīṣyati» iti.

Apare kathayanti, «Pūrṇam api śabdāpayāmaḥ.» anye kathayanti, «kiṃ tasya kṛpaṇasy' âsti yaḥ śabdyate» iti.

Tena khalu samayena Pūrṇo bahir nirgataḥ. tena śrutaṃ, «mahā|samudrāt pañca vaṇik|śatāni saṃsiddha|yāna|pātrāṇi Sūrpārakaṃ nagaram anuprāptāni» iti. so 'praviśy' âiva nagaraṃ teṣāṃ sakāśam upasaṃkrāntaḥ. pṛcchati, «bhavantaḥ, kim idaṃ dravyam?» iti.

Te kathayanti, «idaṃ c' êdaṃ ca» iti.

2.95 «Kiṃ mūlyam?»

Te kathayanti, «sārtha|vāha, dūram api param api gatvā, tvam eva praṣṭavyaḥ.»

«Yady apy evaṃ, tath" âpy ucyatāṃ mūlyam.» tair aṣṭādaśa suvarṇa|lakṣā mūlyam upadiṣṭam. sa kathayati, «bhavantaḥ, tisro lakṣā avadraṅgaṃ gṛhṇīta mam' âitat. paṇyam avaśiṣṭaṃ dāsyāmi.»

«Tathā bhavatu.» tena tisro lakṣā ānāyya dattāḥ. sva|mudrā|lakṣitaṃ ca kṛtvā prakrāntaḥ.

Just then five hundred merchants, sailing in from the great ocean, their ship safe and sound, arrived in the city of Surpáraka. The merchants' guild of Surpáraka then made a rule: "No one of us—who must act in unison—may approach these visiting merchants independently. Only the guild as a body may purchase their goods."

Some of the merchants said, "Let us inform Purna too." Others declared, "What does that wretch have that he should be informed?"

Just then, Purna went outside, where he learned, "Five hundred merchants have arrived in Surpáraka from across the great ocean with their ships safe and sound." Without entering the city, he went directly into their presence and asked them, "Sirs, what goods have you got?"

Said they, "Some of this and some of this."

"What is the price?" 2.95

They replied, "Caravan-leader, since you have travelled far and wide and know the value of things, only you can name a price."

"That may be so," said Purna. "Nevertheless, name your price." They indicated a price of one million eight hundred thousand gold coins. Purna said, "Sirs, take three hundred thousand as a deposit; I have that much. I shall give you the balance later."

"Very well." So Purna had three hundred thousand gold coins brought and paid them to the visiting merchants. He then affixed his seal to the merchandise and departed.

Tato vaṇig|grāmeṇ' âvacarakāḥ puruṣāḥ preṣitāḥ: «paśyata. kiṃ dravyam?» iti. tair gatvā pṛṣṭāḥ, «kiṃ dravyam.» «idaṃ c' êdaṃ ca.»

2.100 «Asmākam īdṛśena pūrṇāni kośa|koṣṭh'|âgārāṇi tiṣṭhanti.» «pūrṇāni vā bhavantu mā vā—api vikrītam.»

«Kasy' ântike?»

«Pūrṇasya.»

«Prabhūtam āsādayiṣyatha Pūrṇasy' ântike vikrīya?»

2.105 Te kathayanti, «yat ten' âvadraṅge dattam, tad yūyaṃ mūlye 'pi na dāsyatha.»

«Kiṃ ten' âvadraṅge dattam?»

«Tisraḥ suvarṇa|lakṣāḥ.»

«Su|muṣitās tena bhrātaraḥ kṛtāḥ!»

Tair āgatya vaṇig|grāmasy' ārocitam. «tat paṇyaṃ vikrītam.»

2.110 «Kasy' ântike?»

«Pūrṇasya.»

«Prabhūtam āsādayiṣyanti Pūrṇasy' ântike vikrīya?»

«Yat ten' âvadraṅge dattam, tad yūyaṃ mūlye 'pi na dāsyatha.»

«Kiṃ ten' âvadraṅge dattam?»

2.115 «Tisraḥ suvarṇa|lakṣāḥ.

«Sumuṣitās tena te bhrātaraḥ kṛtāḥ!»

Meanwhile, the merchants' guild dispatched their agents: "Take a look. What merchandise have they got?" The agents went and asked, "What have you got?" "Some of this and some of this."

"Our storerooms and warehouses are filled with such mer- 2.100
chandise."

"They may be full or not—everything's already sold."

"To whom?"

"To Purna."

"Will you make a good profit by having sold it all to Purna?"

Said the merchants, "What he paid as deposit you would 2.105
not even pay as the full price."

"What did he give as deposit?"

"Three hundred thousand gold coins."

"He has well and truly robbed his brothers!"

The agents returned and informed the merchants' guild. "The merchandise has already been sold."

"To whom?" 2.110

"To Purna."

"Will they make a good profit by having sold it to Purna?"

"What he paid in deposit you wouldn't even pay as the full price."

"What did he pay as deposit?"

"Three hundred thousand gold coins." 2.115

"He has well and truly robbed his brothers!"

Sa tair āhūy' ôktaḥ, «Pūrṇa, vaṇig|grāmeṇa kriyā|kāraḥ kṛtaḥ: ‹na kena cid ekākinā grahītavyam. vaṇig|grāma eva grahīṣyati› ity eva. kasmāt te gṛhītam?»

Sa kathayati, «bhavantaḥ, yadā yuṣmābhiḥ kriyā|kāraḥ kṛtaḥ, tadā kim ahaṃ śabdito mama bhrātā vā? yuṣmābhir eva kriyā|kāraḥ kṛtaḥ, yūyam eva pālayata.»

Tato vaṇig|grāmeṇa saṃjāt'|âmarṣeṇa ṣaṣṭeḥ kārṣāpaṇānām arthāy' ātape dhāritaḥ. rājñaḥ pauruṣeyair dṛṣṭaḥ. tai rājña ārocitam. rājā kathayati, «bhavantaḥ, śabdayat' âitān.» taiḥ śabditāḥ. kathayati rājā, «bhavantaḥ, kasy' ârthe yuṣmābhiḥ Pūrṇa ātape vidhāritaḥ?»

2.120 Te kathayanti, «Deva, vaṇig|grāmeṇa kriyā|kāraḥ kṛtaḥ: ‹na kena cit ekākinā paṇyaṃ grahītavyam› iti. tad anen' âikākinā gṛhītam.»

Pūrṇaḥ kathayati. «Deva, samanuyujyantāṃ yad" âibhiḥ kriyā|kāraḥ kṛtaḥ, tadā kim aham ebhiḥ śabdito mama bhrātā vā.»

Te kathayanti, «Deva, na» iti.

Rājā kathayati, «bhavantaḥ, śobhanaṃ Pūrṇaḥ kathayati.» sa tair vrīḍitair muktaḥ.

The merchants' guild summoned Purna and told him: "Purna, the merchants' guild made a rule, that 'No one should independently purchase merchandise from the visiting merchants; only the guild as a body would do so.' Why, then, did you purchase the goods on your own?"

Purna answered, "Sirs, when you made the rule, were either my brother Bhávila or myself informed? It was you alone who made the rule and it is you alone who must abide by it."

At that, the members of the merchants' guild became angry and forcibly exposed Purna in the scorching sun in order to make him pay the fine of sixty silver coins. Officers of the crown saw Purna and they apprised the king of his predicament. The king said, "Sirs, summon those men." Purna and the members of the merchants' guild were summoned. Said the king, "Why did you forcibly expose Purna in the scorching sun?"

The guild members replied, "Your majesty, the mer- 2.120
chants' guild made a rule, that 'No one should independently purchase thatmerchandise.' Purna, however, did just that."

Purna spoke up. "Your majesty, ask them whether, when they made this rule, they informed either myself or my brother."

The guild members admitted, "No, your majesty, we did not."

Declared the king, "Sirs, Purna speaks truly." Ashamed, the guild members released Purna.

Yāvad apareṇa samayena rājñas tena dravyeṇa prayojanam utpannam. tena vaṇig|grāma āhūy' ôktaḥ, «bhavanto mam' āmukena dravyeṇa prayojanam. anuprayacchata» iti.

2.125 Te kathayanti, «Deva, Pūrṇasy' âsti.»

Rājā kathayati, «bhavantaḥ, n' âhaṃ tasy' ājñāṃ dadāmi. yūyam eva tasy' ântikāt krītv" ânuprayacchata.»

Taiḥ Pūrṇasya dūtaḥ preṣitaḥ. «vaṇig|grāmaḥ śabdayati» iti.

Sa kathayati, «n' âham āgacchāmi.»

Te vaṇig|grāmāḥ sarva eva saṃbhūya, tasya niveśanaṃ gatvā, dvāri sthitvā, tair dūtaḥ preṣitaḥ. «Pūrṇa, nirgaccha! vaṇig|grāmo dvāri tiṣṭhati» iti. sa s'|âhaṃ|kāra|kāma|kāra|madatvān nirgataḥ.

2.130 Vaṇig|grāmaḥ kathayati, «sārtha|vāha, yathā|krītakaṃ paṇyam anuprayaccha.»

Sa kathayati, «ativāṇijako 'haṃ yadi yathā|krītaṃ paṇyam anuprayacchāmi» iti.

Te kathayanti, «sārtha|vāha, dvi|guṇa|mūlyen' ânuprayaccha—vaṇig|grāmaḥ pūjito bhavati» iti.

Sa saṃlakṣayati, «pūjanīyo vaṇig|grāmo dadāmi» iti. tena dvi|guṇa|mūlyena dattam.

Pañca|daśa lakṣāṇi teṣāṃ vaṇijāṃ dattam avaśiṣṭaṃ sva|gṛhaṃ praveśitam. sa saṃlakṣayati, «kiṃ śakyam avaśyāya|bindunā kumbhaṃ pūrayitum? mahā|samudram avatarāmi» iti.

On another occasion, a need arose on the part of the king for some of that merchandise. He summoned the members of the merchants' guild and told them, "Sirs, I have need of some of that merchandise. You shall supply it."

They said, "Your majesty, it belongs to Purna." 2.125

The king told them, "Sirs, I do not give orders to him. You shall purchase it from him and supply it to me."

The merchants' guild sent a messenger to Purna: "The merchants' guild summons you."

But Purna replied, "I shall not come."

Then all the merchants of the guild assembled, went to Purna's house, stood at the gate and again sent in a messenger. "Purna, please come out! The merchants' guild members are waiting at the gate." Impelled by pride, his own wishes and a sense of his own importance, Purna came out.

The guild members said, "Caravan-leader, sell us some 2.130
merchandise for the same price you paid."

Purna said, "A fine trader I would be were I to sell you merchandise for the same price I paid!"

They replied, "O caravan-leader, sell it for twice what you paid—the members of the guild are respected men."

Purna reflected, "The members of the guild should be treated respectfully; I will sell it at that price." And he sold the merchandise for twice the price he had paid.

Purna paid a million and a half gold coins to the foreign merchants; the rest he stored in his house. Then he thought, "Is it possible to fill a jar with dewdrops? I will cross the great ocean."

2.135 Tena Sūrpārake nagare ghaṇṭ"|âvaghoṣaṇaṃ kāritam: «śṛṇvantu, bhavantaḥ Saurpārakīyā vaṇijaḥ! Pūrṇaḥ sārtha|vāho mahā|samudram avatarati! yo yuṣmākam utsahate Pūrṇena sārtha|vāhena sārdham, aśulken' âgulmen' âtara|paṇyena, mahā|samudram avatartuṃ, sa mahā|samudra|gamanīyaṃ paṇyaṃ samudānayatu» iti.

Pañca|mātrair vaṇik|śatair mahā|samudra|gamanīyaṃ paṇyaṃ samudānītam. tataḥ Pūrṇaḥ sārtha|vāhaḥ kṛta|kautūhala|maṅgala|svasty|ayanaḥ, pañca|vaṇik|śata|parivāraḥ, mahā|samudram avatīrṇaḥ. sa saṃsiddha|yāna|pātraś ca pratyāgataḥ. evaṃ yāvat ṣaṭ|kṛtvaḥ. sāmantakena śabdo viśrutaḥ: «Pūrṇaḥ ṣaṭ|kṛtvo mahā|samudram avatīrṇaḥ, saṃsiddha|yāna|pātraś ca pratyāgataḥ» iti.

Śrāvasteyā vaṇijaḥ paṇyam ādāya, Sūrpārakaṃ nagaraṃ gatāḥ. te mārga|śramaṃ prativinodya, yena Pūrṇaḥ sārtha|vāhas ten' ôpasaṃkrāntāḥ. upasaṃkramya kathayanti, «sārtha|vāhaḥ, mahā|samudram avatarāmaḥ» iti.

Sa kathayati, «bhavanto 'sti kaś cid yuṣmābhir dṛṣṭaḥ śruto vā ṣaṭ|kṛtvo mahā|samudrāt saṃsiddha|yāna|pātr'|āgataḥ saptamaṃ vāram avataran?»

Te kathayanti, «Pūrṇa, vayaṃ tvām uddiśya dūrād āgatāḥ. yadi n' âvatarasi, tvam eva pramāṇam» iti.

Purna had the proclamation bell rung in Surpáraka City: 2.135
"Hear ye, gentlemen, merchants of Surpáraka! Purna, the caravan-leader, is crossing over the great ocean! Whosoever among you ventures to cross the great ocean with the caravan-leader Purna, free from customs duties, escort charges and freight fees, is to gather together the trade-goods for transport across the great ocean."

Merchants numbering five hundred gathered together trade-goods to take across the great ocean. Then the caravan-leader Purna, having performed the rites to ensure a safe and successful journey, accompanied by those five hundred merchants, set out across the great ocean. And in time he returned, his ship safe and sound. Six times he crossed the great ocean in this way. The word spread about in the vicinity: "Six times Purna has crossed the great ocean and returned, his ship safe and sound."

Meanwhile, some merchants from Shravásti, equipping themselves with trade-goods, travelled overland to the city of Surpáraka. After recovering from the fatigue of travel, they went to see Purna, the great caravan-leader. When they arrived at Purna's house, they said to him, "Great caravan-leader, let us cross the great ocean."

Purna said, "Sirs, have you seen or heard about someone who has returned six times from across the great ocean, his ship safe and sound, and who is setting out a seventh time?"

They replied, "Purna, from afar we have come to seek you out, but if you won't cross the ocean, that's up to you."

2.140 Sa saṃlakṣayati, «kiṃ c' âpy ahaṃ dhanen' ânarthī tath" âpy eṣām arthāy' âvatarāmi» iti. sa taiḥ sārdhaṃ mahā|samudraṃ saṃprasthitaḥ.

Te rātryāḥ pratyūṣa|samaya Udānaṃ Pār'|âyaṇaṃ Satya|dṛṣṭiṃ Sthavira|gāthāḥ Śaila|gāthā Muni|gāthā Artha|vargīyāṇi ca Sūtrāṇi vistareṇa svareṇa svādhyāyaṃ kurvanti. tena te śrutāḥ. sa kathayati, «bhavantaḥ, śobhanāni gītāni gāyatha!»

Te kathayanti, «sārtha|vāha, n' âitāni gītāni. kiṃ nu khalv etad Buddha|vacanam?»

Sa «Buddhaḥ» ity aśruta|pūrvaṃ śabdaṃ śrutvā, sarva|roma|kūpāny āhṛṣṭāni. sa ādara|jātaḥ pṛcchati, «bhavantaḥ, ko 'yaṃ Buddha|nāma» iti.

Te kathayanti, «asti śramaṇo Gautamaḥ, Śākya|putraḥ, Śākya|kulāt, keśa|śmaśrūṇy avatārya, kāṣāyāṇi vastrāṇy ācchādya, samyag eva śraddhay" âgārād anagārikāṃ pravrajitaḥ. so 'nuttarāṃ samyak|saṃbodhim abhisaṃbuddhaḥ. sa eṣa, sārtha|vāha, ‹Buddho› nāma.»

2.145 «Kutra, bhavantaḥ, sa bhagavān etarhi viharati?»

«Sārtha|vāha, Śrāvastyāṃ Jeta|vane 'nāthapiṇḍadasy' ārāme.»

Purna reflected, "Though I do not seek any more wealth, 2.140
I shall nevertheless cross the ocean for their sake." And so Purna, accompanied by those merchants, set out on the great ocean.

At night, at the time just before dawn, those merchants recited, in their entirety, "The Exultations," "The Way to the Further Shore," "Discerning the Truth," "Verses of the Elders," "Verses Concerning Shaila," "The Sage's Verses" and "Sayings Concerning the Goal." After listening to them, Purna exclaimed, "Sirs, you sing beautiful songs!"

They replied, "Caravan-leader, these are not mere songs! What are they but the words of the Awakened One, the Buddha?"

Hearing the title "the Buddha," which he had never heard before, Purna got goose bumps all over. Very respectfully, he asked, "Sirs, who is this one called 'the Buddha'?"

The Shravásti merchants told him, "There is an ascetic by the name of Gáutama, a son of the Shakya people, who, having cut off his beard and hair and donned yellow garments, with right faith went forth from his home into the homeless life. He has fully awakened to Supreme, Perfect Awakening. He, O caravan-leader, is called 'the Buddha,' the Awakened One."

"Sirs, where is this holy one now staying?" 2.145

"Caravan-leader, he is staying in Shravásti, in Anátha·píndada's park in Prince Jeta's Grove."

Sa taṃ hṛdi kṛtvā, taiḥ sārdhaṃ mahā|samudram avatīrṇaḥ saṃsiddha|yāna|pātraś ca pratyāgataḥ. bhrāt" âsya Bhavilaḥ saṃlakṣayati, «parikhinno 'yaṃ mahā|samudra|gamanena niveśo 'sya kartavyaḥ» iti. sa ten' ôktaḥ, «bhrātaḥ. kathaya katarasya dhaninaḥ sārtha|vāhasya vā tav' ârthāya duhitaraṃ prārthayāmi» iti.

Sa kathayati, «n' âhaṃ kāmair arthī. yady anujānāsi, pravrajāmi» iti.

Sa kathayati, «yad" âsmākaṃ gṛhe vārttā n' âsti, tadā na pravrajitaḥ. idānīṃ kim|arthaṃ pravrajasi?»

2.150 Pūrṇaḥ kathayati, «bhrātaḥ, tadānīṃ na śobhate, idānīṃ tu yuktam.» sa ten' âvaśyaṃ nirbandhaṃ jñātv" ânujñātaḥ.

Sa kathayati, «bhrātaḥ, mahā|samudro bahv|ādīnavo 'lp'|āsvādaḥ. bahavo 'vataranty alpā vyuttiṣṭhanti. sarvathā na tvayā mahā|samudram avatartavyam. nyāy'|ôpārjitaṃ te prabhūtaṃ dhanam asty eṣāṃ tu tava bhrātṝṇām anyāy'|ôpārjitam. yady ete kathayanti, ‹ekadhye vasāmaḥ› iti, na vastavyam.» ity uktv" ôpasthāyakam ādāya, Śrāvastīṃ saṃprasthitaḥ. anupūrveṇa Śrāvastīm anuprāptaḥ.

Śrāvastyām udyāne sthiten' Ânāthapiṇḍadasya gṛha|pater dūto 'nupreṣitaḥ. tena gatv" ânāthapiṇḍadasya gṛha|pater ārocitam, «gṛha|pate, Pūrṇaḥ sārtha|vāha udyāne tiṣṭhati, gṛha|patiṃ draṣṭukāmaḥ» iti.

Bearing the Buddha in his heart, Purna, accompanied by those merchants, crossed the great ocean and then returned with the ship safe and sound. Purna's brother Bhávila thought, "He has been exhausted by his voyages across the great ocean. I should arrange a marriage for him." And so he said to Purna, "Tell me, brother. Of the two—a rich landowner or a caravan-leader—which should I ask on your behalf for his daughter in marriage?"

Purna replied, "I am not seeking the pleasures of love. If you will permit it, I shall go forth into the homeless life of a religious mendicant."

Said Bhávila, "When there was nothing to live on in our house, you did not go forth into the homeless life. Why do you wish to go forth now that we are rich?"

Purna told him, "Brother, then it held no attraction for 2.150
me; now it is the right thing to do." Realizing that Purna was resolutely determined, Bhávila gave his permission.

Then Purna said, "Brother, on the great ocean there are many hazards and few pleasures. Many cross; few return. You must on no account cross the great ocean. Your considerable wealth has been justly acquired, but not so that of your brothers. If they should say, 'Let us all live together again,' you must refuse." Having spoken thus, Purna took one servant and set out for Shravásti. In due course he arrived in that city.

In Shravásti, Purna settled himself in a park and then dispatched a messenger to the householder Anátha·píndada. The messenger went and said to the householder Anátha·píndada, "Householder, the caravan-leader Purna, who

Anāthapiṇḍado gṛha|patiḥ saṃlakṣayati, «nūnaṃ jala|yānena khinna idānīṃ sthala|yānen' āgataḥ.» tataḥ pṛcchati, «bhoḥ puruṣa, kiyat|prabhūtaṃ paṇyam ānītam?»

Sa kathayati, «kuto 'sya paṇyam? upasthāyaka|dvitīyaḥ. sa c' âhaṃ ca.»

2.155 Anāthapiṇḍadaḥ saṃlakṣayati, «na mama prati|rūpaṃ yad ahaṃ pradhāna|puruṣam asat|kāreṇa praveśayeyam» iti. sa tena mahatā sat|kāreṇa praveśita udvartitaḥ snāpito bhojitaḥ. svair'|ālāpen' âvasthitayor Anāthapiṇḍadaḥ pṛcchati, «sārtha|vāha, kim āgamana|prayojanam?»

«Gṛha|pate, icchāmi sv|ākhyāte Dharma|Vinaye pravrajyām upasaṃpadaṃ bhikṣu|bhāvam» iti.

Tato 'nāthapiṇḍado gṛha|patiḥ pūrvaṃ kāyam abhyunnamayya, dakṣiṇaṃ bāhuṃ prasārya, udānam udānayati: «aho Buddhaḥ, aho Dharmaḥ, aho Saṃghaḥ! sv|ākhyātatā. yatr' êdānīm īdṛśāḥ pradhāna|puruṣā vistīrṇa|sva|jana|bandhu|vargam apahāya, sphītāni ca kośa|koṣṭh'|âgārāṇy ākāṅkṣanti sv|ākhyāte Dharma|Vinaye pravrajyām upasaṃpadaṃ bhikṣu|bhāvam» iti. tato 'nāthapiṇḍado gṛha|patiḥ Pūrṇaṃ sārtha|vāham ādāya yena Bhagavāṃs ten' ôpasaṃkrāntaḥ.

is staying in a park in Shravásti, wishes to see the master of the house."

Anátha·píndada reflected, "It must be that he is tired of ocean travel and has now come trading overland." So he asked, "Good fellow, how great a quantity of trade-goods has he brought?"

The messenger replied, "How would he have trade-goods? But for one manservant, he has come alone. There's just he and I."

Thinking, "It would be improper of me to bring this em- 2.155
inent man into my home without offering him my hospitality," Anátha·píndada received Purna into his home with grand hospitality: he was bathed, massaged with scented oils and given a meal. Afterward, as the two men sat and talked freely, Anátha·píndada asked, "Caravan-leader, what is your purpose in coming here?"

"Householder, I wish to receive the lower and higher ordinations and become a monk in accordance with the Doctrine and Discipline which are so well expounded."

At that, the householder Anátha·píndada sat up straight, stretched out his right arm, and pronounced this solemn but joyous utterance: "Ah, the Buddha! Ah, the Dharma! Ah, the Sangha! Justly celebrated are they! For now such eminent men as this are leaving behind all their relatives, both close and distant, as well as their rich treasuries and warehouses, and seeking to receive the lower and higher ordination, to become monks, in accordance with the Doctrine and Discipline, which are so well expounded." The householder Anátha·píndada then took along with him the caravan-leader Purna, and together they set out to see the Lord.

Tena khalu samayena Bhagavān aneka|śatāyā bhikṣu|pariṣadaḥ purastān niṣaṇṇo Dharmaṃ deśayati. adrākṣīd Bhagavān Anāthapiṇḍadaṃ gṛha|patiṃ sa|prābhṛtam āgacchantam. dṛṣṭvā ca punar bhikṣūn āmantrayate sma: «eṣaḥ, bhikṣavaḥ, Anāthapiṇḍado gṛha|patiḥ saprābhṛta āgacchati. n' âsti Tathāgatasy' âivaṃ|vidhaḥ prābhṛto yathā vaineya|prābhṛtaḥ» iti.

Tato 'nāthapiṇḍado gṛha|patir Bhagavataḥ pād'|âbhivandanaṃ kṛtvā, Pūrṇena sārtha|vāhena sārdham ek'|ânte niṣaṇṇaḥ. ek'|ânta|niṣaṇṇaḥ, Anāthapiṇḍado gṛha|patir Bhagavantam idam avocat: «ayam, Bhadanta, Pūrṇaḥ sārtha|vāha ākāṅkṣati sv|ākhyāte Dharma|Vinaye pravrajyām upasaṃpadaṃ bhikṣu|bhāvam. taṃ Bhagavān pravrājayat' ûpasaṃpādayed anukampām upādāya» iti.

2.160 Adhivāsayati Bhagavān Anāthapiṇḍadasya gṛha|pates tūṣṇī|bhāvena. tato Bhagavān Pūrṇaṃ sārtha|vāham āmantrayate: «ehi, bhikṣo, cara brahma|caryam» iti.

Sa Bhagavato vāc"|âvasāne: muṇḍaḥ saṃvṛttaḥ, saṃghāṭi|prāvṛtaḥ, pātra|karaka|vyagra|hastaḥ, sapt'|âh'|âvaropita|keśa|śmaśruḥ, varṣa|śat'|ôpasaṃpannasya bhikṣor īryā|pathen' âvasthitaḥ.

At that time, the Lord was seated before an assembly of several hundred monks giving instruction in the Dharma. The Lord observed the householder Anátha·píndada coming forward, bearing a gift. And, seeing this, he again addressed the monks: "This man, O monks, the householder Anátha·píndada, comes bearing a gift. For the Tathágata, there is no gift comparable to the gift of one who wishes to undertake religious training."

Then the householder Anátha·píndada worshipped the feet of the Lord and, together with the caravan-leader Purna, sat down to one side. Having thus sat down to one side, the householder Anátha·píndada said this to the Lord: "This man, O Venerable sir, the caravan-leader Purna, desires to receive the lower and higher ordinations and become a monk in accordance with the Doctrine and Discipline, which are so well expounded. May the Lord, out of compassion, confer upon him the lower and higher ordinations."

The Lord indicated his consent to the request of the 2.160
householder Anátha·píndada by remaining silent. Then the Lord addressed the caravan-leader Purna. "Come, monk. Practice the holy life."

As soon as the Lord had uttered these words, Purna was transformed: shaven-headed he became, clad in monastic robes, almsbowl and water pot in his hands, with a week's growth of hair and beard and the deportment of a monk of a hundred years' standing.

«Eh' îti» c' ôktaḥ sa Tathāgatena
muṇḍaś ca saṃghāti|parīta|dehaḥ.
sadyaḥ praśānt'|êndriya eva tasthau
evaṃ sthito Buddha|mano|rathena.

Ath' âpareṇa samayen' Āyuṣmān Pūrṇo yena Bhagavāṃs ten' ôpasaṃkrāntaḥ. upasaṃkramya Bhagavataḥ pādau śirasā vanditv" âik'|ânte 'sthāt. ek'|ânte sthita Āyuṣmān Pūrṇo Bhagavantam idam avocat: «sādhu me Bhagavāṃs tathā saṃkṣiptena Dharmaṃ deśayatu, yath" âhaṃ Bhagavato 'ntikāt saṃkṣiptena Dharmaṃ śrutvā, eko vyapakṛṣṭo 'pramatta ātāpī prahit'|ātmā vihareyam. yad|arthaṃ kula|putrāḥ keśa|śmaśrūṇy avatārya, kāṣāyāṇi vastrāṇy ācchādya, samyag eva śraddhay" âgārād anagārikāṃ pravrajanti, tad anuttaraṃ brahma|carya|paryavasānaṃ dṛṣṭa|dharme svayam abhijñāya, sākṣāt|kṛtvā, upasaṃpadya, pravrajayeyaṃ kṣīṇā me jātiḥ, uṣitaṃ brahma|caryaṃ, kṛtaṃ karaṇīyaṃ, n' âparam asmād bhavaṃ prajānāmi» iti.

Evam ukte, Bhagavān Āyuṣmantaṃ Pūrṇam idam avocat: «sādhu, Pūrṇa! sādhu khalu tvam, Pūrṇa, yas tvam evaṃ vadasi, ‹sādhu me Bhagavāṃs tathā saṃkṣiptena Dharmaṃ deśayatu, yath" âhaṃ Bhagavato 'ntikāt saṃkṣiptena Dharmaṃ śrutvā, eko vyapakṛṣṭo 'pramatta ātāpī prahit'|ātmā vihareyam. yad|arthaṃ kula|putrāḥ keśa|śmaśrūṇy avatārya, kāṣāyāṇi vastrāṇy ācchādya, samyag eva śraddhay" âgārād

Again told "Come" by the Tathágata, he,
Shaven-headed and body enfolded in monastic
robes,
Instantly attained tranquility of the senses
And thus remained, by the will of the Buddha.

Some time later, the Venerable Purna paid a visit to the Lord. He approached the Lord, reverently knelt with his head at the Buddha's feet, and stood to one side. Standing there to one side, Purna said this to the Lord: "Well would it be for me if the Lord were to concisely expound the Dharma so that, having heard from the Lord the Dharma thus concisely expounded, I may abide alone, secluded, attentive, ardent and self-controlled. That for the sake of which sons of good family cut off hair and beard, don yellow garments and with right faith go forth from home into homelessness—in this very life and by my own efforts may I know, realize and attain that supreme end of the holy life and go forth to that which is expressed by 'Exhausted for me is birth, accomplished the course of the holy life; what was to be done has been done; I will know no birth beyond this one.'"

When he had so spoken, the Lord answered to the Venerable Purna, "Well spoken, Purna! Well spoken indeed is it for you to have said: 'Well would it be for me were the Lord to concisely expound the Dharma so that, having heard from the Lord the Dharma thus concisely expounded, I may abide alone, secluded, attentive, ardent and self-controlled. That for the sake of which sons of good family cut off hair and beard, don yellow garments and with right faith go forth

anagārikāṃ pravrajanti, tad anuttaraṃ brahma|carya|paryavasānaṃ dṛṣṭa|dharme svayam abhijñāya, sākṣāt|kṛtv" ôpasaṃpadya, pravrajayeyam. kṣīṇā me jātir uṣitaṃ brahma|caryaṃ, kṛtaṃ karaṇīyaṃ, n' âparam asmād bhavaṃ prajānāmi› iti.»

2.165 tena hi, Pūrṇa, śṛṇu sādhu ca, suṣṭhu ca manasi kuru, bhāṣiṣye. santi, Pūrṇa, cakṣur|vijñeyāni rūpāṇi, iṣṭakāni, kāntāni, priyāṇi, manāpāni, kām'|ôpasaṃhitāni, rañjanīyāni. tāni ced bhikṣur dṛṣṭvā, abhinandati, abhivadati, adhyavasyati, adhyavasāya tiṣṭhati, tāny abhinandato 'bhivadato 'dhyavasato 'dhyavasāya tiṣṭhataḥ, ānandī bhavati. ānandyā, nandī|saumanasyaṃ bhavati. nandī|saumanasye sati, saṃrāgo bhavati. nandī|saṃrāge sati, nandī|saṃrāga|saṃyojanaṃ bhavati. nandī|saṃrāga|saṃyojana|saṃyuktaḥ, Pūrṇa, bhikṣur ārād nirvāṇasy' ôcyate.

Santi, Pūrṇa, śrotra|vijñeyāḥ śabdāḥ, ghrāṇa|vijñeyā gandhāḥ, jihvā|vijñeyā rasāḥ, kāya|vijñeyāni spraṣṭavyāni, mano|vijñeyā dharmāḥ, iṣṭāḥ, kāntāḥ, priyāḥ, manāpāḥ, kām'|ôpasaṃhitāḥ, rañjanīyāḥ. tāṃś ca bhikṣur dṛṣṭvā, abhinandati, abhivadati, adhyavasyati, adhyavasāya tiṣṭhati, tāny abhinandato 'bhivadataḥ, adhyavasataḥ, adhyavasāya tiṣṭhataḥ, ānandī bhavati. ānandyā, nandī|saumanasyaṃ bhavati. nandī|saumanasye sati, saṃrāgo bhavati. nandī|saṃrāge sati,

from home into homelessness—in this very life and by my own efforts may I know, realize and attain that supreme end of the holy life and go forth to that which is expressed by "Exhausted for me is birth, accomplished the course of the holy life; what was to be done has been done; I will know no birth beyond this one."'

Therefore, Purna, listen and bear in mind well and care- 2.165
fully; I shall speak. There are, Purna, forms perceptible to the eye which are desirable, agreeable, pleasing, captivating, connected with sensual pleasure and which arouse desire. And if a monk, seeing such forms, approves them, welcomes them, clings to and continues clinging to them, then, as a result of approving, welcoming, clinging to and continuing to cling to them, he comes to enjoy them. With enjoyment comes the satisfaction of enjoyment. When there is the satisfaction of enjoyment, passion arises. When there is passion for enjoyment, bondage to passion for enjoyment arises. Purna, a monk in bondage to passion for enjoyment is said to be far from nirvana.

There are, Purna, sounds perceptible to the ear, smells perceptible to the nose, flavors perceptible to the tongue, tactile objects perceptible to the body, thoughts perceptible to the mind, which are desirable, agreeable, pleasing, captivating, connected with sensual pleasure and which arouse desire. And if a monk, becoming aware of these, approves them, welcomes them, clings to and continues to cling to them, then, as a result of approving them, welcoming them, clinging to and continuing to cling to them, he comes to

nandī|saṃrāga|saṃyojanaṃ bhavati. nandī|saṃrāga|saṃyojana|saṃyuktaḥ, Pūrṇa, bhikṣur ārān nirvāṇasy' êty ucyate.

Santi tu, Pūrṇa, cakṣur|vijñeyāni rūpāṇ' îṣṭāni, kāntāni, priyāṇi, manāpāni, kām'|ôpasaṃhitāni, rañjanīyāni. tāni tu bhikṣur dṛṣṭvā, n' âbhinandati, n' âbhivadati, n' âdhyavasyati, adhyavasāya na tiṣṭhati, tāny anabhinandato 'nabhivadato 'nadhyavasato 'dhyavasāya tiṣṭhataḥ, ānandī na bhavati. anānandyā, nandī|saumanasyaṃ na bhavati. nandī|saumanasye 'sati, saṃrāgo na bhavati. nandī|saṃrāge 'sati, nandī|saṃrāga|saṃyojanaṃ na bhavati. nandī|saṃrāga|saṃyojan'|â|saṃyuktaḥ, Pūrṇa, bhikṣuḥ śukla|pakṣeṇ' ântike nirvāṇasy' êty ucyate.

Santi, Pūrṇa, śrotra|vijñeyāḥ śabdāḥ, ghrāṇa|vijñeyā gandhāḥ, jihvā|vijñeyā rasāḥ, kāya|vijñeyāni spraṣṭavyāni, mano|vijñeyā dharmāḥ, iṣṭāḥ, kāntāḥ, priyāḥ, manāpāḥ, kām'|ôpasaṃhitāḥ, rañjanīyāḥ. tāṃś ca bhikṣur dṛṣṭvā, n' âbhinandati, n' âbhivadati, n' âdhyavasyati, adhyavasāya na tiṣṭhati, tāny anabhinandato 'nabhivadataḥ, anadhyavasataḥ, adhyavasāya na tiṣṭhataḥ, ānandī na bhavati. anānandyā, nandī|saumanasyaṃ na bhavati. nandī|saumanasye 'sati,

enjoy them. With enjoyment comes the satisfaction of enjoyment. When there is the satisfaction of enjoyment, passion arises. When there is passion for enjoyment, bondage to passion for enjoyment arises. Purna, a monk in bondage to passion for enjoyment is said to be far from nirvana.

There are, Purna, forms perceptible to the eye which are desirable, agreeable, pleasing, captivating, connected with sensual pleasure and which arouse desire. But if a monk, seeing such forms, does not approve them, does not welcome them, does not cling to them, then, as a result of not approving, welcoming, or clinging to them, he does not come to enjoy them. When there is no enjoyment, the satisfaction of enjoyment does not arise. When there is no satisfaction of enjoyment, passion does not arise. When there is no passion for enjoyment, bondage to passion for enjoyment does not arise. Purna, a monk not in bondage to passion for enjoyment is progressing like the waxing moon, is near to nirvana.

There are, Purna, sounds perceptible to the ear, smells perceptible to the nose, flavors perceptible to the tongue, tactile objects perceptible to the body, thoughts perceptible to the mind, which are desirable, agreeable, pleasing, captivating, delightful, connected with sensual pleasure and which arouse desire. But if a monk, becoming aware of these, does not delight in them, does not welcome them, does not cling to them, then, as a result of not approving, welcoming, or clinging to them, he does not enjoy them. Where there is no enjoyment, the satisfaction of enjoyment does not arise. When there is no satisfaction of enjoyment,

saṃrāgo na bhavati. nandī|saṃrāge 'sati, nandī|saṃrāga|saṃyojanaṃ na bhavati. nandī|saṃrāga|saṃyojan'|â|saṃyuktaḥ, Pūrṇa, bhikṣuḥ śukla|pakṣeṇ' ântike nirvāṇasy' êty ucyate.

Anena tvam, Pūrṇa, mayā saṃkṣipten' âvavādena coditaḥ. kutr' êcchasi vastum? kutr' êcchasi vāsaṃ kalpayitum?»

2.170 «Anen' âham, Bhadanta, Bhagavatā saṃkṣipten' âvavādena coditaḥ, icchāmi Śroṇāparāntakeṣu jana|padeṣu vastum, Śroṇāparāntakeṣu jana|padeṣu vāsaṃ kalpayitum.»

«Caṇḍāḥ, Pūrṇa, Śroṇāparāntakā manuṣyāḥ, rabhasāḥ, karkaśāḥ, ākrośakāḥ, roṣakāḥ, paribhāṣakāḥ. sacet tvām, Pūrṇa, Śroṇāparāntakā manuṣyāḥ saṃmukhaṃ pāpikay" âsabhyayā, paruṣayā vāc" ākrokṣyanti roṣayiṣyanti paribhāṣiṣyante, tatra te kathaṃ bhaviṣyati?»

«Sacen mām, Bhadanta, Śroṇāparāntakā manuṣyāḥ saṃmukhaṃ pāpikay" â|sabhyayā, paruṣayā vāc" ākrokṣyanti roṣayiṣyanti paribhāṣiṣyante, tatra mam' âivaṃ bhaviṣyati: ‹bhadrakā bata Śroṇāparāntakā manuṣyāḥ, snigdhakā bata Śroṇāparāntakā manuṣyāḥ, ye māṃ saṃmukhaṃ pāpikay" âsabhyayā paruṣayā vāc" ākrośanti roṣayanti paribhāṣante, no tu pāṇinā vā loṣṭena vā praharanti› iti.»

«Caṇḍāḥ, Pūrṇa, Śroṇāparāntakā manuṣyāḥ, rabhasāḥ, karkaśāḥ, ākrośakāḥ, roṣakāḥ, paribhāṣakāḥ. sacet tvām, Pūrṇa, Śroṇāparāntakā manuṣyāḥ pāṇinā vā loṣṭena vā prahariṣyanti, tatra te kathaṃ bhaviṣyati?»

passion does not arise. Where there is no passion for enjoyment, bondage to passion for enjoyment does not arise. Purna, a monk not in bondage to passion for enjoyment, progressing like the waxing moon, is near to nirvana.

This, Purna, is the concise advice by which I exhort you. Now, where do you wish to live? Where do you wish to make your home?"

"Venerable sir, thus exhorted by the Lord by means of this 2.170
concise advice, I wish to live among the people of Shronáparántaka, to make my home among the people of Shronáparántaka."

"Purna, the people of Shronáparántaka are fierce, violent, cruel, abusive, wrathful and contemptuous. Purna, if the people of Shronáparántaka curse, abuse and revile you face-to-face with evil, indecent and harsh speech, what will you think?"

"Venerable sir, if the people of Shronáparántaka curse, abuse and revile me face-to-face with evil, indecent and harsh speech, then I shall think, 'Good are the people of Shronáparántaka, affectionate are the people of Shronáparántaka: face-to-face they curse, abuse and revile me with evil, indecent and harsh speech, but they do not strike me with their fists or with clods of earth.'"

"Purna, the people of Shronáparántaka are fierce, violent, cruel, abusive, wrathful and contemptuous. If the people of Shronáparántaka strike you with their fists or with clods of earth, what will you think?"

«Sacen mām, Bhadanta, Śroṇāparāntakā manuṣyāḥ, pāṇinā vā loṣṭena vā prahariṣyanti, tatra mam' âivaṃ bhaviṣyati: ‹bhadrakā bata Śroṇāparāntakā manuṣyāḥ, snehakā bata Śroṇāparāntakā manuṣyāḥ, ye māṃ pāṇinā vā loṣṭena vā praharanti, no tu daṇḍena vā śastreṇa vā praharanti› iti.»

2.175 «Caṇḍāḥ, Pūrṇa, Śroṇāparāntakā manuṣysāḥ, rabhasāḥ, karkaśāḥ, ākrośakāḥ, roṣakāḥ, paribhāṣakāḥ. sacet tvām, Pūrṇa, Śroṇāparāntakā manuṣyā daṇḍena vā śastreṇa vā prahariṣyanti, tatra te kathaṃ bhaviṣyati?»

«Sacen mām, Bhadanta, Śroṇāparāntakā manuṣyā daṇḍena vā śastreṇa vā prahariṣyanti, tatra mam' âivaṃ bhaviṣyati: ‹bhadrakā bata Śroṇāparāntakā manuṣyāḥ, snehakā bata Śroṇāparāntakā manuṣyāḥ, ye māṃ daṇḍena vā śastreṇa vā praharanti, no tu sarveṇa sarvaṃ jīvitād vyaparopayanti.›»

«Caṇḍāḥ, Pūrṇa, Śroṇāparāntakā manuṣyāḥ, rabhasāḥ, karkaśāḥ, ākrośakāḥ, roṣakāḥ, paribhāṣakāḥ. sacet tvām, Pūrṇa, Śroṇāparāntakā manuṣyāḥ sarveṇa sarvaṃ jīvitād vyaparopayiṣyanti, tatra te kathaṃ bhaviṣyati?»

«Sacen mām, Bhadanta, Śroṇāparāntakā manuṣyāḥ sarveṇa sarvaṃ jīvitād vyaparopayiṣyanti, tatra ma evaṃ bhaviṣyati: ‹santi Bhagavataḥ śrāvakāḥ, ye 'nena pūti|kāyen' ārdīyamānā jehrīyamāṇā vijigupsamānāḥ, śastram apy ādhārayanti, viṣam api bhakṣayanti, rajjvā baddhā api mriyante, prapātād api prapatanty api. bhadrakā bata Śroṇāparāntakā manuṣyakāḥ, snehakā bata Śroṇāparāntakā manuṣyāḥ, ye mām asmāt pūti|kalevarād alpa|kṛcchreṇa parimocayanti› iti.»

"Venerable sir, if the people of Shronáparántaka strike me with their fists or with clods of earth I shall think, 'Good are the people of Shronáparántaka, affectionate are the people of Shronáparántaka: they strike me with their fists or with clods of earth, but they do not use weapons to beat me or stab me.'"

"Purna, the people of Shronáparántaka are fierce, violent, 2.175
cruel, abusive, wrathful and contemptuous. If the people of Shronáparántaka but they do not use weapons to beat me or stab me, what will you think?"

"Venerable sir, if the people of Shronáparántaka attack me with swords or clubs, I shall think, 'Good are the people of Shronáparántaka, affectionate are the people of Shronáparántaka: they use weapons to beat me or stab me but do not deprive me utterly of life.'"

"Purna, the people of Shronáparántaka are fierce, violent, cruel, abusive, wrathful and contemptuous. If the people of Shronáparántaka deprive you utterly of life, what will you think?"

"Venerable sir, if the people of Shronáparántaka deprive me utterly of life, I shall think, 'The Lord has disciples who are so tormented, shamed and disgusted by this stinking body that they even wield a knife against themselves, even eat poison, even hang themselves, even fling themselves from a cliff. Good are the people of Shronáparántaka, affectionate are the people of Shronáparántaka: they set me free with little difficulty from this stinking carcass!'"

«Sādhu, sādhu, Pūrṇa! śakyas tvam, Pūrṇa, anena kṣānti|sauratyena samanvāgataḥ Śroṇāparāntakeṣu jana|padeṣu vastum, Śroṇāparāntakeṣu vāsaṃ kalpayitum. gaccha tvam, Pūrṇa! muktaḥ, mocaya! tīrṇaḥ, tāraya! āśvastaḥ, āśvāsaya! parinirvṛtaḥ, parinirvāpaya!» iti.

2.180 Ath' Āyuṣmān Pūrṇo Bhagavato bhāṣitam abhinandy' ânumodya, Bhagavataḥ pādau śirasā vanditvā, Bhagavato 'ntikāt prakrāntaḥ. ath' Āyuṣmān Pūrṇas tasyā eva rātrer atyayāt pūrv'|âhṇe nivāsya, pātra|cīvaram ādāya, Śrāvastīṃ piṇḍāya prāvikṣat. Śrāvastīṃ piṇḍāya caritvā, kṛta|bhakta|kṛtyaḥ paścād|bhakta|piṇḍa|pātraḥ pratikrāntaḥ. yathā|paribhukta|śayan'|āsanaṃ pratisamayya, samādāya pātra|cīvaraṃ, yena Śroṇāparāntakā jana|padās tena cārikāṃ caran, Śroṇāparāntakān jana|padān anuprāptaḥ.

Ath' Āyuṣmān Pūrṇaḥ pūrv'|âhṇe nivāsya, pātra|cīvaram ādāya, Śroṇāparāntakaṃ piṇḍāya prāvikṣat.

Anyatamaś ca lubdhako dhanuṣ|pāṇir mṛgayāṃ nirgacchati. tena dṛṣṭaḥ. sa saṃlakṣayati, «a|maṅgalo 'yaṃ muṇḍakaḥ śramaṇo mayā dṛṣṭaḥ» iti viditvā, ā karṇād dhanuḥ pūrayitvā, yen' Āyuṣmān Pūrṇas tena pradhāvitaḥ. sa Āyuṣmatā Pūrṇena dṛṣṭaḥ. dṛṣṭvā c' ôttar'|āsaṅgaṃ vivartya, kathayati, «bhadra|mukha, asya duṣ|pūrasy' ârthe praviśāmi. atra prahara!» iti. gāthāṃ ca bhāṣate:

"Well spoken, Purna, well spoken! With your forbearance and meekness, you are well able to live among the people of Shronáparántaka, well able to make your home among the people of Shronáparántaka. Go, then, Purna! Attain liberation, then liberate others! Cross over, then convey others across! Consoled, console others! Achieve final emancipation, then emancipate others!"

Then, rejoicing in and approving the words of the Lord, 2.180
the Venerable Purna reverently knelt with his head at the Lord's feet and departed. After passing the night, early the next morning the Venerable Purna dressed, took his alms-bowl and outer robe and went into Shravásti for alms. He made his alms-round in Shravásti, ate the food he had collected and in the afternoon returned from his alms-round. Then, putting away the bed and seat he had used and again taking up his robe and bowl, he set out for the land of Shrona·parántaka and in due course reached that country.

The following morning, the Venerable Purna got dressed, took up his robe and bowl, and entered Shronáparántaka for alms.

Just then, a certain hunter, bow in hand, was on his way out to hunt. He caught sight of Purna and thought, "This is inauspicious, seeing this shaven-headed ascetic!" He drew the bowstring to his ear and rushed after the Venerable Purna. The Venerable Purna saw him. Seeing him, he displaced his outer robe, and declared, "Good sir, I have come here for the sake of this one that is never satisfied. Strike here!" And he recited this verse:

Yasy' ârthe gahane caranti vihagāḥ
 gacchanti bandhaṃ mṛgāḥ
saṃgrāme śara|śakti|tomara|dharāḥ
 naśyanty ajasraṃ narāḥ;
dīnā durdina|cāriṇaś ca kṛpaṇāḥ
 matsyā grasanty āyasam
asy' ârtha udarasya pāpa|kalile
 dūrād ih' âbhyāgataḥ. iti

Sa saṃlakṣayati, «ayaṃ pravrajita īdṛśena kṣānti|sauratyena samanvāgataḥ! kim asya praharāmi» iti matvā, abhiprasannaḥ. tato 'sy' Āyuṣmatā Pūrṇena Dharmo deśitaḥ śaraṇa|gamana|śikṣā|padeṣu ca pratiṣṭhāpitaḥ. anyāni ca pañc'|ôpāsikā|śatāni. pañca|vihāra|śatāni kāritāny anekāni ca mañca|pīṭha|vṛṣi|kocava|bimb'|ôpadhāna|caturasraka|śatāny anupradāpitāni.

2.185 Tasy' âiva ca tri|māsasy' âtyayāt tisro vidyāḥ kāyena sākṣāt|kṛtāḥ. arhan saṃvṛttaḥ: trai|dhātuka|vīta|rāgaḥ: sama|loṣṭa|kāñcanaḥ, ākāśa|pāṇi|tala|sama|cittaḥ, vāsī|candana|kalpaḥ, vidyā|vidārit'|âṇḍa|kośaḥ, vidy"|âbhijñā|pratisaṃvit|prāptaḥ, bhava|lābha|lobha|sat|kāra|parāṅ|mukhaḥ, s'|êndr'|ôpendrāṇāṃ devānāṃ pūjyo mānyo 'bhivādyaś ca saṃvṛttaḥ.

For the sake of which birds and wild animals are
caught in snares and nets,
And men bearing arrows, swords and spears
forever perish in battle;
For the sake of which those wretched dwellers in
darkness, the pitiful fish, swallow the hook:
It is for the sake of this belly that I have come from
afar to this cesspool of wickedness!

The hunter reflected, "This renunciate possesses such forbearance and meekness!," and, thinking further, "Why should I attack him?," became well disposed toward Purna. He then received instruction in the Dharma from the Venerable Purna and was thereby established in Going for Refuge to the Buddha, Dharma and Sangha and in the five moral precepts. Purna also converted five hundred other male lay disciples and five hundred female lay disciples. In addition, Purna had his disciples build five hundred monastic dwellings and furnish them with many hundreds of beds, stools, cushions, pillows, woollen blankets and shawls.

And after the passage of three months Purna realized the 2.185
Three Knowledges with his body and became an Arhat. He was freed from desire for anything in the three worlds: to him, a lump of gold and a clod of earth were the same; so, too, the palm of the hand and the open sky; so, too, being cut with a hatchet and being rubbed with sandalwood paste. With knowledge he cracked open the shell of that egg, the mundane world: he realized the Three Knowledges, the Six Superknowledges and the Four Analytical Knowledges. From conditioned existence, with its gain and greed, fame

Yāvad apareṇa samayena Dārukarṇi|bhrātror bhogās tanutvaṃ parikṣayaṃ paryādānaṃ gatāḥ. tau kathayataḥ, «gato 'sāv asmākaṃ gṛhāt kāla|karṇi|prakhyaḥ. āgaccha, ekadhye prativasāmaḥ.»

Sa kathayati, «kataro 'sau kāla|karṇi|prakhyaḥ?»

Tau kathayataḥ, «Pūrṇaka|śrīḥ.»

«Sā mama gṛhān niṣkrāntā—n' âsau kāla|karṇi|prakhyaḥ.»

2.190 Tau kathayataḥ, «śrīr vā bhavatu kāla|karṇī vā—āgaccha, ekadhye prativasāmaḥ.»

Sa kathayati, «yuvayor a|nyāy'|ôpārjitaṃ dhanaṃ, mama nyāy'|ôpārjitam. n' âhaṃ yuvābhyāṃ sārdham ekadhye vāsaṃ kalpayāmi» iti.

Tau kathayataḥ, «tena dāsī|putreṇa mahā|samudram avatīry' âvatīrya bhogāḥ samudānītā, yena tvaṃ bhuñjāno vikatthase. kutas tava sāmarthyaṃ mahā|samudram avatartum?» iti.

Sa tābhyāṃ mānaṃ grāhitaḥ. sa saṃlakṣayati, «aham api mahā|samudram avatarāmi.» tena Sūrpārake nagare ghaṇṭ"|âvaghoṣaṇaṃ kāritam: «śṛṇvantu, bhavantaḥ Saurpārakīyā vaṇijaḥ! Dārukarṇī sārtha|vāho mahā|samudram avatarati. yo yuṣmākam utsahate Dārukarṇinā sārtha|vāhena sārdham, aśulken' âgulmen' âtara|paṇyena mahā|samudram avatartum, sa mahā|samudra|gamanīyaṃ paṇyaṃ samudānayatu» iti.

and honor, he had turned away. He became worthy of the respectful salutation, honor and worship of the gods themselves, not excepting Indra and Upéndra.

Time passed, and the wealth of Daru·karnin's two brothers dwindled, shrank and finally was exhausted. Those two said to their elder brother, "He is gone from our house, that one who is like a vision of misfortune. Come, let us live together."

Bhávila said, "Who is it that is like a vision of misfortune?"

The other two told him, "Your precious Púrnaka."

"Fortune has indeed departed from my house—Purna is no vision of misfortune!"

The two replied, "Call him good fortune or vision of 2.190
misfortune—it doesn't matter. Come, let us live together."

Bhávila replied, "You two acquired your wealth by immoral means; my own was acquired justly. I shall not set up housekeeping with you two."

The two brothers said, "That son of a slave girl crossed and recrossed the great ocean and brought riches so that you can enjoy them and be arrogant. What ability have you to set out on the great ocean?"

In this way, the two caused Bhávila to cling to his pride. He thought, "Well, then, I will cross the great ocean!" He had the proclamation bell rung in Surpáraka City. "Hear ye, merchants of Surpáraka! Daru·karnin, the caravan-leader, is crossing the great ocean! Whosoever among you ventures to cross the great ocean with the caravan-leader Daru·karnin, free from customs duties, escort charges and freight fees, is to gather together the trade-goods for transport across the great ocean."

Pañca|mātrair vaṇik|śatair mahā|samudra|gamanīyaṃ paṇyaṃ samudānītam. tata Dārukarṇī sārtha|vāhaḥ, kṛta|kautūhala|maṅgala|svasty|ayanaḥ, pañca|vaṇik|śata|parivāraḥ, mahā|samudram avatīrṇaḥ. yāvat tad vahanaṃ vāyunā Go-śīrṣa|candana|vanam anupreritam. karṇa|dhāraḥ kathayati, «bhavantaḥ, yat tac chrūyate ‹Go|śīrṣa|candana|vanam› it' îdaṃ tad gṛhṇantv atra yat sāram» iti.

2.195 Tena khalu samayena Go|śīrṣa|candana|vanam Maheśvarasya yakṣasya parigraho 'bhūt. sa ca yakṣāṇāṃ yakṣa|samitiṃ gataḥ. tato Go|śīrṣa|candana|vane pañca|mātrāṇi kuṭhāra|śatāni voḍhum ārabdhāni. adrākṣīd Apriy'|ākhyo yo yakṣo Go|śīrṣa|candana|vane pañca|mātrāṇi kuṭhāra|śatāni vahataḥ. dṛṣṭvā ca yena Maheśvaro yakṣas ten' ôpasaṃkrāntaḥ. upasaṃkramya Maheśvaraṃ yakṣam idam avocat: «yat khalu, grāma|ṇīḥ, jānīyā Go|śīrṣa|candana|vane pañca|mātrāṇi kuṭhāra|śatāni vahanti. yat te kṛtyaṃ vā karaṇīyaṃ vā tat kuruṣva» iti.

Atha Maheśvaro yakṣo yakṣāṇāṃ samitim asamitiṃ kṛtvā, saṃjāt'|âmarṣo mahā|kālikā|vāta|bhayaṃ saṃjanya, yena Go|śīrṣa|candana|vanaṃ tena saṃprasthitaḥ.

Karṇa|dhāreṇ' ārocitam, «śṛṇvantu bhavantaḥ, Jāmbudvīpakā vaṇijaḥ! yat tac chrūyate ‹Mahā|kālikā|vāta|bhayam› iti idaṃ tat. kiṃ|kartavyatāṃ manyadhvam» iti.

Tatas te vaṇijaḥ, bhītāḥ, trastāḥ, saṃvign'|āhṛṣṭa|roma|kūpāḥ, devat"|āyācanaṃ kartum ārabdhāḥ:

Merchants numbering five hundred gathered together trade-goods for transport across the great ocean. Then the caravan-leader Daru·karnin, having performed the rites to ensure a safe and successful journey, accompanied by those five hundred merchants, set out across the great ocean. The winds brought his ship to the Yellow Sandalwood Forest. The helmsman called out, "Sirs, this is what people call the 'Yellow Sandalwood Forest'! Let the men take what is best from this place!"

At that time, the Yellow Sandalwood Forest was the prop- 2.195
erty of the ogre Mahéshvara, but he was away attending the Ogre Assembly. Then five hundred axes began cutting down the trees in the Yellow Sandalwood Forest. An ogre named Ápriya, "Inimical," saw men plying five hundred axes in the Yellow Sandalwood Forest, and went after to the ogre Mahéshvara. Approaching the ogre Mahéshvara, he said this to him: "Headman, you should know that five hundred axes are cutting down the trees in the Yellow Sandalwood Forest. Do what you need to do, sir; do what must be done."

Enraged, the ogre Mahéshvara dissolved the Ogre Assembly, produced a fearsome , apocalyptic cyclone and set out for the Yellow Sandalwood Forest.

The helmsman of Bhávila's ship cried out, "Listen, sirs, merchants of India! This is what people call the 'Cyclone of the Apocalypse'! Think what is to be done?"

Those merchants, terrified and shuddering with fear, the hair of their bodies standing on end, began to supplicate the gods:

Śiva|Varuṇa|Kubera|Vāsav'|ādyāḥ
sura|manuj'|ôraga|yakṣa|dānav'|êndrāḥ!
vyasanam atibhayaṃ vayaṃ prapannāḥ!
vigata|bhayā hi bhavantu no 'dya nāthāḥ!

2.200 Ke cin namasyanti Śacī|patiṃ narāḥ,
Brahmāṇam anye Hari|Śaṃkarāv api,
bhūmy|āśritān vṛkṣa|van'|āśritāṃś ca
trāṇ'|ârthino vāta|piśāca|daṣṭhāḥ.

Dārukarṇy alp'|ôtsukas tiṣṭhati. vaṇijaḥ kathayanti, «sārtha|vāha, vayaṃ kṛcchra|saṃkaṭa|saṃbādha|prāptāḥ! kim|artham alp'|ôtsukas tiṣṭhasi» iti.

Sa kathayati, «bhavanto 'haṃ bhrātr" âbhihitaḥ, ‹mahā|samudro 'lp'|āsvādo bahv|ādīnavaḥ. tṛṣṇ"|ândhāḥ, bahavo 'vataranti; svalpā vyutpatsyanti. na tvayā kena cit prakāreṇa mahā|samudram avatartavyam› iti. so 'haṃ tasya vacanam avacanaṃ kṛtvā, mahā|samudram avatīrṇaḥ. kim idānīṃ karomi?»

«Kas tava bhrātā?»

«Pūrṇaḥ.»

2.205 Vaṇijaḥ kathayanti, «bhavantaḥ, sa eva, Ārya|pūrṇaḥ, puṇya|maheś'|ākhyaḥ! tam eva śaraṇaṃ prapadyāma!» iti. tair eka|svareṇa sarvair evaṃ nādo muktaḥ, «namas tasmai, Āryāya Pūrṇāya! namaḥ, namas tasmai, Āryāya Pūrṇāya!» iti.

Atha yā devatā Āyuṣmati Pūrṇe 'bhiprasannā, sā yen' Āyuṣmān Pūrṇas ten' ôpasaṃkrāntā. upasaṃkramy' Āyuṣmantaṃ Pūrṇam idam avocat: «Ārya, bhrātā te kṛcchra|saṃkaṭa|saṃbādha|prāptaḥ—samanvāhara!» iti.

O Shiva, Váruna, Kubéra, Vásava and the other deities!
Lords over gods, humans, serpents, ogres and demons!
A frightful calamity has befallen us!
May these fearless ones this day be our protectors!
Some of the men supplicated the Lord of Shachi; 2.200
Others, Brahma, Hari or Shánkara,*
Or the gods of earth, tree and forest:
Assailed by that demon-wind,
Those merchants pleaded for protection.

Daru·karnin remained indifferent. The merchants said, "Caravan-leader, we are trapped, beset and in great danger! How can you remain indifferent?"

Bhávila replied, "Sirs, I was told by my brother, 'On the great ocean there are few pleasures and many hazards. Blinded by greed, many cross; few will return. You must by no means cross the great ocean.' I myself, ignoring his words, crossed the great ocean. What am I to do now?"

"Who is your brother?"

"Purna."

The merchants said, "Sirs, that very one, the holy Purna, 2.205
he is a great man by reason of his merit! Let us go for refuge to that very man!" Then all those merchants cried out with one voice, "Reverence to him, the Holy Purna! Reverence, reverence to him, the Holy Purna!"

At that, the Venerable goddess who had faith in the Venerable Purna approached the Venerable Purna and, having approached him, said this: "Holy One, your brother

Tena samanvāhṛtam. tata Āyuṣmān Pūrṇas tad|rūpaṃ samādhiṃ samāpanno yathā, samāhite citte, Śroṇāparāntake 'ntarhitaḥ, mahā|samudre vahana|sīmāyāṃ paryaṅkaṃ baddhv" âvasthitaḥ. tato 'sau kālikā|vātaḥ Sumeru|pratyāhata iva pratinivṛttaḥ.

Atha Maheśvaro yakṣaḥ saṃlakṣayati, «pūrvam, yat kiṃ cid vahanaṃ kālikā|vātena spṛśyate, tat tūla|picu|vat kṣipyate viśīryate ca. idānīṃ ko yogo yena kālikā|vātaḥ Sumeru|pratyāhata iva pratinivṛttaḥ?» sa itaś c' âmutaś ca pratyavekṣitum ārabdhaḥ, yāvat paśyaty Āyuṣmantaṃ Pūrṇaṃ vahana|sīmāyāṃ paryaṅkaṃ baddhv" âvasthitam. dṛṣṭvā ca punaḥ kathayati, «Ārya Pūrṇa, kiṃ viheṭhayasi?» iti.

Āyuṣmān Pūrṇaḥ kathayati, «jarā|dharmo 'haṃ—kiṃ tvāṃ viheṭhayāmi? tvam eva māṃ viheṭhayasi! yadi may" ēdṛśā guṇa|guṇā n' âdhigatāḥ syuḥ, bhrātā me tvayā nām'|âvaśeṣaḥ kṛtaḥ syāt.»

2.210 Maheśvaro yakṣaḥ kathayati, «Ārya, idaṃ Go|śīrṣa|candana|vanaṃ rājñaś cakra|vartino 'rthāya dhāryate.»

«Kiṃ manyase, grāma|ṇīḥ? kiṃ varam—rājā cakra|varty uta Tathāgataḥ, Arhan, samyak|saṃbuddhaḥ?»

«Kim, Ārya? Bhagavān loka utpannaḥ?»

«Utpannaḥ.»

is trapped, beset and in great danger—focus your mind on him!"

Purna focussed his mind on Bhávila. Then the Venerable Purna entered into a meditation such that, as soon as his mind was fully concentrated, he vanished from Shronápa-rántaka and appeared in the great ocean, seated cross-legged in meditation, on the edge of his brother's ship. Then that cyclone turned back as if repelled by Mount Suméru.

At that, the ogre Mahéshvara reflected, "In the past, any ship touched by that cyclone capsized and broke apart like a tuft of cotton! Now through what yoga has the cyclone turned back as if repelled by Mount Suméru?" He began to look here and there until he saw the Venerable Purna seated cross-legged on the edge of the ship. Seeing Purna, the ogre said, "Holy Purna, why do you harass me?"

The Venerable Purna replied, "Why do I, an old man, harass you? It is you who are harassing me! Had I not mastered such powers as I have, you would have reduced my brother to nothing more than a name."

Replied the ogre Mahéshvara, "Holy One, this Yellow 2.210
Sandalwood Forest is maintained for the use of a universal monarch."

"What do you think, headman? Which is superior—a king who is a universal monarch or a Tathágata, an Arhat, a Fully Awakened One?"

"Holy One, has such a Lord appeared in the world?"

"Such a one has appeared."

«Yady evam, yad a|paripūrṇam, tat paripūryatām!» tatas te vaṇijaḥ, gata|pratyāgata|prāṇāḥ, Āyuṣmati Pūrṇe cittam abhiprasādya, tad vahanaṃ go|śīrṣa|candanasya pūrayitvā, saṃprasthitāḥ. anupūrveṇa, Sūrpārakaṃ nagaram anuprāptāḥ.

2.215 Tata Āyuṣmān Pūrṇo bhrātuḥ kathayati, «yasya nāmnā vahanaṃ saṃsiddha|yāna|pātram āgacchati, tat tasya gamyaṃ bhavati. tvam eṣāṃ vaṇijāṃ ratna|saṃvibhāgaṃ kuru. aham, anena go|śīrṣa|candanena, Bhagavato 'rthāya Candana|mālaṃ prāsādaṃ kārayāmi» iti. tena teṣāṃ vaṇijāṃ ratnaiḥ saṃvibhāgaḥ kṛtaḥ. tata Āyuṣmān Pūrṇo go|śīrṣa|candanena prāsādaṃ māpayitum ārabdhaḥ. tena śilpān āhūy' ôktāḥ, «bhavantaḥ, kiṃ divase divase pañca kārṣāpaṇa|śatāni gṛhṇīdhvam āhosvid go|śīrṣa|candana|cūrṇasya biḍāla|padam?»

Te kathayanti, «Ārya, go|śīrṣa|candana|cūrṇasya biḍāla|padam.»

Yāvad alpīyasā kālena Candana|mālaḥ Prāsādaḥ kṛtaḥ. rājā kathayati, «bhavantaḥ, śobhanaṃ prāsādam! sarva|jāta|kṛta|niṣṭhitaḥ saṃvṛttaḥ!»

Yat tatra saṃkalikā cūrṇaṃ c' âvaśiṣṭaṃ, tat piṣṭvā tatr' âiva pralepo dattaḥ. te ca bhrātaraḥ paras|paraṃ sarve kṣamitā uktāś ca, «Buddha|pramukhaṃ bhikṣu|saṃgham upanimantrya bhojayata.»

"If that is so, then let that which has not been finished be finished!" Thereupon, those merchants, having recovered their lives, became filled with faith in the Venerable Purna and, loading their ship with yellow sandalwood, they departed. In due course they reached Surpáraka City.

At that point, the Venerable Purna said to his brother 2.215 Bhávila, "This cargo must go to him through whose name your ship has returned safe and sound. Divide these jewels among the merchants. With the yellow sandalwood I shall have built for the use of the Lord a grand edifice, the 'Sandalwood Pavilion.'" And so Bhávila distributed the jewels among the merchants. The Venerable Purna, using the yellow sandalwood, began the construction of the pavilion. He summoned artisans and said to them, "Sirs, will you accept as your daily payment five hundred coins or would you prefer one measure of powdered yellow sandalwood the size of a cat's footprint?"

They replied, "Holy One, one measure of yellow sandalwood powder."

In a short time, the Sandalwood Pavilion was completed. The king declared, "Sirs, the pavilion is exquisite! It is completed, finished and entirely perfect!"

The sandalwood shavings and sawdust that were left over were ground up and the sandal-paste was donated to the monastery to be used as salve. And Purna made all the brothers forgive each other and instructed them, "Invite the community of monks, led by the Buddha, and serve them a meal."

«Ārya, kutra Bhagavān?»

«Śrāvastyām.»

«Kiyad dūram itaḥ Śrāvastī?»

«S'|âtirekaṃ yojana|śatam.»

«Rājānaṃ tāvad avalokayāmaḥ.»

«Evaṃ kuruta.»

Te rājñaḥ sakāśam upasaṃkrāntāḥ. upasaṃkramya, śirasā praṇāmaṃ kṛtvā, kathayanti, «Deva, icchāmo vayaṃ Buddha|pramukhaṃ bhikṣu|saṃgham upanimantrya bhojayitum. Devo 'smākaṃ sāhāyyaṃ kalpayatu.»

Rājā kathayati, «tataḥ śobhanam. tathā bhavatu. kalpayāmi.»

Tata Āyuṣmān Pūrṇaḥ śaraṇa|pṛṣṭham abhiruhya, Jeta|van'|âbhimukhaṃ sthitvā, ubhe jānu|maṇḍale pṛthivyāṃ pratiṣṭhāpya, puṣpāṇi kṣiptvā, dhūpaṃ cārya, āgārikena ca sauvarṇa|bhṛṅgāraṃ grāhayitv" ārādhituṃ pravṛttaḥ:

Viśuddha|śīlin! suviśuddha|buddhe!
  bhakt'|âbhisāre satat'|ârtha|darśin!
anātha|bhūtān prasamīkṣya, sādho!
  kṛtvā kṛpām, āgamanaṃ kuruṣva! iti

Tatas tāni puṣpāṇi Buddhānāṃ Buddh'|ânubhāvena devatānāṃ ca devat"|ânubhāven' ôpari puṣpa|maṇḍapaṃ kṛt-

"Holy One, where is the Lord?"

"In Shravásti." 2.220

"How far is Shravásti from here?"

"More than a hundred leagues."

"First we should see the king."

"Yes, do that."

So Purna's brothers went before the king. They drew near, 2.225
performed obeisance with their heads at his feet and said, "Sire, we wish to invite the community of monks, led by the Buddha, in order to serve them a meal. May your majesty make arrangements to assist us."

Said the king, "Fine! So be it. I shall make the arrangements."

Then the Venerable Purna climbed onto the roof of the daïs for the ritual of taking refuge, and stood facing the Jeta Grove. He knelt down on both knees, strewed flowers, waved incense; then, handed a golden vase by a lay disciple, he proceeded to worship in order to obtain a boon:

O you of purified conduct! O you of perfectly purified
Intelligence!
You who always see the benefit of meeting your devotees!
Behold those beings who are without a protector,
O Great One! Exercise compassion and come to this
place!

Then, through the spiritual power of the Buddhas and the divine power of the gods, the flowers fashioned themselves into an airborne pavilion and were transported to the Jeta Grove. There they settled down at the end of the line

vā, Jeta|vane gatvā, vṛddh'|ânte sthitāni, dhūpo 'bhra|kūṭa|vad, udakaṃ vaidūrya|śalāka|vat.

2.230 Āyuṣmān Ānando nimitta|kuśalaḥ. sa kṛta|kara|puṭaḥ, Bhagavantaṃ papraccha, «kutaḥ, Bhagavan, nimantraṇam āgatam?»

«Sūrpārakāt, Ānanda, nagarāt.»

«Kiyad dūre, Bhadanta, Sūrpārakaṃ nagaram?»

«S'|âtirekam, Ānanda, yojana|śatam.»

«Gacchāmaḥ?»

2.235 «Ānanda, bhikṣūn ārocaya, ‹yo yuṣmākam utsahate śvaḥ Sūrpārakaṃ nagaraṃ gatvā bhoktuṃ, sa śalākāṃ gṛhṇātu› iti.»

«Evam, Bhadanta,» ity Āyuṣmān Ānando Bhagavataḥ pratiśrutya, śalākāṃ gṛhītvā, Bhagavataḥ purastāt sthitaḥ. Bhagavatā śalākā gṛhītā, sthavira|sthaviraiś ca bhikṣubhiḥ.

Tena khalu samayena, Āyuṣmān Pūrṇaḥ, Kuṇḍ'|ôpadhānīyakaḥ sthaviraḥ, prajñā|vimuktaḥ, tasyām eva pariṣadi saṃniṣaṇṇo 'bhūt. saṃnipatitaḥ, so 'pi śalākāṃ gṛhītum ārabdhaḥ. tam Āyuṣmān Ānando gāthayā pratyabhāṣata:

N' âitad bhoktavyam, Āyuṣman,
Kośal'|âdhipater gṛhe,
āgāre vā Sudattasya
Mṛgāra|bhavane 'thavā.

of senior monks, while the incense appeared there like a canopy of clouds and the water from the vase like a staff of lapis lazuli.

Now, the Venerable Anánda was skilled in the interpre- 2.230
tation of signs and portents. Raising his joined hands in respectful salutation, he asked the Lord, "Lord, from where does this invitation come?"

"From the city of Surpáraka, Anánda."

"Venerable sir, how far away is the city of Surpáraka?"

"More than a hundred leagues, Anánda."

"We are going there?"

"Anánda, make this announcement to the monks: 'Who- 2.235
ever among you is able to travel to Surpáraka tomorrow to accept an invitation for a meal should now take a food-ticket.'"

"So be it, Venerable sir," said Anánda in agreement. He took a food-ticket and took his place before the Lord. Then the Buddha and the most senior monks took food-tickets.

Now, at that time another Venerable Purna, the Elder Kundópadhaníyaka, who had been liberated through insight,* was seated in that very assembly. Being among those assembled, he also went to take a food-ticket. But the Venerable Anánda addressed him with these verses:

Venerable sir, this is not a meal
At the palace of the King of Kóshala,
Nor in Mrigára's mansion
Nor at the house of Sudátta.

S'|âdhikaṃ yojana|śataṃ
Sūrpārakam itaḥ puram;
ṛddhibhir yatra gantavyaṃ
tūṣṇī tvaṃ bhava, Pūrṇaka. iti

2.240 Sa prajñā|vimuktaḥ. tena' rddhir n' ôtpāditā. tasy' âitad abhavat, «yena mayā sakalaṃ kleśa|gaṇaṃ vāntaṃ charditaṃ tyaktaṃ pratiniḥsṛṣṭaṃ so 'haṃ tīrthika|sādhāraṇāyām ṛddhyāṃ niṣaṇṇaḥ.» tena vīryam āsthāya, ṛddhim utpādya, yāvad Āyuṣmān Ānandas tṛtīya|sthavirasya śalākāṃ na dadāti, tāvat tena gaja|bhuja|sadṛśaṃ bāhum abhiprasārya, śalākā gṛhītā. tato gāthāṃ bhāṣate:

Na vapurmatayā śrutena vā
na balāt|kāra|guṇaiś ca, Gautama,
prabalair api vāṅ|mano|rathaiḥ
ṣaḍ|abhijñatvam ih' âdhigamyate.
Śama|śīla|vipaśyanā|balair
vividhair dhyāna|balaiḥ parīkṣitāḥ,
jaray" âpi nipīḍita|yauvanāḥ
ṣaḍ|abhijñā hi bhavanti mad|vidhāḥ. iti

Tatra Bhagavān bhikṣūn āmantrayate sma, «eṣo 'gro me, bhikṣavaḥ, bhikṣūṇāṃ mama śrāvakāṇāṃ caitya|śalākā|grahaṇe. tat prathamataḥ śalākāṃ gṛhṇatāṃ yad uta Pūrṇa Kuṇḍ'|ôpadhānīyakaḥ sthaviraḥ.»

More than a hundred leagues from here
Is the city of Surpáraka;
To get there one needs psychic powers,
So be silent, Purnaka.

Purna, who had been liberated through insight and so had 2.240
not developed psychic powers, said to himself, "Although I have vomited forth, expelled, abandoned and driven away all defilements, I am left standing when it comes to psychic powers common in other sects." Then, generating spiritual energy, he produced psychic power. Before the Venerable Anánda could give a food-ticket to a third monk, Purna stretched out his arm as long as an elephant's trunk and took the food-ticket. Thereupon he recited these verses:

It is not with beauty or learning,
O Gáutama, nor with physical force,
Nor yet with powerful expressed wishes
Does one in this life master the Six Super-
knowledges.
Tried and tested by the manifold powers of tranquility,
Moral discipline, insight and meditation,
Even those like me whose youth is eclipsed by
declining years,
Acquire the Six Superknowledges.

The Lord then announced to the monks, "O my monks, this one is foremost among my monastic disciples in taking ecclesiastical food-tickets.* Among those who take food-tickets, this Purna, the Elder Kundópadhaníyaka, is foremost."

Tatra Bhagavān Āyuṣmantam Ānandam āmantrayate. «gaccha, Ānanda, bhikṣūṇām ārocaya: ‹kiṃ c' âpy uktaṃ mayā, praticchanna|kalyāṇair vo bhikṣavo vihartavyaṃ vivṛta|pāpair iti, api tu tīrthik'|âvastabdhaṃ tan nagaram. yo vo yasyā ṛddher lābhī, tena tayā tatra Sūrpārakaṃ nagaraṃ gatvā bhoktavyam› iti.»

2.245 «Evam, Bhadanta,» ity Āyuṣmān Ānando Bhagavataḥ pratiśrutya, bhikṣūṇām ārocayati, «āyuṣmantaḥ, Bhagavān evam āha, ‹kiṃ c' âpy uktaṃ mayā praticchanna|kalyāṇair vo bhikṣavo vihartavyaṃ vivṛta|pāpair iti, api tu tīrthik'|âvastabdhaṃ tan nagaram. yo vo yasyā ṛddher lābhī, tena tayā tatra Sūrpārakaṃ nagaraṃ gatvā bhoktavyam› iti.»

Tataḥ Sūrpāraka|rājñā Sūrpāraka|nagaram apagata|pāṣāṇa|śarkara|kaṭhalaṃ vyavasthāpitaṃ, candana|vāri|pariṣiktaṃ, nānā|vidha|surabhi|dhūpa|ghaṭikā|samalaṃkṛtam, āmukta|paṭṭa|dāma|kalāpam, nānā|puṣp'|âbhikīrṇam—ramaṇīyam!

Sūrpārakasya nagarasy' âṣṭā|daśa dvārāṇi. tasy' âpi rājñaḥ sapta|daśa putrāḥ. pratyekam ek'|âikasmin dvāre, paramayā vibhūtyā rāja|putrā vyavasthitāḥ. mūla|dvāre ca, mahatā rāj'|ânubhāvena Sūrpārak'|âdhipatī rājā, Āyuṣmān Pūrṇaḥ, Dārukarṇī, Stavakarṇī, Trapukarṇī ca vyavasthitāḥ.

The Lord then addressed the Venerable Anánda. "Go, Anánda, announce this to the monks: 'I have declared, monks, that you should live with your virtues concealed and your sins displayed. However, that city, Surpáraka, is stiff with unbelievers. Therefore, whoever among you has acquired psychic powers is to travel to Surpáraka by means of those powers and there take his meal.'"

"Very well, Venerable sir," said Anánda, assenting to the 2.245
Lord. He then announced to the monks: "Venerables, the Lord says, 'I have declared, monks, that you should live with your virtues concealed and your vices displayed. However, that city, Surpáraka, is overrun with unbelievers. Therefore, whomever among you has acquired psychic powers are to travel to Surpáraka by means of those powers and there accept the invitation for a meal.'"

In the meantime, the King of Surpáraka had the streets of Surpáraka City swept clean of stones, pebbles and gravel, sprinkled with sandalwood-water, lined with many kinds of urns wafting fragrant incense, decorated with rows of silk banners and strewn with various flowers. It was indeed lovely!

Surpáraka had eighteen gates. And the king had seventeen sons. One prince was stationed in royal splendor at each gate. And in all his royal splendor, the king, sovereign ruler of Surpáraka, stationed himself at the main gate, accompanied by the Venerable Purna, Daru·karnin Bhávila, Stava·karnin Bhava·nandin and Trapu·karnin Bhava·trata.

Yāvat pattra|cārikā ṛddhyā, harita|cārikāḥ, bhājana|cārikāś c' āgatāḥ. tān dṛṣṭvā, rājā kathayati, «Bhadanta Pūrṇa, kiṃ Bhagavān āgataḥ?»

Āyuṣmān Pūrṇaḥ kathayati, «Mahā|rāja, pattra|cārikāḥ, harita|cārikāḥ, bhājana|cārikāś c' âite; na tāvat Bhagavān.»

2.250 Yāvat sthavira|sthavirā bhikṣavo 'neka|vidhābhir dhyāna|samāpattibhiḥ saṃprāptāḥ. punar api pṛcchati, «Bhadanta Pūrṇa, kiṃ Bhagavān āgataḥ?»

Āyuṣmān Pūrṇaḥ kathayati, «Mahā|rāja, na Bhagavān, api tu khalu sthavira|sthavirā eva te bhikṣavaḥ» iti. ath' ânyatam'|ôpāsakas tasyāṃ velāyāṃ gāthāṃ bhāṣate:

Siṃha|vyāghra|gaj'|âśva|nāga|vṛṣabhān
  āśritya ke cic chubhān
ke cid ratna|vimāna|parvata|tarūñ
  citrān rathāṃś c' ôjjvalān.
Anye toya|dharā iv' âmbara|tale
  vidyul|lat"|âlaṃkṛtāḥ
ṛddhyā Deva|purīm iva pramuditāḥ
  gantuṃ samabhyudyatāḥ.
Gāṃ bhittvā hy utpatanty eke
  patanty anye nabhas|talāt.
āsane nirmitāś c' âike
  paśya* ṛddhimatāṃ balam. iti.

Tato Bhagavān bahir vihārasya pādau prakṣālya, vihāraṃ praviśya, prajñapta ev' āsane niṣaṇṇaḥ, ṛjuṃ kāyaṃ praṇidhāya, pratimukhaṃ smṛtim upasthāpya. yāvad Bhagavatā

Then by means of their psychic powers monks came flying in on leaves, grass and domestic vessels. Seeing them, the king asked, "Venerable Purna, has the Lord arrived?"

Replied the Venerable Purna, "Great king, these travel on leaves, grass and domestic vessels. The Lord is not yet here."

Then, through exercise of the various stages of medi- 2.250
tation and yogic absorption, the most senior monks arrived.* And again the king asked, "Venerable Purna, has the Lord arrived?"

Replied the Venerable Purna, "Great king, the Lord has not yet arrived. These monks are his most senior disciples." Then one of the lay disciples recited these verses:

Some ride on splendid lions, tigers, elephants,
Horses, divine serpents or bulls;
Some choose jewelled aerial cars, mountains,
Trees or glittering, many-colored chariots;
Others, like thunderclouds, fly through the sky
adorned with tendrils of lightning;
By means of their psychic powers they ascend,
Rejoicing, as if en route to the City of the Gods.
Some part the earth and rise up
Or descend from the sky,
Some appear by magic on their seats:
Behold the might of these who command the
powers of the mind!

Then in the Jeta Grove outside Shravásti, the Lord washed his feet, entered the monastery, sat down on the specially appointed seat, assumed an upright posture and established himself in full mindfulness. As soon as the Lord, with fixed

gandha|kuṭyāṃ s"|âbhisaṃskāraṃ pādo nyastaḥ, ṣaḍ|vikāraḥ pṛthivī|kampo jātaḥ: iyaṃ mahā|pṛthivī calati, saṃcalati, saṃpracalati; vyadhati, pravyadhati, saṃpravyadhati. pūrva|dig|bhāga unnamati, paścimo 'vanamati. paścima unnamati, pūrvo 'vanamati. dakṣiṇa unnamati, uttaro 'vanamati. uttara unnamati, dakṣiṇo 'vanamati. anta unnamati, madhyo 'vanamati. madhya unnamati, anto 'vanamati.

2.255 Rāj" Āyuṣmantaṃ Pūrṇaṃ pṛcchati, «Ārya Pūrṇa, kim etat?»

Sa kathayati, «Mahā|rāja, Bhagavatā gandha|kuṭyāṃ s'|âbhisaṃskāraḥ pādo nyastaḥ; tena ṣaḍ|vikāraḥ pṛthivī|kampo jātaḥ.»

Tato Bhagavatā kanaka|marīci|varṇa|prabh" ôtsṛṣṭā, yayā Jambu|dvīpo vilīna|kanak'|âvabhāsaḥ saṃvṛttaḥ. punar api rājā vismay'|ôtphulla|locanaḥ pṛcchati, «Ārya Pūrṇ' êdaṃ kim?»

Sa kathayati, «Mahā|rāja, Bhagavatā kanaka|marīci|varṇa|prabh" ôtsṛṣṭā» iti.

Tato Bhagavān, dānto dānta|parivāraḥ, śāntaḥ śānta|parivāraḥ, pañcabhir Arhac|chataiḥ sārdham, Sūrpārak'|âbhimukhaḥ saṃprasthitaḥ. atha yā Jeta|vana|nivāsinī devatā, sā bakula|śākhāṃ gṛhītvā, Bhagavataś chāyāṃ kurvantī, pṛṣṭhataḥ saṃprasthitā. tasyā Bhagavat" āśay'|ânuśayaṃ dhātuṃ prakṛtiṃ ca jñātvā, tādṛśī catur|Ārya|satya|saṃprativedhakī Dharma|deśanā kṛtā, yāṃ śrutvā, tayā devatayā,

determination of mind, set foot in his perfumed chamber, the earth shook in six different ways: the great earth stirred, quivered and quaked; it shook, trembled and shuddered. The eastern quarter rose up, the western sank down. The western quarter rose up, the eastern sank down. The southern quarter rose up, the northern sank down. The northern quarter rose up, the southern sank down. The periphery rose up, the middle sank down. The middle rose up, the periphery sank down.

The king asked the Venerable Purna, "Holy Purna, what 2.255
is this?"

He replied, "Great king, the Lord, with fixed determination of mind, has stepped into his perfumed chamber; this has caused the earth to shake in six different ways."

Then, from his body the Lord emitted an effulgent stream of golden light by which all of India was made to look like molten gold. Once again, the king, wide-eyed with astonishment, asked, "Holy Purna, what is this?"

He replied, "Great king, the Lord is emitting an effulgent stream of golden light."

Then the Lord, senses restrained and surrounded by those whose senses were restrained, tranquil and surrounded by those who were tranquil, accompanied by five hundred Arhats, set out in the direction of Surpáraka. At the same time, the goddess who dwelled in the Jeta Grove, taking a branch of a *bákula* tree, followed behind the Lord, shading him. Knowing her mental disposition, character and circumstances, the Lord imparted to her such instruction in the Dharma in elucidation of the Four Noble Truths

viṃśati|śikhara|samudgataṃ sat|kāya|dṛṣṭi|śailaṃ jñāna|vajreṇa bhittvā, Śrota|āpatti|phalaṃ sākṣāt|kṛtam.

2.260 Yāvad anyatamasmin pradeśe pañca|mātrāṇi ghariṇī|śatāni prativasanti. adrākṣus tā Buddhaṃ Bhagavantaṃ, dvā|triṃśatā Mahā|puruṣa|lakṣaṇaiḥ samalaṃkṛtam aśīty" ânuvyañjanaiḥ, virājita|gātraṃ, vyāma|prabh"|âlaṃkṛtaṃ, sūrya|sahasr'|âtireka|prabhaṃ, jaṅgamam iva ratna|parvataṃ, samantato bhadrakam. saha|darśanāc ca tāsāṃ bhagavati mahā|prasāda utpannaḥ. dharmat" âiṣā: na tathā dvā|daśa|varṣ'|âbhyastaḥ śamathaś cittasya kalyatāṃ janayati, a|putrasya ca putra|lābhaḥ, daridrasya vā nidhi|darśanaṃ, rājy'|âbhinandino vā rājy'|âbhiṣekaḥ, yath" ôpacita|kuśala|mūla|hetukasya sattvasya tat prathamato Buddha|darśanam.

Tato Bhagavāṃs tāsāṃ vinaya|kālam avekṣya, purastād bhikṣu|saṃghasya prajñapta ev' āsane niṣaṇṇaḥ. tā api Bhagavataḥ pādau śirasā vanditv" âik'|ânte niṣaṇṇāḥ. tato Bhagavatā tāsām āśay'|ânuśayaṃ dhātuṃ prakṛtiṃ ca jñātvā, tādṛśī catur|Ārya|satya|saṃprativedhakī Dharma|deśanā kṛtā, yāṃ śrutvā, tābhir ghariṇībhir viṃśati|śikhara|samudgataṃ sat|kāya|dṛṣṭi|śailaṃ jñāna|vajreṇa bhittvā, Śrota|āpatti|phalaṃ sākṣāt|kṛtam. tā dṛṣṭa|satyāḥ, trir udānam udānayanti:

that, listening to it, the goddess, shattering with the thunderbolt of insight the twenty-peaked mountain that is the erroneous belief in a permanently existent self, attained the fruit of Entrance into the Stream.

Meanwhile, in a certain district there lived five hundred matrons. And they saw the Lord Buddha, his lustrous 2.260
body adorned with the thirty-two primary and eighty secondary physical features of a Great Man, surrounded by a fathom-wide halo, more dazzling than a thousand suns, like a jewelled mountain in motion, wholly auspicious. At the mere sight of him, on their part arose great faith in the Lord. This is in the nature of things: meditative cultivation of calm awareness, practised for twelve years, could not produce such mental receptivity, nor could the birth of a son for a man without sons, nor the sight of a treasure trove for a poor man, nor royal consecration for one who glories in kingship, as does the first sight of a Buddha for a living being who has planted the roots of spiritual merit over many lifetimes.

Then the Lord, perceiving that the time was right for the women's spiritual training, sat down in front of the community of monks on the seat that had been especially provided. As for those women, they honored the Lord by touching their heads to his feet, then sat down to one side. Knowing their mental dispositions, their character and circumstances, the Lord imparted to them such instruction in the Dharma in elucidation of the Four Noble Truths that, listening to it, those women, shattering with the thunderbolt of insight the twenty-peaked mountain that is the erroneous belief in a permanently existent self, attained the fruit of Entrance into

«Idam asmākam, Bhadanta, na mātrā kṛtam, na pitrā kṛtam, na rājñā, n' êṣṭa|sva|jana|bandhu|vargeṇa, na devatābhiḥ, na pūrva|pretaiḥ, na śramaṇa|brāhmaṇaiḥ, yad Bhagavat" âsmākaṃ tat kṛtam. ucchoṣitā rudhir'|âśru|samudrāḥ, laṅghitā asthi|parvatāḥ, pihitāny apāya|dvārāṇi pratiṣṭhāpitā vayaṃ deva|manuṣyeṣv atikrānt'|âbhikrāntāḥ. etā vayaṃ Bhagavantaṃ śaraṇaṃ gacchāmo Dharmaṃ ca Bhikṣu|saṃghaṃ ca. upāsikāś c' âsmān Bhagavān dhārayatu.» tata utthāy' āsanāt yena Bhagavāṃs ten' âñjaliṃ praṇamya, Bhagavantam idam avocan: «aho bata Bhagavān asmākaṃ kiṃ cid atra prayacched yatra vayaṃ kārāṃ kariṣyāmaḥ.» tato Bhagavata" rddhyā keśa|nakham utsṛṣṭam. tābhir Bhagavataḥ Keśa|nakha|stūpaḥ pratiṣṭhāpitaḥ.

Tatas tayā Jeta|vana|nivāsinyā devatayā, tasmin stūpe medhyām, sā bakula|śākh"|āropitā, Bhagavāṃś c' ôktaḥ, «Bhagavan, aham asmin stūpe kārāṃ kurvantī tiṣṭhāmi» iti. sā tatr' âiv' āsthitā. tatra ke cit ‹Ghariṇī|stūpaḥ› iti saṃjānate, ke cid ‹Bakula|medhi› iti, yam ady' âpi caitya|vandakā bhikṣavo vandante.

Tato Bhagavān saṃprasthitaḥ.

the Stream. Having seen the truth, they thrice proclaimed with calm joy:

"Such a kind favor as you have done for us, Venerable sir, was never done by our mothers or fathers, nor by the king or by any of our relatives or immediate family, nor by the gods or by our ancestors, nor by any priest or ascetic. The oceans of blood and tears are dried up! The mountains of bones have been surmounted! The gates to misery are shut fast! We are established among gods and humans* and have surpassed the most excellent among them. We here go for refuge to the Lord, the Dharma and the Community of Monks. May the Lord accept us as lay disciples!" They then rose from their seats, made reverence to the Lord with joined palms and said to the Lord, "Please! May the Lord give us something here to which we may offer worship." And so the Lord, using his psychic powers, let go some of his hair and fingernails. Then the women constructed a reliquary mound (Stupa) containing the Lord's hair and fingernails.

The goddess who dwelled in the Jeta Grove planted that *bákula* branch on the central shaft of that Stupa, then addressed the Lord: "Lord, I shall remain worshipping here at this Stupa," and there she stationed herself. Some people call the shrine "Matrons' Stupa"; others, "*Bákula*-Shaft," and to this day it is venerated by those monks who are given to the veneration of shrines.

Then the Lord set out.

2.265 Yāvad anyasminn āśrama|pade, pañca' ṛṣi|śatāni prativasanti. tat teṣām āśrama|padaṃ puṣpa|phala|salila|saṃpannam. te tena madena mattā na kiṃ cin manyante. tato Bhagavāṃs teṣāṃ vinaya|kālam avekṣya, tad āśrama|padam upasaṃkrāntaḥ. upasaṃkramya, tasmād āśrama|padāt puṣpa|phalam ṛddhyā śāmitam, salilaṃ śoṣitam, harita|śādvalaṃ kṛṣṭam, sthaṇḍilāni pātitāni.

Tatas ta ṛṣayaḥ, kare kapolaṃ dattvā, cintā|parā vyavasthitāḥ. tato Bhagavat" âbhihitāḥ, «Mahā|ṛṣayaḥ, kim|arthaṃ cintā|parās tiṣṭhatha» iti.

Te kathayanti, «Bhagavan, tvaṃ dvi|pādakaṃ puṇya|kṣetram iha praviṣṭo 'smākaṃ c' ēdṛśī samavasthā.»

Bhagavān āha, «ṛṣayaḥ, kiṃ puṣpa|phala|salila|saṃpannam āśrama|padaṃ vinaṣṭam? kiṃ yathā|paurāṇaṃ bhavatu?»

«Bhavatu, Bhagavan!» tato Bhagavata" rddhiḥ prasrabdhā, yathā|paurāṇaṃ saṃvṛttam.

2.270 Tatas te paraṃ vismayam upagatāḥ, bhagavati cittam abhiprasādayām āsuḥ. tataḥ, Bhagavatā, teṣām āśay'|ânuśayaṃ dhātuṃ prakṛtiṃ ca jñātvā, tādṛśī catur|Ārya|satya|saṃprativedhakī Dharma|deśanā kṛtā, yāṃ śrutvā, taiḥ pañcabhir ṛṣi|śatair Anāgāmi|phalaṃ sākṣāt|kṛtam, ṛddhiś c' âbhinirhṛtā. tato yena Bhagavāṃs ten' âñjaliṃ praṇamya,

At that time, in a certain hermitage, dwelled five hundred sages. Their hermitage was well provided with water, fruit and flowers. Those sages were drunk with their own self-importance and had no respect for anyone. And so the Lord, perceiving that the time was ripe for their spiritual training, approached their hermitage. And, having approached, he employed his psychic powers to cause the flowers and fruit to disappear from the hermitage, the water to dry up, the lush meadows to be plowed up and the fields to die. 2.265

Then those sages, holding their heads in their hands, lost themselves in anxious thought. They were then addressed by the Lord. "Great sages, why are you lost in anxious thought?"

They told him, "Lord, you, a field of merit in human form, entered this place and now we find ourselves in such a state as this."

Said the Lord, "Sages, has your hermitage, so well provided with water, fruit and flowers, been destroyed? Do you wish it as it was before?"

"Let it be so, Lord!" The Buddha then abated the activity of his psychic powers and the hermitage became as before.

At this, those sages were greatly astonished and their 2.270
hearts were inspired with faith in the Lord. Then, knowing their mental dispositions, character and circumstances, the Lord imparted to them such instruction in the Dharma in elucidation of the Four Noble Truths that, listening to it, those five hundred sages all attained the fruit of a Never-Returner as well as developing psychic powers. Then, having venerated the Lord with joined hands, they said this to the Lord: "Let us receive the lower and higher ordinations and become monks in the Doctrine and Discipline, which are so

Bhagavantam idam avocan: «labhema vayaṃ, Bhadanta, sv|ākhyāte Dharma|vinaye pravrajyām upasaṃpadaṃ bhikṣu|bhāvam. carema vayaṃ Bhagavato 'ntike brahma|caryam.»

Tatas te, Bhagavatā, ehi|bhikṣukay" ābhāṣitāḥ: «eta, bhikṣavaḥ, carata brahma|caryam» iti. Bhagavato vācāvasāne muṇḍāḥ saṃvṛttāḥ, saṃghāṭi|prāvṛtāḥ, pātra|karaka|vyagra|hastāḥ, sapt'|âh'|âvaropita|keśa|śmaśravaḥ, varṣa|śat'|ôpasaṃpannasya bhikṣor īryā|pathen' âvasthitāḥ.

«Eh' îti», c' ôktā hi Tathāgatena
muṇḍāś ca saṃghāṭi|parīta|dehāḥ,
sadyaḥ praśānt'|êndriyā eva tasthuḥ
evaṃ sthitā Buddha|mano|rathena.

Tair yujyamānair ghaṭamānair vyāyacchamānair idam eva pañca|gaṇḍakaṃ saṃsāra|cakraṃ cal'|âcalaṃ viditvā, sarva|saṃskāra|gatīḥ śatana|patana|vikiraṇa|vidhvaṃsana|dharmatayā parāhatya, sarva|kleśa|prahāṇād Arhattvaṃ sākṣāt|kṛtam. arhantaḥ saṃvṛttāḥ, trai|dhātuka|vīta|rāgāḥ, sama|loṣṭa|kāñcanāḥ, ākāśa|pāṇi|tala|sama|cittāḥ, vāsī|candana|kalpāḥ, vidyā|vidārit'|âṇḍa|kośāḥ, vidy"|âbhijñā|pratisaṃvit|prāptāḥ, bhava|lābha|lobha|sat|kāra|parāṅ|mukhāḥ. s'|êndr'|ôpendrāṇāṃ pūjyāḥ, mānyāḥ, abhivādyāś ca saṃvṛttāḥ.

well expounded. Let us practice the holy life in the presence of the Lord."

Then they were addressed thus by the Lord: "Come, monks! Practice the holy life." As soon as the Lord had uttered these words, the sages were transformed: shaven-headed they became, clad in monastic robes, almsbowls and water pots in their hands, with a week's growth of hair and beard and the deportment of monks of a hundred years' standing.

Again told "Come!" by the Tathágata,
They, shaven-headed and bodies robed,
Instantly attained tranquility of the senses
And thus remained, by the will of the Buddha.

Through intensive practice, sustained effort and zealous striving, those sages came to understand the nature of this transitory, five-spoked wheel of birth-and-death. They cut off rebirth in all realms of conditioned existence due to their being characterized by ruin, decline, death and destruction, and, by abandoning all defilements, attained Arhatship. Arhats they became, free from passion for anything in the three worlds: to them, a lump of gold and a clod of earth were the same; so, too, the palm of the hand and the open sky; so, too, being cut with a hatchet and being rubbed with sandalwood paste. With knowledge they cracked open the shell of that egg, the mundane world: they realized the Three Knowledges, the Six Superknowledges and the Four Analytical Knowledges. From conditioned existence, with its gain and greed, fame and honor, they had turned away. They became worthy of the respectful salutation, honor

Yas teṣām ṛṣir avavādakaḥ, sa kathayati, «Bhagavan, may" ânena veṣeṇa mahā|jana|kāyo vipralabdhaḥ. taṃ yāvad abhiprasādayāmi, paścāt pravrajiṣyām' îti.»

2.275 Tato Bhagavān pañcabhir ṛṣi|śataiḥ pūrvakaiś ca pañcabhir bhikṣu|śatair ardha|candr'|ākār'|ôpagūḍhas tata eva' rddhy" ôpari vihāyasā prakrānto 'nupūrveṇa Musalakam Parvatam anuprāptaḥ.

Tena khalu samayena Musalake Parvate Vakkalī nāma' rṣiḥ prativasati. adrākṣīt sa ṛṣir Bhagavantaṃ dūrād eva, dvā|triṃśatā Mahā|puruṣa|lakṣaṇaiḥ samalaṃkṛtam aśīty" ânuvyañjanaiḥ, virājita|gātram, vyāma|prabh"|âlaṃkṛtaṃ sūrya|sahasr'|âtireka|prabham, jaṅgamam iva ratna|parvatam, samantato bhadrakam. saha|darśanāc c' ânena Bhagavato 'ntike cittam abhiprasāditam. sa, prasāda|jātaḥ, cintayati, «yan nv ahaṃ parvatād avatīrya, Bhagavantaṃ darśanāy' ôpasaṃkramiṣyāmi. Bhagavān vainey'|âpekṣay" âtikramiṣyati. yan nv aham ātmānaṃ parvatān muñceyam» iti.

Tena parvatād ātmā muktaḥ. a|saṃmoṣa|dharmāṇo Buddhā Bhagavantaḥ. Bhagavata" rddhyā pratīṣṭaḥ. tato 'sya Bhagavat" āśay'|ânuśayaṃ dhātuṃ prakṛtiṃ ca jñātvā, tādṛśī Dharma|deśanā kṛtā, yāṃ śrutvā, Vakkalin" Ânāgāmi|phalaṃ sākṣāt|kṛtam ṛddhiś c' âbhinirhṛtā.

and worship of the gods themselves, not excepting Indra and Upéndra.

Then the sage who was their teacher spoke up: "Lord, with this false appearance, I have deceived a great many people. When I have led them to faith in the Lord, I shall seek ordination."

Then, with those five hundred sages and the five hun- 2.275
dred original monks deployed around him in the shape of a crescent moon, the Lord, using his psychic powers, set out through the sky, and in due course reached Mount Músalaka.

Now, at that time there lived on Mount Músalaka a sage by the name of Vákkalin. From afar that sage saw the Lord approaching, his lustrous body adorned with the thirty-two primary and eighty secondary physical features of a Great Man, surrounded by a fathom-wide halo, more dazzling than a thousand suns, like a jewelled mountain in motion, wholly auspicious. At that sight, the mind of the sage became filled with faith in the Lord. With faith arisen, he thought, "Suppose now, in order to see the Lord, I descend the mountain and approach him. In that case, the Lord, looking around for those ripe for spiritual training, will pass on without noticing me. Suppose, rather, I fling myself off the mountain."

And so Vákkalin flung himself off the mountain. But the Lord Buddhas are always mentally alert and, using his psychic powers, the Lord caught Vákkalin. Then, knowing his mental predispositions, his character and circumstances, the Lord imparted to him such instruction in the Dharma

Tato Bhagavantam idam avocat: «labhey' âham, Bhadanta, sv|ākhyāte Dharma|Vinaye pravrajyām upasaṃpadaṃ bhikṣu|bhāvam. carāmy ahaṃ Bhagavato 'ntike brahma|caryam.»

Tataḥ sa Bhagavatā «ehi|bhikṣukayā» ābhāṣitaḥ: «ehi, bhikṣo! cara brahma|caryam» iti. Bhagavato vāc"|âvasāne, muṇḍaḥ saṃvṛttaḥ, saṃghāṭi|prāvṛtaḥ, pātra|karaka|vyagra|hastaḥ, sapt'|âh'|âvaropita|keśa|śmaśruḥ, varṣa|śat'|ôpasaṃpannasya bhikṣor īryā|pathen' âvasthitaḥ.

2.280 «Eh' îti!» c' ôkto hi Tathāgatena
muṇḍaś ca saṃghāṭi|parīta|dehaḥ,
sadyaḥ praśānt'|êndriya eva tasthau
evaṃ sthito Buddha|mano|rathena.

Tatra Bhagavān bhikṣūn āmantrayate sma, «eṣo 'gro me, bhikṣavaḥ, bhikṣūṇāṃ mama śraddh"|âdhimuktānāṃ yad uta Vakkalī bhikṣur» iti.

Tato Bhagavān, bhikṣu|sahasra|parivṛtaḥ, vicitrāṇi prātihāryāṇi kurvan, Sūrpārakaṃ nagaram anuprāptaḥ. Bhagavān saṃlakṣayati, «yady ekena dvāreṇa praviśāmi, apareṣāṃ bhaviṣyaty anyathātvam. yan nv aham ṛddhy" âiva praviśeyam» iti. tata ṛddhy" ôpari vihāyasā madhye Sūrpārakasya nagarasy' âvatīrṇaḥ.

that, listening to it, Vákkalin attained the fruit of a Never-Returner and also gained psychic powers.

Then Vákkalin said to the Lord: "Let me receive the lower and higher ordinations and become a monk in the Doctrine and Discipline, which are so well expounded. I shall practice the holy life in the presence of the Lord."

In response, Vákkalin was addressed by the Lord with the formula for ordination: "Come, monk! Practice the holy life." As soon as the Lord had uttered these words, Vákkalin was transformed: shaven-headed he became, clad in monastic robes, almsbowl and water pot in his hands, with a week's growth of hair and beard and the disciplined comportment of a monk of a hundred years' standing.

Again told "Come!" by the Tathágata, he, 2.280
  Shaven-headed and body robed,
  Instantly attained tranquility of the senses
  And thus remained, by the will of the Buddha.

At that the Lord announced to the monks, "O my monks, this one—namely the monk Vákkalin—is foremost among my monks who are committed to their faith in me."

Then the Lord, accompanied by those thousand monks, performing as he went all manner of miraculous feats, reached the city of Surpáraka. The Lord reflected, "If I enter by one particular gate, those at the other gates will be alienated. Suppose, now, I were to enter the city simply by the exercise of psychic powers." And so, exercising his psychic powers, he ascended into the sky, then came down in the middle of Surpáraka City.

Tataḥ Sūrpārak'|âdhipatī rājā, Āyuṣmān Pūrṇaḥ, Dārukarṇī, Stavakarṇī, Trapukarṇī, te ca sapta|daśa rāja|putrāḥ, svaka|svakena parivāreṇa, yena Bhagavāṃs ten' ôpasaṃkrāntāḥ, anekāni ca prāṇi|śata|sahasrāṇi. tato Bhagavān, anekaiḥ prāṇi|śata|sahasrair anugamyamānaḥ, yena Candana|mālaḥ Prāsādas ten' ôpasaṃkrāntaḥ. upasaṃkramya purastād bhikṣu|saṃghasya prajñapta ev' āsane niṣaṇṇaḥ.

Sa jana|kāyo Bhagavantam apaśyan, Candana|mālaṃ Prāsādaṃ bhettum ārabdhah. Bhagavān saṃlakṣayati, «yadi Candana|mālaḥ Prāsādo bhetsyate, dātṝṇāṃ puṇy'|ântarāyo bhaviṣyati. yan nv aham enaṃ sphaṭika|mayaṃ nirminuyām» iti.

2.285 Sa Bhagavatā sphaṭika|mayo nirmitaḥ. tato Bhagavatā tasyāḥ pariṣada āśay'|ânuśayaṃ dhātuṃ prakṛtiṃ ca jñātvā, tādṛśī Dharma|deśanā kṛtā, yāṃ śrutvā, anekaiḥ prāṇi|śata|sahasrair mahān viśeṣo 'dhigataḥ. kaiś cin mokṣa|bhāgīyāni kuśala|mūlāny utpāditāni, kaiś cin nirvedha|bhāgīyāni, kaiś cit Śrota|āpatti|phalaṃ sākṣāt|kṛtaṃ; kaiś cit Sakṛd|āgāmi|phalam, kaiś cid Anāgāmi|phalam. kaiś cit sarva|kleśa|prahāṇād Arhattvaṃ sākṣāt|kṛtam. kaiś cit Śrāvaka|bodhau cittāny utpāditāni, kaiś cit Pratyeka|bodhau, kaiś cid anuttarāyāṃ samyak|saṃbodhau cittāny utpāditāni. yad bhūyasā, sā parṣad Buddha|nimnā Dharma|pravaṇā Saṃgha|prāg|bhārā vyavasthāpitā.

Thereupon the king, sovereign ruler of Surpáraka, the Venerable Purna, Daru·karnin, Stava·karnin, Trapu·karnin and the seventeen princes, together with all their attendants, approached the Lord, as did many hundreds of thousands of living beings. The Lord, followed by those many hundreds of thousands of living beings, approached the Sandalwood Pavilion. Having thus approached, the Lord entered the pavilion and sat down before the Community of Monks on the seat that had been especially provided.

The crowd of people, unable to see the Lord, began to force its way into the Sandalwood Pavilion. The Lord reflected, "If the Sandalwood Pavilion is wrecked, the merit of the donors will be obstructed. Suppose, now, I were to transform the pavilion into crystal."

And the Lord transformed the pavilion into crystal. Then, 2.285
knowing the mental dispositions, the natures and circumstances of the members of that assembly, the Lord gave an exposition of the Dharma such that, listening to it, those hundreds of thousands of living beings attained spiritual distinction. Some were inspired to plant roots of merit conducive to liberation; some, roots of merit conducive to attainment of the Four States of Penetration; some attained the fruit of Entrance into the Stream; some, the fruit of a Once-Returner; some, the fruit of a Never-Returner. Some, as a result of the abandonment of all defilements, attained Arhatship. Some were inspired to produce the resolve for the Awakening of a Disciple; some, for the Awakening of a Solitary Buddha; and some were inspired to produce the resolve

Atha Dārukarṇī, Stavakarṇī, Trapukarṇī śuci praṇītaṃ khādanīyaṃ bhojanīyaṃ samudānīya, āsanāni prajñapya, Bhagavato dūtena kālam ārocayanti: «samayaḥ, Bhadanta. sajjaṃ bhaktaṃ yasy' êdānīṃ Bhagavān kālaṃ manyate» iti.

Tena khalu samayena Kṛṣṇa|Gautamakau nāga|rājau ma-hā|samudre prativasataḥ. tau saṃlakṣayataḥ, «Bhagavān Sū-rpārake nagare Dharmaṃ deśayati. gacchāvo Dharmaṃ śro-ṣyāvaḥ» iti.

Tatas tau, pañca|nāga|śata|parivārau, pañca|nadī|śatāni saṃjanya, Sūrpārakaṃ nagaraṃ saṃprasthitau. a|saṃmoṣa|dharmāṇo Buddhā Bhagavantaḥ. Bhagavān saṃlakṣayati, «imau Kṛṣṇa|Gautamakau nāga|rājau—yadi Sūrpārakaṃ nagaram āgamiṣyato '|gocarī|kariṣyataḥ.»

Tatra Bhagavān Āyuṣmantaṃ Maudgalyāyanam āmant-rayate, «pratigṛhāṇa, Mahāmaudgalyāyana, Tathāgatasy' ātyayika|piṇḍa|pātam. tat kasya hetoḥ? pañca ime, Maudgal-yāyana, ātyayika|piṇḍa|pātāḥ. katame pañca? āgantukasya, gamikasya, glānasya, glān'|ôpasthāyakasya, upadhi|vārikas-ya ca. asmiṃs tv arthe Bhagavān upadhau vartate.»

for Supreme, Perfect Awakening. Over all, that assembly became devoted to the Buddha, intent on the Dharma and committed to the Monastic Community.

After that, Daru·karnin, Stava·karnin and Trapu·karnin, having prepared the finest pure foods, both hard and soft, and having arranged the required seating, informed the Lord by messenger that it was time for the meal: "It is time, Venerable. The food is ready if the Lord thinks now is the right time."

At that time, Krishna and Gáutamaka, two serpent-kings, were living in the great ocean. Those two thought, "The Lord is expounding the Dharma in Surpáraka City. Let us go there! Let us hear the Dharma!"

Then those two produced five hundred rivers and, attended by five hundred serpents, set out for Surpáraka City. However, the Lord Buddhas are always mentally alert, and the Lord reflected, "Here are two serpent-kings, Krishna and Gáutamaka—if they come to Surpáraka, they will wreak havoc."

So the Lord summoned the Venerable Maudgalyáyana: "Maudgalyáyana, go and accept from Purna's brothers, on the Tathágata's behalf, some 'irregular' almsfood. Why should you do so? There are five types of irregular almsfood, Maudgalyáyana. What are these five? The almsfood for a monk who has just arrived at a monastery, that for one who is setting out on a journey, for one who is ill, for one who is caring for the sick and that for a monk who is guarding monastic property. In this case, the Lord is acting in regard to the material property of the Order."

2.290 Atha Bhagavān, Maudgalyāyana|sahāyaḥ, yena Kṛṣṇa|Gautamakau nāga|rājau ten' ôpasaṃkrāntaḥ. upasaṃkramya kathayati, «samanvāharata, nāg'|êndrau, Sūrpārakaṃ nagaraṃ m" â|gocarī|bhaviṣyati.»

Tau kathayataḥ, «tādṛśena, Bhadanta, prasādena vayam āgatāḥ, yan na śakyam asmābhiḥ kunta|pipīlikasy' âpi prāṇinaḥ pīḍām utpādayitum, prāg eva Sūrpāraka|nagara|nivāsino jana|kāyasya» iti.

Tato Bhagavatā Kṛṣṇa|Gautamakayor nāga|rājayos tādṛśo Dharmo deśito yaṃ śrutvā, Buddhaṃ śaraṇaṃ gatau, Dharmaṃ Saṃghaṃ ca śaraṇaṃ gatau, śikṣā|padāni ca gṛhītāni.

Bhagavān bhakta|kṛtyaṃ kartum ārabdhaḥ. ek'|âiko nāgaḥ saṃlakṣayati, «aho bata, Bhagavān mama pānīyaṃ pibatu» iti.

Bhagavān saṃlakṣayati, «yady ekasya pānīyaṃ pāsyāmi, apareṣāṃ bhaviṣyaty anyathātvam. upāya|saṃvidhānaṃ kartavyam» iti. tatra Bhagavān Āyuṣmantaṃ Mahāmaudgalyāyanam āmantrayate, «gaccha, Maudgalyāyana, yatra pañcānāṃ nadī|śatānāṃ saṃbhedaḥ, tasmād udakasya pātra|pūram ānaya.»

2.295 «Evam, Bhadanta» ity Āyuṣmān Mahāmaudgalyāyano Bhagavataḥ pratiśrutya, yatra pañcānāṃ nadī|śatānāṃ saṃbhedaḥ, tatr' ôdakasya pātra|pūram ādāya, yena Bhagavāṃs ten' ôpasaṃkrāntaḥ. upasaṃkramya, Bhagavata udakasya pātra|pūram upanāmayati. Bhagavatā gṛhītvā paribhuktam.

After that, the Lord, accompanied by Maudgalyáyana, 2.290
approached those two serpent-kings, Krishna and Gáutamaka, and, having approached, he told them, "Take care, serpent-lords, that Surpáraka City is not devastated."

The two replied, "Venerable sir, we have come in such tranquil faith that we could never cause injury to any living being, even to a tiny ant, much less to the host of people who live in Surpáraka."

Then the Lord expounded the Dharma to those two serpent-kings, Krishna and Gáutamaka, such that, after listening to it, they went for refuge to the Buddha, the Dharma and the Monastic Community and also accepted the Five Rules of Training.

Then the Lord began his meal. Each of those five hundred serpents thought, "Ah! May the Lord drink the water from my river!"

The Lord thought, "If I drink the beverage of only one of these serpents, the others will be alienated. Some strategy for dealing with this must be devised." So the Lord instructed the Venerable Maha·maudgalyáyana: "Go, Maudgalyáyana, to the common source of those five hundred rivers and bring back from there a bowlful of water."

"Very well," replied Maudgalyáyana, consenting to the 2.295
Lord, and at the common source of the those five hundred rivers he filled a bowl full of water and returned to the Lord. Approaching the Lord, he presented to him the bowlful of water. The Lord accepted the water and drank it.

Āyuṣmān Mahāmaudgalyāyanaḥ saṃlakṣayati, «pūrvam uktaṃ Bhagavatā, ‹duṣ|kara|kārakau hi, bhikṣavaḥ, putrasya mātā|pitarau: āpyāyakau, poṣakau, saṃvardhakau, stanyasya dātārau, citrasya Jambu|dvīpasya darśayitārau. eken' âṃśena putro mātaram, dvitīyena pitaram, pūrṇa|varṣa|śataṃ pariharet, yad v" âsyāṃ mahā|pṛthivyāṃ maṇayaḥ, muktā, vaidūrya|śaṅkha|śilā|pravālam, rajatam, jāta|rūpam, aśma|garbhaḥ, musāra|galvaḥ, lohitikā dakṣiṇ'|āvartā iti, evaṃ|rūpe vā vividh'|âiśvary'|âdhipatye pratiṣṭhāpayet—n' êyatā putreṇa mātā|pitroḥ kṛtaṃ vā syād upakṛtaṃ vā.

Yas tv asāv a|śrāddhaṃ mātā|pitaraṃ śraddhā|saṃpadi samādāpayati, vinayati, niveśayati, pratiṣṭhāpayati; duḥ|śīlaṃ śīla|saṃpadi, matsariṇaṃ tyāga|saṃpadi, duṣprajñaṃ prajñā|saṃpadi samādāpayati, vinayati, niveśayati, pratiṣṭhāpayati—iyatā putreṇa mātā|pitroḥ kṛtaṃ vā syād upakṛtaṃ vā› iti.

Mayā ca mātur na kaś cid upakāraḥ kṛtaḥ! yan nv ahaṃ samanvāhareyam—kutra me māt" ôpapann" êti.»

Then Venerable Maha·maudgalyáyana reflected. "On a previous occasion the Lord said, 'Monks, the mother and father of a son indeed performer difficult feats: they nourish and nurture the child; they raise him, provide milk and are his guides to the diverse beauties of this Rose-Apple Continent. Were a son to serve with half his energy his mother and with the other half his father for a full hundred years; or were he to present them with all the jewels, pearls, lapis lazuli, mother-of-pearl, coral, silver, gold, emeralds, tiger's-eyes, rubies and conch shells with spirals turning to the right which are found on this great earth; or were he to establish them in supreme sovereignty and royal power—even having done so much, that son would not have repaid or helped his mother and father.

But a son who introduces to the riches of faith a mother or father without faith, who inspires them with it, trains them in it and establishes them in it; who introduces to the riches of moral discipline a mother or father who lacks moral discipline; who introduces to the riches of giving a mother or father who are jealous and covetous; who introduces to the riches of spiritual insight a mother or father who lack insight; who inspires them with these qualities, trains them in these qualities and establishes them therein—the son who does these things does indeed repay and help his mother and father.'

And yet I never performed such service for my mother! Suppose now I concentrate my mind on where my mother has been reborn."

Samanvāhartuṃ saṃvṛttaḥ, paśyati Marīcike loka|dhātāv upapannā. sa saṃlakṣayati, «kasya vineyā?» paśyati Bhagavataḥ. tasy' âitad abhavat, «dūraṃ vayam ih' āgatāḥ. yan nv aham etam arthaṃ Bhagavato nivedayeyam» iti. Bhagavantam idam avocat: «uktam, Bhadanta, Bhagavatā pūrvaṃ, ‹duṣ|kara|kārakau hi, bhikṣavaḥ, putrasya mātā|pitarau› iti. tan mama mātā Marīcike loka|dhātāv upapannā, sā ca Bhagavato vineyā. tad arhati Bhagavān tāṃ vinetum anukampām upādāya» iti.

2.300 Bhagavān kathayati, «Maudgalyāyana, kasya' rddhyā gacchāmaḥ?»

«Bhagavan, madīyayā.» tato Bhagavān, Āyuṣmāṃś ca Mahāmaudgalyāyanaḥ Sumeru|mūrdhni pādān sthāpayantau, saṃprasthitau. saptame divase, Marīcikaṃ loka|dhātum anuprāptaḥ.

Adrākṣīt sā Bhadrakany" Āyuṣmantaṃ Mahāmaudgalyāyanaṃ dūrād eva. dṛṣṭvā ca punaḥ sa|saṃbhramāt tat|sakāśam upasaṃkramya kathayati, «cirād bata putrakaṃ paśyāmi» iti.

Tato jana|kāyaḥ kathayati, «bhavanto 'yaṃ pravrajito vṛddhaḥ, iyaṃ ca kanyā! katham asya mātā bhavati?» iti.

Āyuṣmān Maudgalyāyanaḥ kathayati, «bhavantaḥ, mam' ême skandhā anayā saṃvṛddhāḥ. tena mam' êyaṃ mātā» iti.

And, in thus concentrating his mind, Maudgalyáyana saw that she had been reborn in the world called Marícika, "Radiant." He reflected, "Who is to undertake her spiritual training?" Then he saw that it would be undertaken by the Lord. He said to himself, "We in this world are far from there. Suppose now I were to inform the Lord of this matter." And so he said this to the Lord: "Venerable sir, on a previous occasion the Lord said, 'Monks, the mother and father of a son indeed perform difficult feats!' My mother has been reborn in the Marícika world and she is to be given spiritual training by the Lord. Therefore, the Lord should so train her. Please exercise your compassion!"

The Lord said, "Maudgalyáyana, by means of whose psy- 2.300
chic power shall we travel to that world?"

"By means of mine, Lord." And so the Lord and the Venerable Maha·maudgalyáyana set their feet on the peak of Mount Suméru, set out, and in seven days reached the Marícika world.

The maiden called Bhadra·kanya saw the Venerable Mahamaudgalyáyana coming from afar and, seeing him once again, she excitedly ran up to him, saying, "Ah! After so long I see my little son again!"

At that, a large group of people declared, "Sirs, this person is an aged religious mendicant, while this one is just a young girl! How can she be his mother?"

Replied the Venerable Maudgalyáyana, "Sirs, the five constituents of my personality originated with her. Therefore she is my mother."

2.305 Tato Bhagavatā tasyā Bhadrakanyāyā āśay'|ânuśayaṃ dhātuṃ prakṛtiṃ ca jñātvā, tādṛśī catur|Ārya|satya|saṃprativedhakī Dharma|deśanā kṛtā, yāṃ śrutvā, tayā Bhadra|kanyayā viṃśati|śikhara|samudgataṃ sat|kāya|dṛṣṭi|śailaṃ jñāna|vajreṇa bhittvā, Śrota|āpatti|phalaṃ sākṣāt|kṛtam. sā dṛṣṭa|satyā trir udānam udānayati:

«Idaṃ mama, Bhadanta, na mātrā kṛtam, na pitrā kṛtam, na rājñā, n' êṣṭa|sva|jana|bandhu|vargeṇa, na devatābhiḥ, na pūrva|pretaiḥ, na śramaṇa|brāhmaṇaiḥ, yad Bhagavatā me tat kṛtam. ucchoṣitā rudhir'|âśru|samudrāḥ! laṅghitā asthi|parvatāḥ! pihitāny apāya|dvārāṇi! pratiṣṭhāpit" âhaṃ deva|manuṣyeṣu.» āha ca:

Tav' ânubhāvāt pihitaḥ sughoro hy
 apāya|mārgo bahu|doṣa|duṣṭaḥ,
apāvṛtā svarga|gatiḥ supuṇyā
 nirvāṇa|mārgaṃ ca may" ôpalabdham.
Tvad|āśrayāc c' āptam apeta|doṣaṃ
 mam' âdya śuddhaṃ suviśuddha|cakṣuḥ,
prāptaṃ ca kāntaṃ padam Ārya|kāntaṃ
 tīrṇā ca duḥkh'|ârṇava|pāram asmi.

Then the Lord, knowing Bhadra·kanya's mental dispositions resulting from the traces of previous deeds, her character and nature, gave an exposition of the Dharma in elucidation of the Four Noble Truths such that, listening to it, Bhadra·kanya, shattering with the thunderbolt of insight the twenty-peaked mountain that is the erroneous view of a permanently existent self, attained the fruit of Entering into the Stream. Realizing the truth, she thrice proclaimed: 2.305

"Such a kind favor as you have done for me, Venerable sir, was never done by my mother or father, nor by the king nor by any of my relatives or immediate family, nor by the gods nor by my ancestors, nor by any priest or ascetic. The oceans of blood and tears are dried up! The mountains of bones have been surmounted! The gates of misery are shut fast! I am established among gods and humans!" And then she declaimed these verses :

Through your spiritual power, closed is the path to
evil rebirths,
So frightful, so filled with sin and wickedness;
Opened for me is the meritorious way to heaven
And gained by me the path to nirvana.
Through taking refuge in you, I have this day
Acquired the faultless, pure, wholly purified vision,
And have attained that longed-for goal sought by
the Holy Ones—
I have crossed to the further shore of the ocean of
suffering.

Jagati daitya|nar'|âmara|pūjita,
vigata|janma|jarā|maraṇ'|āmaya,
bhava|sahasra|sudurlabha|darśana
sa|phalam adya, mune, tava darśanam!

2.310 «Atikrānt" âham, Bhadanta, atikrāntā! eṣ" âhaṃ Bhagavantaṃ śaraṇaṃ gacchāmi, Dharmaṃ ca, Bhikṣu|saṃghaṃ ca. upāsikāṃ ca māṃ dhāray' âdy' âgreṇa yāvaj|jīvam—prāṇ'|ôpetāṃ śaraṇaṃ gatām abhiprasannām. adhivāsayatu me Bhagavān adya piṇḍa|pātena sārdham Ārya|Mahāmaudgalyāyanena» iti. adhivāsayati Bhagavān tasyā Bhadrakanyāyās tūṣṇī|bhāvena.

Atha sā Bhadrakanyā Bhagavantam Āyuṣmantaṃ ca Mahāmaudgalyāyanaṃ sukh'|ôpaniṣaṇṇaṃ viditvā, śucinā praṇītena khādanīyena bhojanīyena sva|hastaṃ saṃtarpya, saṃpravārya, Bhagavantaṃ bhuktavantaṃ viditvā, dhauta|hastam apanīta|pātraṃ nīca|taram āsanaṃ gṛhītvā, Bhagavataḥ purastān niṣaṇṇā Dharma|śravaṇāya. Bhagavatā tasyā Dharmo desitaḥ. Āyuṣmān Mahāmaudgalyāyano Bhagavataḥ pātra|grāhakaḥ pātraṃ niryātayati. Bhagavat" âbhihitaḥ «Maudgalyāyana, gacchāmaḥ.»

«Gacchāmaḥ, Bhagavan.»

O you who in this world are honored by gods, men
and demons,
Who are freed from birth, old age, disease and death,
The sight of whom is so exceedingly difficult to gain
even in a thousand births—
O Sage, seeing you this day has borne great fruit!

"I have gone beyond the cycle of birth and death, Venerable sir, I have gone beyond! I, this very person, go for refuge to the Lord, to the Dharma and to the Monastic Community. Please accept me as a lay disciple from this day forth for as long as I shall live—in faith I have gone for refuge as long as I breathe. May the Lord, accompanied by the Holy Maha·maudgalyáyana, now consent to receive alms from me." The Lord indicated his consent to Bhadra·kanya's request by remaining silent. 2.310

Then, after ensuring that the Lord and the Venerable Maha·maudgalyáyana were comfortably seated, with her own hands Bhadra·kanya served and satisfied them with the finest pure foods, both hard and soft. When she saw that the Lord had finished eating, had washed his hands and had set aside his bowl, she took a low stool and sat down before the Lord in order to hear the Dharma. The Lord then expounded the Dharma to her. The Venerable Maha·maudgalyáyana retrieved the Lord's bowl, which had been washed, and returned it to him.* Then the Lord said, "Maudgalyáyana, let us go."

"Yes, Lord, let us go."

«Kasya ṛddhyā?»

«Tathāgatasya, Bhagavataḥ.»

2.315 «Yady evam, samanvāhara Jeta|vanam.»

«Āgatāḥ smaḥ, Bhagavan!»

«Āgatāḥ, Maudgalyāyana.»

Tato vismay'|āvarjita|matiḥ kathayati, «kiṃ nām' êyam, Bhagavan, ṛddhiḥ?»

«‹Manojavā›, Maudgalyāyana.»

2.320 «Na mayā, Bhadanta, vijñātam evaṃ gambhīrā Buddha|dharmā iti. yadi vijñātam abhaviṣyat, tilaśo 'pi me saṃcūrṇita|śarīreṇ' Ânuttarāyā samyak|saṃbodheś cittaṃ vyāvartitaṃ n' âbhaviṣyat. idānīṃ kiṃ karomi, dagdh'|êndhanaḥ?» iti.

Tato bhikṣavaḥ saṃśaya|jātāḥ sarva|saṃśaya|chettāraṃ Buddhaṃ Bhagavantaṃ papracchuḥ, «kim, Bhadanta, Āyuṣmatā Pūrṇena karma kṛtam, yen' āḍhye mahā|dhane mahā|bhoge kule jātaḥ? kiṃ karma kṛtaṃ yena dāsyāḥ kukṣāv upapannaḥ, pravrajya ca, sarva|kleśa|prahāṇād Arhattvaṃ sākṣāt|kṛtam?»

Bhagavān āha, «Pūrṇena, bhikṣavaḥ, bhikṣuṇā karmāṇi kṛtāny upacitāni, labdha|saṃbhārāṇi, pariṇata|pratyayāni, oghavat pratyupasthitāni, avaśyaṃ|bhāvīni. Pūrṇena karmāṇi kṛtāny upacitāni. ko 'nyaḥ pratyanubhaviṣyati? na, bhikṣavaḥ, karmāṇi kṛtāny upacitāni bāhyaḥ pṛthivī|dhātau vipacyante, n' âb|dhātau, na tejo|dhātau, na vāyu|dhātau,

"By means of whose psychic power?"

"By means of the Lord's, the Tathágata's."

"If so, then focus your mind on the Jeta Grove." 2.315

". . . We have arrived, Lord!"

"Maudgalyáyana, we have arrived."

Then, his mind quite overcome by astonishment, Maudgalyáyana said, "Lord, what is the name of this psychic power?"

"'Mind-Speed,' Maudgalyáyana."

"Venerable sir, I did not realize that the powers of the 2.320
Buddha were so profound. Had I known this, my mind would never have been turned back from Supreme, Perfect Awakening* even were my body to have been ground into particles as tiny as sesame seeds! Now that my fuel is spent, what can I do?"

Later, their doubts aroused, the monks questioned the Buddha, who resolves all doubts: "Venerable sir, what deed did the Venerable Purna perform as a result of which he was born into a wealthy family possessed of great riches and extensive properties? And what deed did he perform as a result of which he was born in the womb of a slave girl and then, going forth into the homeless life, attained Arhatship by abandoning all defilements?"

The Lord replied, "Monks, the monk Purna performed and accumulated many deeds, the bases of which are about to ripen, which exist in a multitude and the effects of which are inevitable. Purna himself performed and accumulated these deeds. Who else could experience their effects? Monks, deeds performed and accumulated do not manifest

api t' ûpātteṣv eva skandha|dhātv|āyataneṣu karmāṇi kṛtāny upacitāni vipacyante, śubhāny aśubhāni ca.

Na praṇaśyanti karmāṇi
kalpa|koṭi|śatair api:
sāmagrīṃ prāpya kālaṃ ca
phalanti khalu dehinām.

Bhūta|pūrvam, bhikṣavo 'sminn eva Bhadra|kalpe, viṃśati|varṣa|sahasr'|āyuṣi prajāyām, Kāśyapo nāma samyak|saṃbuddho loka udapādi, vidyā|caraṇa|saṃpannaḥ, Sugataḥ, loka|vid anuttaraḥ, puruṣa|damya|sārathiḥ, śāstā devānāṃ manuṣyāṇāṃ ca. Buddho Bhagavān Vārāṇasīṃ nagarīm upaniśritya, viharati. tasy' âyaṃ śāsane pravrajitaḥ. Tri|piṭakaḥ saṃvṛttaḥ Saṃghasya ca Dharma|vaiyāvṛtyaṃ karoti.

2.325 Yāvad anyatamasy' ārhata upadhi|vāraḥ prāptaḥ. sa vihāraṃ saṃmārṣṭum ārabdhaḥ. vāyun' êtaś c' âmutaś ca saṃkāro nīyate. sa saṃlakṣayati, ‹tiṣṭhatu tāvad yāvad vāyur upaśamaṃ gacchati› iti.

their effects without, in the earth-element or in the water-element, in the fire-element or in the air-element. Rather, deeds that are performed and accumulated manifest their effects in the five constituents of the personality, in the whole complex of embodied experience of the six senses, where they were performed, and these results may be wholesome or unwholesome.

> Deeds are never destroyed,
> Even after myriads of aeons:
> In the fullness of time, and in the right circumstances,
> They inevitably bear fruit for living beings.

Long ago, monks, yet in this present Auspicous Aeon, when people had a life span of twenty thousand years, there arose in the world a Fully Awakened Buddha named Káshyapa, perfect in wisdom and conduct, a blessed one, unexcelled in his knowledge of the world, a charioteer of men, who need to be broken in, a teacher of gods and men. At one time that Lord Buddha was staying near Varánasi. Purna went forth into homelessness under his tutelage. He mastered the Threefold Collection of Scripture and worked as overseer of Dharma for the order.

On one occasion it was the turn of a certain Arhat to 2.325
look after the property. He began sweeping the monastery. The sweepings were blown hither and thither by the wind. He thought, 'Let me wait until the wind dies down.'

Vaiyāvṛtya|kareṇ'â|saṃmṛṣṭo vihāro dṛṣṭaḥ. tena tīvreṇa paryavasthānena khara|vāk|karma niścāritam: ‹kasya dāsī|putrasy' ôpadhi|vāra› iti.

Ten' Ârhatā śrutam. sa saṃlakṣayati, ‹paryavasthito 'yam. tiṣṭhatu tāvat. paścāt saṃjñāpayiṣyāmi. . . › iti.

Yad" âsya paryavasthānaṃ vigatam, tadā tasya sakāśam upasaṃkramya kathayati, ‹jānīṣe tvaṃ ko 'ham?› iti.

Sa kathayati, ‹jāne tvaṃ Kāśyapasya samyak|saṃbuddhasya śāsane pravrajito 'ham api› iti.

2.330 Sa kathayati, ‹yady apy evaṃ, tath" âpi tu yan mayā pravrajya karaṇīyam, tat kṛtam—ahaṃ sakala|bandhan'|âbaddhaḥ. tvaṃ sakala|bandhana|baddhaḥ kharaṃ te vāk|karma niścāritam. atyayam atyayato deśaya! apy ev' âitat karma tanutvaṃ parikṣayaṃ paryādānaṃ gacchet› iti.

Ten' âtyayam atyayato deśitam. yat tena naraka upapadya dāsī|putreṇa bhavitavyam, tan narake n' ôpapannaḥ, pañca tu janma|śatāni dāsyāḥ kukṣāv upapannaḥ. yāvad etarhy api carame bhave dāsyā eva kukṣāv upapannaḥ. yat Saṃghasy' ôpasthānaṃ kṛtaṃ ten' āḍhye mahā|dhane mahā|bhoge kule jātaḥ. yat tatra paṭhitaṃ sv'|âdhyāyitaṃ skandha|kauśalaṃ ca kṛtam, tena mama śāsane pravrajya, sarva|kleśa|prahāṇād Arhattvaṃ sākṣāt|kṛtam.

Meanwhile, Purna, as overseer, noticed that the monastery remained unswept. Quite overcome with rage, he committed the deed of harsh speech, shouting, 'What slave girl's son is the duty cleaner?'

The Arhat heard him and thought, 'That monk is overcome with rage. Let me wait awhile. Later I shall inform him. . .'

When Purna's fit of rage had passed, that monk approached him and said, 'Do you know who I am?'

Replied Purna, 'I know that you, like myself, have gone forth into the homeless life under the tutelage of the Fully Awakened Buddha, Káshyapa.'

Said the Arhat, 'That may be so, but since going forth 2.330
into the religious life I have done what was to be done—I am liberated from all bonds. You, however, still bound by those bonds, committed the deed of harsh speech. Confess the offense! Then maybe the offense will be a small one and will wane and completely exhaust itself.'

Purna confessed the offense. Now, Purna would have been reborn in hell and thereafter as the son of a slave girl, but, because he had confessed, he was not reborn in hell. However, for five hundred births he was reborn in the womb of a slave girl. Even in this, his final birth, he was born again in the womb of a slave girl. However, because of Purna's service to the Monastic Community, he was born into a wealthy family, one possessed of great riches and extensive properties. And because he read and studied and worked for the welfare of many, he went forth into homelessness under my tutelage and by freeing himself from all defilements attained Arhatship.

Iti hi, bhikṣavaḥ, ek'|ânta|kṛṣṇānāṃ karmaṇām ek'|ânta|kṛṣṇo vipākaḥ; ek'|ânta|śuklānāṃ karmaṇām ek'|ânta|śuklo vipākaḥ; vyatimiśrāṇāṃ karmaṇāṃ vyatimiśro vipākaḥ. tasmāt tarhi, bhikṣavaḥ, ek'|ânta|kṛṣṇāni karmāṇy apāsya vyatimiśrāṇi c' âik'|ânta|śukleṣv eva karmasv ābhogaḥ karaṇīyaḥ. ity evaṃ vaḥ, bhikṣavaḥ, śikṣitavyam.»

Idam avocad Bhagavān. ātta|manasaḥ, te bhikṣavo Bhagavato bhāṣitam abhyanandann iti.

iti Śrī|divy'|âvadāne
Pūrṇ'|âvadānaṃ dvitīyam.

Therefore, monks, it is said, 'The fruit of wholly black deeds is itself wholly black; the fruit of wholly white deeds is itself wholly white; and the fruit of mixed deeds is itself mixed.' Therefore, then, monks, abandon wholly black deeds as well as mixed deeds and direct your own earnest efforts toward wholly white deeds. In this way, monks, should you train yourselves."

Thus spoke the Lord. Their hearts gladdened, the monks rejoiced at the Lord's words.

Thus concludes "The Glorious Deeds of Purna,"
the second story in "The Heavenly Exploits."

30
THE STORY OF PRINCE SÚDHANA

Punar api, mahā|rāja, yan may" ânuttara|samyak|saṃbodhi|prāptaye, dānāni dattāni, puṇyāni kṛtāni, Vīrya|pāramitā ca paripūritā, anuttarā samyak|saṃbodhir n'|ārādhitā, tac chrūyatām:

«Bhūta|pūrvam, mahā|rāja, Pāñcāla|viṣaye rājānau babhūvatuḥ, Uttara|pāñcālo Dakṣiṇa|pāñcālaś ca. tatr' Ôttara|pāñcālo Mahādhano nāmnā Hastināpure rājyaṃ kārayati, ṛddhaṃ ca sphītaṃ ca kṣemaṃ ca subhikṣaṃ c' ākīrṇa|bahu|jana|manuṣyaṃ ca praśānta|kali|kalaha|ḍimba|ḍamaraṃ taskara|durbhikṣa|rog'|âpagataṃ śāl'|īkṣu|go|mahiṣī|saṃpannam. dhārmiko dharma|rājo dharmeṇa rājyaṃ kārayati.

Tasmiṃś ca nagare mahān hrada utpala|kumuda|puṇḍarīka|saṃpanno haṃsa|kāraṇḍava|cakravāk'|ôpaśobhito ramaṇīyas. tatra ca hrade Janmacitro nāma nāga|potaḥ prativasati. sa kālena kālaṃ samyag|vāri|dhārām anuprayacchati. atīva śasya|saṃpattir bhavati śasyavatī vasu|matī. subhikṣ'|ânna|pāno deśaḥ, dāna|māna|satkāravāṃś ca lokaḥ śramaṇa|brāhmaṇa|kṛpaṇa|vaṇīpak'|ôpabhojyaḥ.

Dakṣiṇa|pāñcālas tu rājā 'dharma|bhūyiṣṭhaś caṇḍo rabhasaḥ karkaśo 'dharmeṇa rājyaṃ kārayati. nityaṃ daṇḍana|tāḍana|ghātana|dhāraṇa|bandhana|haḍi|nigaḍ'|ôparodhai rāṣṭra|nivāsinaṃ trāsayati. adharma|bhūyiṣṭhatayā c' âsya devo na kālena kālaṃ samyag|vāri|dhārām utsṛjati. tato 'sau

LISTEN, GREAT KING, to how yet again, when I had not yet attained unexcelled, Supreme, Perfect Awakening, in order to attain it, I practised giving, performed meritorious deeds and fulfilled the Perfection of Energy:

"In a previous existence, great king, in the Panchála country, there were two kings, he of North Panchála and he of South Panchála. The ruler of North Panchála, named Maha·dhana, 'Great Wealth,' ruled, from his capital, Hástina·pura, a kingdom that was prosperous, wealthy, secure, well provided with food, filled with crowds of people, free from strife, discord, riot and tumult as well as from thieves, famine and disease, and rich in rice, sugarcane, cattle and water buffalo. Committed to Dharma, that monarch of Dharma ruled in accordance with Dharma.

Now, in that city, Hástina·pura, there was a large and beautiful lake, covered with blue, red and white lotuses and resplendent with swans, ducks and geese. And in that pool dwelled a young divine serpent by the name of Janma·chitra. He, from time to time, would send forth the right amount of rain. As a result, the country was exceedingly fertile and bore rich crops. For alms, the region offered excellent food and drink, while the people, generous, respectful and hospitable, fed ascetics, priests, poor people and beggars.

The King of South Panchála, however, utterly disdained Dharma, was fierce, violent and harsh, and in no way ruled his kingdom in accordance with Dharma. Punishments, beatings, executions, arrests, imprisonments and wooden and iron fetters kept the inhabitants of his kingdom in a constant state of fear. And because he utterly disdained Dharma, the god did not, from time to time, send forth the

mahā|jana|kāyaḥ saṃtrastaḥ sva|jīvit'|âpekṣayā rāṣṭra|parityāgaṃ kṛtv" Ôttara|pāñcālasy' âiva rājño viṣayaṃ gatvā prativasati.

30.5 Yāvad apareṇa samayena Dakṣiṇa|pāñcālo rājā mṛgayā|vyapadeśena jana|padān vyavalokanāya nirgataḥ. yāvat paśyati grāma|nagarāṇi śūnyāni, udyāna|deva|kulāni bhinna|prabhagnāni. ‹sa jana|kāyaḥ—kva gataḥ?› iti kathayati.

Amātyāḥ kathayanti, ‹Deva, Uttara|pāñcālasya rājño viṣayaṃ gataḥ.›

‹Kim|artham?›

‹Deva, abhayaṃ prayaccha. kathayāmaḥ.›

‹Dattam, bhavantaḥ. kathayata.›

30.10 Tatas te kathayanti, ‹Deva, Uttara|pāñcālo rājā dharmeṇa rājyaṃ kārayati. tasya janapadā ṛddhāś ca sphītāś ca kṣemāś ca subhikṣāś c' ākīrṇa|bahu|jana|manuṣyāś ca praśānta|kali|kalaha|ḍimba|ḍamara|taskara|durbhikṣa|rog'|âpagatāḥ śāl'|īkṣu|go|mahiṣī|saṃpannāḥ. dāna|māna|sat|kāravāṃś ca lokaḥ śramaṇa|brāhmaṇa|vaṇīpak'|ôpabhojyaḥ. Devas tu caṇḍo rabhasaḥ karkaśo nityaṃ daṇḍana|tāḍana|ghātana|dhāraṇa|bandhana|haḍi|nigaḍ'|ôparodhai rāṣṭra|nivāsinaṃ trāsayati. yato 'sau jana|kāyaḥ, saṃtrastaḥ saṃvegam āpannaḥ, Uttara|pāñcālasya rājño viṣayaṃ gataḥ.›

right amount of rain, as a result of which a great many people, terrified and panic-stricken, abandoned the kingdom out of regard for their lives, fled to the realm of the king of North Panchála, and dwelled there.

Later, on another occasion, the King of South Panchála, 30.5
under the pretext of going hunting, went out to inspect his dominions. When he saw the emptied villages and cities and ruined gardens and temples, he asked, 'The people—where have they gone?'

His ministers answered, 'Your majesty, they have gone to the realm of the King of North Panchála.'

'For what reason?'

'Your majesty, grant immunity. Then we will speak.'

'Granted, gentlemen. Speak.'

At that, they told him, 'Your majesty, the King of North 30.10
Panchála rules in accordance with Dharma. His kingdom is prosperous, wealthy, secure, well provided with food, filled with crowds of people, free from strife, discord, riot and tumult as well as from thieves, famine and disease, and rich in rice, sugarcane, cattle and water buffalo. Moreover, the people are generous, respectful and hospitable, and feed ascetics, priests, poor people and beggars. Your majesty, however, is fierce, violent and harsh: punishments, beatings, executions, arrests, imprisonments and wooden and iron fetters keep the inhabitants of your kingdom in a constant state of fear. As a result, a great many people, terrified and panic-stricken, have fled to the realm of the king of North Panchála.'

Dakṣiṇa|pāñcālo rājā kathayati, ‹bhavantaḥ, ko 'sāv upāyaḥ syād yen' âsau jana|kāyaḥ punar āgaty' âiṣu grāma|nagareṣu prativaset?›

Amātyāḥ kathayanti, ‹yadi Deva Uttara|pāñcālavad dharmeṇa rājyaṃ kārayati, maitra|citto hita|citto 'nukampā|cittaś ca sva|rāṣṭraṃ pālayati, na cirād asau jana|kāyaḥ punar āgaty' âiṣu grāma|nagareṣu prativaset.›

Dakṣiṇa|pāñcālo rājā kathayati, ‹bhavantaḥ, yady evam, aham apy Uttara|pāñcālavad dharmeṇa rājyaṃ kārayāmi, maitra|cittaḥ, hita|cittaḥ, anukampā|cittaś ca, rāṣṭraṃ paripālayāmi. yūyaṃ tathā kuruta, yath" âsau jana|kāyaḥ punar āgaty' âiṣu grāma|nagareṣu prativasati› iti.

‹Deva, aparo 'pi tatr' ânuśaṃso 'sti. tasmin nagare mahān hrada utpala|kumuda|puṇḍarīka|saṃchanno haṃsa|kāraṇḍava|cakravāk'|ôpaśobhitaḥ. tatra Janmacitrako nāma nāga|potakaḥ prativasati. sa kālena kālaṃ samyag|vāri|dhārām anuprayacchati. atīva śasya|saṃpattir bhavati. tena tasya śasyavatī vasumatī subhikṣ'|ânnapānaś ca deśaḥ.›

30.15 ‹Ko 'sāv upāyaḥ syād yen' âsau nāga|pota ih' ānīyeta?›

‹Deva, vidyā|mantra|dhāriṇas tam ānayanti. te samanviṣyantām.›

The King of South Panchála said, 'Gentlemen, what measures will induce these people to return and again take up residence in these villages and cities?'

His ministers replied, 'If your majesty, like the King of North Panchála, rules the kingdom in accordance with Dharma, and if, with an attitude of amity and compassion and dedication to the common good, he governs his kingdom, it will be no long time until those people return and again take up residence in these villages and cities.'

The King of South Panchála told them, 'Gentlemen, if that is so, then I, too, like the king of North Panchála, shall rule the kingdom in accordance with Dharma; with an attitude of amity and compassion and dedication to the common good, I will properly govern my kingdom. You ministers will act accordingly, so that the people will return and again take up residence in these villages and cities.'

'Your majesty, Hástina·pura has yet another advantage. In that city, there is a great lake, covered with blue, red and white lotuses and resplendent with swans, ducks and geese. There dwells the young divine serpent named Janma·chítraka. He, from time to time, sends forth the right amount of rain. Accordingly, the country produces exceedingly rich crops. The earth is fertile and the land yields excellent alms, food and drink.'

'What measures will bring that young divine serpent here, 30.15
to South Panchála?'

'Your majesty, those who know spells and magical formulae can bring him. Let us seek them out.'

Tato rājñā, suvarṇa|piṭakaṃ dhvaj'|âgre baddhvā, sarva|vijite ghaṇṭ"|âvaghoṣaṇaṃ kāritam: ‹ya Uttara|pāñcāla|viṣayāj Janmacitraṃ nāga|potam ānayet, tasy' êmaṃ suvarṇa|piṭakaṃ dāsyāmi, mahatā ca sat|kāreṇa satkariṣyāmi› iti.

Yāvad anyatamo 'hi|tuṇḍiko 'mātyānāṃ sakāśaṃ gatvā, kathayati, ‹mam' âitat suvarṇa|piṭakam anuprayacchata—ahaṃ Janmacitraṃ nāga|potam apahṛty' ānayāmi› iti.

Amātyāḥ kathayanti, ‹eṣaṃ gṛhāṇa.›

30.20 sa kathayati, ‹yo yuṣmākaṃ śraddhitaḥ pratyayitaś ca, tasya haste tiṣṭhatu. ānīte Janmacitre nāga|pote grahīṣyami› iti.

‹Evaṃ kuruṣva› iti.

Tato 'sāv ahi|tuṇḍikaḥ pratyayitasya puruṣasya haste suvarṇa|piṭakaṃ sthāpayitvā, Hastināpuraṃ nagaraṃ gataḥ. tatas ten' âsau hradaḥ samantato vyavalokitaḥ. ‹nimittī|kṛtaṃ c' âsau Janmacitro nāga|pota etasmin pradeśe tiṣṭhati› iti. tato baly|upahāra|nimittaṃ punaḥ pratyāgataḥ. Amātyānāṃ kathayati, ‹baly|upahāraṃ me prayacchata. saptame divase taṃ nāga|potam apahṛty' ānayāmi› iti.

sa c' âhi|tuṇḍikas tena saṃlakṣitaḥ, ‹mam' âsāv apaharaṇāy' āgataḥ. saptame divase mām apahariṣyati. mātā|pitṛ|viyoga|jaṃ mahad duḥkhaṃ bhaviṣyati. kiṃ karomi? kaṃ śaraṇaṃ prapadye?› iti.

At that, the king tied a golden basket to the end of a flagpole and, throughout his realm had the proclamation bell rung: 'He who brings the young divine serpent Janma·chitra from the realm of North Panchála, on him I shall bestow this golden basket and great honor and favor as well.'

Soon after, a snake charmer appeared before the ministers, saying, 'Bestow this golden basket on me—I shall capture and bring back the young divine serpent Janma·chitra!'

Said the ministers, 'Take it yourself.'

Replied the snake charmer, 'He among you who is trust- 30.20
worthy and reliable—let it stay in his hands. When I have brought back the young divine serpent Janma·chitra, I will take it.'

'Do so.'

Then the snake charmer placed the golden basket in the hands of a trustworthy man and proceeded to the city of Hástina·pura. Then he examined the lake on all sides. 'The signs show that the young divine serpent Janma·chitra dwells in this part of the lake.' He then returned to South Panchála for offerings and oblations. To the ministers he said, 'Give me gifts to use as offerings. In seven days, I'll capture that young divine serpent and bring him to you.'

Now, the serpent, who had noticed the snake charmer, thought, 'This fellow has come to capture me, and in seven days he will carry me off. Separation from my mother and father will cause me great distress. What shall I do? To what refuge can I turn?'

Tasya ca hradasya n'|âtidūre dvau lubdhakau prativasataḥ, Sārakaḥ Phalakaś ca. tau taṃ hradam āśritya jīvikāṃ kalpayataḥ. ye sthala|gatāḥ prāṇino mṛga|śaśa|śarabha|sūkar'|ādayas tadd|hradam upasarpanti, tān praghātayataḥ, ye 'pi jala|gatā matsya|kacchapa|maṇḍūk'|ādayaḥ. tatra ca Sārakaḥ kāla|gataḥ. Phalako jīvati.

30.25 Janmacitro nāga|potaḥ saṃlakṣayati, ‹n' ânyo 'sti mama śaraṇam ṛte Phalakād lubdhakāt.› tato manuṣya|veśam āsthāya, Phalakasya sakāśaṃ gataḥ. gatvā, kathayati, ‹bhoḥ puruṣa, kiṃ tvaṃ jānīṣe kasy' ânubhāvāt Dhanasya Rājño jana|padā ṛddhāś ca sphītāś ca kṣemāś ca subhikṣāś c' ākīrṇa|bahu|jana|manuṣyāś ca praśānta|kali|kalaha|ḍimba|ḍamarās taskara|durbhikṣa|rog'|âpagatāḥ śāl'|īkṣu|go|mahiṣī|saṃpannāḥ?› iti.

sa kathayati, ‹jāne sa rājā dhārmiko dharmeṇa rājyaṃ kārayati, maitra|citto hita|citto 'nukampā|cittaś ca rāṣṭraṃ pālayati› iti.

sa kathayati, ‹kim etad ev' âth' āsty anyad api?› iti

Lubdhakaḥ kathayati, ‹asty anyo 'py anuśaṃsaḥ. yo 'smin hrade Janmacitro nāma nāga|potaḥ prativasati, sa kālena kālaṃ samyag|vāri|dhārām anuprayacchati. atīva śasya|saṃpattir bhavati, śasyavatī vasumatī subhikṣ'|ânna|pānaś ca deśaḥ› iti.

Not far from Janma·chitra's lake dwelled a pair of hunters, Sáraka and Phálaka, who, by frequenting the lake, earned their livelihood. Those land animals—antelopes, rabbits, deer, wild boar and others—that came to the lake, they killed, as they did creatures that lived in the water—fish, turtles, frogs and others. Now, around that time, Sáraka died, while Phálaka lived on.

The serpent Janma·chitra reflected, 'There is no one to 30.25
whom I can go for refuge except the hunter Phálaka.' So, taking on the form of a man, he approached Phálaka. Having done so, he said, 'Good fellow, do you know through what power King Dhana's territories came to be prosperous, wealthy, secure, well provided with food, filled with crowds of people, free from strife, discord, riot and tumult as well as from thieves, famine and disease, and rich in rice, sugarcane, cattle and water buffalo?'

The hunter replied, 'I know that the king is devoted to Dharma, rules the kingdom in accordance with Dharma, and with an attitude of amity, compassion and dedication to the common good governs the kingdom.'

The disguised serpent replied, 'Is this the only reason, or is there another?'

Said the hunter, 'He also has another advantage. He who dwells in this lake, the young divine serpent called Janma·chitra, from time to time sends forth the right amount of rain. Accordingly, the country produces exceedingly rich crops. The earth is fertile and the land yields excellent alms, food and drink.'

Janmacitraḥ kathayati, ‹yadi kaś cit taṃ nāga|potam ito viṣayād apaharet, tasya nāga|potasya kiṃ syān mātā|pitṛ|viyoga|jam asya duḥkham, syād rājño rāṣṭrasya ca? yo 'paharati, tasya tvaṃ kiṃ kuryāḥ?›

30.30 ‹Jīvitād vyavaropayeyam›

‹Jānīṣe tvaṃ kataro 'sau nāga|potaḥ?› iti

‹Na jāne.›

›Aham ev' âsau nāgaḥ! Dakṣiṇa|pāñcāla|viṣayiken' âhi|tuṇḍiken' âpahṛtya nīye! sa baly|upahāra|vidhān'|ârthaṃ gataḥ, saptame divasa āgamiṣyati. āgaty' âsya hradasya catasṛṣu dikṣu khadira|kīlakān nikhanya, nānā|raṅgaiḥ sūtrair veṣṭayitvā, mantrān āvartayiṣyati. tatra tvayā pracchannaṃ saṃnikṛṣṭe sthāne sthātavyam. yadā ten' âyam evaṃ|rūpaḥ prayogaḥ kṛto bhavati, tadā hrada|madhyāt kvathamānaṃ pānīyam utthāsyati—ahaṃ c' ôtthāsyāmi. tadā tvay" âsāv ahi|tuṇḍikaḥ śareṇa marmaṇi tāḍayitavyaḥ, āśu c' ôpasaṃkramya vaktavyaḥ, «mantrān upasaṃhara! mā ta utkṛtta|mūlaṃ śiraḥ kṛtvā pṛthivyāṃ nipātayiṣyāmi» iti. yady asau mantrān anupasaṃhṛtya prāṇair viyokṣyate, tadā tasmin mṛte, ahaṃ yāvaj|jīvam eva mantra|pāśa|baddhaḥ syām› iti.

Lubdhakaḥ prāha, ‹yadi tav' âikasy' âivaṃ guṇaḥ syāt, tath" âpy aham evaṃ kuryām, prāg eva sakalasya rāṣṭrasya. gaccha! ahaṃ te trātā› iti.

Janma·chitra continued, 'If someone were to take that young divine serpent away from this land, would separation from his mother and father cause the young serpent distress? What would happen to the king and his kingdom? And the one who carried the serpent off—what would you do to him?'

'I'd deprive him of his life!' 30.30

'Do you know this serpent?'

'No, I don't.'

'I am that very serpent! A snake charmer from South Panchála is going to carry me off and take me back with him! He has returned to make arrangements for oblations and offerings and will return in seven days. When he returns, he will drive in posts of acacia-wood at the four corners of this lake, wind round them threads of various colors, and recite spells. During all that, you must remain hidden nearby. Now, when he conducts a ritual of this sort, the water will come boiling up from the middle of the lake and overflow—and I will come out. Then you must wound that snake charmer in a vulnerable spot with an arrow, approach quickly, and say, "Retract the spells! If you do not, I shall chop your head from your neck and cast it on the ground!" But if he breathes his last breath without retracting the spells, then, even though he is dead, for the rest of my life I will be caught in the snare of those spells.'

The hunter responded, 'If it were of benefit to you alone, even so I would do it; how much more so for the entire kingdom! Go! I shall save you.'

30.35 Tataṣ tena nāga|potena tasy' âika|pārśve guptaṃ sthānam upadarśitam. yāvad asau lubdhakaḥ saptame divase pratigupte pradeśa ātmānaṃ gopayitv" âvasthitaḥ. sa c' âhituṇḍika āgatya baly|upahāraṃ kartum ārabdhaḥ. tena catasṛṣu dikṣu catvāraḥ khadira|kīlakā nikhātāḥ. nānā|raṅgaiḥ sūtrair veṣṭayitvā mantrā āvartitāḥ. tatas tat pānīyam utkvathitum ārabdham. lubdhakena śareṇa marmaṇi tāḍito niṣkośaṃ c' âsiṃ kṛtv" âbhihitaḥ, ‹tvam asmad|viṣaya|nivāsinaṃ nāga|potakaṃ mantreṇ' âpaharasi. mantrān upasaṃhara! mā te utkṛtta|mūlaṃ śiraḥ kṛtvā pṛthivyāṃ nipātayiṣyāmi› iti.

Tato 'hi|tuṇḍikena duḥkha|vedan'|âbhibhūtena maraṇa|bhaya|bhītena mantrā vyāvartitāḥ. tena ca samanantaraṃ lubdhakena jīvitād vyavaropitaḥ. tato nāga|poto mantra|pāśa|bandhanād vinirmuktaḥ, hradād abhyudgatya, taṃ lubdhakaṃ pariṣvaktavān, evaṃ c' āha: ‹tvaṃ me mātā, tvaṃ me pitā! yan mayā tvām āgamya mātā|pitṛ|viyoga|jaṃ duḥkhaṃ n' ôtpannam. āgaccha! Bhuvanaṃ gacchāvaḥ.› ten' âsau sva|bhuvanaṃ nītaḥ, nānā|vidhena c' ânna|pānena saṃtarpitaḥ, ratnāni c' ôpadarśitāni, mātā|pitroś ca niveditam: ‹Amba! Tāta! eṣa me suhṛc charaṇaṃ bāndhavaḥ. asy' ânubhāvān mama yuṣmābhiḥ saha viyogo na jātaḥ› iti. tābhyām apy asau vareṇa pravāritaḥ, vividhāni ratnāni dattāni. sa tāny ādāya tasmādd hradād vyutthitaḥ.

The young serpent then showed him a hiding spot nearby. When seven days had passed, the hunter concealed himself in that secret place and waited. The snake charmer arrived and began to prepare the implements and offerings. At the four sides of the lake he drove in the acacia-wood posts. Then he ran threads of various colors around the posts and began reciting spells. At that, the lake water began to boil. The hunter wounded the snake charmer in a vulnerable spot with an arrow, drew his sword and declared, 'You are using spells to carry off the young divine serpent who dwells in our realm! Retract the spells! If you do not, I shall chop your head from your neck and cast it on the ground!' 30.35

The snake charmer, overwhelmed by intense pain and terrified of death, retracted the spell. Immediately the hunter killed him. Then the young serpent, released from the snare of those spells, came up out of the lake, embraced the hunter and declared, 'You are my mother! You are my father! Because I came to you, I need not endure the pain of separation from them. Come! Let us go to my palace.' He then led the hunter to his palace, satiated him with various kinds of food and drink, showed him his jewels, and informed his parents: 'Mother! Father! This is my friend, refuge and kinsman. His power has saved me from being separated from you.' As for the couple, they offered the hunter a reward and gave him various kinds of jewels. After accepting these, he came back up out of the lake.

Tasya hradasya n'|âtidūre puṣpa|phala|saṃpannaṃ nānā|śakunibhir nikūjitam āśrama|padam. tatra' rṣiḥ prativasati, maitry|ātmakaḥ, kāruṇikaḥ, sattva|vatsalaḥ. tato 'sau lubdhakas tasya' rṣes tri|kālam upasaṃkramitum ārabdhaḥ. yac c' âsya Janmacitreṇa nāga|potena sārdhaṃ vṛttaṃ tat sarvaṃ vistareṇa samākhyātam. tato 'sāv ṛṣiḥ kathayati, ‹kiṃ ratnaiḥ kiṃ vā te suvarṇena? tasya bhuvane 'mogho nāma pāśas tiṣṭhati. taṃ yācasv' êti›.

Tato lubdhako 'mogha|pāśe jāta|tṛṣṇaḥ. ṛṣi|vacanam upaśrutya, punar api nāga|bhuvanaṃ gataḥ. yāvat paśyati, nāga|bhuvana|dvāre, tam Amoghaṃ pāśam. tasy' âitad abhavat, ‹eṣa sa pāśo yo mayā prārthanīyaḥ› iti viditvā, nāga|bhuvanaṃ praviṣṭaḥ. tato Janmacitreṇa nāga|poten' ânyaiś ca nāga|potaiḥ sa|saṃbhramaṃ pratisaṃmodito ratnaiś ca pravāritaḥ, sa kathayati, ‹alaṃ me ratnaiḥ! kiṃ tv etad Amoghaṃ pāśaṃ mam' ânuprayaccha› iti.

Janmacitraḥ kathayati, ‹tav' ânena kiṃ prayojanam? asmākaṃ tu mahat prayojanam! yadā garutmat" ôpadrutā bhavāmas, tad" ânen' ātmānaṃ rakṣāmaḥ.›

30.40 Lubdhakaḥ kathayati, ‹yuṣmākam eṣa kadā cit karhi cid garutmat" ôpadrutānām upayogaṃ gacchati, mama tv anena satatam eva prayojanam. yady asti kṛt'|ôpakṛta|jñat" ânuprayaccha› iti.

Janmacitrasya nāga|potasy' âitad abhavat, ‹mam' ânena bah' ûpakṛtam. mātā|pitarāv avalokya, dadāmi› iti. tena mātā|pitarāv avalokya, sa pāśo dattaḥ. tato 'sau lubdhakaḥ pṛthivī|labdha|prakhyena sukha|saumanasyen' âpyāyitama-

Not far from that lake, rich in flowers and fruits and filled with the warbling of many kinds of birds, was a hermitage. A sage dwelled there, filled with amity, compassion and tenderness toward living creatures. The hunter began to visit the sage three times a day, dawn, noon and dusk. And to him the hunter recounted all that had happened with the young divine serpent Janma·chitra. Then the sage said, 'What use to you are jewels or gold? In the serpent's palace is the noose called "Infallible." Ask him for that!'

After that, the hunter longed for the Infallible Noose. After he had listened to the sage's words, he went back to the serpent's palace. Right away he saw at the palace entrance the Infallible Noose. Realizing, 'This is the noose for which I should ask!,' he entered the serpent's palace. Then, when the young serpent Janma·chitra and others of his kind greeted him eagerly and presented him with yet more jewels, he said, 'That's enough jewels for me! It's that Infallible Noose that you should bestow upon me.'

Janma·chitra said, 'What use can it be to you? For us, however, it is of great utility. When the Gáruda* attacks us, we protect ourselves with this.'

The hunter replied, 'You use the noose at the rare times 30.40
when the Gáruda attacks, but I have constant need of it. If you value the service I have done you, bestow it upon me.'

The young serpent Janma·chitra thought, 'He has done me a great service. I'll ask permission of my mother and father, then give it to him.' And, after asking their permission, he gave it to Phálaka. Then the hunter, filled with happiness and good cheer as if he had won the earth, took

no 'mogham pāśam ādāya, nāga|bhuvanād abhyudgamya sva|gṛhaṃ gataḥ.

Yāvad apareṇa samayena, Dhano Rājā devyā sārdhaṃ krīḍati, ramate, paricārayati. tasya krīḍato ramamāṇasya paricārayataḥ, na putro na duhitā. sa kare kapolaṃ dattvā, cintā|paro vyavasthitaḥ: ‹aneka|dhana|samuditaṃ me gṛham, na me putro na duhitā. mam' âtyayāt sva|kula|vaṃśa|chede, rāṣṭr'|âpahāraḥ sarva|saṃmataḥ.* svāpateyam aputram iti kṛtvā, anya|rāja|vidheyaṃ bhaviṣyati› iti.

Sa śramaṇa|brāhmaṇa|suhṛt|saṃbandhi|bāndhavair ucyate, ‹Deva, kim asi cintā|paraḥ?› iti. sa etat prakaraṇaṃ teṣāṃ vistareṇ' ārocayati. te kathayanti, ‹devat"|ārādhanaṃ kuru! putras te bhaviṣyati› iti.

So 'putraḥ, putr'|ābhinandī, Śiva|Varuṇa|Kubera|Śakra|Brahm'|ādīn anyāṃś ca devatā|viśeṣān āyācate, tadyath" ārāma|devatāḥ, vana|devatāḥ, catvara|devatāḥ, śṛṅgāṭaka|devatāḥ, bali|pratigrāhikā devatāḥ. saha|jāḥ saha|dharmikā nity'|ânubaddhā api devatā āyācate.

30.45 Asti c' âiṣa loka|pravādo yad āyācana|hetoḥ putrā jāyante duhitaraś c' êti. tac ca n' âivam. yady evam abhaviṣyad ek'|âikasya putra|sahasram abhaviṣyat tad|yathā rājñaś cakra|vartinaḥ. api tu trayāṇāṃ sthānānāṃ saṃmukhī|bhāvāt putrā jāyante duhitaraś ca. katameṣāṃ trayāṇām? mātā|pitarau raktau bhavataḥ saṃnipatitau, mātā kalyā bhavati'

the Infallible Noose, rose up from the serpents' palace and returned to his own home.

Some time later, King Dhana was frolicking, making love and dallying with his queen. But, despite frolicking, love-making and dalliance, neither son nor daughter was born to him. The king sat alone, with his head in his hands, lost in anxious thought: 'Although my lineage has accumulated many treasures, I have neither son nor daughter. After my passing, when my family's line is cut off, all will approve if the kingdom is appropriated. And so my estate will be at another king's mercy when he sees that it lacks an heir.'

Ascetics, priests, friends and relatives, both near and distant, asked King Dhana, 'Your majesty, why are you lost in anxious thought?' When he explained the matter to them in full, they told him, 'Propitiate the gods! Then you will have a son!'

Having no son and being one who delights in sons, he entreated Shiva, Váruna, Kubéra, Shakra, Brahma and the other gods, that is to say, the garden deities, the forest deities, the deities who dwell at the crossroads and the deities who accept non-vegetarian offerings. He entreated, too, his hereditary tutelary deities, who shared his traditions.

It is popularly said that as a result of such entreaties sons 30.45
are born and daughters, too. But this is not so. If it were, every man would have a thousand sons, just like a universal monarch. Rather, it is due to a conjunction of three conditions that sons are born and daughters, too. What three? The father and mother, full of passion, unite; the mother is healthy and in her fertile period; and a being in the intermediate stage between births is at hand. These are the three

rtumatī, gandharvaś ca pratyupasthito bhavati. eṣāṃ trayāṇāṃ sthānānāṃ saṃmukhī|bhāvāt putrā jāyante duhitaraś ca. sa c' âivam āyācana|paras tiṣṭhati.

Anyatamaś ca Bhadra|kalpiko Bodhisattvas tasyā agra|mahiṣyāḥ kukṣim avakrāntaḥ. Pañc'|āveṇikā dharmā ekatye paṇḍita|jātīye mātṛ|grāme. katame pañca? raktaṃ puruṣaṃ jānāti, viraktaṃ jānāti. Kālaṃ jānāti, ṛtuṃ jānāti. garbham avakrāntaṃ jānāti. yasya sa|kāśād garbho 'vakrāmati, taṃ jānāti. dārakaṃ jānāti, dārikāṃ jānāti. Saced dārako bhavati, dakṣiṇaṃ kukṣiṃ niśritya tiṣṭhati. saced dārikā bhavati, vāmaṃ kukṣiṃ niśritya tiṣṭhati.

Sā, ātta|man'|ātta|manāḥ, svāmina ārocayati, ‹diṣṭyā, ārya|putra, vardhase! āpanna|satv" âsmi saṃvṛttā! yathā ca me dakṣiṇaṃ kukṣiṃ niśritya tiṣṭhati, niyataṃ dārako bhaviṣyati› iti.

So 'py ātta|man'|ātta|manāḥ pūrvaṃ kāyam abhyunnamayya, dakṣiṇaṃ bāhum abhiprasārya, udānam udānayati: ‹apy ev' âhaṃ cira|kāl'|âbhilaṣitaṃ putra|mukhaṃ paśyeyam. Jāto me syān n' âva|jātaḥ. kṛtyāni me kurvīta. bhṛtaḥ pratibibhṛyāt. dāy'|ādyaṃ me pratipadyeta. kula|vaṃśo me cira|sthitikaḥ syāt. asmākaṃ c' âpy atīta|kāla|gatānām alpaṃ vā prabhūtaṃ vā dānāni dattvā, puṇyāni kṛtvā, asmākaṃ nāmnā dakṣiṇām ādekṣyati. idaṃ tayor yatra tatr' ôpapannayor gacchator anugacchatu› iti.»

conditions through the conjunction of which sons are born and daughters too.* Nevertheless, King Dhana continued to devote himself, as before, to entreating the gods.

Now, a certain future Buddha of this present auspicious aeon, who was about to take up his final birth, descended into the queen's womb. A woman born with intelligence possesses five special qualities. What are these five? She recognizes a man who is impassioned and one who is not. She recognizes the right time for lovemaking, that is to say, when she is fertile. She recognizes when the new life has entered her womb. And she knows the conditions on which such entry depends. She knows whether the child will be a boy or a girl: if a boy, it attaches itself on the right side of the womb; if a girl, on the left.

The queen, her mind transported by delight, declared to her husband, 'Thanks be to heaven, noble one! You have cause for congratulation! I am with child—and since it has attached itself on the right side of my womb, it will certainly be a boy!'

King Dhana, also transported by delight, sat up straight, stretched out his right arm and made this joyous declaration: 'I, too, shall look upon the face of the son for whom I have yearned for such a long time! May the son born to me not be misbegotten! He shall carry on my work! When I have supported him may he in turn support me. May he inherit from me. My family's lineage will endure for a long time! Moreover, when I have become a has-been, he shall give gifts, great or small, perform meritorious deeds and make over to me the benefit of having done so, saying, "Wherever my parents are reborn, may this merit follow them."'

Āpanna|sattvāṃ c' âināṃ viditvā, upari prāsāda|tala|gatām ayantritāṃ dhārayati śīte śīt'|ôpakaraṇair uṣṇa uṣṇ'|ôpakaraṇair vaidya|prajñaptair āhārair n'|âti|tiktair n'|âty|amlair n'|âti|lavaṇair n'|âti|madhurair n'|âti|kaṭukair n'|âti|kaṣāyais tikt'|âmla|lavaṇa|madhura|kaṭuka|kaṣāya|vivarjitair āhāraiḥ, hār'|ârdha|hāra|vibhūṣita|gātrīm apsarasam iva Nandana|vana|vicāriṇīṃ mañcān mañcaṃ pīṭhāt pīṭhaṃ carantīm an|avatarantīm adhar imāṃ bhūmim.

30.50 Na c' âsyāḥ kiṃ cid a|manojña|śabda|śravaṇaṃ yāvad eva garbhasya paripākāya. s" âṣṭānāṃ vā navānāṃ vā māsānām atyayāt prasūtā. dārako jātaḥ, abhirūpaḥ, darśanīyaḥ, prāsādikaḥ, gauraḥ, kanaka|varṇaḥ, chatr'|ākāra|śirāḥ, pralamba|bāhuḥ, vistīrṇa|lalāṭaḥ, ucca|ghoṣaḥ, saṃgata|bhrūḥ, tuṅga|nāsaḥ, sarv'|âṅga|pratyaṅg'|ôpetaḥ.

Tasya jātāv ānanda|bheryas tāḍitāḥ. śrutvā, rājā kathayati, ‹kim etat?› iti.

Antaḥ|purikābhir rājñe niveditam, ‹Deva, diṣṭyā vardhase! putras te jātaḥ› iti.

Tato rājñā sarvaṃ tan nagaram apagata|pāṣāṇa|śarkara|kaṭhallaṃ vyavasthāpitam. candana|vāri|pariṣiktam ucchrita|dhvaja|patākaṃ surabhi|dhūpa|ghaṭik"|ôpanibaddhaṃ nānā|puṣp'|âvakīrṇaṃ ramaṇīyam. ājñā ca dattā: ‹śramaṇa|

On learning that she was with child, King Dhana maintained his wife—now ensconced at her ease on the flat roof of their mansion—with everything needed in cold or heat, with foods, recommended by a physician, that were neither too bitter, too sour, too salty, too sweet, too pungent nor too astringent, with a diet free from all those flavors. Adorned with pearl necklaces of sixty-four and one hundred and eight strings, she was like a nymph wandering in the Garden of Delight in Indra's heaven who makes her way from one couch to another and from one seat to another without descending to this earth below.

Nor did the queen hear a single displeasing sound during 30.50
the entire course of her pregnancy. After the passage of eight or nine months, she gave birth. It was a boy. He was well formed, good-looking, handsome, with a pale golden complexion, a large, round head, long arms, a broad brow, eyebrows that joined, a strong voice, a prominent nose and complete in all his limbs.

At the boy's birth, the drums that announce glad tidings were sounded. Hearing these, the king said, 'What is happening?'

The palace women informed him, 'Your majesty, thanks be to heaven! You have cause for celebration! A son is born to you!'

Then the king had all the city streets swept clean of stones, pebbles and gravel, sprinkled with sandalwood-water, decorated with rows of silk banners, lined with many kinds of urns wafting fragrant incense and strewn with many varieties of flowers. It was lovely! And he commanded, 'Give

brāhmaṇa|kṛpaṇa|vanīpakebhyo dānaṃ prayacchata. sarva|bandhana|mokṣaṃ kuruta› iti.

Tasy' âivaṃ trīṇi saptakāny eka|viṃśati|divasān vistareṇa jātasya jāti|mahaṃ kṛtvā, nāma|dheyaṃ vyavasthāpyate. ‹kiṃ bhavatu dārakasya nāma?› iti.

30.55 Amātyāḥ kathayanti, ‹ayaṃ dārako Dhanasya Rājñaḥ putraḥ. bhavatu dārakasya «Sudhanaḥ» iti nāma› iti. tasya ‹Sudhanaḥ› iti nāma|dheyaṃ vyavasthāpitam.

Sudhano dārako 'ṣṭābhyo dhātrībhyo 'nupradattaḥ: dvābhyām aṃsa|dhātrībhyām, dvābhyāṃ kṣīra|dhātrībhyām, dvābhyāṃ mala|dhātrībhyām, dvābhyāṃ krīḍanikābhyāṃ dhātrībhyām. so 'ṣṭābhir dhātrībhir unnīyate, vardhyate kṣīreṇa dadhnā nava|nītena sarpiṣā sarpi|maṇḍen' ânyaiś c' ôttapt'|ôttaptair upakaraṇa|viśeṣaiḥ. āśu vardhate hrada|stham iva paṅka|jam.

Sa yadā mahān saṃvṛttaḥ, tadā lipyām upanyastaḥ, saṃkhyāyām, gaṇanāyām, mudrāyām, uddhāre, nyāse, nikṣepe, vastu|parīkṣāyām, dāru|parīkṣāyām, kumāra|parīkṣāyām, kumārikā|parīkṣāyām, ratna|parīkṣāyām, hasti|parīkṣāyām, aśva|parīkṣāyām, vastra|parīkṣāyām. so 'ṣṭāsu parīkṣās' ûdghaṭako vācakaḥ paṇḍitaḥ paṭu|pracāraḥ saṃvṛttaḥ.

Sa yāni tāni bhavanti rājñāṃ kṣatriyāṇāṃ mūrdhn" âbhiṣiktānāṃ jana|pad'|âiśvaryam anuprāptānāṃ mahāntaṃ pṛthivī|maṇḍalam abhinirjitya, adhyāvasatāṃ pṛthag|bhavanti śilpa|sthāna|karma|sthānāni—tad|yathā hasti|grīvāyām, aśva|pṛṣṭhe, rathe, tsarau, dhanuṣi, apayāne, niryāṇe, aṅkuśa|grahe, pāśa|grahe, chedye, bhedye, muṣṭi|bandhe, śikhā|bandhe, pada|bandhe, dūra|vedhe, śabda|vedhe, marma|

gifts to ascetics, priests, poor people and beggars. And release all prisoners!'

After three weeks, that is, twenty-one days, King Dhana performed the full birth-ceremony and settled upon a name. 'What name should this boy be given?'

His ministers said, 'This boy is the son of King Dhana. 30.55
Let him, therefore, have the name Súdhana.' And so he was named Súdhana.

The boy Súdhana was given over to the care of eight nurses: two to carry him about, two as wet nurses, two to bathe him and two to play with him. Raised by those eight nurses, who nourished him with milk, yoghurt, fresh butter, clarified butter and its by-products, and other pure and choice foods, he grew rapidly, like a lotus in a deep lake.

When he grew older, Súdhana was entrusted to teachers of letters, arithmetic, accounting, finance, debt-collection and commercial law. He also learned to inspect and assess real estate, lumber, young men and women, jewels, elephants, horses and textiles. He became an expounder, an explainer, a scholar, an expert in the evaluation of these eight valuable commodities.

Whatever skills in the practical arts are distinctive to consecrated kings of noble lineage who wield sovereignty over the people and have established dominion over the great orb of the earth—that is to say, riding on the neck of an elephant, on horseback and in a chariot; wielding sword and bow; retreating and attacking; wielding goad and snare, cutting and hacking; wielding the bow using the fist, the top of the head and the feet; hitting a target from afar, by its

vedhe, akṣaṇa|vedhe, dṛḍha|prahāritāyām—pañca|sthāneṣu kṛtāvī saṃvṛttaḥ.

Tasya pitrā trīṇi vāsa|gṛhāṇi māpitāni, haimantikaṃ graiṣmikaṃ vārṣikam. trīṇy udyānāni māpitāni, haimantikaṃ graiṣmikaṃ vārṣikam. trīṇy antaḥ|purāṇi vyavathāpitāni, Jyeṣṭhaṃ Madhyaṃ Kanīyasam. tataḥ Sudhanaḥ Kumāraḥ, upari|prāsāda|tala|gataḥ, niṣpuruṣeṇa tūryeṇa, krīḍati, ramate, paricārayati.

30.60 Yāvad apareṇa samayena, Phalako lubdhakaḥ, mṛgān anveṣamāṇaḥ, tena ten' ânuvicaran, anyatamaṃ parvatam anuprāptaḥ. tasya ca parvatasy' âdhastād ṛṣer āśrama|padaṃ paśyati, puṣpa|phala|saṃpannaṃ nānā|pakṣi|gaṇa|vicaritam, mahāntaṃ ca hradam utpala|kumuda|puṇḍarīka|saṃchannaṃ haṃsa|kāraṇḍava|cakravāk'|ôpaśobhitam. sa tam āśrama|padaṃ paribhramitum ārabdho yāvat tam ṛṣiṃ paśyati, dīrgha|keśa|śmaśru|nakha|romāṇam, vāt'|ātapa|karṣita|śarīram, cīvara|valkala|dhāriṇam, anyatama|vṛkṣa|mūl'|āśrayam, tṛṇa|kuṭikā|kṛta|nilayam. dṛṣṭvā ca punaḥ, pād'|âbhivandanaṃ kṛtvā kṛt'|âñjali|puṭaḥ papraccha, ‹Bhagavan, kiyac ciram asmin pradeśe tava prativasataḥ?›

‹Catvāriṃśad varṣāṇi.›

‹Asti tvay" êyatā kālen' âsmin pradeśe kaś cid āścary'|âdbhuto dharmo dṛṣṭaḥ śruto vā?›

sound alone and where it is weakest, and dealing stalwart blows—all these skills Súdhana mastered.*

Súdhana's father had three palaces constructed, one each for the cool, hot and rainy seasons. He also had three parks constructed, one each for the cool, hot and rainy seasons. And he established three groups of palace women to wait upon Súdhana—Senior, Intermediate and Junior. Ensconced on the flat roof of his palace, with music played only by women, Prince Súdhana enjoyed himself with, made love to and otherwise dallied with them.

Some time later, the hunter Phálaka, while roaming on 30.60
the lookout for game, came to a certain mountain. And he saw, at the foot of that mountain, a sage's hermitage, lush with flowers and fruit, traversed by flocks of many kinds of birds and provided with a substantial lake covered with blue, red and white lotuses and resplendent with swans, geese and ducks. Phálaka wandered around the hermitage until he caught sight of the sage, with his long hair, beard, nails and body hair, body roughened by wind and sun, clad in a bark garment and seated in a grass hut at the foot of a tree. Seeing him, Phálaka repeatedly touched his head to the sage's feet, placed his palms together in respectful greeting, and asked, 'Lord, for how long have you dwelled in this place?'

'Forty years.'

'In all that time in this spot, did you ever see or hear anything extraordinary?'

Praśānt'|ātma" ṛṣir mandaṃ mandam uvāca, ‹bhadra|mukha, dṛṣṭas te 'yaṃ hradaḥ?›

‹Dṛṣṭaḥ, bhagavan.›

30.65 ‹Eṣā Brahma|sabhā nāma puṣkariṇī, utpala|padma|kumuda|puṇḍarīka|saṃchannā, nānā|pakṣi|gaṇa|niṣevitā, hima|rajata|tuṣāra|gaur'|âmbu|saṃpūrṇā, surabhi|kusuma|parivāsita|toyā. asyāṃ puṣkariṇyām, pañca|daśyāṃ pañca|daśyām, Manoharā nāma Drumasya Kinnara|rājasya duhitā, pañca|kinnarī|śata|parivṛtā, nānā|vidha|śiraḥ|snān'|ôdvartanair āgatya, snāti. snāna|kāle c' âsya madhura|nṛtya|gīta|vādita|śabdena mṛga|pakṣiṇo 'pahriyante. aham api, taṃ śabdaṃ śrutvā, mahatā prīti|saumanasyena sapt'|âham atināmayāmi. etad āścaryam, bhadra|mukha, mayā dṛṣṭam› iti.

Atha Phalakasya lubdhakasy' âitad abhavat, ‹śobhano 'yaṃ may" Âmoghaḥ Pāśo nāgād labdhas—taṃ Manoharāyāḥ kinnaryāḥ kṣepsyāmi› iti. so 'pareṇa samayena pūrṇa|pañca|daśyām, Amoghaṃ Pāśam ādāya, hrada|tīra|samīpe puṣpa|phala|viṭapa|vṛkṣa|gahanam āśritya, avadhāna|tat|paro 'vasthitaḥ. yāvan Manoharā kinnarī, pañca|śata|kinnarī|parivṛtā, mahatyā vibhūtyā Brahma|sabhāṃ puṣkariṇīm avatīrṇā snātum.

The tranquil sage replied in measured tones, 'Good fellow, do you see that lake?'

'I see it, Lord.'

'This is the lotus pool called Brahma·sabha, "Brahma's 30.65
Meeting Place." It is covered with blue, red, yellow and white lotuses, frequented by flocks of various kinds of birds, filled with shining waters the color of snow, silver and hoarfrost that are perfumed by the fragrant blossoms. In this lotus pool, on the fifteenth day of each month, Mano·hara, "She Who Captivates the Mind," daughter of Druma, king of the *kínnaras*, comes to bathe, bringing many kinds of unguents for washing and anointing the head, and attended by five hundred *kínnaris*. And when she bathes, the sweet sounds of her company's dancing, singing and musical instruments enchants even the birds and beasts. Even I, having heard those sounds, pass seven full days of delight and good cheer. This is the extraordinary thing, good fellow, that I see in this place.'

Then it occurred to the hunter Phálaka, 'Well it is that I have acquired the Infallible Noose from the divine serpent—I'll cast it over the *kínnari* Mano·hara!' So, sometime later, on the day of the full moon, the fifteenth day of the month, he took the Infallible Noose, concealed himself among the flowers, fruit and foliage in a thicket of trees and attentively waited. After a while, the *kínnari* Mano·hara, attended by five hundred *kínnaris*, with great splendor descended into the Brahma·sabha lotus pool to bathe.

Tat|samanantaraṃ ca Phalakena lubdhaken' Âmoghaḥ Pāśaḥ kṣipto yena Manoharā kinnarī baddhā. tay" Âmogha|pāśa|pāśitayā hrade mahān upamardaḥ kṛto vibhīṣaṇaś ca śabdo niścāritaḥ. yaṃ śrutvā pariśiṣṭaḥ kinnarī|gaṇaḥ, itaś c' âmutaś ca saṃbhrāntaḥ, Manoharāṃ kinnarīṃ nirīkṣitum ārabdhaḥ. paśyanti baddhām, dṛṣṭvā ca punar bhītā niṣpalāyitāḥ. adrakṣīt sa lubdhakas tāṃ parama|rūpa|darśanīyām, dṛṣṭvā ca, ‹punar upaśliṣṭo grahīṣyāmi› iti.

S" āha, ‹hā hat" âsmi! hā manda|bhāgyā! mam' ēdṛśy avasth" āptā!

Mā n' âiṣīs tvaṃ hi mā sprākṣīr
  n' âitat tava su|ceṣṭitam
rāja|bhogyā su|rūp" âhaṃ
  na sādhu grahaṇaṃ tava! iti.›

30.70 Lubdhakaḥ prāha, ‹yadi tvāṃ na gṛhṇāmi, niṣpalāyase.›

Sā kathayati, ‹n' âhaṃ niṣpalāye. yadi na śraddadhāsi, imaṃ cūḍā|maṇiṃ gṛhāṇa. asy' ânubhāven' âham upari|vihāyasā gacchāmi› iti.

Lubdhakaḥ kathayati, ‹kathaṃ jāne?›

Tayā śiraḥ|sthaś cūḍā|maṇir datta uktaś ca, ‹etac|cūḍā|maṇir yasya hasta|sthas—tasy' âhaṃ vaśā bhavāmi.› tato lubdhaken' âsau maṇir gṛhītaḥ, pāśa|baddhām iv' âināṃ gṛhītvā, saṃprasthitaḥ.

Immediately, the hunter Phálaka cast the Infallible Noose, which bound the *kínnari* Mano·hara. Snared by the Infallible Noose, she pulled at it frantically, crying out with terror. Hearing this, the band of *kínnaris* scattered, and, rushing here and there, began to look for Mano·hara. They saw she was trapped, and, seeing this, fled in terror. As for the hunter, he saw that she was exquisitely formed and beautiful and, so seeing, thought, 'I'll draw near and seize her'—and so he did.

Mano·hara cried out, 'Alas, stricken am I! Ill-fortuned am I to have come to such a pass!

You must neither desire nor touch me!
Such deeds are not for you!
For a king's pleasure is my lovely form.
It is improper for you to seize me!'

The hunter replied, 'If I do not seize you, you'll flee.' 30.70

She said, 'I shall not flee. If you do not trust me, take my head-jewel. It is by its power that I fly through the air.'

Said the hunter, 'How would I know?'

She gave him the jewel from her head, saying, 'He who holds this head-jewel—to him I am subject.' The hunter accepted the jewel and, taking her, as if still bound by the noose, set out.

Tena khalu samayena Sudhanaḥ Kumāro mṛgayāṃ nirgataḥ. adrākṣīt sa lubdhakaḥ Sudhanaṃ Kumāram, abhirūpaṃ darśanīyaṃ prāsādikam, dṛṣṭvā ca punar asy' âitad abhavat, ‹ayaṃ ca rāja|kumāraḥ, iyaṃ ca parama|rūpa|darśanīyā. yady enāṃ drakṣyati, balād grahīṣyati. yan nv aham enāṃ prābhṛta|nyāyena svayam ev' ôpanayeyam.›

30.75 Tatas tāṃ pāśa|baddhām iv' ādāya, yena Sudhano rāja|kumāras ten' ôpasaṃkrāntaḥ. upasaṃkramya, pādayor nipatya, kathayati, ‹idaṃ mayā devasya strī|ratnaṃ prābhṛtam ānītaṃ pratigṛhyatām› iti.

Adrākṣīt Sudhano Rāja|kumāro Manoharāṃ kinnarīm, abhirūpām, darśanīyām, prāsādikām, paramayā varṇa|puṣkalatayā samanvāgatām, sarva|guṇa|samuditām, aṣṭā|daśabhiḥ strī|lakṣaṇaiḥ samalaṃkṛtām, jana|pada|kalyāṇīm, kāñcana|kalaśa|kūrma|pīn'|ônnata|kaṭhinasaṃhata|sujāta|vṛtta|pragalbhamāna|stanīm, abhinīla|rakt'|âṃśuka|visṛt'|āyata|nava|kamala|sadṛśa|nayanām, su|bhruvam, āyata|tuṅga|nāsām, vidruma|maṇi|ratna|bimba|phala|saṃsthāna|sadṛś'|âdhar'|âuṣṭhīm, sa|dṛḍha|paripūrṇa|gaṇḍa|pārśvām aty|artha|rati|kara|viśeṣa|kara|kapola|tilakām, anupūrva|racita|saṃhata|bhruvam aravinda|vikaca|sadṛśa|paripūrṇa|vimala|śaśi|vapuṣīm, pralamba|bāhum, gambhīra|tri|valīka|saṃnata|madhyām, stana|bhār'|âvanāmyamāna|pūrv'|ârdhām, rath'|âṅga|saṃsthita|su|jāta|jaghanām, kadalī|garbha|sadṛśa|karām, pūrv'|ânuvartita|saṃhata|su|jāta|kara|bhorum,

At this same time, Prince Súdhana was out hunting. The hunter caught sight of Prince Súdhana, who was well formed, good-looking and handsome, and, on seeing him, it occurred to Phálaka, 'Now, that one is the son of a king and this one is a beautiful woman with an exquisite figure. If he sees her, he'll take her by force. Suppose instead that, of my own free will, I offer her as a gift.'

So the hunter, leading Mano·hara as if she were still 30.75
bound by the noose, approached Prince Súdhana. Having approached, he fell at his feet, saying, 'May his lordship accept as a gift this jewel of a woman I have brought.'

Prince Súdhana looked upon the *kínnari* Mano·hara. She was exquisitely formed, lovely to look at, beautiful, with a perfect complexion. Endowed with all good qualities and adorned with all eighteen physical characteristics of the ideal woman, she was the loveliest in the land. Like golden calabashes or tortoises were her full, upstanding, firm, closely placed, large, prominent, round breasts. Dark, with tiny red veins and elongated, her eyes resembled new lotuses. Well shaped were her eyebrows, high-bridged and prominent her nose. Like coral, rubies or *bimba*-fruit were her lips. Her cheeks, full and round, were distinguished by exceedingly lovely freckles. Her perfectly symmetrical eyebrows joined in form like a blooming lotus or a spotless full moon. Long were her arms, rounded her belly with three deep folds. Her upper body bent forward from the weight of her breasts; her shapely hips and bottom were round like a discus. Delicate as the pith of a plantain tree were her hands. Her well-formed thighs resembled a pair of elephant's trunks close together. On each well-made limb, the delicate veins were

su|nigūḍha|su|racita|sarv'|âṅga|sundara|sirām, saṃhita|ma-ṇi|cūḍām, ārakta|kara|talām, praharṣa|nūpura|valaya|hār'|ârdha|hāra|nirghoṣa|vilasita|gatim, āyata|nīla|sūkṣma|keśīṃ Śacīm iva, bhraṣṭa|kāñcī|guṇām, nūpur'|âvacchādita|pādām. Chāt'|ôdarīṃ tāṃ prakīrṇa|hārām uttapta|jāmbū|nada|cā-ru|varṇāṃ dṛṣṭvā, kumāraḥ sahasā papāta baddho dṛḍhaṃ rāga|pāśena.

Tatra sa rāga|vahṇau dahana|pataṅga|sadṛśena, jala|ca-ñcala|candra|vimal'|ôjjvala|svabhāvena durgrāhya|tareṇa, nadī|taraṅga|jhaṣa|makara|duradhigamena, garuḍa|pavana|java|sama|gatinā, tula|parivartana|laghu|tarena, vānar'|âva-sthita|capal'|ôdbhrānta|tareṇa, satat'|âbhyāsa|kleśa|niṣeva-ṇa|rāga|sukh'|āsvāda|lolena, sarva|kleśa|viṣama|durga|prapā-ta|niḥsaṃgena parama|līnena cittena, tad|bhūt'|ânurāgatay" âyoniśo|manaskāra|dhanur|visṛtena saṃyog'|âbhilaṣita|para-ma|rahasya|śabdena, kāma|śareṇa hṛdaye viddhaḥ. āha ca,

scarcely visible. She wore the jewel on her forehead and the palms of her hands were reddened with henna. The delightful sounds of her anklets, bracelets and pearl necklaces of sixty-four and one hundred and eight strings accompanied her rhythmic gait. Long, black and fine was her hair, like that of Shachi, Indra's consort. From her ornamented belt hung more strings of pearls and the anklets covered her feet. Looking upon that slender-waisted woman, with her pearl necklaces in disarray and her lovely complexion like burnished gold, the prince succumbed straightaway, caught firmly in passion's snare.

At that moment, Súdhana was shot through the heart by the arrow of desire, that passionate desire which is like a moth in a flame; which, having the nature of a spotless, luminous moon trembling in water, is exceedingly difficult to grasp; which, like a sea monster among the billows in a torrent, is hard to catch; which moves with the wind's or a Gáruda's speed; which, being exceedingly light, whirls about like a cotton tuft; which leaps about, always in motion, like a monkey; which ever seeks the flavor of passion's happiness, which feeds the impurities; which, entirely absorbing all thought, is careless of that rough and dangerous precipice that leads to all those impurities—which, with the supremely mysterious sound that is the yearning for union, is loosed from the bow of false understanding. And so it is said,

Dṛṣṭvā ca tāṃ Sudhana indu|samāna|vaktrāṃ
prāvṛḍ|ghan'|ântara|viniścarat" îva vidyut
tat|sneha|manmatha|vilāsa|samudbhavena
sadyaḥ sa cetasi tu rāga|śareṇa viddhaḥ.

Saḥ, tām ati|manoharāṃ Manoharāṃ gṛhītvā, Hastināpuraṃ gataḥ. sa ca lubdhako grāma|vareṇ'|ācchāditaḥ. tataḥ Sudhanaḥ Kumāro Manoharayā sārdham upari|prāsāda|tala|gataḥ, krīḍati, ramate, paricārayati. Manoharayā rūpa|yauvana|guṇena, Sudhanaḥ Kumāro 'nekaiś c' ôpacāra|śatais tath" âpahṛto yathā Sudhanaḥ Kumāro muhūrtam api tāṃ na jahāti.

30.80 Yāvad apareṇa samayena jana|padād dvau brāhmaṇāv abhyāgatau. tatr' âiko rājānaṃ saṃśritaḥ, dvitīyaḥ Sudhanaṃ Kumāram. yo rājānaṃ saṃśritaḥ, sa rājñā purohitaḥ sthāpito bhogaiś ca saṃvibhaktaḥ. yas tu Sudhanaṃ Kumāraṃ saṃśritaḥ, sa bhoga|mātreṇa saṃvibhaktaḥ. sa kathayati, ‹Kumāra, yadā tvaṃ pitur atyayād rājye pratiṣṭhāsyasi, tadā me kiṃ kariṣyasi?› iti.

Sudhanaḥ Kumāraḥ kathayati, ‹yathā tava sahāyo brāhmaṇo mama pitrā paurohitye sthāpitaḥ, evam ahaṃ tvām api paurohitye sthāpayāmi› iti.

As when, in the rainy season, lightning issues forth
from a cloud,
When he beheld her whose face was as lovely as the
moon, Súdhana,
With affection, love and amorous feelings toward
her springing up,
At once was pierced through the heart by passion's
arrow.

Súdhana took the ravishingly beautiful Mano·hara and returned to Hástina·pura. And he rewarded the hunter with the gift of a village. Then, accompanied by Mano·hara, Prince Súdhana ensconced himself on the flat roof of his palace, where he frolicked, dallied and took his pleasure with her. And with Mano·hara's qualities of youth and beauty and her constant attentiveness to him, Prince Súdhana, utterly captivated, did not leave her side even for a moment.

Some time later, two Brahmans arrived from the coun- 30.80
tryside. One entered the king's service; the other, Prince Súdhana's. The one who entered the king's service was appointed royal chaplain by the king, who also bestowed upon him much wealth and property. But the one who entered Prince Súdhana's service, he had bestowed upon him a mere fraction of that. He said, 'Prince, when, after your father's passing, you are established as sovereign, what will you do for me?'

Prince Súdhana replied, 'Just as that Brahman who is your friend my father appointed to the office of royal chaplain, in the same way, you, too, I will appoint to the office of royal chaplain.'

Eṣa ca vṛtt'|ântas tena brāhmaṇena karṇa|paraṃparayā śrutaḥ. tasy' âitad abhavat, ‹ahaṃ tathā kariṣyāmi, yathā kumāro rājyam eva n' āsādayiṣyati. kutas taṃ purohitaṃ sthāpayiṣyati?› iti.

Yāvad apareṇa samayena, tasya rājño vijite 'nyatamaḥ kārvaṭikaḥ prativiruddhaḥ. tasya samucchittaye rājñ" âiko daṇḍaḥ preṣitaḥ. sa hata|vihata|vidhvastaḥ pratyāgataḥ. evaṃ yāvat sapta daṇḍāḥ preṣitāḥ. te 'pi hata|vihata|vidhvastāḥ pratyāgatāḥ. Amātyai rājā vijñaptaḥ, ‹Deva, kim|arthaṃ svabalaṃ hāpyate, para|balaṃ vardhyate? yāvat kaś cid Deva|vijite śastra|bal'|ôpajīvī sarvo 'sāv āhūyatām› iti.

Brāhmaṇaḥ purohitaḥ saṃlakṣayati, ‹ayaṃ kumārasya vadh'|ôpāya|kālaḥ› iti. tena rājā vijñaptaḥ, ‹Deva, n' âivam asau śakyaḥ saṃnāmayitum.›

30.85 Rājā kathayati, ‹kiṃ mayā svayaṃ gantavyam?›

Purohitaḥ kathayati, ‹kim|arthaṃ Devaḥ svayaṃ gacchati? ayaṃ Sudhanaḥ Kumāraḥ, bala|darpa|yuktaḥ! eṣa daṇḍa|sahīyaḥ preṣyatām› iti.

Rājā kathayati, ‹evam astu› iti. tato rājā, kumāram āhūya, kathayati, ‹gaccha, kumāra, daṇḍa|sahīyaḥ, kārvaṭikaṃ saṃnāmaya.›

‹Evaṃ Deva,› iti Sudhanaḥ Kumāro rājñaḥ pratiśruty' ântaḥ|puraṃ praviṣṭaḥ. Manoharā|darśanāc c' âsya sarvaṃ vismṛtam. punar api rājñ' âbhihitaḥ, punar api tad|darśanāt sarvaṃ vismṛtam.

Now, this news reached the other Brahman through a succession of ears. And it occurred to him, 'I shall manage it such that the prince does not acquire sovereignty. Then how will he appoint the other fellow as royal chaplain?'

Some time later, in one of the king's vassal territories, a hill-tribe chieftain rebelled. With the aim of utterly destroying him, the king sent out a punitive force. It returned, defeated, vanquished and decimated. In the same way, seven armies were dispatched. They, too, returned defeated, vanquished and decimated. His ministers addressed the king, 'Your majesty, why do you allow your own forces to dwindle away and those of the enemy to grow in strength? Those in your majesty's dominions who earn their living by force of arms—let all of them be conscripted.'

That Brahman, the royal chaplain, reflected, 'Here is the occasion and the means to bring about the prince's death.' He addressed the king, 'Your majesty, not in that way can the rebel be made to submit.'

Said the king, 'Should I then march out myself?' 30.85

Replied the royal chaplain, 'Why should your majesty go himself? Here's Prince Súdhana, proud of his strength! Let him be sent out with your forces.'

Said the king, 'So be it!' Then, summoning the prince, he told him, 'Go, prince, take with you a punitive force, and force that hill-tribe chieftain to submit.'

'So I shall, your majesty,' replied Prince Súdhana, and then entered the women's quarters of his palace. But, at the sight of Mano·hara, he forgot entirely about it. Again the king spoke to him and again, at the sight of Mano·hara, he forgot entirely about it.

Tataḥ purohitena rāj" âbhihitaḥ, ‹Deva, Sudhanaḥ Kumāraḥ, Manoharay" âtīva|saktaḥ, na śakyate preṣayitum. sādhanaṃ sajjīkriyatām. nirgataḥ kumāro 'ntaḥ|purāt preṣayitavyo yathā Manoharāyāḥ sakāśaṃ na praviśati› iti.

30.90 Rājñ" âmātyānām ājñā dattā, ‹bhavantaḥ, evaṃ kurudhvam› iti.

Amātyai rājñaḥ pratiśrutya, bal'|âugho hasty|aśva|ratha|padāti|sampanno 'neka|praharaṇ'|ôpakaraṇa|yuktaḥ sajjīkṛtaḥ. tataḥ kumāraḥ, nirgataḥ, uktaḥ, ‹gaccha, kumāra, sajjo bal'|âughaḥ› iti.

sa kathayati, ‹Deva, gamiṣyāmi Manoharāṃ dṛṣṭvā.›

Rājā kathayati, ‹kumāra, na draṣṭavyā—kālo 'tivartate.›

‹Tāta, yady evam, mātaraṃ dṛṣṭvā, gacchāmi.›

30.95 ‹Gaccha, kumāra; avalokaya jananīm.›

sa Manoharā|santakaṃ cūḍā|maṇim ādāya, mātuḥ sakāśam upasaṃkrāntaḥ, pādayor nipatya, kathayati, ‹Amba, ahaṃ kārvaṭikaṃ saṃnāmanāya gacchāmi. ayaṃ cūḍā|maṇiḥ su|guptaḥ sthāpayitavyo; na kathaṃ cin Manoharāyā deyo 'nyatra prāṇa|viyogāt› iti. sa evaṃ mātaraṃ saṃdiśy' âbhivādya ca, nānā|yodha|bal'|âugha|tūrya|ninādaiḥ saṃprasthitaḥ. anupūrveṇa jana|padān atikramya, tasya kārvaṭikasya n'|âtidūre 'nyatamad vṛkṣa|mūlaṃ niśritya, vāsam upagataḥ.

At that, the royal chaplain spoke to the king. 'Your majesty, because Prince Súdhana is excessively attached to Mano·hara, it is impossible to send him out. Therefore, ready the troops. This time, when the prince leaves the women's quarters of his palace, order him to set out without going to see Mano·hara again.'

The king gave the command to his ministers: 'Gentle- 30.90
men, do as he says.'

Assenting to the king's command, the ministers readied the army of elephant and horse cavalry, chariots and infantry, who were equipped with all manner of weapons and implements. Then, when the prince came out of the women's quarters of his palace, they addressed him, 'Go, prince: the army is ready.'

Súdhana told the king, 'Your majesty, I shall set out after I have seen Mano·hara.'

Replied the king, 'Prince, do not go see her—time is passing.'

'Father, if that is so, I'll see my mother and then go.'

'Go, prince; see your mother.' 30.95

Súdhana took Mano·hara's crest-jewel, went before his mother, fell at her feet, and said, 'Mother, I am leaving to subdue a mountain chieftain. Keep this crest-jewel well hidden; on no account give it to Mano·hara unless her life is in danger.' Having thus instructed his mother and respectfully taken his leave of her, he set out, with the diverse host of warriors, to the sound of musical instruments. By stages, he advanced through a number of districts; then, not far from that hill-tribe chieftain's territory, he took shelter at the foot of a tree and made camp for the night.

Tena khalu samayena, Vaiśravaṇo Mahā|rājaḥ, aneka|yakṣa|parivāraḥ, aneka|yakṣa|śata|parivāraḥ, aneka|yakṣa|sahasra|parivāraḥ, aneka|yakṣa|śata|sahasra|parivāraḥ, tena pathā yakṣāṇāṃ yakṣa|samitaṃ saṃprasthitaḥ. tena tasya pathā gacchataḥ, khaga|pathe yānam avasthitam. tasy' âitad abhavat, ‹bahuśo 'ham anena pathā samatikrāntaḥ, na ca me kadā cid yānaṃ pratihatam. ko 'tra hetur yena yānaṃ pratihatam?› iti. sa paśyati Sudhanaṃ Kumāram. tasy' âitad abhavat, ‹ayaṃ Bhadra|kalpiko Bodhi|sattvaḥ khedam āpatsyati, yuddhāy' âbhiprasthitaḥ! sāhāyyam asya karaṇīyam. ayaṃ kārvaṭakaḥ saṃnāmayitavyo na ca kasya cit prāṇinaḥ pīḍā kartavyā› iti viditvā, Pāñcikaṃ mahā|yakṣa|senā|patim āmantrayate: ‹ehi tvam, Pāñcika! Sudhanasya Kumārasya kārvaṭakam ayuddhena saṃnāmaya, na ca te kasya cit prāṇinaḥ pīḍā kartavyā› iti.

‹Tathā› iti Pāñcikena mahā|yakṣa|senā|patinā Vaiśravaṇasya Mahā|rājasya pratiśrutya, divyaś catur|aṅgo bala|kāyo nirmitas: tāla|mātra|pramāṇāḥ puruṣāḥ, parvata|pramāṇā hastinaḥ, hasti|pramāṇā aśvāḥ. tato nānā|khaḍga|musala|tomara|prāsa|cakra|śakti|śara|paraśvadha|śastra|viśeṣeṇa nānā|vāditra|saṃkṣobheṇa ca mahā|bhayam upadarśayan, mahatā bal'|âughena Pāñcikaḥ karvaṭam anuprāptaḥ.

At that very time, the great king Vaishrávana, attended by many *yakshas*,* many hundreds, many thousands, many hundreds of thousands of *yakshas*, was travelling that way to a meeting of the *yakshas*. As he proceeded along the way, his chariot was halted in midair. Vaishrávana thought, 'Many a time have I travelled this way, and never before has my chariot been stopped. What now is the cause of this?' Then he caught sight of Prince Súdhana and it occurred to him, 'This is the Bodhi·sattva of the present Auspicious Aeon; he is headed for disaster, setting out for battle! I should help him out. That hill-tribe chieftain must be made to submit, but without harm being inflicted on any living being.' Knowing this, he summoned Pánchika, the great field marshal of the *yakshas*: 'Come, Pánchika! Make the hill-tribe chieftain submit to Prince Súdhana without a fight and without harm being inflicted on any living being.'

'Very well,' Pánchika, the great field marshal of the *yakshas*, replied to the great king Vaishrávana, and he created the four divisions of a divine army: men as tall as palm trees, elephants the size of mountains and horses the size of elephants. Then, using both all manner of weapons, such as swords, clubs, lances, javelins, discuses, pikes and axes, and the cacophony of massed musical instruments to inspire great fear, Pánchika and that mighty host reached the hill-tribe village.

Hasty|aśva|ratha|nirghoṣa|nānā|vāditra|nisvanāt
yakṣāṇāṃ sva|prabhāvāc ca prākārāḥ prapapāta vai.

30.100 Tatas te, karvaṭaka|nivāsinas taṃ bal'|âughaṃ dṛṣṭvā, tac ca prākāra|patanam, paraṃ viṣādam āpannāḥ, papracchuḥ, ‹kuta eṣa bal'|âugha āgacchati?› iti.

Te kathayanti, ‹śīghraṃ dvārāṇi muñcata! eṣa pṛṣṭhataḥ Sudhanaḥ Kumāra āgacchati, tasy' âiṣo bal'|âughaḥ. yadi ciraṃ dhārayiṣyatha, sarvathā svasthā na bhaviṣyatha› iti.

Te kathayanti,

Vyutpannā na vayaṃ rājño na kumārasya dhīmataḥ,
nṛpa|pauruṣakebhyaḥ smo bhītāḥ saṃtrāsam āgatāḥ.

Tair dvārāṇi muktāni. tataḥ, ucchrita|dhvaja|patākaiḥ, pūrṇa|kalaśaiḥ, nānā|vidha|tūrya|ninādaiḥ, Sudhanaṃ Kumāraṃ pratyudgatāḥ. tena ca samāśvāsitāḥ, tad|abhiprāyāś ca rāja|bhaṭāḥ sthāpitāḥ, nipakāś ca nigṛhītāḥ, kara|pratyāyāś ca nibaddhāḥ. tatas taṃ karvaṭakaṃ sphītīkṛtya, Sudhanaḥ Kumāraḥ pratinivṛttaḥ.

30.105 Dhanena ca Rājñā tām eva rātriṃ svapno dṛṣṭo: gṛdhreṇ' āgatya, rājña udaraṃ sphoṭayitvā, antrāṇy ākṛṣya, sarvaṃ tan nagaram antrair veṣṭitam. sapta ca ratnāni gṛhaṃ praveśyamānāni dṛṣṭāni. tato rājā, bhītas trasta āhṛṣṭa|roma|kūpaḥ, laghu|laghv ev' ôtthāya, mah"|ârha|śayane niṣadya,

The elephants, horses and chariots made such an
uproar, the many musical instruments made
such a racket,
And the divine power of the *yakshas* was so great,
that the village's stockade collapsed.

The inhabitants of the village, seeing that mighty host 30.100
and the collapse of their stockade, gave way to utter despair, asking, 'From where does this mighty host come?'

The soldiers replied, 'Open the gates with all speed! Prince Súdhana is coming up behind; his is this vast army. If you continue to resist, you will certainly lose everything.'

The villagers declared,

We are against neither the king nor the prince, who
is wise:
It is royal officials who have reduced us to fear and
terror.

The villagers opened the gates. Then, with flags and pennants raised high, with brimming urns, and to the sound of all manner of musical instruments, they went out to meet Prince Súdhana. The prince reassured them, appointed representatives of the crown who shared his attitude, took their chiefs into custody and imposed tribute and taxes. Then, having enlarged the village, Prince Súdhana returned home.

That night, King Dhana dreamed this dream: a vulture 30.105
came, tore open his belly, pulled out his entrails and draped them around the entire city. And the seven treasures* were seen entering the palace. Then the king, his skin crawling with alarm and fear, rose swiftly, and, seated in his splendid bedchamber with his head in his hands, gave himself up to

kare kapolaṃ dattvā, cintā|paro vyavasthitaḥ. ‹mā h" âiva me 'tonidānaṃ rājyāc cyutir bhaviṣyati jīvitasya v" ântarāya› iti. sa prabhātāyāṃ rajanyāṃ taṃ svapnaṃ brāhmaṇāya purohitāya nivedayām āsa.

sa saṃlakṣayati, ‹yādṛśo Devena svapno dṛṣṭaḥ, niyataṃ kumāreṇa karvaṭako nirjitaḥ. vitatha|nirdeśaḥ karaṇīyaḥ.› iti viditvā, kathayati, ‹Deva, na śobhanaḥ svapnaḥ. niyatam atonidānaṃ Devasya rājyāc cyutir bhaviṣyati jīvitasya v" ântarāyaḥ. kevalaṃ tv atr' âsti pratīkāraḥ sa ca brāhmaṇakeṣu mantreṣu dṛṣṭaḥ.›

‹Ko 'sau pratīkāraḥ?›

‹Deva, udyāne puṣkariṇī surūpā puruṣa|prāmāṇikā kartavyā. tataḥ sudhayā praleptavyā. su|saṃmṛṣṭāṃ kṛtvā, kṣudra|mṛgāṇāṃ rudhireṇa pūrayitavyā. tato Devena snāna|prayatena tāṃ puṣkariṇīm ekena sopānen' âvataritavyam. eken' âvatīrya, dvitīyen' ôttaritavyam. dvitīyen' ôttīrya, tṛtīyen' âvataritavyam. tṛtīyen' âvatīrya, caturthen' ôttaritavyam. tataś caturbhir brāhmaṇair Veda|Ved'|âṅga|pāra|gair Devasya pādau jihvayā nirleḍhavyau, kinnara|vasayā ca dhūpo deyaḥ. evaṃ Devo vidhūta|pāpaś ciraṃ rājyaṃ pālayiṣyati› iti.

Rājā kathayati, ‹sarvam etac chakyam; yad idaṃ kinnara|medam atīva|dur|labham.›

anxious thought. 'Alas! Let this not be a sign that I shall lose my kingdom or my life!' When night gave way to morning, he described the dream to that Brahman, the royal chaplain.

The chaplain reflected, 'Since the king had such a dream, the prince has certainly defeated the mountaineers. I must therefore come up with some false instructions.' Knowing this, he said, 'Your majesty, that was not an auspicious dream. You will certainly lose your kingdom or your life. Nevertheless, for this there is a remedy that is found in the sacred lore of the Brahmans.'

'What is this remedy?'

'Your majesty, in a park, let a splendid lotus tank, one that will accommodate a man, be dug. Then have it lined with mortar. Have the walls made perfectly smooth, then have it filled with the blood of young deer. Then, when your majesty is properly prepared for ritual ablution, you must descend into the tank to the first step. Having descended to the first step, descend to the second. Having descended to the second step, descend to the third. Having descended to the third step, descend to the fourth. Then four Brahmans who have mastered the Veda and its ancillary literature will lick your majesty's feet with their tongues and anoint them with the fat of a *kínnara*. In this way your majesty will be cleansed of evil and will rule the kingdom for many years to come.'

Replied the king, 'All that is possible; yet the fat of a *kínnara* is exceedingly difficult to obtain.'

30.110 Purohitaḥ kathayati, ‹Deva, yad eva dur|labham, tad eva su|labham.›

Rājā kathayati, ‹yathā katham?›

Purohitaḥ kathayati, ‹Deva, nanv iyaṃ Manoharā kinnarī.›

Rājā kathayati, ‹purohita! mā m" âivaṃ vada! kumārasy' âtra prāṇāḥ pratiṣṭhitāḥ.›

sa kathayati, ‹nanu Devena śrutam?

30.115 Tyajed ekaṃ kulasy' ârthe,
grāmasy' ârthe kulaṃ tyajet;
grāmaṃ jana|padasy' ârthe,
ātm" ârthe pṛthivīṃ tyajet.
Dṛḍhena hy ātmanā, rājan,
kumārasy' âsya dhīmataḥ
śakṣyasi hy aparāṃ kartuṃ
ghātay' âināṃ Manoharām.› iti

Ātm"|âbhinandino na kiṃ cin na pratipadyante, iti ten' âdhivāsitam. tato yathā|diṣṭaṃ purohitena kārayitum ārabdham. puṣkariṇī khātā, sudhay" ôpaliptā, saṃmṛṣṭā, kṣudra|mṛgāṇāṃ ca rudhiram upāvartitam. sa ca prayogaḥ Sudhanasy' ântaḥ|pura|janen' ôpalabdhaḥ, tāḥ prīti|manasaḥ saṃvṛttāḥ: ‹vayaṃ rūpa|yauvana|saṃpannā—idānīm asmākaṃ Sudhanaḥ Kumāraḥ paricārayiṣyati› iti.

Said the royal chaplain, 'Your majesty, what is difficult to 30.110
obtain—that very thing is easy to obtain.'

The king said, 'How is that?'

The chaplain replied, 'Your majesty, is Mano·hara not a female *kínnara*?'

The king retorted, 'Chaplain! Speak not so! On her the prince's very life depends.'

His chaplain responded, 'Has your majesty not heard this saying?

Forsake an individual for the sake of the family; 30.115
for the sake of the village, forsake a family;
Forsake a village for the sake of the country;
for one's own sake, forsake the earth.
If you stand firm, O king,
for the wise prince
You can find another wife,
after you have had Mano·hara put to death.'

Now, those who delight in themselves alone, there is nothing they will not do—and so the king gave the chaplain his consent. Then the chaplain undertook to do exactly as instructed: the lotus tank was dug, lined with mortar and made perfectly smooth, then filled with the blood of young deer. And when the women of Súdhana's palace learned about the preparations, they were delighted: 'We who are endowed with youth and beauty—finally Prince Súdhana will take his pleasure with us!'

Tāḥ pramuditā dṛṣṭvā, Manoharā pṛcchati, ‹kiṃ yūyam atīva|praharṣitāḥ?› iti. yāvad aparayā sa vṛtt'|ânto Manoharāyai niveditaḥ. tato Manoharā, saṃjāta|duḥkha|daurmanasyā, yena Sudhanasya Kumārasya jananī ten' ôpasaṃkrāntā. upasaṃkramya, pādayor nipatya, karuṇa|dīna|vilambitair akṣarair etam arthaṃ nivedayām āsa.

Sā kathayati, ‹yady evam, sv|āgamitaṃ kuru; vicārayiṣyāmi› iti. Manoharay" āgamayya punar api samākhyātam. tay" âpi vicāritam, paśyati bhūtam. tatas tayā sa cūḍā|maṇir vastrāṇi ca Manoharāyai dattāni, uktā ca, ‹putrike, prāpte te kāla āgantavyam; evaṃ mam' ôpālambho na bhaviṣyati› iti.

Tato rājā, yathā|nirdiṣṭena krameṇa snāna|prayataḥ, rudhira|pūrṇāṃ puṣkariṇīm avatīrṇ'|ôttīrṇaḥ. tato 'sya brāhmaṇair jihvayā pādau līḍhau. ‹aciram—ānīyatāṃ kinnarī› iti ca samādiṣṭam. tat|samanantaram eva Manoharā gagana|talam utplutya, gāthāṃ bhāṣate:

30.120 Sparśa|saṃgamane mahyaṃ, hasitaṃ ramitaṃ ca me
nāg" îva bandhanān muktā, eṣā gacchāmi sāṃpratam.

iti. Rājñā ca dṛṣṭā vāyu|pathena gacchantī. saḥ, bhītaḥ, purohitam āmantrayate: ‹yad|arthaṃ kṛto yatnaḥ, sa na saṃpannaḥ. Manoharā kinnarī palāyate› iti.

On seeing them thus overjoyed, Mano·hara asked, 'Why are you so exceedingly delighted?' Then one of them explained to Mano·hara what was happening. At that, Mano·hara, anguished and despondent, went to see Prince Súdhana's mother. She approached, knelt respectfully at her mother-in-law's feet, and in words expressive of her wretchedness and distress explained the matter.

The queen replied, 'If that is so, think it over carefully, as shall I.' When Mano·hara returned, she spoke about it again. As for the queen, she had thought it over and had realized the true state of affairs. Accordingly, she gave the crest-jewel and a set of clothes to Mano·hara, and said, 'Child, only if your life was in danger was this to be returned to you; therefore, no blame will fall on me.'

A little while later, the king, having prepared for the bath as instructed, climbed into, then out of, the blood-filled tank. Then the Brahmans licked his feet. 'Quickly—let the *kínnari* be brought forward!' they instructed. At that very moment Mano·hara ascended into air, declaiming this verse:

Intimacy and close union, 30.120
    laughter and pleasure, have been mine;
Now, like an elephant freed from her bonds,
    I am gone!

The king saw her flying through the air. Alarmed, he summoned the royal chaplain: 'The object for which we have taken such pains is not yet achieved—and Mano·hara, the *kínnari*, is escaping!'

Purohitaḥ kathayati, ‹Deva, siddho 'rthaḥ! Apagata|pāpo Devaḥ saṃvṛttaḥ sāṃpratam› iti.

Tato Manoharāyāḥ khaga|pathena gacchantyā etad abhavat, ‹yad aham etām avasthāṃ prāptā, tat tasya' ṛṣer vyapadeśāt. yadi tena n' ākhyātam abhaviṣyat, n' âhaṃ grahaṇaṃ gat" âbhaviṣyam. tena hi yāsyāmi tāvat tasya' ṛṣeḥ sakāśam› iti. sā tasy' āśrama|padaṃ gatā.

Pād'|âbhivandanaṃ kṛtvā, tam ṛṣim uvāca, ‹maha"|ṛṣe, tvad|vyapadeśād ahaṃ grahaṇaṃ gatā, manuṣya|saṃsparśaṃ ca saṃprāptā, jīvit'|ântarāyo me c' âitat saṃvṛttaḥ. tad vijñāpayāmi: yadi yadā kadā cit Sudhanaḥ Kumāra āgacchen māṃ samanveṣamāṇaḥ, tasy' êmām aṅguli|mudrāṃ dātum arhasi, evaṃ ca vaktum: «kumāra, viṣamāḥ panthāno durgamāḥ. khedam āpatsyase. nirvartasva» iti. yadi ca nirvāyamāṇo nas tiṣṭhet, tasya mārgaṃ vyapadeṣṭum arhasi: «kumāra, Manoharayā samākhyātam. . .

30.125 Uttare dig|bhāge, trayaḥ kāla|parvatāḥ. tān atikramya, apare trayaḥ. tān atikramya, apare trayaḥ. tān atikramya, apare trayaḥ. tān atikramya, Himavān parvata|rājaḥ. tasy' ôttareṇa, Utkīlaka|parvatas; tataḥ Kūjakaḥ, Jala|pathaḥ, Khadirakaḥ, Eka|dhārakaḥ, Vajrakaḥ, Kāma|rūpī, Kīlakaḥ, Airāvatakaḥ, Adhunānaḥ, Pramokṣaṇaḥ. ete te parvatāḥ samatikramaṇīyāḥ. tatra Khadirake Parvate guhā|praveśaḥ, Eka|dhārake ca Utkīlake. Vajrake tu pakṣi|rājena praveśaḥ. ebhir upāyais te parvatā atikramaṇīyāḥ. yantrāṇi ca bhaṅktavyāni,

The royal chaplain told him, 'Your majesty, we have achieved our purpose! Your majesty is now cleansed of all evil!'

To Mano·hara, as she proceeded through the air, the thought occurred, 'That I have come to this pass is due to that sage's directions. Had he not spoken as he did, I would not have been captured. Therefore I shall now pay him a visit.' And so she went to that sage's hermitage.

After kneeling and touching his feet, she said to the sage, 'Great sage, it is due to your directions that I was captured and came into contact with humans, which almost cost me my life. This I request of you: if at any time Prince Súdhana should come searching for me, please give him this ring and tell him this: "Prince, dangerous are these paths, and very hard going. You will suffer terribly. Turn back!" But, if he cannot endure turning back, please show him the way, saying, "Prince, as Mano·hara explained. . .

To the north, there are three black mountains. Scale 30.125
them, and there will be three more. Scale those, and there will be three more. Scale those, and there will be yet three more. Scale those, and there will be the Himalaya, the king of mountains. To the north of the Himalaya is Mount Utkílaka; after that, the mountains Kújaka, Jala·patha, Khádiraka, Eka·dháraka, Vájraka, Kama·rupin, Kílaka, Airávataka, Adhunána and Pramókshana. These you must also scale. There is a cave entrance to Mount Khádiraka, as there is to Eka·dháraka and Utkílaka. But at Vájraka the procedure is to employ Gáruda, the king of birds. Use these methods to cross those mountains. Also, there are magical creatures you will have to overcome, including one like a ram with

aja|vaktro meṇḍhakaḥ, puruṣo rākṣasa|rūpī piṅgalo hantavyaḥ. guhāyāṃ lālā|srotasā mahān aja|garo vegena pradhāvati—sa te vikrameṇa hantavyaḥ.

Ardh'|ântara|gataṃ nāgaṃ yatra paśyet Kirīṭakam
cāpa|muktena bāṇena hantavyo mama kāraṇāt.
Yatra paśyeta dvau meṣau saṃghaṭṭantau parasparam
tayoḥ śṛṅgam ekaṃ bhaṅktvā mārgaṃ pratilapsyase.
Āyasau puruṣau dṛṣṭvā śastra|pāṇī mahā|bhayau
tayor ekaṃ tāḍayitvā mārgaṃ pratilapsyase.
Saṃkocayantīṃ prasārayantīṃ rākṣasīm āyasaṃ
mukham
yadā paśyet tadā kīlaṃ lalāṭe tasyā nikhānayet.
Śil"|āvartas tathā kūpo vilaṅghyas te ṣaṣṭi|hastakaḥ
hari|piṅgala|keś'|âkṣo dāruṇo yakṣa|rākṣasaḥ.
Kārmukaṃ maṇḍalaṃ kṛtvā hantavyaś ca dur'|āsadaḥ
nadyaś ca bahavas tāryā nakra|grāha|samākulāḥ:
Naṅgā Pataṅgā Tapanī Citrā Rudanī Hasanī Āśī|viṣā
Vetravatī ca.
Naṅgāyāṃ rākṣasī kopā, Pataṅgāyām a|manuṣyakāḥ
Tapanyāṃ grāha|bahulatvam, Citrāyāṃ
kāma|rūpiṇaḥ.

a goat's face and a yellow man, who looks like a demon, whom you will have to slay. In the cave, a great serpent, with its streams of poisonous saliva, strikes quickly—it you must subdue by force.

When you see the serpent Kirítaka half in the cave,
Loose an arrow from your bow and slay it for my sake.
When you see two rams butting each other,
Break off a horn from each and you will regain the way.
When you see two iron men wielding terrifying weapons,
Strike down one of them, you will regain the way.
A demoness, opening and closing her iron mouth—
When you see her, you must bury a stake in her forehead.
You must leap across a crevasse, a whirlpool in the stone sixty hands wide.
Vicious ogres and demons with yellow-brown hair and eyes—
Bend your bow into a circle and slay them, dangerous to approach.
And many rivers you must cross, all infested with crocodiles and hippos:
Then there are the rivers Crocodile, Butterfly, Burning, Marvelous, Weeping, Laughing, Snake-Poison and Reedy.
In the Crocodile is an angry demoness; in the Butterfly, there are demons;
In the Burning River, hosts of water monsters; in the Marvelous, shape-shifters;

Rudanyāṃ kinnarī|ceṭyaḥ, Hasanyāṃ kinnarī|snuṣāḥ
Āśī|viṣāyāṃ nānā|vidhāḥ sarpāḥ, Vetra|nadyāṃ tu
śālmaliḥ.
Naṅgāyāṃ dhairya|karaṇam, Pataṅgāyāṃ
parākramaḥ
Tapanyāṃ grāha|mukha|bandhaḥ, Citrāyāṃ
vividhaṃ gītam.

30.130 Rudanyāṃ saumanasyena samuttāraḥ, Hasanyāṃ tūṣṇīṃ|bhāva|yogena, Āśī|viṣāyāṃ sarpa|viṣa|mantra|prayogena. Vetra|vatyāṃ tīkṣṇa|śastra|saṃpāta|yogena samuttāraḥ. nadīḥ samatikramya, pañca|yakṣa|śatānāṃ gulmaka|sthānam. tad dhairyam āsthāya, vidrāvyam. tataḥ kinnara|rājasya bhavanam» iti.› tato Manoharā, tam ṛṣim evam uktvā, pād'|âbhivandanaṃ kṛtvā, prakrāntā.

Yāvat, Sudhanaḥ Kumāraḥ, taṃ karvaṭakaṃ saṃnāmya, gṛhīta|prābhṛtaḥ, Hastināpuram anuprāptaḥ. śrutvā ca, rājā parāṃ prītim upagataḥ. tataḥ kumāro mārga|śramaṃ prativinodya, pituḥ sakāśaṃ gataḥ. praṇāmaṃ kṛtvā, purastān niṣaṇṇaḥ. rājñā paramayā saṃtoṣaṇayā saṃbhāṣita uktaś ca, ‹Kumāra, śivena tvam āgataḥ›

‹Deva, tava prasādāt karvaṭakaḥ saṃnāmitaḥ, nipakā gṛhītāḥ, cintakaḥ sthāpitaḥ. ime tu kara|pratyayāḥ, paṇy'|āgāraś ca sthāpyatām› iti.

In the Weeping, *kínnari* maidservants; in the Laughing, a *kínnari* matron;
In the Snake-Poison, many kinds of snakes; and in the Reedy River, a silk-cotton tree.
At the Crocodile, you must be brave and resolute, at the Butterfly, heroic;
At the Burning, you must bind the water monsters' jaws, and at the Marvelous, you must sing diverse songs.

At the Weeping River, a cheerful attitude will enable you to cross; at the Laughing, silence; at the Venomous Serpent, spells against snake venom. At the Reedy River, beating sharp weapons together will enable you to cross. After crossing these rivers, you will reach a semi-forested area inhabited by five hundred ogres—stand firm and you will drive them off. After that, you will reach the *kínnara* king's palace."' At that, Mano·hara, having delivered her message to the sage, touched her head to his feet and departed. 30.130

Just then, Prince Súdhana, having subdued the hill tribe and accepted their offerings, reached Hástina·pura. When he heard this, the king's joy was extreme. After he had dispelled the fatigue of the journey, the prince went to see his father. He made obeisance and sat down to one side. The king, speaking with immense satisfaction, said, 'Prince, you have returned successful!'

'Your majesty, through your favor the hill tribe was overcome, its leaders were taken hostage and representatives of the crown appointed. And here are taxes and tribute—let it all be placed in the treasury.'

Rājā kathayati, ‹putra, śobhanaṃ pratigṛhītam.› tataḥ pituḥ praṇāmaṃ kṛtvā, saṃprasthitaḥ. rājā kathayati, ‹Kumāra, tiṣṭha! prābhṛtaṃ sahitāv eva bhokṣyāmaḥ.›

‹Deva, gacchāmi. ciram adṛṣṭā me Manoharā.›

30.135 ‹Alam, Kumāra, adya gamanena! tiṣṭha! śvo gamiṣyasi.› iti.

So 'nurudhyamāna evam āha, ‹tāta, ady' âiva may" âvaśyaṃ gantavyam.› rājā tūṣṇīm avasthitaḥ. tataḥ kumāraḥ, sva|gṛhaṃ gataḥ, paśyati śrī|vivarjitam antaḥ|pura|dvāram. sa cintā|paraḥ, praviśya, Manoharāṃ na paśyati. itaś c' âmutaś ca saṃbhrāntaḥ, śūnya|hṛdayaḥ, śabdaṃ kartum ārabdhaḥ, ‹Manohare! Manohare!,› iti yavad antaḥ|puram saṃnipatitam. tāḥ striyaḥ kṣepaṃ kartum ārabdhāḥ. viddho 'sau hṛdaya|śalyena, sutarāṃ praṣṭum ārabdhaḥ. tābhir yathā|bhūtaṃ samākhyātam—saḥ śokena saṃmuhyate.

Tāḥ striyaḥ kathayanti, ‹Deva, antaḥ|pure tat|prativiśiṣṭatarāḥ striyaḥ santi. kim|arthaṃ śokaḥ kriyate?›

sa pitur nairguṇyam upaśrutya kṛta|ghnatāṃ ca, mātuḥ sakāśam upasaṃkrāntaḥ. pādayor nipatya, kathayati: ‹amba,

Manoharāṃ na paśyāmi, manoratha|guṇair yutām
sādhu|rūpa|samāyuktā. kva gatā me Manoharā?

The king declared, 'My son, you have done splendidly!' At that, Súdhana touched his head to his father's feet and went to leave. The king called after him, 'Prince, stop! These offerings—let us enjoy them together!'

'Your majesty, I am going. It is a long time that I have not seen Mano·hara.'

'Prince, never mind going today! Stay here! Go tomor- 30.135
row.'

Súdhana, his way barred, said, 'Father, I shall certainly go see Mano·hara this very day.' The king remained silent. The prince then returned to his own palace, where he did not see his princess waiting at the door of the palace women's quarters. Filled with anxiety, he entered, but did not see Mano·hara. Rushing hither and thither, his heart bereft, he began to call out, 'Mano·hara! Mano·hara!,' until all the palace women came out and began to complain. Pierced to the heart by grief's dart, he questioned them relentlessly. They explained exactly what had happened—he was stupefied with grief.

The women said, 'Your highness, in this palace there are much better women than she. Why grieve?'

When Súdhana had learned of his father's wickedness and of the slaughter he had caused, he hurried into his mother's presence, threw himself at her feet, and said: 'Mother,

I cannot find Mano·hara, who is endowed with all
the virtues my heart desires
As well as with the most exquisite beauty. Where
has my Mano·hara gone?

30.140 Manasā saṃpradhāvāmi, mano me saṃpramuhyati
hṛdayaṃ dahyate c' âiva rahitasya tayā bhṛśam.
Mano|bhirāmā ca Manoharā ca sā
mano|nukūlā ca mano|ratiś ca me
saṃtapta|deho 'smi Manoharāṃ vinā;
kuto mam' êdaṃ vyasanaṃ samāgatam?› iti

Sā kathayati, ‹putra, kṛcchra|saṃkaṭa|saṃbādha|prāptā Manohar' êti mayā pramuktā.›

‹Amba, yathā katham?› tayā yathā|vṛttaṃ sarvaṃ vistareṇa samākhyātam. saḥ, pitur nairguṇyam akṛta|jñatāṃ c' ôktvā, kathayati, ‹amba, kutra gatā? katareṇa pathena?› iti.

Sā kathayati, ‹putra,

30.145 Dīrgho 'sau vidyate mārga ṛṣi|siṃha|niṣevitaḥ
uṣito dharma|rājena yatra yātā Manoharā.› iti

Saḥ, Manoharā|viyoga|duḥkh'|ārtaḥ, kṛcchraṃ vilalāpa, karuṇaṃ paridevamānaḥ:

Manoharāṃ na paśyāmi, manoratha|guṇair yutām
sādhu|rūpa|samāyuktā. kva gatā me Manoharā?
Manasā saṃpradhāvāmi, mano me saṃpramuhyati
hṛdayaṃ dahyate c' âiva rahitasya tayā bhṛśam.

My mind, searching for her everywhere, is bewildered, stupefied, 30.140
And my heart burns painfully because I am bereft of her.
Dear to my heart is Mano·hara, agreeable to my mind and its chief delight.
My body burns without Mano·hara! How has this calamity befallen me?'

The queen replied, 'My son, trouble, difficulty and affliction came upon Mano·hara, and so I let her go.'

'Mother, how did this happen?' She explained everything in detail, just as it had happened. Súdhana denounced his father's wickedness and ingratitude, then asked, 'Mother, where has she gone? What route has she taken?'

She replied, 'My son,

Long is that road, frequented by sages and lions 30.145
And by Yama, Lord of Justice, on which Mano·hara has set out.'

Súdhana, afflicted and in pain due to separation from Mano·hara, wailed miserably and lamented piteously:

I cannot find Mano·hara, who is endowed with all the virtues my heart desires
As well as with the most exquisite beauty. Where has my Mano·hara gone?
My mind, searching for her everywhere, is bewildered, stupefied,
And my heart burns painfully because I am bereft of her.

Tato mātr" âbhihitaḥ, ‹putra, santy asminn antaḥ|pure tat|prativiśiṣṭatarāḥ striyaḥ. kim|arthaṃ śokaḥ kriyate?› iti.

30.150 Kumāraḥ kathayati, ‹amba, kuto me ratir a|prāptāyāṃ tasyām?› iti. saḥ, tayā samāśvāsyamāno 'pi, śoka|saṃtāpa|saṃtaptaḥ, tasyāḥ pravṛttiṃ samanveṣamāṇa itaś c' âmutaś ca, paribhramitum ārabdhaḥ. tasya buddhir utpannā: ‹yata eva labdhā, tam eva tāvat pṛcchāmi› iti. saḥ, Phalakasya lubdhakasya sakāśaṃ gataḥ, pṛcchati, ‹Manoharā—kutas tvayā labdhā?› iti.

sa kathayati, ‹amuṣmin parvata|pārśva ṛṣiḥ prativasati. tasy' āśrama|pade Brahma|sabhā nāma puṣkariṇī. tasyāṃ snātum avatīrṇā, ṛṣi|vyapadeśena labdhā› iti.

sa saṃlakṣayati, ‹ṛṣir idānīm abhigantavyaḥ. tasmāt pravṛttir bhaviṣyati› iti.

Eṣa ca vṛtt'|ânto rājñā śrutaḥ: ‹Manoharā|viyogāt kumāro 'tīva viklavaḥ› iti. tato rājñ" âbhihitaḥ, ‹Kumāra, kim asi viklavaḥ? idānīṃ tat|prativiśiṣṭam antaḥ|puraṃ vyavasthāpayiṣyāmi› iti.

sa kathayati, ‹tāta, na śakyaṃ mayā, tām an|ānīya, antaḥ|puraḥ|sthena bhavitum.› saḥ, rājñā bahv apy ucyamānaḥ, na nivartate. Tato rājñā nagara|dvāra|prākāra|śṛṅgāṭakeṣv ārakṣakāḥ puruṣāḥ sthāpitā yathā ‹Kumāro na niṣkāsati› iti.

At that, his mother said, 'Son, there are, in your palace, women who are far better than she. Why grieve?'

Replied the prince, 'Mother, how can I take pleasure in 30.150
anything without having found Mano·hara?' Although she sought to console him, Súdhana, scorched by grief's fire, began to rush about hither and thither, seeking news of Mano·hara. Then the idea came to him: 'The very place she was caught—that's where I'll ask about her!' So Súdhana made his way to the hunter Phálaka, whom he asked, 'Mano·hara—where did you capture her?'

The hunter told him, 'On that mountain slope dwells a sage. In his hermitage there is a lotus pool called Brahma·sabha. When Mano·hara descended into it to bathe, I captured her by following the sage's instructions.'

Súdhana reflected, 'I must go now to that sage. He will have news of her.'

When the king learned about Súdhana's efforts to find Mano·hara, he thought, 'Separation from Mano·hara has made the prince excessively overwrought.' So he told his son, 'Prince, why are you so overwrought? Now I shall bestow upon you a woman far better than Mano·hara.'

The prince replied, 'Father, it is impossible for me, without having brought her back, to accept any other palace woman.' And although the king spoke to him at length, Súdhana would not relent. So the king stationed guards at the city gates, on the ramparts and at the crossroads, with the order that 'The prince does not pass.'

30.155 Kumāraḥ kṛtsnāṃ rātriṃ jāgartu|kāmaḥ. uktaṃ ca, ‹pañc' ême, rātryām, alpaṃ svapanti, bahu jāgrati. katame pañca? puruṣaḥ striyām avekṣyavān pratibaddha|cittaḥ, strī puruṣe, utkrośa|kārī, caura|senā|patiḥ, bhikṣuś c' ārabdha|vīryaḥ› iti.

Atha kumārasy' âitad abhavat, ‹yadi dvāreṇa yāsyāmi, rājño dvāra|pālaka|rakṣakāś caṇḍā bhavanti, te māṃ daṇḍayiṣyanty utsādayiṣyanti vā. yan nv aham a|rakṣitena pathā gaccheyam› iti. sa rātryāṃ vyutthāya, nīl'|ôtpala|mālā|baddha|śirāḥ, yena rakṣiṇaḥ puruṣā na santi, tena tāṃ mālāṃ dhvaje baddhv" âvatīrṇaḥ. candraś ca coditaḥ. tato 'sau candram avekṣya, Manoharā|virahitaḥ, evaṃ vilalāpa:

Bhoḥ pūrṇa|candra! rajanī|kara! tāra|rājā!
tvaṃ Rohiṇī|nayana|kānta! Su|s'|ârtha|vāha!
kac cit priyā mama manohara n' ôtpal'|âkṣā
dṛṣṭā tvayā bhuvi Manohara|nāma|dheyā? iti

Anubhūta|pūrva|ratim anusmaran, jagāma. dadarśa mṛgīm, tām apy uvāca:

That entire night the prince remained awake. It is said, 'Five are those who, at night, sleep little and remain much awake. Which five? The man who watches for his woman with infatuated mind—or the woman for her man—the night watchman, the robber chieftain and the monk who is energetic in his spiritual practice.' 30.155

It then occurred to Súdhana, 'If I leave by the gate, the royal guards and gatekeepers, who are fierce, will beat or arrest me. Suppose rather I were to leave by an unguarded way.' So during the night he got up and, with a garland of blue and red lotuses tied around his head, he went to an unguarded part of the wall, tied the garland to a flagpole and, using it as a rope, climbed over and down—just as the moon was rising. Gazing at the moon, and bereft of Mano·hara, he lamented:

O full moon! Maker of night! King of the stars!
Dear to Róhini's eyes are you! Excellent caravan-leader!
My beloved, stealer of my heart, that lotus-eyed woman—
Have you not seen anywhere on this earth the one named Mano·hara?

Remembering the pleasures he had previously enjoyed, he went on. He saw a gazelle and to her, too, he spoke:

He tvaṃ kuraṅgi! tṛṇa|vāri|palāśa|bhakṣe!
svasty astu te! cara sukhaṃ! na mṛg'|ârir asmi!
dīrgh'|ēkṣaṇā mṛga|vadhū|kamanīya|rūpā
dṛṣṭā tvayā mama Manohara|nāma|dheyā?

30.160 Saḥ, tām atikramy' ânyatamaṃ pradeśaṃ gataḥ, dadarśa vanaṃ nānā|puṣpa|phal'|ôpaśobhitaṃ bhramarair upabhujyamāna|sāram. tato 'nyatamaṃ bhramaram uvāca:

Nīl'|āñjan'|âcala|sa|varṇa madhu|dvi|rephaḥ
vaṃś'|ântar'|âmbu|ruha|madhya|kṛt'|âdhivāsa!
varṇ'|âli|pattra|sadṛś'|āyata|keśa|hastā!
dṛṣṭā tvayā mama Manohara|nāma|dheyā?

Tasmād api pradeśād atikrāntaḥ, paśyaty āśī|viṣaṃ, dṛṣṭvā c' āha:

Bhoḥ kṛṣṇa|sarpa! taru|pallava|lola|jihva!
vaktr'|ântar'|ôtpatita|dhūma|kal"|āpa|vaktra!
rāg'|âgninā tava samo na viṣ'|âgnir ugraḥ
dṛṣṭā tvayā bhuvi Manohara|nāma|dheyā?

Tam api pradeśaṃ samatikrāntaḥ, dadarś' âparaṃ vanaṃ kokil'|âbhināditam, dṛṣṭvā ca punas taṃ kokilam uvāca:

Greetings to you, gazelle, enjoyer of grass, water and leaves!
Most welcome are you! Roam happily! No enemy to gazelles am I!
My long-eyed one, that doe, so desirable her figure–
Have you seen the one who is called Mano·hara?

Súdhana left the gazelle behind, went on to another spot, 30.160
and saw a wood, resplendent with many kinds of flowers and fruit, in which bees busied themselves. Then, to one particular bee, he spoke:

Dark as a mountain, your hue, O honey bee!
In bamboo stalks and lotuses you make your dwelling.
She whose long hair is dark as a bee's wing in color—
Have you seen my woman, the one who is called Mano·hara?

Passing on also from that spot, Súdhana saw a venomous serpent, and, seeing it, declared:

Greetings, O cobra! Your tongue flickers like trees' leaves tremble!
From your mouth issues forth masses of smoke!
She who is intense like the fire of passion, not like the fire of your poison—
Have you seen on this earth the one who is called Mano·hara?

Moving on to another spot, Súdhana saw another wood in which a cuckoo was singing, and catching sight of the cuckoo, once again spoke:

30.165 Bhoḥ kokil'|ôttama! van'|ôttama|vṛkṣa|vāsin!
nārī|manohara! patatri|gaṇasya rājan!
nīl'|ôtpal'|âmala|sam'|āyata|cāru|netrā!
dṛṣṭā tvayā mama Manohara|nāma|dheyā?

Tam api pradeśaṃ samatikrāntaḥ, dadarś' âśoka|vṛkṣaṃ sarva|puṣpa|pariphullam.

Maṅgalya|nām'|ântara|nāma|yuktaḥ,
sarva|drumāṇām adhirāja|bhūtaḥ,
Manoharā|śoka|vimūrchitaṃ mām
eṣo 'ñjalis te kuru vīta|śokam.

Saḥ, evaṃ viklavaḥ, anupūrveṇa tasya' rṣer āśrama|padam anuprāptaḥ. saḥ, tam ṛṣiṃ sa|vinayaṃ praṇipaty' ôvāca,

Cīr'|âjin'|âmbara|dhara, kṣamayā viśiṣṭa,
mūl'|âṅkur'|āmalaka|vilva|kapittha|bhakta—
vande, ṛṣe, nata|śirāḥ, vada me laghu tvam
dṛṣṭā tvayā mama Manohara|nāma|dheyā?

30.170 Tataḥ sa ṛṣiḥ, Sudhanaṃ Kumāraṃ sv|āgata|vacan'|āsana|dāna|kriy"|ādi|puraḥ|saraṃ pratisaṃmody' ôvāca,

Greetings, most excellent of cuckoos who dwells in a tree in this most excellent of woods! 30.165
Stealer of women's hearts! King of the bird-flock!
Like spotless blue lotuses are her long, lovely eyes—
Have you seen my woman, the one who is called Mano·hara?

Moving on to yet another spot, Súdhana saw an *ashóka* tree, blooming all over with flowers.

Bearing a name that is another word for well-being,
Great king of all the trees,
This respectful greeting is for you:
Free from grief one who is faint with grief over Mano·hara.

Such was the state of agitation and confusion in which Súdhana eventually reached the sage's hermitage. He flung himself down before the sage and said:

O you who bark and antelope-skin garments wear, who by forbearance are distinguished,
And who on roots, shoots and on *ámalaka, vilva* and *kapíttha* fruit dine—
I honor you, O sage, with bowed head. Tell me quickly,
Have you seen my woman, the one who is called Mano·hara?

At that, the sage, with words of welcome, a seat and other such hospitable offerings, greeted Prince Súdhana in return, and said: 30.170

Dṛṣṭā sā: paripūrṇa|candra|vadanā,
nīl'|ôtpal'|ābhāsvarā,
rūpeṇa priya|darśanā, su|vadanā,
nīl'|âñcita|bhrū|latā.
tvaṃ sva|stho bhuvi, bhujyatāṃ hi vividhaṃ
mūlaṃ phalaṃ ca prabhaḥ
paścāt svasti gamiṣyas'|îti—manasā
n' âtr' âsti me saṃśayaḥ.
Idaṃ hy avocad vacanaṃ ca su|bhrūḥ:
«kumāra, tṛṣṇā tvayi bādhate me,
mahac ca duḥkhaṃ vasatāṃ vaneṣu,
yātāṃ ca māṃ drakṣyasi niścayena.» iti.

Iyaṃ ca tay" âṅguli|mudrikā dattā, kathayati ca, «Kumāra, viṣamāḥ panthānaḥ, dur|gamāḥ. khedam āpatsyase. nivartasva! iti. yadi ca nivāryamāṇo na tiṣṭhet, tasya mārgam upadeṣṭum arhasi.» Kumāra, idaṃ ca tayā samākhyātam:

«Uttare dig|bhāge trayaḥ kāla|parvatāḥ. tān atikramya, apare trayaḥ. tān atikramya, apare trayaḥ. tān atikramya, apare trayaḥ. tān apy atikramya, Himavān parvata|rājaḥ. tat| praveśena, tvay" êmāni bhaiṣajyāni samudānetavyāni, tad| yathā Sudhā nām'|âuṣadhiḥ. tayā ghṛtaṃ paktvā, pātavyaṃ tena ca te na tṛṣā na bubhukṣā smṛti|balaṃ ca vardhayati. Vānaraḥ samudānetavyaḥ, mantram adhyetavyam, saśaraṃ dhanur grahītavyam, maṇayo 'vabhās'|ātmakāḥ, agadaḥ, viṣa|ghātakaḥ, ayaḥ|kīlās trayaḥ, vīṇā ca. Himavataḥ parvata|rājasy' ôttareṇa, Utkīlakaḥ parvataḥ. tataḥ Kūjakaḥ,

I have seen her: a face like the full moon,
blue eyes bright as lotuses,
A shapely figure lovely to behold, a beautiful countenance, and dark arched eyebrows.
Seat yourself comfortably on the ground;
enjoy varied roots and fruits, O mighty one.
Eventually you will achieve success—
in my mind there is no doubt of that.
For this is what she said, she of the lovely eyebrows:
"O prince, longing for you oppresses me,
As does the great suffering of those who dwell in the woods,
But I who have fled, you will find, that's certain."

And she gave me this signet ring, along with the message, "Prince, difficult are the paths, and hard to find. Catastrophes will befall you. Turn back! But if he cannot bear to turn back, please point out the way to him." And this, Prince, is how she explained it:

"To the north there are three black mountains. Scale them, and there will be three more. Scale those, and there will be three more. Scale those, and there will be yet three more. Scale those, and there will be the Himalaya, the king of mountains. Proceed into the Himalaya and gather remedies, in particular the medicinal herb called Sudha, 'divine nectar.' After simmering it in clarified butter, drink it and you will know neither thirst nor hunger and your memory and strength will increase. There is also a monkey you must capture, a spell you must memorize and recite, and you must carry off a bow and arrows as well as luminous jewels, an antidote, a deadly poison, three iron stakes and

Jala|pathaḥ, Khadirakaḥ, Eka|dhārakaḥ, Vajrakaḥ, Kāma|rūpī, Utkīlakaḥ, Airāvatakaḥ, Adhunānaḥ, Pramokṣaṇaḥ. ete parvatāḥ, sarve te samatikramaṇīyāḥ. tatra Khadirake parvate guhā|praveśa Eka|dhārake ca Utkīlake, Vajrake tu pakṣi|rājena praveśaḥ. Ebhir upāyais te sarve parvatāḥ samatikramaṇīyāḥ. yantrāṇi ca bhaṅktavyāni, aja|vaktro meṇḍhakaḥ puruṣaḥ Piṅgala|rākṣasa|rūpī hantavyaḥ. guhāyām, lālā|srotasā mahat" âja|garo vegena pradhāvati—sa te vikrameṇa hantavyaḥ.

30.175 Ardh'|ântara|gataṃ nāgaṃ yatra paśyeḥ Kirīṭakam
cāpa|muktena bāṇena hantavyo mama kāraṇāt.
Yatra paśyeta dvau meṣau saṃghaṭṭantau parasparam
tayoḥ śṛṅgam ekaṃ bhaṅktvā mārgaṃ pratilapsyase.
Āyasau puruṣau dṛṣṭvā śastra|pāṇī mahā|bhayau
tayor ekaṃ tāḍayitvā mārgaṃ pratilapsyase.
Saṃkocayantīṃ prasārayantīṃ rākṣasīm āyasaṃ mukham
yadā paśyet tadā kīlaṃ lalāṭe tasyā nikhānayet.
Śil"|āvartas tathā kūpo vilaṅghyas te ṣaṣṭī|hastakaḥ
hari|piṅgala|keś'|âkṣo dāruṇo yakṣa|rākṣasaḥ.

a lute. To the north of the Himalaya, the king of mountains, is Mount Utkílaka. After that, there are Kújaka, Jala·patha, Khádiraka, Eka·dháraka, Vájraka, Kama·rupin, Utkílaka, Airávataka, Adhunána and Pramókshana. All these mountains you must also scale. There is a cave entrance to Mount Khádiraka, as there is to Eka·dháraka and Utkílaka, but Vájraka you must cross on a Gáruda, the king of birds. These methods will enable you to cross all those mountains. There are also magical creatures you will have to overcome, including one like a ram with a goat's face and a yellow man, who looks likes the demon Píngala, whom you will have to slay. In the cave, a great serpent, with its streams of poisonous saliva, strikes quickly—you must subdue it by force.

When you see the serpent Kirítaka half in the cave, 30.175
Loose an arrow from your bow and slay it for me.
When you see two rams butting each other,
Break off a horn from each and regain the way.
When you see two terrifying iron men wielding weapons,
Strike down one of them and regain the way.
A demoness, opening and closing her iron mouth—
When you see her, you must bury a stake in her forehead.
Over a whirlpool, too—a crevasse sixty hands across—you must leap.
Vicious ogres and demons with yellow-brown hair and eyes—

Kārmukaṃ maṇḍalaṃ kṛtvā hantavyaś ca dur|āsadaḥ
nadyaś ca balatas tāryā nakra|grāha|samākulāḥ—

Naṅgā, Pataṃ|gā, Tapanī, Citrā, Rudanī, Hasanī, Āśī|viṣā, Vetravatī ca—

Naṅgāyāṃ rākṣasī|kopaḥ,
 Pataṃ|gāyām a|manuṣyakāḥ
Tapanyāṃ grāha|bahulatvam,
 Citrāyāṃ Kāma|rūpiṇaḥ.
Rudanyāṃ kinnarī|ceṭyaḥ,
 Hasanyāṃ kinnarī|snuṣāḥ
Āśī|viṣāyāṃ nānā|vidhāḥ sarpāḥ,
 Vetra|nadyāṃ tu śālmaliḥ.
Naṅgāyāṃ dhairya|karaṇam,
 Pataṃ|gāyāṃ parākramaḥ
Tapanyāṃ grāha|mukha|bandhaḥ,
 Citrāyāṃ vividhaṃ gītam.

«Rudanyāṃ saumanasyena samuttāraḥ, Hasanyāṃ tūṣṇīṃ|bhāvena. Āṣī|viṣāyāṃ sarpa|viṣa|mantra|prayogena samuttāraḥ. Vetra|nadyāṃ tīkṣṇa|śastra|saṃpāta|yogena samuttāraḥ. nadīḥ samatikramya, pañca|yakṣa|śatānāṃ gulmaka|sthāne. tad dhairyam āsthāya, vidrāvyam. tato Drumasya Kinnara|rājasya bhavanam' iti.»›

Bend your bow into a circle and slay them,
dangerous to approach.
And many rivers you must cross, all infested with
crocodiles and hippos—

The rivers Crocodile, Butterfly, Burning, Marvelous, Weeping, Laughing, Snake-Poison and Reedy—

In the Crocodile is an angry demoness;
in the Butterfly, demons;
In the Burning River, hosts of water monsters;
in the Marvelous, shape-shifters;
In the Weeping, *kínnari* maidservants;
in the Laughing, *kínnari* matrons;
In the Snake-Poison, many kinds of snakes;
and in the Reedy River, a silk-cotton tree.
At the Crocodile, you must be brave and resolute;
at the Butterfly, heroic;
At the Burning, you must bind the water monsters'
jaws,
And at the Marvelous, you must sing various songs.

"At the Weeping River, a cheerful attitude will enable you to cross; at the Laughing, silence; at the Snake-Poison, spells to counter snake venom. At the Reedy River, beating sharp weapons together will enable you to cross. After crossing these rivers, you will reach a semi-forested area inhabited by five hundred ogres—stand firm and you will drive them off. After that, you will reach the palace of Druma, king of the *kínnaras*.'"

30.180 Tataḥ Sudhanaḥ Kumāro yath"|ôpadiṣṭān oṣadha|mantr'|âgada|prayogān samudānayanāya, tasya' rṣeḥ pād'|âbhivandanaṃ kṛtvā, prakrāntaḥ. tatas tena, yath"|ôpadiṣṭāḥ, sarve samudānītāḥ, sthāpayitvā vānaram. tatas tān ādāya, punar api tasya' rṣeḥ sakāśam upasaṃkrāntaḥ, uktaś ca, ‹alam, Kumāra! kim anena vyavasāyena? kiṃ Manoharayā? tvam, ekākī, asahāyaḥ, śarīra|saṃśayam avāpsyasi› iti.

Kumāraḥ prāha, ‹Maha"|rṣe, avaśyam ev' âhaṃ prayāsyām' îti. kutaḥ,

Candrasya khe vicarataḥ, kva sahāya|bhāvaḥ?
damṣṭrā|balena balinaś ca mṛg'|âdhipasya,
agneś ca dāva|dahane, kva sahāya|bhāvaḥ?
asmad|vidhasya ca sahāya|balena kiṃ syāt?
Kiṃ bhoḥ! mah"|ârṇava|jalaṃ na vigāhitavyam?
kiṃ sarpa|daṣṭa iti n' âiva cikitsanīyaḥ?
vīryaṃ bhajet su|mahad ūrjita|sattva|dṛṣṭaṃ,
yatne kṛte, yadi na sidhyati, ko 'tra doṣaḥ. iti.›

Tataḥ Sudhanaḥ Kumāraḥ, Manohar"|ôpadiṣṭena vidhinā, saṃprasthitaḥ. anupūrveṇa parvata|nadī|guhā|prapāt'|ādīni bhaiṣajya|mantr'|âgada|prayogena vinirjitya, Druma-

Then, in order to acquire the remedy, the spell and the antidote as instructed, Prince Súdhana respectfully took his leave of the sage and set out. Of the items indicated, he acquired all except for the monkey. So, taking them with him, he again approached the sage, who told him, 'Enough, Prince! What is the use of your strenuous efforts? What is the use of Mano·hara? Alone, without companions, you are risking your life!' 30.180

The prince replied, 'Great sage, most certainly I am going. For,

The moon traversing the heavens,
where is its companion?
The mighty king of beasts, with its powerful fangs,
And the fire that consumes the forest,
where are their companions?
For those like us, what need is there of a
companion's strength?
Into the water of the great ocean should one not
plunge?
Is there a snakebite that can in no way be cured?
One should cultivate enormous energy that mighty
beings witness,
And if, despite the efforts made, one does not
succeed, what fault is there?'

Then Prince Súdhana set out on the route that Mano·hara had indicated. In due course, he traversed the mountains, rivers, caves, precipices and other obstacles by employing the remedy, the spells and the antidote, and reached the

sya Kinnara|rājasya bhavana|samīpaṃ gataḥ. kumāro 'paśyat,

Tan nagaram adūraṃ śrīmad|udyān'|ôpaśobhitam,
nānā|puṣpa|phal'|ôpetaṃ, nānā|vihaga|sevitam,
Taḍāga|dīrghik"|āvāpī|kinnaraiḥ samupāvṛtam
kinnarīs tatra c' âpaśyat pānīy'|ârtham upāgatāḥ.

30.185 Tatas tāḥ Sudhana|kumāreṇ' âbhihitāḥ, ‹kim anena bahunā pānīyena kriyate?› iti.

Tāḥ kathayanti, ‹asti Drumasya Kinnara|rājasya duhitā, Manoharā nāma. sā manuṣya|hasta|gatā babhūva. tasyāḥ sa manuṣya|gandho na naśyati.›

Sudhānaḥ Kumāraḥ pṛcchati, ‹kim ete ghaṭāḥ samastāḥ sarve tasyā upari nipātyanta āhosvid ānupūrveṇa?› iti.

Tāḥ kathayanti, ‹ānupūrvyā.›

sa saṃlakṣayati, ‹śobhano 'yam upāya—imām aṅguli|mudrām ekasmin ghaṭe prakṣipāmi› iti. ten' âikasyāḥ kinnaryā ghaṭe 'nālakṣitaṃ prakṣiptā, sā ca kinnary abhihitā, ‹anena tvayā ghaṭena Manoharā tat|prathamataraṃ snāpayitavyā.›

30.190 Sā saṃlakṣayati, ‹nūnam atra kāryeṇa bhavitavyam.› tatas tay" âsau ghaṭaḥ prathamataraṃ Manoharāyā mūrdhni nipātitaḥ, yāvad aṅguli|mudr" ôtsaṅge nipatitā. sā Manoharayā pratyabhijñātā.

vicinity of the palace of Druma, king of the *kínnaras*. The prince beheld

That city, not far off, surrounded by lovely parks and gardens,
With many kinds of flowers and fruit, frequented by various species of birds,
Provided with ponds and tanks and filled with *kínnaris*.
And there Súdhana saw some *kínnaris* who had come to draw water.

Prince Súdhana addressed them, 'What will you do with all this water?' 30.185

They told him, 'Druma, king of the *kínnaras*, has a daughter, Mano·hara by name, who fell into the hands of humans. From her the stink of humanity is not yet washed off.'

Prince Súdhana asked, 'Are these jars of water to be poured over her all at once or one after the other?'

The *kínnaris* replied, 'One after the other.'

He reflected, 'Here's a splendid strategy—I'll drop this signet ring into one of the jars.' Unnoticed, he dropped the ring into one *kínnari*'s jar, and to her he said, 'You should use this jar first to bathe Mano·hara.'

She thought, 'Certainly there's some purpose behind this.' 30.190
Later, that jar she did empty out first over Mano·hara's head, until the ring rolled out into her lap. Mano·hara recognized it at once.

Tataḥ kinnarīṃ pṛcchati, ‹mā tatra kaś cin manuṣyo 'bhyāgataḥ?›

S" āha, ‹abhyāgataḥ.›

‹Gaccha! enaṃ pracchannaṃ praveśaya.› tayā praveśitaḥ sugupte pradeśe sthāpitaḥ.

Tato Manoharā, pituḥ pādayor nipatya, kathayati, ‹tāta, yady asau Sudhanaḥ Kumāra āgacchet—yen' âhaṃ hṛtā—tasya tvaṃ kiṃ kuryāḥ?›

30.195 sa kathayati, ‹tam ahaṃ khaṇḍa|śataṃ kṛtvā, catasṛṣu dikṣu kṣipeyam! manuṣyo 'sau. kiṃ tena?› iti.

Manoharā kathayati, ‹tāta, manuṣya|bhūtasya kuta ih' āgamanam? aham evaṃ bravīmi› iti.

Tato Drumasya Kinnara|rājasya paryavasthāno vigataḥ. tataḥ, vigata|paryavasthānaḥ, kathayati, ‹yady asau kumāra āgacchet, tasy' âhaṃ tvāṃ sarv'|âlaṃkāra|vibhūṣitāṃ prabhūta|vitt'|ôpakaraṇa|kinnarī|sahasra|parivṛtāṃ bhāry"|ârthaṃ dadyām› iti.

Tato Manoharayā hṛṣṭa|tuṣṭa|pramuditayā, Sudhanaḥ Kumāro divy'|âlaṃkāra|vibhūṣito Drumasya Kinnara|rājasy' ôpadarśitaḥ. tato Drumaḥ Kinnara|rājaḥ Sudhanaṃ Kumāraṃ dadarśa—abhirūpam, darśanīyam, prāsādikam, paramayā śubha|varṇa|puṣkalatayā samanvāgatam—dṛṣṭvā ca, punaḥ paraṃ vismayam upagataḥ. tatas, tasya jijñāsāṃ kartukāmena, sapta sauvarṇāḥ stambhā ucchritāḥ, sapta tālāḥ, sapta bheryaḥ, sapta śūkarāḥ. āha ca,

She then asked that *kínnari*, 'Has a male human not come here?'

She replied, 'One has come.'

'Go! Bring him to a secluded place.' The *kínnari* brought Súdhana to a well-concealed spot and bid him wait.

Then Mano·hara threw herself at her father's feet and asked, 'Father, if that Prince Súdhana—by whom I was carried off—were to arrive, what would you do with him?'

King Druma replied, 'Him I would cut into a hundred pieces, which I would then cast to the ten directions! He is a human. What value has he?' 30.195

Mano·hara said, 'Father, how could one who is a human come here? That's what I say.'

At that, King Druma's anger abated. Then, his anger abated, he said, 'If the prince were to come here, to him I would give you, adorned with all your jewelry and accompanied by much wealth and a thousand *kínnari* serving maids, to be his wife.'

Then Mano·hara, pleased, delighted and, indeed, overjoyed, presented Prince Súdhana, adorned with divine jewelry, to Druma, king of the *kínnara*s. King Druma beheld Prince Súdhana—well built, good-looking, gracious, with a fine, glowing complexion—and, beholding him, was utterly astonished. So, wishing to put Súdhana to the test, he had arranged seven golden pillars, seven palm trees, seven kettledrums and seven wild boars. Then he said,

Tvayā kāntyā jitās tāvad ete kinnara|dārakāḥ,
saṃdarśita|prabhāvas tu, divya|saṃbandham arhasi.
Atyāyataṃ śara|vanaṃ kṛtv" ôddhṛtya śaraṃ kṣaṇāt.
vyuptam anyūnam uccitya punar dehi til'|āḍhakam.
Saṃdarśaya dhanur|vede, dṛḍha|lakṣ'|ādi|kauśalam:
tataḥ kīrti|patāk" êyaṃ tav' āyattā Manoharā.

30.200 Sudhanaḥ Kumāro Bodhi|sattvaḥ, kuśalāś ca bhavanti bodhi|sattvās teṣu teṣu śilpa|sthāna|karma|sthāneṣu. devatāś c' âiṣām autsukyam āpatsyante 'vighna|bhāvāya. tato Bodhi|sattvo nṛtya|gīta|vīṇā|paṇava|sughoṣaka|vallarī|mṛdaṅg'|ādi|nānā|vidhena, daivaty" ôpasaṃhatena vāditra|viśeṣeṇa, samantād āpūryamāṇo 'nekaiḥ kinnara|sahasraiḥ parivṛtaḥ.

Śata|kratu|samādiṣṭair yakṣaiḥ śūkara|rūpibhir
utpāṭite śara|vaṇe same, vyuptaṃ til'|āḍhakam
ekīkṛtaṃ samuccitya, Śakra|sṛṣṭaiḥ pipīlakaiḥ,
kumāraḥ kinnar'|êndrāya vismitāya nyavedayat.

Granted, you, by your handsome appearance, have
surpassed these *kínnara* youths;
But only he who displays true might is worthy to
be the kinsman of a divine race.
You must discharge a forest of arrows, then instantly
pluck one out of the air,
You must pick up and return an entire *ádhaka** of
sesame seeds lying scattered about,
Display, in your mastery of the bow, skill at hitting
fixed and moving targets:
Then this pennant of celebrity, Mano·hara, you will
have won.

Now, Prince Súdhana was a Bodhi·sattva, and Bodhi·sattvas are expert in every kind of art, craft and skill. Moreover, for them, the gods are eager to remove obstacles. Then the Bodhi·sattva, amid singing and dancing and superb music played by the gods on lutes, small drums, cymbals, three-string lutes, large drums and many other instruments, was joined on all sides my many thousands of *kínnaras*. 30.200

After *yakshas* in the form of boars, directed by
Indra, king of the gods,
Had extracted the right arrow, and the scattered
ádhaka of sesame seed
Had been gathered into one heap by ants that issued
forth from Indra,
The prince informed the *kínnara* king, who was
astonished.

Nīl'|ôtpala|dal'|ābhen' âsinā gṛhītena, paśyato Drumasya Kinnara|rājasya sauvarṇa|stambha|samīpaṃ gatvā, tān stambhān, kadalī|cchedena, khaṇḍa|khaṇḍaṃ chettum ārabdhaḥ. tataḥ, tān tilaśo 'vakīrya, sapta|tālān sapta|bherīḥ sapta ca śūkarān bāṇena vidhya, Sumeruvad akampyo 'vasthitaḥ. tato gagana|tala|sthābhir devatābhiś ca kinnara|śata|sahasrair hāhākāra|kilikilā|prakṣveḍ'|ôccair nādo muktaḥ, yaṃ dṛṣṭvā ca kinnara|rājaḥ paraṃ vismayam upagataḥ. tataḥ kinnarī|sahasrasya Manoharā|samāna|rūpasya madhye Manoharāṃ sthāpayitvā, Sudhanaḥ Kumāro 'bhihitaḥ, ‹ehi, kumāra! pratyabhijānāsi Manoharām?› iti. tataḥ, Sudhanaḥ Kumāraḥ, tāṃ pratyabhijñāya, gāth"|âbhigīten' ôktavān,

Yathā Drumasya duhitā tvaṃ mam' êṣṭā Manoharā,
śīghram, etena satyena, padaṃ vraja, Manohare.

Tataḥ sā druta|padam abhikrāntā. Kinnarāḥ kathayanti, ‹Deva, ayaṃ Sudhanaḥ Kumāraḥ, bala|vīrya|parākrama|samanvitaḥ, Manoharāyāḥ pratirūpaḥ! kim|arthaṃ vipralabhya? dīyatām asya Manoharā› iti.

30.205 Tato Drumaḥ Kinnara|rājaḥ, kinnara|gaṇena saṃvarṇitaḥ, Sudhanaṃ kinnar'|âbhimatena mahatā satkāreṇa puraskṛtya, Manoharāṃ divy'|âlaṃkāra|vibhūṣitāṃ vāmena pāṇinā gṛhītvā, dakṣiṇena sauvarṇa|bhṛṅgāraṃ, Sudhanaṃ Kumāram abhihitaḥ, ‹Kumāra, eṣā te Manoharā, kinnarī|pa-

Wielding a sword shaped like the leaf of a blue lotus, as King Druma looked on, Súdhana approached the golden pillars and proceeded to cut them into pieces as if he were slicing up plantain trees. Then he scattered the pieces, as tiny as sesame seeds, shot an arrow through the seven palm trees, the seven kettledrums and the seven boars, and stood back, as unperturbed as Mount Suméru. At that, the deities who were floating in the air and the hundreds of thousands of *kínnara*s let out loud ooohs and aaahs of astonishment and approval. Observing all this, the king of the *kínnara*s was, again, utterly astonished. After that, Druma placed Mano·hara amid a thousand *kínnari*s each of whom looked exactly like her, and said to Prince Súdhana, 'Come, prince! Do you recognize Mano·hara?' Prince Súdhana, so that he might recognize her, pronounced this verse:

> As you are Druma's daughter, my chosen one,
> Mano·hara,
> By this truth, step quickly forward, Mano·hara.

Mano·hara took a quick step forward. The *kínnara*s cried, 'Your majesty, Prince Súdhana is mighty, manly and heroic, and deserving of Mano·hara! Why cheat him? Give her to him!'

At that, Druma, king of the *kínnara*s, applauded by the 30.205
kínnara host, honored Súdhana with the great celebration for which the *kínnara*s had longed. Taking Mano·hara, adorned in her heavenly ornaments, with his left hand, and, in his right, a golden pitcher, he addressed Prince Súdhana: 'Prince, this woman, Mano·hara, together with her retinue,

rivṛtā, bhāry"|ârthāya dattā. a|paricitā mānuṣā: yath" âināṃ na parityakṣyasi› iti.

‹Param, tāta› iti Sudhanaḥ Kumāro Drumasya Kinnara|rājasya pratiśrutya, kinnara|bhavana|sthaḥ, Manoharayā sārdham, niṣpuruṣeṇa tūryeṇa, krīḍate, ramate, paricārayati.

Saḥ, apareṇa samayena, sva|deśam anusmṛtya, mātā|pitṛ|viyogajena duḥkhen' âbhyāhataḥ, Manoharāyā nivedayati, ‹mātā|pitṛ|viyogajaṃ me duḥkhaṃ bādhate› iti.

Tato Manoharay" âiṣa vṛtt'|ânto vistareṇa pitur niveditaḥ. sa kathayati, ‹gaccha kumāreṇa sārdham, apramādayā te bhavitavyaṃ, vipralambhakā manuṣyāḥ.› tato Drumeṇa Kinnara|rājena, prabhūtaṃ maṇi|muktā|suvarṇ'|ādīn dattvā, anupreṣitaḥ.

Saḥ, Manoharayā sārdham, upari|vihāyasā, kinnara|khaga|pathena, saṃprasthitaḥ, anupūrveṇa Hastināpura|nagaram anuprāptaḥ. tato Hastināpuraṃ nagaraṃ nānā|manohareṇa surabhiṇā gandha|viśeṣeṇa sarvadig āmoditam. śrutvā Dhanena Rājñ" ānanda|bheryaś ca tāḍitāḥ, sarvaṃ ca tan nagaram apagata|pāṣāṇa|śarkara|kaṭhallaṃ kāritam, candana|vāri|siktam, āmukta|paṭṭa|dāma|kalāpaṃ samucchrita|dhvaja|patākaṃ surabhi|dhūpa|ghaṭik'|ôpanibaddham, nānā|puṣp'|âvakīrṇa|ramaṇīyam. tataḥ kumāraḥ, aneka|nara|vara|sahasra|parivṛtaḥ, Manoharayā sārdham, Hastināpuraṃ nagaraṃ praviṣṭaḥ. tato mārga|śramaṃ prativinodya,

I give to be your wife. However, humans are untrustworthy: never forsake her!'

'Absolutely not, father!' replied Prince Súdhana to Druma, king of the *kínnaras*. Then, retiring to a *kínnara* palace, to the sound of musical instruments played only by women, he took his pleasure with, made love to and otherwise dallied with Mano·hara.

After a time, Súdhana began to think about his native land and, stricken by suffering produced by separation from his mother and father, told Mano·hara, 'Separation from my parents is causing pain that torments me.'

Mano·hara explained to her father in detail what had happened. He said, 'Go with the prince, but take heed, as humans are deceivers.' Then King Druma gave her quantities of jewels, pearls, gold and other precious substances, and sent her off.

Súdhana set out with Mano·hara, travelling through the air along the bird paths used by the *kínnaras*, and in due course reached Hástina·pura. The city of Hástina·pura was made fragrant in every quarter with a variety of captivating, delicious and choice scents. When he learned of this, King Dhana beat the drum that announced glad tidings, had the entire city swept clean of stones, pebbles and gravel, sprinkled with sandalwood-water and decorated with rows of jewelled silk banners. He had flags and pennants put up, urns wafting fragrant incense set out, and many kinds of lovely flowers scattered about. Then the prince, surrounded by many thousands of eminent men, and accompanied by Mano·hara, entered the city of Hástina·pura. After dispelling his travel weariness, he took a variety of jewels and

vividhāni ratnāny ādāya, pituḥ sakāśam upsaṃkrāntaḥ. pitrā kaṇṭhe pariṣvaktaḥ, pārśve rāj'|āsane niṣaṇṇaḥ, kinnara|nagara|gaman'|āgamanaṃ ca vistareṇa samākhyātam.

30.210 Tato Dhanena Rājñā, atibala|vīrya|parākrama iti viditvā, rājy'|âbhiṣekeṇ' âbhiṣiktaḥ. Sudhanaḥ Kumāraḥ saṃlakṣayati, ‹yan mama Manoharayā sārdhaṃ samāgamaḥ saṃvṛttaḥ, rājy'|âbhiṣekaś c' ânuprāptaḥ, tat pūrva|kṛta|hetu|viśeṣāt: yan nv aham idānīṃ dānāni dadyām, puṇyāni kuryām› iti. tena Hastināpure nagare dvādaśa|varṣāṇi nirargalo yajña iṣṭaḥ.

Syāt khalu te, Mahā|rāja, anyaḥ sa tena kālena, tena samayena, Sudhanaḥ Kumāro v" êti. na khalv evaṃ draṣṭavyam, api tv aham eva, tena kālena, tena samayena, bodhi|sattva|caryāyāṃ vartamānaḥ, Sudhano nāma rājā babhūva. yan mayā Manoharā|nimittaṃ bala|vīrya|parākramo darśitaḥ, dvādaśa|varṣāṇi nirargalo yajña iṣṭo—na tena may" ân|uttarā samyak|saṃbodhir adhigatā, kiṃ tu tad dānaṃ tac ca vīryam an|uttarāyāḥ samyak|saṃbodher hetu|mātrakaṃ pratyaya|mātrakaṃ saṃbhāra|mātrakam.»

Ity avocad Bhagavān, ātta|manasas te ca sarve lokā Bhagavato bhāṣitam abhyanumodan.

Iti Sudhana|kumār'|âvadānaṃ samāptam.

went into his father's presence. King Dhana clasped him around the neck, then seated him beside his royal throne. Then Súdhana recounted in full his trip to and from the city of the *kínnaras*.

Then King Dhana, knowing Súdhana's great power, man- 30.210
liness and heroism, consecrated him king. Prince Súdhana reflected, 'That I came to be united with Mano·hara and consecrated king is due to the cause of having, in the past, performed virtuous deeds: suppose, then, I now give gifts and perform other meritorious deeds.' And for twelve years, in the city of Hástina·pura, Súdhana unstintingly carried out sacrificial rituals.

It may occur to you, great king, that someone else, at that time, on that occasion, was Prince Súdhana. On no account should you think thus, for it was I who, at that time and on that occasion, was advancing in the Bodhi·sattva practice as the king named Súdhana. As for my demonstrating might, manliness and heroism on account of Mano·hara and for twelve years unstintingly carrying out sacrificial rituals—at that time I had not attained unexcelled, Supreme, Perfect Awakening, but rather that liberality and energy were no more than causes, bases, prerequisites of unexcelled, Supreme, Perfect Awakening."

Thus spoke the Lord and all those present, their minds uplifted, rejoiced at the Lord's words.

Thus ends "The Story of Prince Súdhana."

36
THE STORY OF MAKÁNDIKA THE WANDERER

Buddho Bhagavān, Kuruṣu jana|pada|cārikāṃ caran, Kalmāṣa|damyam anuprāptaḥ.

Tena khalu punaḥ samayena, Kalmāṣa|damye, Mākandiko nāma parivrājakaḥ prativasati. tasya Sākalir nāma patnī. tasya duhitā jātā, abhirūpā, darśanīyā, prāsādikā, sarv'|âṅga|pratyaṅg'|ôpetā. tasyā asthīni sūkṣmāṇi, su|sūkṣmāṇi, na śakyata upamā kartum.

Tasyās trīṇi sapt'|âhāny eka|viṃśati divasān vistareṇa jāti|mahī saṃvṛttā. yāvaj jāta|mahaṃ kṛtvā, nāma|dheyaṃ vyavasthāpyate, «kiṃ bhavatu dārikāyā nāma» iti.

Jñātaya ūcuḥ, «iyaṃ dārikā, abhirūpā, darśanīyā, prāsādikā, sarv'|âṅga|pratyaṅg'|ôpetā. tasyā asthīni sūkṣmāṇi, su|sūkṣmāṇi, na śakyata upamā kartum. bhavatu dārikāyāḥ ‹Anupamā› iti nāma.» tasyāḥ «Anupamā» iti nāma|dheyaṃ vyavasthāpitam.

36.5 S" ônnītā, vardhitā. Mākandikaḥ saṃlakṣayati, «iyaṃ dārikā na mayā kasya cit kulena dātavyā, na dhanena, n' âpi śrutena, kiṃ tu yo 'syā rūpeṇa samo v" âpy adhiko vā, tasya mayā dātavyā» iti.

Atr'|ântare Bhagavān, Kuruṣu jana|padeṣu cārikāṃ caran, Kalmāṣa|damyam anuprāptaḥ. Kalmāṣa|damye viharati, Kurūṇāṃ nigame viharati.

The Lord Buddha, travelling through the countryside among the Kurus, arrived at the town of Kalmásha·damya, "Spotted Bullock."

At that very time, a wanderer, Makándika by name, was also staying in Kalmásha·damya. He had a wife whose name was Sákali. A daughter had been born to him: she was well formed, good-looking, lovely and sound in every part. Her frame was delicate, exceedingly delicate, delicate beyond compare.

After three weeks, that is, twenty-one days, had passed, a grand birthday celebration was held for her and, after having concluded the celebration, Makándika proceeded to give her a name: "What name shall this girl have?"

Makándika's relatives said, "This girl is well formed, good-looking, lovely and sound in every part. Her frame is delicate, exceedingly delicate, delicate beyond compare. Let this girl's name be Anúpama, 'Incomparable.'" And so she was given the name Anúpama.

Anúpama was brought up and reached maturity. Ma- 36.5
kándika thought, "I shall not give this girl in marriage to anyone merely on account of his lineage, wealth or learning, but only to a man who is equally or more beautiful than she shall I give her."

Meanwhile, the Lord, travelling through the countryside among the Kurus, arrived at Kalmásha·damya and stopped in that town of the Kurus.

Atha Bhagavān pūrv'|âhṇe nivāsya, pātra|cīvaram ādāya, Kalmāṣa|damyaṃ piṇḍāya prāvikṣat. Kalmāṣa|damyaṃ piṇḍāya caritvā, kṛta|bhakta|kṛtyaḥ paścād|bhakta|piṇḍa|pātraḥ, pratikrāntaḥ. pātra|cīvaraṃ pratiśāmya, pādau prakṣālya, anyatama|vṛkṣa|mūlaṃ niśritya, niṣaṇṇaḥ supt'|ôraga|rāja|bhoga|paripiṇḍī|kṛtaṃ paryaṅkaṃ baddhvā.

Tena khalu samayena, Mākandikaḥ parivrājakaḥ puṣpa|samidhasy' ârthe nirgato 'bhūt. adrākṣīn Mākandikaḥ parivrājako Bhagavantaṃ dūrād ev' ânyatara|vṛkṣa|mūlaṃ niśritya, supt'|ôraga|rāja|bhoga|paripiṇḍī|kṛtaṃ paryaṅkaṃ baddhvā, niṣaṇṇam, prāsādikam, pradarśanīyam, śānt'|êndriyam, śānta|mānasam, parameṇa citta|vyupaśamena samanvāgatam, suvarṇa|yūpam iva, śriyā jvalantam. dṛṣṭvā ca punaḥ prīti|pramodya|jātaḥ.

sa saṃlakṣayati, «yādṛśo 'yaṃ śramaṇaḥ prāsādikaḥ, pradarśanīyaḥ, sakala|jana|manohārī. durlabhas tu sarva|strī|janasya patiḥ pratirūpaḥ prāg ev' Ânupamāyāḥ. labhdo me jāmātā!» iti.

36.10 Yena svaṃ niveśanaṃ ten' ôpasaṃkrāntaḥ. upasaṃkramya patnīm āmantrayate, «yat khalu, bhadre, jānīyā labdho me duhitur jāmātā. alaṃkuruṣv' Ânupamāṃ dadāmi» iti.

Sā kathayati, «kasya prayacchasi» iti.

Sa kathayati, «śramaṇasya Gautamasya» iti.

Then, after passing the night, in the morning he dressed himself, took up his outer robe and bowl and went into Kalmásha·damya for alms. He completed his alms-round in Kalmásha·damya, ate his meal and put away his alms-bowl. Having put away his robe and bowl, he washed his feet, then seated himself at the foot of a tree and assumed a cross-legged posture, limbs arranged like the piled-up coils of a sleeping serpent-king.

Just then the wanderer Makándika came along, looking for flowers and firewood. From quite a distance the wanderer Makándika caught sight of the Lord, seated in a cross-legged posture at the foot of the tree, limbs arranged like the piled-up coils of a sleeping serpent-king, handsome, exceedingly good-looking, senses quiescent, thought quiescent, possessed of perfect mental tranquility, and shining brightly like a golden sacrificial pillar. Makándika looked at him once more, and joy and delight arose in his mind.

He reflected, "O! How handsome and good-looking is this ascetic! His beauty would captivate anyone! A suitable husband is hard to find for any woman, how much more so for Anúpama. I've found a son-in-law!"

Then he returned home and, having returned, declared 36.10
to his wife, "Allow me to inform you, dear, that I have found a husband for our daughter! Dress her in her finery. I am going to give Anúpama in marriage!"

His wife said, "To whom will you give her?"

He replied, "To the ascetic Gáutama."

Sā kathayati, «gacchāvas tāvat paśyāvaḥ» iti. Mākandikas tayā sārdhaṃ gataḥ. dūrāt tayā dṛṣṭaḥ. tasyā antar|mārge smṛtir upapannā, gāthāṃ bhāṣate:

Dṛṣṭo mayā, vipra, sa piṇḍa|hetoḥ
  Kalmāṣa|damye vicaran maha'|rṣiḥ.
bhū|ratna|bhā|saṃtatir asti tasya
  pragacchato 'tyunnamate na c' âiva.
n' âsau bhartā bhajate kumārikām.
  nivarta! yāsyāmaḥ svaṃ niveśanam.

36.15 So 'pi gāthāṃ bhāṣate:

Amaṅgale Sākalike!
  tvaṃ māṅgalya|kāle vadase hy amaṅgalam!
saced drutaṃ samadhikṛtaṃ
  bhaviṣyati punar apy asau kāma|guṇeṣu raṃsyate.

iti.

S" Ânupamāṃ vastr'|âlaṃkārair alaṃkṛtya, saṃprasthitā. Bhagavān api tasmād vana|ṣaṇḍād anya|vana|ṣaṇḍaṃ saṃprasthitaḥ. adrākṣīn Mākandikaḥ parivrājako Bhagavantaṃ tṛṇa|saṃstaraṇakam. dṛṣṭvā ca, punaḥ patnīm āmantrayate, «yat khalu, bhavati, jānīyā eṣa te duhitus tṛṇa|saṃstaraṇakaḥ» iti.

Sā gāthāṃ bhāṣate:

She returned, "Let's go take a look at him." So Makándika set off with her. Sákali caught sight of the Buddha from a distance and there, in the middle of the road, the memory came to her and she spoke these verses:

O brahmin, I saw that great sage in Kalmásha·damya,
Making his alms-round.
Being the jewel-on-earth, he leaves a trail of radiance where he walks,
And it is ever perfectly level.
That one is no husband who will love our daughter.
Turn back! Let's go home.

As for Makándika, he spoke this verse: 36.15

Inauspicious Sákalika!
On such an auspicious occasion you speak so inauspiciously!
If he can quickly be made irresolute,
Then he will once again desire sensual pleasures.

Sákali dressed Anúpama in fine garments and ornaments and then set out. As for the Lord, he had moved from one thicket of trees to another. The wanderer Makándika saw the Lord strewing grass to make a bed and, seeing that, he again declared to his wife, "Allow me to inform you, my lady, that this one is strewing grass to make a bed for your daughter."

She spoke these verses:

Raktasya śayyā bhavati vikopitā,
dviṣṭasya śayyā sahasā nipīḍitā.
mūḍhasya śayyā khalu pādato gatā,
suvīta|rāgeṇa nisevitā nv iyam.
n' âsau bhartā bhajate kumārikām.
nivarta! yāsyāmaḥ svaṃ niveśanam.
36.20 Amaṅgale Sākalike!
tvaṃ māṅgalya|kāle vadase hy amaṅgalam!
saced drutaṃ samadhikṛtaṃ
bhaviṣyati punar apy asau kāma|guṇeṣu raṃsyate.
iti.

Adrākṣīn Mākandikaḥ parivrājako Bhagavataḥ padāni dṛṣṭvā, punaḥ patnīm āmantrayate: «imāni te bhavanti, bhadre, duhitur jāmātuḥ padāni.»

Gāthāṃ bhāṣate:

Raktasya puṃsaḥ padam utpaṭaṃ syāt,
nipīḍitaṃ dveṣa|vataḥ padaṃ ca.
padaṃ hi mūḍhasya visṛṣṭa|dehaṃ
suvīta|rāgasya padaṃ tv ih' êdṛśam.
n' âsau bhartā bhajate kumārikām.
nivarta! yāsyāmaḥ svaṃ niveśanam.
Amaṅgale Sākalike!
tvaṃ māṅgalya|kāle vadase hy amaṅgalam!
saced drutaṃ samadhikṛtaṃ
bhaviṣyati punar apy asau kāma|guṇeṣu raṃsyate.
iti.

An impassioned man's bed is in disarray;
That of a man inclined to hatred, violently pressed down;
A deluded man's bed is arranged backward,
But this bed is used by a dispassionate man.
That one is no husband who will love our daughter.
Turn back! We're going home.
Inauspicious Sákalika! 36.20
On such an auspicious occasion you speak so inauspiciously!
If he can quickly be made irresolute,
Then he will once again desire sensual pleasures.

The wanderer Makándika looked. He saw the Lord's footprints and again addressed his wife: "These, my dear, are the footprints of your daughter's future husband."

In reply, she spoke this verse:

An impassioned man's footprint is almost effaced;
That of one subject to hatred, deeply imprinted;
A deluded man's footprint has a splayed-out shape,
But a footprint like the one here belongs to one
Who is completely free from the passions.
This is not a husband who will love our daughter.
Turn back! We're going home!
Inauspicious Sákalika!
On such an auspicious occasion you speak so inauspiciously!
If he can quickly be made irresolute,
Then he will once again desire sensual pleasures.

36.25 Bhagavat"|ôtkāśa|śabdaḥ kṛtaḥ. aśrauṣīn Mākandikaḥ parivrājako Bhagavata utkāśana|śabdaṃ śuśrāva. śrutvā ca, punaḥ punaḥ patnīm āmantrayate: «eṣa te bhavati duhitur jāmātur utkāśana|śabdaḥ» iti.

Sā gāthāṃ bhāṣate:

Rakto naro bhavati hi gadgada|svaraḥ;
dviṣṭo naro bhavati hi khakkhaṭā|svaraḥ.
mūḍho naro hi bhavati samākula|khara
Buddho hy ayaṃ brāhmaṇa|dundubhi|svaraḥ.
n' âsau bhartā bhajate kumārikām.
nivarta! yāsyāmaḥ svaṃ niveśanam.
Amaṅgale Sākalike!
tvaṃ māṅgalya|kāle vadase hy amaṅgalam!
saced drutaṃ samadhikṛtaṃ
bhaviṣyati punar apy asau kāma|guṇeṣu raṃsyate.

iti.

Bhagavatā Mākandikaḥ parivrājako dūrād avalokitaḥ. adrākṣīn Mākandikaḥ parivrājako Bhagavantam avalokayantam, dṛṣṭvā ca, punaḥ patnīm āmantrayate sma, «eṣa te bhavati duhitur jāmātā nirīkṣate» iti.

36.30 Sā gāthāṃ bhāṣate:

Rakto naro bhavati hi cañcal'|ēkṣaṇaḥ,
dviṣṭo bhujaga|ghora|viṣo yath" ēkṣate.
mūḍho naraḥ saṃtamas' îva paśyati,
dvija, vīta|rāgo yuga|mātra|darśī.
na eṣa bhartā bhajate kumārikām.

The Lord spoke aloud. The wanderer Makándika, listening, heard the Lord speak aloud and, hearing him do so, announced to his wife repeatedly, "This, my lady, is our daughter's future husband speaking aloud." 36.25

Sákali spoke this verse:

An impassioned man has a stammering voice,
That of one subject to hatred is harsh;
A deluded man's voice is greatly agitated,
But this man is an Awakened One,
With a voice like a brahmin's kettledrum.
This one is no husband who will love our daughter.
Turn back! We're going home.
Inauspicious Sákalika!
On such an auspicious occasion you speak so inauspiciously!
If he can quickly be made irresolute,
Then he will once again desire sensual pleasures.

The Lord regarded the ascetic Makándika from a distance. The ascetic Makándika saw the Lord regarding him from a distance and, seeing him so doing, again called to his wife, "That one, my dear, who is looking me over—he is the husband for our daughter."

Sákali pronounced these verses: 36.30

An impassioned man's eyes dart back and forth;
One subject to hatred stares as if having imbibed virulent snake venom.
A deluded man appears as if staring into darkness,
O twice-born, but the gaze of this passionless one is directed a yoke's length in front of him.

nivarta! yāsyāmaḥ svakaṃ niveśanam.
Amaṅgale Sākalike!
tvaṃ māṅgalya|kāle vadase hy amaṅgalam!
saced drutaṃ samadhikṛtaṃ
bhaviṣyati punar apy asau kāma|guṇeṣu raṃsyate.
iti.

Bhagavāṃś caṅkramyate. adrākṣīn Mākandikaḥ parivrājako Bhagavantaṃ caṅkramyamānaṃ dṛṣṭvā ca, punaḥ patnīm āmantrayate, «eṣa duhitur jāmātā caṅkramyate» iti. Sā gāthāṃ bhāṣate:

36.35 Yath" âsya netre ca yath" âvalokitaṃ
yath" âsya kāle sthitir eva gacchataḥ,
yath" âiva padmaṃ stimite jale 'sya
netraṃ viśiṣṭe vadane virājate,
na eṣa bhartā bhajate kumārikām.
nivarta! yāsyāmaḥ svakaṃ niveśanam.
Amaṅgale Sākalike!
tvaṃ māṅgalya|kāle vadase hy amaṅgalam!
saced drutaṃ samadhikṛtaṃ
bhaviṣyati punar apy asau kāma|guṇeṣu raṃsyate.
iti.

This is no husband who will love our daughter.
Turn back! We're going home!
Inauspicious Sákalika!
On such an auspicious occasion you speak so inauspiciously!
If he can quickly be made irresolute,
Then he will once again desire sensual pleasures.

The Lord began walking up and down. The ascetic Makándika saw the Lord walking up and down and, seeing him so doing, once again called to his wife: "This one walking up and down is the husband for our daughter."

Sákali pronounced this verse:

From his eyes and his gaze, 36.35
From his staying still and moving only at the right time,
From the way his eyes shine
In his distinguished countenance like a lotus in still water,
I can see this one is no husband who will love our daughter.
Turn back! We're going home.
Inauspicious Sákalika!
On such an auspicious occasion you speak so inauspiciously!
If he can quickly be made irresolute,
Then he will once again desire sensual pleasures.

Vaśiṣṭh'|Ôśīra|Mauna|Lāyanā
apatya|hetor atat|kāma|mohitāḥ.
dharmo munīnāṃ hi sanātano hy ayam
apatyam utpāditavān sanātanaḥ.

Atha Mākandikaḥ parivrājako yena Bhagavāṃs ten' ôpasaṃkrāntaḥ. upasaṃkramya, Bhagavantam idam avocat:

Imāṃ Bhagavān paśyatu me sutāṃ
satīṃ rūp'|ôpapannāṃ pramadām alaṃkṛtām.
kām'|ârthinīṃ yad bhavate pradīyate
sah' ânayā sādhur iv' ācaratāṃ bhavān,
sametya candro nabhas' îva Rohiṇīm.

36.40 Bhagavān saṃlakṣayati, «yady aham Anupamāyā anunaya|vacanaṃ brūyām, sthānam etad vidyate, yad Anupamā rāgeṇa svinnā kālaṃ kurvāṇā bhaviṣyati. tat tasyāḥ pratigha|vacanaṃ brūyām» iti viditvā, gāthāṃ bhāṣate:

Dṛṣṭā mayā Māra|sutā hi, vipra,
tṛṣṇā na me n' âpi tathā ratiś ca.
chando na me kāma|guṇeṣu kaś cit:
tasmād imāṃ mūtra|purīṣa|pūrṇāṃ
spraṣṭuṃ hi padbhyām api n' ôtsaheyam.

Mākandiko gāthāṃ bhāṣate:

Sutām imāṃ paśyasi kiṃ madīyāṃ
hīn'|âṅginīṃ rūpa|guṇair viyuktām?
chandaṃ na yen' âtra karoṣi cārau
vivikta|bhāveṣv iva kāma|bhogī? iti

Vasíshtha, Úshira, Mauna and Láyana,
For the sake of offspring, were deluded by desire.
For the law of the sages is eternal—indeed,
That eternal law has caused me
To produce this child, Anúpama.

Then the ascetic Makándika approached the Lord and, having approached, said this to the Lord:

May the Lord behold my virtuous daughter,
A beautiful and shapely young woman beautifully adorned.
Since I give this amorous girl to you,
Live with her like a true sage,
Like the moon in the sky with Róhini.

The Lord reflected, "If I speak conciliatory words to An- 36.40
úpama, what will happen is that she will die, sweating with passion. Therefore I shall speak repellent words to her," and, so thinking, he pronounced this verse:

Even when I beheld Mara's daughters, O brahmin,
I felt neither craving nor sexual desire.
I have no desire whatever for sensual pleasures:
Therefore this girl, filled with urine and excrement,
I could not bear to touch even with my foot.

Makándika spoke this verse:

Do you regard this daughter of mine as ill-formed,
As without the qualities of beauty?
Thus you feel no desire for this lovely girl,
As a sensualist feels none for those bereft of strong emotion?

Bhagavān api gāthāṃ bhāṣate:

36.45 Yasmād ih' ârthī viṣayeṣu mūḍhaḥ,
sa prārthayet, vipra, sutāṃ tav' êmām;
rūp'|ôpapannāṃ viṣayeṣu saktām
avīta|rāgo 'tra janaḥ pramūḍhaḥ.
Ahaṃ tu Buddhaḥ, muni|sattamaḥ, kṛtī
prāptā mayā bodhir anuttarā śivā.
padmaṃ yathā vāri|kaṇair aliptam,
carāmi loke 'nupalipta eva.
Nīl'|âmbujāṃ kardama|vāri|madhye
yathā ca paṅkena ca n' ôpaliptam,
tathā hy ahaṃ, brāhmaṇa, loka|madhye
carāmi kāmeṣu vivikta eva. iti

Ath' Ânupamā, Bhagavatā mūtra|purīṣa|vādena samudācaritā, vigata|harṣā durmanāḥ saṃvṛttā. tasyā yad rāga|paryavasthānam, tad vigatam, dveṣa|paryavasthānam utpannam, sthūlībhūt'|ārya|sphītik'|âvarībhūt'|ēkṣiṇī.

Tena sa khalu samayen' ânyatamo mahallo Bhagavataḥ pṛṣṭhataḥ sthito 'bhūt. atha mahallo Bhagavantam idam avocat:

36.50 Samanta|dṛṣṭe, pratigṛhya nārīm
asmat|sametām, Bhagavan, prayaccha!
ratā vayaṃ hi, pramadām alaṃkṛtāṃ
bhokṣyāmahe, dhīra, yath"|ânulomam. iti

The Lord replied with these verses:

O brahmin, a deluded man, intent on objects of sense, 36.45
Would in these circumstances desire this daughter of yours;
Such a deluded fellow, who is not free from passion,
Would desire a beautiful girl who is attached to objects of sense.
But I am an Awakened One, supreme among sages, who has done the work
And attained Awakening, the felicity supreme.
Just as a lotus is not sullied by droplets of water,
So I wander in the world, completely undefiled.
And just as a blue lotus growing in muddy water
Remains unsullied by the mud,
So I, O brahmin, live in this world,
Utterly untouched by sensual desires.

At that, Anúpama, whom the Lord had described using the words "urine and excrement," lost all her joy and became depressed. Passion lost its hold over her, hatred replaced it, and her eyes, wide open and staring, glazed over.

Just then a certain aged monk was standing behind the Lord. That aged monk said this to the Lord:

O all-seeing one, accept this woman 36.50
Whom we have encountered, and give her, O Lord, to me!
For I am lustful;
Let me enjoy this beautiful wench, O wise one, as I please.

Evam ukte, Bhagavāṃs taṃ mahallam idam avocat: «apehi, puruṣa, mā me puratas tiṣṭha» iti. sa ruṣito gāthāṃ bhāṣate:

Idaṃ ca te pātram idaṃ ca cīvaraṃ
  yaṣṭiś ca kuṇḍī ca—vrajantu niṣṭhām!
imāṃ ca śikṣāṃ svayam eva dhāraya,
  dhātrī yathā hy aṅka|gataṃ kumārakam! iti

Evam ukte, sa mahallaḥ śikṣāṃ pratyākhyāya, «mahān anāryo 'yam» iti matvā, yena Mākandikaḥ parivrājakas ten' ôpasaṃkrāntaḥ. upasaṃkramya Mākandikaṃ parivrājakam idam avocat: «anuprayaccha mam' ântike 'nupamām» iti.

Sa paryavasthitaḥ kathayati, «mahalla, draṣṭum api te na prayacchāmi, prāg eva spraṣṭum!» iti. evam uktasya Mākandikasya parivrājakasy' ântike tādṛśaṃ paryavasthānam utpannaṃ yen' ôṣṇaṃ śoṇitaṃ chardayitvā, kāla|gataḥ, narakeṣ' ûpapannaḥ.

36.55 Tato bhikṣavaḥ, saṃśaya | jātāḥ, sarva | saṃśaya | chettāraṃ Buddhaṃ Bhagavantaṃ papracchuḥ, «paśya, Bhadanta, Bhagavat" ôpamā labhyamānā na pratigṛhītā» iti.

Bhagavān āha, «na, bhikṣavaḥ, etarhi yath" âtīte 'py adhvany eṣā mayā labhyamānā, na pratigṛhītā. tac chrūyatām. . .

Bhūta|pūrvam, bhikṣavo 'nyatamasmin karvaṭake, ayas|kāraḥ prativasati. tena sadṛśāt kulāt kalatram ānītam. sa tayā sārdhaṃ krīḍati, ramate, paricārayati. tasya krīḍataḥ, ramamāṇasya, paricārayataḥ, kāl'|ântareṇa patny āpanna|sattvā saṃvṛttā. sāṣṭānāṃ navānāṃ vā māsānām atyayāt, prasūtā.

When addressed thus, the Lord said this to the old monk: "Begone, fellow! Remain not in my presence." Enraged, the old monk pronounced this verse:

This bowl and this robe of yours,
This staff and water pot—to hell with them!
And you can care for your own training,
As a nursemaid cares for a child in her lap!

Having spoken thus, that old monk, repudiating his training, and thinking, "This is just a base fellow," approached the wanderer Makándika, to whom he said, "Give Anúpama to me."

Makándika, incensed, replied, "Old monk, I wouldn't give her to you even to look at, much less to touch." When addressed in this way by the wanderer Makándika, right before him the old monk's intense emotions rose up such that he vomited hot blood, died and was reborn in the hells.

At that, their doubts arisen, the monks questioned the 36.55
Lord Buddha, who resolves all doubts: "Look now, Venerable sir, although she was given to you, you did not accept Anúpama."

Said the Lord, "Not only now, monks, but also in previous births, I was given, but did not accept her. Listen to this. . . .

In a previous existence, monks, in a certain small village, there dwelled a blacksmith. He married a woman from a family similar to his own. He enjoyed himself with her, made love to her and otherwise dallied with her. As he thus enjoyed himself with her, made love to her and dallied with her, his wife became pregnant. After the passage of eight

duhitā jātā, abhirūpā, darśanīyā, prāsādikā. unnītā, vardhitā mahatī saṃvṛttā. ayas|kāraḥ saṃlakṣayati, ‹may" âiṣā duhitā na kasya cit kulena dātavyā, na rūpena, na dhanena, api tu yo mama śilpena samo 'bhyadhiko vā—tasy' âham enāṃ dāsyāmi› iti.

Yāvad anyatamo māṇavo bhikṣ'|ârthī, tasya gṛhaṃ praviṣṭaḥ. sā dārikā, bhaikṣam ādāya, nirgatā. sa māṇavaḥ, tāṃ dṛṣṭvā, kathayati, ‹dārike, tvaṃ kasya cid datt" āhosvin na dattā?› iti.

Sā kathayati, ‹yadā jāt" âham, tad" âiva mat|pit" âiv' âṅgī|kṛtya vadati. duṣ|karam asau māṃ kasya cid dāsyati.›

36.60 ‹Kiṃ tava pitā vadati?›

‹Yo mama śilpena samo 'bhyadhiko v" âsy' âham enāṃ dāsyāmi› iti.

‹Tava pitā, kīdṛśaṃ śilpaṃ jānīte?›

‹Sūcīm īdṛśāṃ karoti yāvad udake plavate.›

Sa māṇavaḥ saṃlakṣayati, ‹kiṃ c' âpy aham anay" ânarthī, mad'|âpanayo 'sya kartavyaḥ› iti.

36.65 Kuśalo 'sau teṣu teṣu śilpa|sthāna|karma|sthāneṣu. ten' âyas|kāra|bhāṇḍikāṃ yācitv" ânyatra gṛhe, su|sūkṣmāḥ sūcyo ghaṭitā yā udake plavante. ekā ca mahatī ghaṭitā yasyāṃ sapta sūcyaḥ pratikṣiptāḥ, saha tayā plavante. sa tāḥ kṛtvā, tasy' âyas|kārasya gṛham āgataḥ. sa kathayati, ‹sūcyaḥ! sūcyaḥ!› iti.

or nine months, she gave birth. It was a daughter. She was well formed, good-looking, a lovely girl. Nurtured, she grew up and reached maturity. The blacksmith reflected, 'I shall not marry my daughter to anyone on account of his family, good looks nor even wealth, but only to a man who is my equal or superior in my own craft—to such a one will I marry her.'

Just then a certain young man seeking alms entered the blacksmith's house. The girl came out, bringing food. The young man saw her and said, 'Girl, have you been given in marriage to someone or have you not?'

She replied, 'When I was born, at that very time my father made a promise that set difficult conditions for giving me in marriage to anyone.'

'What did your father say?' 36.60

'He who is my equal or superior in my own craft—to him I shall give her in marriage.'

'Your father, what craft does he know?'

'He fashions needles such that they float on water.'

The young man reflected, 'I'm certainly not interested in her, but someone should strike a blow to his pride.'

Now, this fellow was skilled in all manner of crafts and 36.65
trades. He then asked for some blacksmith's tools at another house and fashioned some very fine needles that floated on water. He also fashioned one very large needle into which he inserted seven needles that, all together, floated. After fashioning all the needles, he returned to the blacksmith's house, calling out, 'Needles! Needles!'

Tayā dārikayā dṛṣṭaḥ. sā gāthāṃ bhāṣate:

Unmattakas tvaṃ kaṭuko 'tha v" âsy acetanaḥ,
ayas|kāra|gṛhe yas tvaṃ sūcīṃ vikretum āgataḥ. iti

So 'pi gāthāṃ bhāṣate:

N' âham unmattako v" âsmi kaṭuko 'ham acetanaḥ.
mān'|âvatāraṇ'|ârthaṃ tu mayā śilpaṃ pradṛśyate.
Sacet pitā te jānīyāc chilpaṃ mama hi yādṛśam,
tvāṃ c' âiv' ânuprayaccheta anyac ca vipulaṃ dhanam.
iti

Sā kathayati, ‹kīdṛśaṃ tvaṃ śilpaṃ jānīṣe?›
‹Īdṛśāṃ sūcīṃ karomi y" ôdake plavate.›
Tayā mātur niveditam, ‹amba, śilpa|karm' âtr'|âgataḥ› iti.
Sā kathayati, ‹praveśaya› iti. tayā praveśitaḥ.
Ayas|kāra|bhāryā kathayati, ‹kīdṛśaṃ tvaṃ śilpaṃ jānīṣe?› tena samākhyātam. tayā svāmine niveditaḥ, ‹ārya|putra, ayaṃ śilpa|dārakaḥ. īdṛśaṃ jānīte› iti.

Sa kathayati, ‹yady evam, ānaya pānīyam—paśyāmi› iti. tayā pānīyasya bhājanaṃ pūrayitv" ôpanāmitam. ten' âikā sūcī prakṣiptā. sā plotum ārabdhā. evaṃ dvitīyā, tṛtīyā. tataḥ sā mahatī sūcī prakṣiptā. s" âpi plotum ārabdhā. punas tasyām ekā sūcī prakṣiptā. tath" âpi plotum ārabdhā. evaṃ dvitīyām, tṛtīyām, yāvat sapta|sūcīṃ prakṣipya, prakṣiptās tath" âpi plotum ārabdhāḥ.

The blacksmith's daughter saw him and pronounced this verse:

You're either crazy, impetuous or completely brainless,
You who come to sell needles at a blacksmith's house.

As for that young man, he pronounced these verses:

I'm neither crazy nor impetuous nor brainless,
But to quell your father's pride, I display my craft.
If your father knew the extent of my skill, 36.70
He'd give you to me and much wealth besides.

Replied she, 'What craft do you know?'

'I can fashion a needle such that it floats on water.'

She informed her mother, 'Mummy, a craftsman has come.'

Her mother replied, 'Show him in.' The girl showed him in.

The blacksmith's wife said, 'What craft do you know?' 36.75
He explained. She told her husband, 'Arya·putra, this fellow is a craftsman. He knows such-and-such a craft.'

Her husband said, 'If that's the case, bring water—I shall see.' She filled a container with water and placed it before him. The young man threw in a needle. It floated. And so with a second and third needle. Then he threw in the very large needle. It floated, too. Then he inserted one needle into that large needle. It floated, just as before. And so, having inserted two, three, as many as seven needles into it, he threw it in the water and, just as before, it floated.

Ayas|kāraḥ saṃlakṣayati, ‹mam' âiṣo 'dhikataraḥ śilpena! asmai duhitaram anuprayacchāmi› iti viditvā, tāṃ dārikāṃ sarv'|âlaṃkāra|vibhūṣitāṃ kṛtvā, vāmena pāṇinā gṛhītvā, dakṣiṇena pāṇinā bhṛṅgārakam ādāya, māṇavasya purataḥ sthitvā, kathayati, ‹imāṃ te 'ham, māṇavaka, duhitaram anuprayacchāmi bhāry"|ârthāya› iti.

Sa kathayati, ‹n' âham anay" ârthī, kiṃ tu tav' âiva mad'|âpanayaḥ kartavyaḥ, iti mayā śilpam upadarśitam› iti.»

Bhagavān āha, «kiṃ manyadhve, bhikṣavaḥ, yo 'sau māṇavaḥ? aham eva sa tena kālena tena samayena. yo 'sāv ayas|kāraḥ? eṣa eva Mākandikas tena kālena tena samayena. y" âsāv ayas|kāra|bhāryā? eṣ" âiv' âsau Mākandika|bhāryā tena kālena tena samayena. y" âsāv ayas|kāra|duhitā? eṣ" âiv' âsāv Anupamā tena kālena tena samayena. tad" âpy eṣā mayā labhyamānā, na pratigṛhītā. etarhy apy eṣā mayā labhyamānā, na pratigṛhītā.»

36.80 Punar api, bhikṣavaḥ, saṃśaya|jātāḥ, sarva|saṃśaya|chettāraṃ Buddhaṃ Bhagavantaṃ papracchuḥ, «paśya, Bhadanta, ayaṃ mahallako 'nupamām āgamya, anayena vyasanam āpannaḥ» iti.

Bhagavān āha, «na, bhikṣavaḥ, etarhi yath" âtīt' apy adhvany eṣo 'nupamām āgamya, s'|ântaḥ|puro 'nayena vyasanam āpannaḥ. tac chrūyatām. . .

The blacksmith reflected, 'This fellow is a better craftsman than I! I'll give him my daughter in marriage.' Once he decided this, he had his daughter adorned with all her jewelry, took her with his left hand and with his right hand picked up a pitcher. He stood before the young man and said, 'This daugher of mine, young man, I give you to be your wife.'

The young man replied, 'I've no use for her, but someone had to strike a blow to your pride, so I displayed my craft to you.'"

The Lord said, "Now, monks, who do you think that young man was? It was I who was he at that very time. And he who was that blacksmith? It was this very Makándika who was him at that time. And she who was the blacksmith's wife? It was this very wife of Makándika who was she at that time. And she who was the blacksmith's daughter? It was this very Anúpama who was her at that time. Even then I did not accept Anúpama, although she was given to me. Even now, in this life, I did not accept her, although she was given to me."

Again, their doubts arisen, the monks questioned the 36.80
Lord Buddha, who resolves all doubts: "Look, now, Venerable sir, that old monk made improper advances to Anúpama and, because of such conduct, fell into perdition."

Said the Lord, "Not only on this occasion did that old monk make improper advances to Anúpama, but also in a previous birth did he make improper advances to Anúpama and fall into perdition, together with his other wives. Listen to this. . .

Bhūta|pūrvam, bhikṣavaḥ, Siṃha|kalpāyām, Siṃha|kesarī nāma rājā rājyaṃ kārayati, ṛddhaṃ ca, sphītaṃ ca, kṣemaṃ ca, subhikṣaṃ ca, ākīrṇa|bahu|jana|manuṣyaṃ ca, praśānta|kali|kalaha|ḍimba|ḍamaram, taskara|rog'|âpagatam, śāl'|îkṣu|go|mahiṣī|saṃpannam—akhilam akaṇṭakam. dhārmikaḥ, dharma|rājo dharmeṇa rājyaṃ kārayati.

Tena khalu samayena, Siṃha|kalpāyām, Siṃhako nāma sārtha|vāhaḥ prativasati, āḍhyaḥ, Mahādhanaḥ, mahā|bhogaḥ, vistīrṇa|viśāla|parigraho Vaiśravaṇa|dhana|samudito Vaiśravaṇa|dhana|pratispardhī.

Tena sadṛśāt kulāt kalatram ānītam. s" āpanna|sattvā saṃvṛttā. na c' âsyāḥ kiṃ cid amanojña|śabda|śravaṇaṃ yāvad garbhasya paripākāya. sā, aṣṭānāṃ vā navānāṃ vā māsānām atyayāt, prasūtā. dārako jāto 'bhirūpaḥ, darśanīyaḥ, prāsādikaḥ, gauraḥ, kanaka|varṇaḥ, chatr'|ākāra|śirāḥ, pralamba|bāhuḥ, vistīrṇa|lalāṭaḥ, ucca|ghoṇaḥ, saṃgata|bhrūḥ, tuṅga|nāsaḥ, sarv'|âṅga|pratyaṅg'|ôpetaḥ.

36.85 Tasya trīṇi saptakāni, eka|viṃśati divasān, vistareṇa tasya jātasya jāti|mahaṃ kṛtvā, nāma|dheyaṃ vyavasthāpyate: ‹kiṃ bhavatu dārakasya nāma?› iti.

Jñātaya ūcuḥ, ‹ayaṃ dārakaḥ Siṃhasya sārtha|vāhasya putraḥ: bhavatu «Siṃhalaḥ» iti.› nāma tasya Siṃhala iti nāma|dheyaṃ vyavasthāpitam.

In a previous existence, monks, in the city of Simha·kalpa, a king by the name of Simha·késarin, 'Lion Mane,' ruled his kingdom, which was prosperous, thriving, peaceful, endowed with an abundance of food, densely populated, free from riots, fighting, battle and war as well as from thieves and disease, and rich in rice, sugarcane, cattle and water buffalo—entirely without troubles. Being righteous, that righteous king ruled justly.

In Simha·kalpa at that time, there also lived a caravan-leader by the name of Símhaka. He was wealthy, having a great deal of money and other possessions. His properties were extensive and had produced enormous wealth. Indeed, his wealth rivalled that of Vaishrávana, the God of Wealth, himself.

Símhaka took a wife from a family similar to his own. She conceived and no sounds she heard were displeasing to her ears until she was ready to deliver. After the passage of eight or nine months, she gave birth. It was a boy. He was well formed, good-looking, handsome, with a pale golden complexion, a head shaped like a royal parasol, long arms, a broad forehead and a prominent nose, eyebrows that joined and sound in all his limbs.

After three weeks, that is, twenty-one days, Símhaka con- 36.85
ducted the full birth-ceremony for the newborn and, after having done so, settled upon his son a name: 'What name shall this boy be given?'

His relatives said, 'This boy is the son of the caravan-leader Simha: therefore let him be given the name Símhala.' And so he was given the name Símhala.

Siṃhalo dārako 'ṣṭābhyo dhātrībhyo dattaḥ: dvābhyām aṃsa|dhātrībhyām, dvābhyāṃ krīḍanikābhyām, dvābhyāṃ mala|dhātrībhyām, dvābhyāṃ kṣīra|dhātrībhyām. so 'ṣṭābhir dhātrībhir unnīyate vardhyate kṣīreṇa, dadhnā, nava|nītena, sarpiṣā, sarpi|maṇḍen' ânyaiś c' ôttapt'|ôttaptair upakaraṇa|viśeṣaiḥ. āśu vardhate hrada|stham iva paṅka|jam.

Sa, yadā mahān saṃvṛttaḥ, tadā lipyām upanyastaḥ, saṃkhyāyām, gaṇanāyām, mudrāyām, uddhāre, nyāse, nikṣepe, vastu|parīkṣāyām, hasti|parīkṣāyām, aśva|parīkṣāyām, ratna|parīkṣāyām, dāru|parīkṣāyām, vastra|parīkṣāyām, puruṣa|parīkṣāyām, strī|parīkṣāyām. so 'ṣṭāsu parīkṣāsu, ghaṭakaḥ, vācakaḥ, paṇḍitaḥ, paṭu|pracāraḥ saṃvṛttaḥ.

Tasya pitrā trīṇi vāsa|gṛhāṇi māpitāni, haimantikam, graiṣmikam, vārṣikam. trīṇy antaḥ|purāṇi vyavasthāpitāni, jyeṣṭham, madhyam, kanīyasam.

36.90 So 'pareṇa samayena, pitaram āhvayate, ‹tāta, anujānīhi, mahā|samudram avatarāmi› iti.

Sa kathayati, ‹putra, tāvat prabhūtaṃ me dhana|jātam asti, yadi tvaṃ tila|taṇḍula|kulath'|ādi|paribhogena ratnāni me paribhokṣyase, tath" âpi me bhogā na tanutvam, parikṣayam, paryādānaṃ gamiṣyanti. tad, yāvad ahaṃ jīvāmi, tāvat krīḍa, ramasva, paricāraya! mam' âtyayāt, dhanen' ôpārjitaṃ kariṣyasi› iti.

The boy Símhala was given over to the care of eight nurses: two to carry him about, two to play with him, two to bathe him and two as wet nurses. Raised by these eight nurses, who nourished him with milk, clotted milk, fresh butter, clarified butter and its by-products, and other pure and choice foods, the boy Símhala grew rapidly, like a lotus in a deep lake.

When he grew older, Símhala received instruction in letters, arithmetic, accounting, finance, debt-collection and commercial law. He also learned to inspect and assess real estate, elephants, horses, jewels, lumber, textiles and male and female slaves. He became an expounder, an explainer, a scholar, an expert in the evaluation of these eight valuable commodities.

Símhala's father had built for him three mansions, one each for the cool season, the hot season and the rainy season. The women's quarters of the three mansions were designated 'Best,' 'Middling' and 'Lesser.'

On a later occasion, Símhala said to his father, 'Papa, if 36.90
you will permit it, I will cross the great ocean.'

His father said, 'Son, so great is my wealth that, even if, in addition to consuming my rice, sesame and lentils, you were also to enjoy my jewels and other valuables, my wealth will certainly not diminish, wane or be destroyed. Therefore, so long as I am alive, have fun, have a good time, enjoy yourself! After my death, you can acquire wealth on your own.'

Sa bhūyo bhūyaḥ kathayati, ‹tāta, anujānīhi, mahā|samudram avatarāmi› iti.

Sa, ten' âvaśya|nirbandhaṃ jñātvā, uktaḥ, ‹putra, evaṃ kuru, kiṃ tu bhaya|bhairava|sahiṣṇunā te bhavitavyam› iti.

Tena, Siṃha|kalpāyāṃ rāja|dhānyām, ghaṇṭ"|âvaghoṣaṇaṃ kāritaṃ: ‹śṛṇvantu bhavantaḥ Siṃha|kalpā|nivāsino vaṇijaḥ, nānā|deś'|âbhyāgatāś ca! Siṃhala|sārtha|vāho mahā|samudram avatariṣyat' îti. yo yuṣmākam utsahate, Siṃhalena sārtha|vāhena sārdham, aśulken'|âtara|paṇyena, mahā|samudram avatartum, sa mahā|samudra|gamanīyaṃ paṇyaṃ samudānayatu› iti.

36.95 Tataḥ pañcabhir vaṇik|śatair mahā|samudra|gamanīyaṃ paṇyaṃ samudānītam.

Mātā|pitarau, bhṛtyāṃś ca, suhṛt|saṃbandhi|bāndhavān avalokya, divasa|tithi|muhūrta|prayogena, kṛta|kautuka|maṅgala|svasty|ayanaḥ, śakaṭaiḥ, bhāraiḥ, piṭakaiḥ, mūṭaiḥ, uṣṭraiḥ, gobhiḥ, gardabhaiḥ, prabhūtaṃ mahā|samudra|gamanīyaṃ paṇyam ādāya, pañcabhir vaṇik|śataiḥ, sa|parivāraḥ, saṃprasthitaḥ. so 'nupūrveṇa grāma|nagara|nigama|rāṣṭra|rāja|dhānīṣu cañcūryamāṇaḥ, pattanāny avalokayan, samudra|tīram anuprāptaḥ.»

Vistareṇa Rākṣasī|sūtraṃ sarvaṃ vādyam.*

Yet Símhala said repeatedly, 'Papa, if you will permit it, I shall cross the great ocean.'

His father, realizing the degree of his son's pertinacity, said, 'Son, then do so, but you will have to be able to endure fear and terror.'

Then, in the capital, Simha·kalpa, Símhala had the proclamation bell rung: 'Hear ye, gentlemen, merchants living in Simha·kalpa as well as those visiting from various other countries! The caravan-leader Símhala is crossing the great ocean. Whosoever among you dares to cross the great ocean with the caravan-leader Símhala, free from customs duties and freight fees, let him gather together the trade-goods he wishes to take overseas.'

Then five hundred merchants gathered the trade-goods 36.95
they wished to transport across the great ocean.

After taking leave of his mother and father, his servants, friends and relatives, at the appropriate time on the astrologically appropriate day, Símhala performed the rites to ensure a safe journey, packed a great many trade-goods suitable for overseas sale in carts, bales, boxes and baskets, loaded them on camels and oxen and set out, accompanied by the five hundred merchants and his own retinue. Travelling through a succession of villages, towns, districts and royal capitals and surveying the various settlements, he reached the great ocean."

Here the Discourse on the Demons is to be told in its entirety.*

«. . . Sarve te vaṇija, Bālāh'|âśva|rājāt patitāḥ, tābhiś ca rākṣasībhir bhakṣitāḥ. Siṃhalaka ekaḥ, svasti|kṣemābhyām, Jambu|dvīpam anuprāptaḥ.

Siṃhala|bhāryā, yā rākṣasī, sā rākṣasībhir ucyate, ‹bhagini, asmābhiḥ svaka|svakāḥ svāmino bhakṣitāḥ, tvayā svāmī nirvāhitaḥ. yadi tāvat tam ānayiṣyas' îti, evaṃ kuśalam; no cet, tvāṃ bhakṣayāmaḥ!› iti.

36.100 Sā, saṃtrastā, kathayati, ‹yadi yuṣmākaṃ eṣa nirbandhaḥ, māṃ dhariṣyathaḥ, ānayāmi› iti.

Tāḥ kathayanti, ‹śobhanam! evaṃ kuruṣva.› iti.

Sā, parama|bhīṣaṇa|rūpam abhinirmāya, laghu|laghv eva gatvā, Siṃhalasya sārtha|vāhasya purato gatvā sthitā. Siṃhalena sārtha|vāhena niṣkoṣam asiṃ kṛtvā, saṃtrāsit" âpakrāntā.

Yāvan Madhya|deśāt sārtha āgataḥ. sā rākṣasī, sārtha|vāhasya pādayor nipatya, āha, ‹sārtha|vāha, ahaṃ Tāmra|dvīpakasya rājño duhitā. ten' âhaṃ Siṃhala|sārtha|vāhasya bhāry"|ârthaṃ dattā. tasya mahā|samudra|madhy'|âgatasya, makareṇa matsya|jātena, yāna|pātraṃ bhagnam. tena, aham, «amaṅgalā» iti kṛtvā, choritā. tad arhasi taṃ mam' ôpasaṃvarayitum› iti.

‹Ten' âdhivāsitaṃ kṣamāpayāmi!› iti. sa tasya sakāśaṃ gataḥ. viśrambha|kathā|lāpena muhūrtaṃ sthitvā, kathayati, ‹vayasya, rāja|duhit" âsau tvayā pariṇītā—mā tām asthāne parityaja. kṣamasva!› iti.

"... All the merchants fell from Bálaha, the king of horses, and were devoured by the demons. Símhala alone, due to his good fortune and forbearance, reached India.

Símhala's wife, who was also a demon, was addressed by the other demons: 'Sister, each of us has devoured her own husband, but you allowed your husband to escape. If you will now bring him to us, well and good; if not, we shall eat you!'

Terrified, she replied, 'If you insist on this condition, 36.100
spare me and I'll bring him to you.'

The other demons declared, 'Fine! Do so.'

Símhala's wife magically assumed an exceedingly horrific form and, travelling at great speed, appeared before the caravan-leader Símhala. But when the caravan-leader Símhala drew his sword, she became frightened and fled.

Meanwhile, a caravan had arrived from northern India. That demon prostrated herself at the feet of the leader of that caravan and declared, 'O caravan-leader, I am the daughter of the King of Ceylon. My father gave me to the caravan-leader Símhala as his wife. While he was sailing in the middle of the great ocean, his ship was destroyed by a sea monster, a kind of fish. Because of that, he made out that I was inauspicious and cast me away. So please make him accept me again as his wife.'

'I shall make him forgive you and take you back!' That caravan-leader went to see Símhala. After a bit of casual conversation, he said, 'Friend, you married this princess—do not unjustly abandon her. Forgive her!'

36.105 Sa kathayati, ‹vayasya, n' âsau rāja|duhitā Tāmra|dvīpāt—asau rākṣasī!›

‹Atha katham ih' āgatā?› tena vṛttam ārocitam. sa tūṣṇīm avasthitaḥ. Siṃhalaḥ sārtha|vāho 'nukramataḥ sva|gṛham anuprāptaḥ.

S" âpi rākṣasī, svayam atīva|rūpa|yauvana|saṃpanna|mahā|sundarī|mānuṣī|rūpam āsthāya, Siṃhala|sadṛśa|nirviśeṣa|sundaraṃ putraṃ nirmāya, taṃ putram ādāya, Siṃha|kalpāṃ rāja|dhānīm anuprāptā. Siṃhalasya sārtha|vāhasya sva|gṛha|dvāra|mūle 'vasthitā. jana|kāyen' âsau mukha|bimbakena pratyabhijñātaḥ. te kathayanti, ‹bhavantaḥ, jñāyantām ayaṃ dārakaḥ Siṃhalasya sārtha|vāhasya putraḥ› iti.

Rākṣasī kathayati, ‹bhavantaḥ, parijñāto yuṣmābhiḥ! tasy' âiv' âyaṃ putraḥ› iti.

Te kathayanti, ‹bhagini, kuta āgatā, kasya vā duhitā tvam?› iti.

36.110 Sā kathayati, ‹bhavanto 'ham, Tāmra|dvīpa|rājasya duhitā, Siṃhalasya sārtha|vāhasya bhāry"|ârthaṃ dattā. mahā|samudra|madhya|gatasya sārtha|vāhasya, makareṇa matsya|jātena, yāna|pātraṃ bhagnam. ten' âham «amaṅgalā» iti kṛtvā, asthāne choritā . . . kathaṃ cid iha saṃprāptā. kṣudra|putr" âham—arhatha Siṃhalaṃ sārtha|vāhaṃ kṣamayitum!› iti.

Tais tasya mātā|pitror niveditam. sa tābhyām uktaḥ, ‹putra, m" âināṃ tyaja duhitaraṃ rājñaḥ! kṣudra|putr" êyaṃ tapovinī. kṣama!› iti.

Replied Símhala, 'Friend, this is no princess—she's a Ceylonese demon!' 36.105

'Then how did she get here?' Símhala explained what had happened. The merchant remained silent. As for the caravan-leader Símhala, in due course he arrived at his own home.

As for that demoness, she assumed the form of an extraordinarily beautiful, ravishing young woman, then conjured up a 'son,' a handsome child who looked just like Símhala. She took the lad and soon arrived at the royal capital of Simha·kalpa. She waited at the door of the caravan-leader Símhala's own home. A crowd of people recognized the boy by his face. They said, 'Let everyone know that this lad is the son of the caravan-leader Símhala.'

The demon said, 'Gentlemen, you recognize this boy! He is indeed Símhala's son.'

They asked, 'Good lady, from where have you come and whose daughter are you?'

She said, 'Gentlemen, I, daughter of the King of Ceylon, 36.110
was given in marriage to the caravan-leader Símhala. When the caravan-leader was sailing in mid-ocean, his ship was destroyed by a sea monster, a kind of fish. Making out that I was inauspicious, he cast me away . . . somehow I made my way here. I have a small son—please make the caravan-leader Símhala forgive me!'

The people informed Símhala's mother and father, who said to him, 'Son, you must not abandon this princess. She has endured much and has a small son. Forgive her!'

Sa kathayati, ‹tāta, n' âiṣā rāja|duhitā—rākṣasy eṣā Tāmra|dvīpād ih' āgatā!› iti.

Tau kathayataḥ, ‹putra, sarvā eva striyo rākṣasyaḥ. kṣama!› iti.

‹Tāta, yady eṣā yuṣmākam abhipretā, etāṃ gṛhe dhārayata. aham apy anyatra gacchāmi› iti.

36.115 Tau kathayataḥ, ‹putra, sutarāṃ vayam enāṃ tav' âiv' ârthāya dhārayāmaḥ. yady eṣā tava n' âbhipretā, kim asmākam anayā? na dhārayāmaḥ› iti. tābhyāṃ niṣkāsitā.

Sā Siṃha|kesariṇo Rājñaḥ sakāśaṃ gatā. amātyai rājño niveditam, ‹Deva, īdṛśī rūpa|yauvana|saṃpannā strī rāja|dvāre tiṣṭhati› iti.

Rājā kathayati, ‹praveśaya. paśyāmaḥ› iti. sā, taiḥ praveśitā, hāriṇ" îndriyāṇi. rājā, tāṃ dṛṣṭvā, rāgen' ôtkṣiptaḥ. svāgata|vāda|samudācāreṇa tāṃ samudācarya, kathayati, ‹kutaḥ katham atr' āgatā, kasya vā tvam?› iti.

Sā pādayor nipatya, kathayati, ‹Deva, ahaṃ Tāmra|dvīpakasya rājño duhitā, Siṃhalasya sārtha|vāhasya bhāry"|ârthaṃ dattā. tasya mahā|samudra|madhya|gatasya, makareṇa matsya|jātena, yāna|pātraṃ bhagnam. ten' âham «amaṅgalā» iti śrutvā, asthāne choritā. . . kathaṃ cid iha saṃprāptā. kṣudra|putr" âham. tad arhasi, Deva, tam eva Siṃhalaṃ sārtha|vāhaṃ kṣamāpayitum arhasi!›

Tena rājñā samāśvāsitā, amātyānām ājñā dattā: ‹gacchantu bhavantaḥ Siṃhalaṃ sārtha|vāhaṃ śabdayata› iti. tair asau śabditaḥ.

Símhala replied, 'Papa, this is no princess—she's a demon who has come here from Ceylon.'

His parents replied, 'All women are demons. Forgive her!'

'Papa, if you and mother approve of her, then care for her in our home; I shall go live somewhere else.'

Said his parents, 'Son, we would look after her very well, 36.115
but only for your sake. If you don't approve of her, what do we want with her? In that case, we won't take care of her.' And the two of them drove her away.

She then went to King Simha·késarin, whose ministers informed him, 'Your majesty, a beautiful young woman waits at the palace gate.'

Said the king, 'Bring her in. We shall grant her an audience.' The ministers ushered her in and she captivated everyone's senses. Seeing her, the king was overwhelmed by passion. Addressing her with courteous words of welcome, he asked, 'From where and how did you come here? Whose daughter are you?'

She flung herself at the king's feet and said, 'Your majesty, I am the daughter of the King of Ceylon and was given to the caravan-leader Símhala to be his wife. When he was sailing in mid-ocean, a sea monster, a kind of fish, destroyed his ship. Told that I was inauspicious, he cast me away. . . somehow I made my way here. I have a young son. Your majesty, please make the caravan-leader Símhala forgive me!'

The king consoled her and gave this command to his ministers: 'Go, gentlemen, summon the caravan-leader Símhala.' They summoned him.

36.120 Rājā kathayati, ‹Siṃhala, enāṃ rāja|duhitaraṃ dhāraya. kṣamasva!› iti.

Sa kathayati, ‹Deva, n' âiṣā rāja|duhitā—rākṣasy eṣā Tāmra|dvīpād ih' āgatā!› iti.

Rājā kathayati, ‹sārtha|vāha, sarvā eva striyo rākṣasyaḥ! kṣamasva. atha tava n' âbhipretā, mam' ânuprayaccha› iti.

Sārtha|vāhaḥ kathayati, ‹Deva, rākṣasy eṣā! n' âhaṃ dadāmi, na vārayāmi› iti. sā rājñ" ântaḥ|puraṃ praveśitā. tayā rājā vaśī|kṛtaḥ.

Yāvad apareṇa samayena, rājñaḥ s'|ântaḥ|purasy' āsvāpanaṃ dattvā, tāsāṃ rākṣasīnāṃ sakāśaṃ gatvā, kathayati, ‹bhaginyaḥ, kiṃ yuṣmākaṃ Siṃhalena sārtha|vāhena? mayā Siṃha|kesariṇo rājñaḥ s'|ântaḥ|purasy' āsvāpanaṃ dattam. āgacchata! taṃ bhakṣayāma!› iti.

36.125 Tā vikṛta|kara|caraṇa|nāsāḥ parama|bhairavam ātmānam abhinirmāya, rātrau Siṃha|kalpām āgatāḥ. tābhir asau rājā s'|ântaḥ|pura|parivāro bhakṣitaḥ. prabhātāyāṃ rajanyāṃ rāja|dvāraṃ na mucyate. rāja|gṛhasy' ôpariṣṭāt kuṇapa|khādakāḥ pakṣiṇaḥ paribhrāmitum ārabdhāḥ. amātyā bhaṭa|bal'|âgra|naigama|jana|padāś ca rāja|dvāre tiṣṭhanti. eṣa śabdaḥ Siṃha|kalpāyāṃ rāja|dhānyāṃ samantato visṛtaḥ: ‹rāja|dvāraṃ na mucyate! rāja|gṛhasy' ôpariṣṭāt kuṇapa|khādakāḥ pakṣiṇaḥ paribhramanti! amātyā bhaṭa|bal'|âgraṃ naigama|jana|padāś ca rāja|dvāre tiṣṭhanti!› iti.

The king said, 'Símhala, you have to take care of this princess. Forgive her!' 36.120

Símhala replied, 'Your majesty, this is no princess—she's a demon who has come here from Ceylon.'

The king said, 'Caravan-leader, all women are demons! Forgive her. If you don't approve of her, give her to me.'

The caravan-leader declared, 'Your majesty, she's a demon! I won't give her to you nor will I take her for my wife.' But the king admitted her to the royal women's apartments. He had fallen under her power.

Some time later, the demon administered a sleeping potion to the king together with all the palace women, then returned to the other demons and told them, 'Sisters, what use to you is the caravan-leader Símhala? I've given a sleeping potion to King Simha·késarin together with all the palace women. Come! Let us eat them!'

The demons assumed their true, exceedingly terrifying 36.125
forms, with deformed hands, feet and noses, and at night came to Simha·kalpa. They devoured the king together with all the palace women and servants. At dawn, the palace gates were not opened. Carrion-birds began to circle over the royal palace. The ministers and a crowd of townspeople and soldiers stood at the palace gates. The word spread everywhere in the royal capital of Simha·kalpa: 'The palace gates are closed! Carrion-birds are circling over the royal palace! The ministers, the army and a crowd of townspeople are waiting at the palace gates!'

Siṃhalena sārtha|vāhena śrutam. sa tvarita|tvaritaṃ khaḍgam ādāya, gataḥ. sa kathayati, ‹bhavantaḥ, kṣamaṃ cintayata: tayā rākṣasyā rājā khāditaḥ!› iti.

Amātyāḥ kathayanti, ‹katham atra pratipattavyam?› iti.

Sa kathayati, ‹niśrayaṇīm ānayata. paśyāmi› iti. tair ānītā. Siṃhalaḥ sārtha|vāhaḥ, khaḍgam ādāya, nirūḍhaḥ. tena tāḥ saṃtrāsitāḥ. tāsāṃ kāś cidd hasta|pādān ādāya, niṣpalāyitāḥ kāś cic chiraḥ. tataḥ Siṃhalena sārtha|vāhena rāja|kula|dvārāṇi muktāni. amātyai rāja|kulaṃ śodhitam.

Paur'|âmātya|jana|padāḥ, saṃnipatya, kathayanti, ‹bhavantaḥ, rājā s'|ântaḥ|pura|parivāro rākṣasībhir bhakṣitaḥ. kumāro n' âsya—kam atr' âbhiṣiñcāma?› iti.

36.130 Tatr' âike kathayanti, ‹yaḥ sāttvikaḥ prājñaś ca› iti.

Apare kathayanti, ‹Siṃhalāt sārtha|vāhāt ko 'nyaḥ sāttvikaḥ prājñaś ca? Siṃhalaṃ sārtha|vāham abhiṣiñcāma!› iti.

‹Evaṃ kurmaḥ!›

Taiḥ Siṃhalaḥ sārtha|vāha uktaḥ: ‹sārtha|vāha, rājyaṃ pratīccha› iti.

Sa kathayati, ‹ahaṃ vaṇik|saṃvyavahār'|ôpajīvī. kiṃ mama rājyena?› iti.

36.135 Te kathayanti, ‹sārtha|vāha, n' ânyaḥ śaknoti rājyaṃ dhārayitum. pratīccha› iti.

The caravan-leader Símhala heard this. Quickly taking up his sword, he rushed to the palace. He said, 'Gentlemen, consider this carefully: that demon has eaten the king!'

The ministers said, 'What do we do now?'

Símhala replied, 'Bring a ladder. I'll take a look.' They fetched a ladder and the caravan-leader Símhala took his sword and climbed up. The demons were terrified of him. They fled, some of them taking with them half-eaten hands and feet, others heads. Then the caravan-leader Símhala opened the palace gates and the ministers had the palace cleaned up.

The townspeople, the ministers and folk from the country gathered, saying, 'Gentlemen, the king, the palace ladies and their servants have been devoured by demons. The king had no son—in these circumstances whom shall we consecrate as the new king?'

At that, some people called out, 'One who is virtuous 36.130
and wise!'

Others added, 'Who else but the caravan-leader Símhala is so virtuous and wise? Let us consecrate the caravan-leader Símhala!'

'Yes! Let's do that!'

The crowd addressed the caravan-leader Símhala: 'Caravan-leader, please accept the throne.'

He replied, 'I earn my livelihood through trade and commerce. What's kingship got to do with me?'

They said, 'Caravan-leader, no one else is capable of gov- 36.135
erning the kingdom. Please accept.'

Sa kathayati, ‹samayena pratīcchāmi—yadi mama vacan'| ânusāriṇo bhavatha.›

‹Pratīccha! bhavāmaḥ śobhanaṃ te!› tair asau nagara|śobhāṃ kṛtvā, mahatā satkāreṇa, rājye 'bhiṣiktaḥ.

Tena, nānā|deśa|nivāsino vidyā|vādikā āhūya, bhūyasyā mātrayā vidyā śikṣitā, evam iṣv|astr'|ācāryā iṣv|astrāṇi. amātyānāṃ c' ājñā dattā, ‹sajjī|kriyatām, bhavantaḥ, catur|aṅga|bala|kāyam. gacchāmaḥ! tā rākṣasīs Tāmra|dvīpān nirvāsayāmaḥ!› iti

Amātyaiś catur|aṅga|bala|kāyaṃ saṃnāhitam. Siṃhalo Rājā, catur|aṅgād bala|kāyād vara|var'|âṅgān hastino 'śvān, rathān, manuṣyāṃś ca vahaneṣv āropya, Tāmra|dvīpaṃ saṃprasthitaḥ. anupūrveṇa samudra|tīram anuprāptaḥ.

36.140 Tāsāṃ rākṣasīnām āpad|āsthānīyo dhvajaḥ kampitum ārabdhaḥ. tāḥ saṃjalpaṃ kartum ārabdhā: ‹bhavatyaḥ, āpad|āsthānīyo dhvajaḥ kampate. nūnam Jāmbudvīpakā manuṣyāḥ, yuddh'|âbhinandinaḥ, āgatāḥ. samanveṣāmaḥ› iti. tāḥ samudra|tīraṃ gatāḥ. yāvat paśyanty aneka|śatāni yāna|pātrāṇi samudra|tīram anuprāptāni. dṛṣṭvā ca punas tā ardhena pratyudgatāḥ. tato vidyā|dhāribhir āviṣṭāḥ, iṣv|astr'|ācāryaiḥ, saṃpraghātitāḥ. avaśiṣṭā Siṃhalasya Rājñaḥ pādayor nipatya, kathayanti, ‹Deva, kṣamasva!› iti.

Sa kathayati, ‹samayena kṣame—yadi yūyam etan nagaram utkīlayitvā, anyatra gacchatha, na ca mad|vijite kasya cid aparādhyatha› iti.

Replied Símhala, 'I'll accept on one condition—that you will obey my commands.'

'Please accept! We shall obey your commands! Glory to you!' Then the people decorated the city and, amid grand festivities, consecrated Símhala king.

The new king invited professors from various countries and trained intensively, for example, with master archers in archery. Then he commanded his ministers, 'Gentlemen, prepare the four divisions of the army. Let us be off! We'll drive those demons out of Ceylon!'

The ministers prepared the four divisions of the army. King Símhala loaded on boats the best elephants, horses, chariots and men from each of the four divisions of his army and set out for Ceylon. In due course they reached the coast of Ceylon.

The flag* that signals calamity began to flap. The demons 36.140
began talking among themselves: 'Ladies, the flag that signals calamity is flapping. Surely the humans from India are coming, eager for battle. Let's have a look.' They went to the seashore and saw that many hundreds of ships had reached the shore. Seeing that, the demons attacked with half their forces. Overpowered by the master archers, those experts, they were slaughtered. The survivors flung themselves at King Símhala's feet, crying, 'Your majesty, forgive us!'

He said, 'I'll forgive you on one condition—that you leave this city and go elsewhere and that you never again commit an offense against anyone in my kingdom.'

Tāḥ kathayanti, ‹Deva, evaṃ kurmaḥ.›

‹Śobhanam.›

Tan nagaram utkīlayitvā, anyatra gatvā, avasthitāḥ. Siṃhalen' âpi Rājñ" āvāsitam; iti Siṃhala|dvīpaḥ ‹Siṃhaladvīpaḥ› iti saṃjñā saṃvṛttā.

36.145 Kiṃ manyadhve, bhikṣavaḥ? yo 'sau Siṃhalo 'ham eva sa tena kālena, tena samayena. yo 'sau Siṃha|kesarī Rājā, eṣa eva sa mahallas tena kālena, tena samayena. yā sā rākṣasī, eṣ" âiv' Ânupamā tena kālena, tena samayena. tad" âpi, eṣo 'nupamāyā arthe 'nayena vyasanam āpanna—etarhy apy eṣo 'nupamāyā arthe 'nayena vyasanam āpannaḥ.»

Mākandikaḥ parivrājakaḥ, Anupamām ādāya, Kauśāmbīṃ gato 'nyatamasminn udyāne 'vasthitaḥ. udyāna|pālaka|puruṣeṇa Rājña Udayanasya, Vatsa|rājasya, niveditam: «Deva, strī, abhirūpā, darśanīyā, prāsādikā, udyāne tiṣṭhati. Devasy' âiṣā yogyā.»

Iti śrutvā, rājā tad udyānaṃ gataḥ. ten' âsau dṛṣṭā. hāriṇ" îndriyāṇi. saha|darśanād ev' ākṣipta|hṛdayaḥ. tena Mākandikaḥ parivrājaka uktaḥ: «kasy' êyaṃ dārikā?»

Sa āha, «Deva! mad|duhitā, Deva, na kasya cit.»

«Mama kasmān na dīyate?»

36.150 «Deva, dattā bhavatu rājñaḥ.»

They promised, 'Your majesty, we'll do as you say.'

'Good.'

The demons abandoned that city, went to another place and lived there. King Símhala settled the place and in this way Símhala·dvipa, 'Símhala's Island,' received the name by which it is still called.

What do you think, monks? Who was that man Símhala? 36.145
At that time, I was that very man. And that King Simha·késarin? At that time, the old monk was that very man. And that demon? At that time, Anúpama was that very one. Even then, this old monk, because of his improper conduct toward Anúpama, suffered disaster—just as now he suffered disaster on account of his improper conduct toward Anúpama."

The wanderer Makándika took Anúpama and went to Kaushámbi, where he settled in a certain park. The park attendant informed King Udáyana, King of the Vatsas: "Your majesty, there is a woman—shapely, beautiful and lovely—staying in the park. She is worthy of my lord."

Hearing this, the king went to the park. He beheld Anúpama and his senses were captivated. At the mere sight of her, his heart was snatched away. He addressed the wanderer Makándika: "Whose daughter is this girl?"

He said, "Your majesty! She is my daughter, your majesty, no one else's."

"Is there any reason she cannot be given to me?"

"Your majesty, let her be given to the king." 36.150

«Śobhanam!»

Mahā|rājasya bahavaḥ paṇya|pariṇītāḥ. tasya Puṣpa|dantasya pariṇītā. tasyā Puṣpa|dantasya Prāsādasy' ârdhaṃ dattam, pañc'|ôpasthāyikā|śatāni dattāni, pañca ca kārṣāpaṇa|śatāni dine dine gandha|mālya|nimittam. Mākandikaḥ parivrājako 'gr'|âmātyaḥ sthāpitaḥ. tena khalu punaḥ samayen' ^Odayanasya Rājñas trayo 'gr' | âmātyā: Yogāndharāyaṇaḥ, Ghoṣilaḥ, Mākandika iti.

Yāvad apareṇa samayen' Ôdayanasya Rājñaḥ puruṣa upasaṃkrāntaḥ. rājñā pṛṣṭaḥ, «kas tvam?» iti.

Sa kathayati, «Deva, priy'|ākhyāyī» iti.

36.155 Amātyānām ājñā dattā, «bhavantaḥ, prayacchata priy'|ākhyāyino vṛttim» iti. tais tasya vṛttir dattā.

Yāvad aparaḥ puruṣa upasaṃkrāntaḥ. so 'pi rājñā pṛṣṭaḥ, «kas tvam?» iti.

Sa kathayati, «Deva, apriy'|ākhyāyī» iti.

Rājñ" âmātyānām ājñā dattā, «bhavantaḥ, prayacchat' âsy' âpy apriy'|ākhyāyino vṛttim» iti.

Te kathayanti, «mā kadā cid Devo 'priyaṃ śṛṇuyāt.»

36.160 Sa kathayati, «bhavantaḥ, vistīrṇāni rāja|kāryāṇi. prayacchata» iti. tais tasy' âpi vṛttir dattā.

Yāvad apareṇa samayena, Rāj" Ôdayanaḥ, Śyāmāvatī, Anupamā c' âikasmin sthāne tiṣṭhanti. tadā rājñā kṣutaṃ kṛtam.

"Splendid!"

The great king had a great many wives. Anúpama became the wife of the king's Flower-Bower Palace. He made over to her half of the Flower-Bower Palace, five hundred ladies-in-waiting and a daily allowance of five hundred copper coins for fragrant garlands. The wanderer Makándika was appointed a chief minister. At that time, then, King Udáyana had three chief ministers: Yogándharáyana, Ghóshila and Makándika.

On another occasion, a man approached King Udáyana. The king asked him, "Who are you?"

He replied, "Your majesty, I am one who announces glad tidings."

The king commanded his ministers, "Gentlemen, give 36.155
employment to this announcer of glad tidings." They gave him employment.

On yet another occasion, another man approached the king. He, also, was asked by the king, "Who are you?"

The man replied, "I am one who announces ill tidings."

The king commanded his ministers, "Gentlemen, give employment also to this announcer of ill tidings."

Said they, "Never should your majesty listen to ill tidings."

Replied the king, "Gentlemen, a king's duties are many 36.160
and diverse. Give him employment." The ministers gave him employment, too.

Later, on another occasion, King Udáyana, Shyámavati and Anúpama were spending time together in a certain place. Then the king sneezed.

Śyāmāvaty" ôktam, «namo Buddhāya!» iti.

Anupamayā «namo Devasya!» iti. Anupamā kathayati, «Mahā|rāja, Śyāmāvatī Devasya santakaṃ bhaktaṃ bhuṅkte, śramaṇasya Gautamasya namas|kāraṃ karoti» iti.

Rājā kathayati, «Anupame, n' âtra hy evam—Śyāmāvaty upāsikā. avaśyaṃ śramaṇasya Gautamasya namas|kāraṃ karoti» iti. sā tūṣṇīm avasthitā.

36.165 Tasyāḥ preṣya|dārik" ôktā, «dārike, yadā Devaḥ, Śyāmāvatī, ahaṃ ca rahasi tiṣṭhema, tadā tvaṃ sopānake kāṃsikāṃ pātayiṣyasi» iti.

«Evam astu» iti.

Tayā, teṣāṃ rahasy avasthitānām, sopānake kāṃsikā pātitā. Śyāmāvaty" ôktam, «namo Buddhāya» iti.

Anupamā, «namo Devasya» ity uktvā, kathayati, «Devasya santakaṃ bhavatī bhuṅkte, śramaṇasya Gautamasya namas|kāraṃ karoti» iti.

Rājā kathayati, «Anupame, atra mā saṃrambhaṃ kuru. upāsik" âiṣā—n' âtra doṣaḥ» iti.

36.170 Rāj" Ôdayana etasmin divase Śyāmāvatyāḥ sakāśaṃ bhuṅkte, dvitīya|divase 'nupamāyāḥ. rājñā śākunikasy' ājñā dattā, «yasmin divase Śyāmāvatyā bhojana|vāraḥ, tasmin divase jīvantaḥ kapiñjalā ānetavyāḥ» iti. śākunikena jīvantaḥ kapiñjalā rājña upanītāḥ.

Shyámavati exclaimed, "Reverence to the Awakened One!"

Anúpama said, "Reverence to your majesty!" Anúpama continued, "Great king, Shyámavati has long enjoyed your majesty's largesse, yet she offers homage to the ascetic Gáutama."

The king said, "Anúpama, not only here and now does she speak thus—Shyámavati is a lay disciple. She constantly offers homage to the ascetic Gáutama." Anúpama remained silent.

Later, Anúpama told her maidservant, "Girl, when his 36.165
majesty, Shyámavati and I are in private, knock a brass pot down the stairs."

"Very well."

And so, when the three were in private, the maidservant knocked a brass pot down the stairs. Shyámavati declared, "Reverence to the Awakened One!"

Anúpama declared, "Reverence to his majesty," then said, "This lady has long enjoyed your majesty's largesse, yet she offers homage to the ascetic Gáutama."

The king declared, "Anúpama, don't make a fuss about this. Shyámavati is a lay disciple of the Buddha—she commits no fault by speaking so."

Now, King Udáyana was in the habit of dining with 36.170
Shyámavati one day and with Anúpama the next. One day the king commanded the royal fowler: "On the days I dine with Shyámavati, bring live *kapínjala* birds." And so the royal fowler brought the king live *kapínjala* birds.

Rājā kathayati, «Anupamāyāḥ samarpaya» iti. Anupamayā śrutam. sā kathayati, «Deva, na mama vāraḥ; Śyāmāvatyā vāraḥ» iti.

Rājā kathayati, «gaccha, bhoḥ puruṣa, Śyāmāvatyāḥ samarpaya» iti.

Tena Śyāmāvatyāḥ sakāśam upanītaḥ. «Devasy' ârthāya sādhaya» iti.

Sā kathayati, «kim ahaṃ śākunikāyinī? na mama prāṇ'|âtipātaḥ kalpate! gaccha!» iti.

36.175 Tena rājñe gatvā niveditam: «Deva, Śyāmāvatī kathayati, ‹kim ahaṃ śākunikāyinī? na mama prāṇ'|âtipātaḥ kalpate! gaccha!› iti.»

Anupamā, śrutvā, kathayati, «deva, yady asāv ucyate, ‹śramaṇasya Gautamasy' ârthāya sādhaya› iti, sāṃpratam saparivārā sādhayet.»

Rājā saṃlakṣayati, «syād evam.» ten' âsau puruṣa uktaḥ, «gaccha, bhoḥ puruṣa, evaṃ vada, ‹Bhagavato 'rthāya sādhaya› iti.»

Saṃprasthito 'nupamayā pracchannam uktaḥ, «praghātayitvā, ānaya» iti. tena, praghātayitvā, Śyāmāvatyā upanītaḥ. «Devaḥ kathayati, ‹Bhagavato 'rthāya sādhaya› iti.» sā, saparivārā, udyuktā.

Śākunikena, gatvā, rājñe niveditam: «sā, Deva, saparivārā, udyuktā» iti.

36.180 Anupamā kathayati, «śrutaṃ Devena? yadi tāvat prāṇ'|âtipāto na kalpate, śramaṇasy' ârthāya na kalpate, Devasy' âpi na kalpate! ‹Devasya na kalpate.› iti kuta etat?»

"Present them to Anúpama," said the king. Anúpama heard this and said, "Your majesty, it's not my turn; it's Shyámavati's."

Said the king, "Go, my man, present them to Shyámavati."

The fowler brought them to Shyámavati. "Prepare these for the king."

She retorted, "Am I the wife of a fowler? For me taking life is forbidden! Begone!"

The fowler went and informed the king: "Shyámavati 36.175
said, 'Am I the wife of a fowler? For me the taking of life is forbidden! Begone!'"

Hearing this, Anúpama said, "Your majesty, if Shyámavati was told, 'Prepare the birds for the ascetic Gáutama,' she and her retinue would do so at once!"

The king reflected, "That may be so." He addressed the fowler: "Go, my man, and say this to Shyámavati: 'Prepare these birds for the Lord.'"

But after the fowler had left, Anúpama told him secretly, "Kill the birds before bringing them to Shyámavati." He killed them and presented them to Shyámavati, saying, "The king says, 'Prepare these for the Lord.'" Shyámavati and her retinue began preparing the birds.

Meanwhile, the fowler went and informed the king: "Your majesty, Shyámavati and her retinue are preparing the birds."

Anúpama spoke up. "Did your majesty hear that? If in- 36.180
deed, for Shyámavati, taking life is forbidden, it is forbidden on behalf of that ascetic as well as on your majesty's behalf! 'It is forbidden on his majesty's behalf.' How can she say that?"

Rājā, paryavasthitaḥ, dhanuḥ pūrayitvā, saṃprasthitaḥ. mitr'|âmitra|madhyamo lokaḥ. aparayā Śyāmāvatyā niveditam, «Devo 'ty|arthaṃ paryavasthitaḥ, dhanuḥ pūrayitvā, āgacchati! kṣamaya!» iti.

Tayā sv'|ôpaniṣad uktā, «bhaginyaḥ, sarvā yūyaṃ maitrīṃ samāpadyadhvam» iti. tāḥ sarvā maitrī|samāpannāḥ.

Rājñā, ā karṇād dhanuḥ pūrayitvā, śaraḥ kṣiptaḥ. so 'rdha|mārge patitaḥ. dvitīyaḥ kṣiptaḥ. sa, nivartya, rājñaḥ samīpe patitaḥ. tṛtīyaṃ kṣeptum ārabdhaḥ. Śyāmāvatī kathayati, «Deva, mā kṣepsyasi! mā sarveṇa sarvaṃ bhaviṣyati» iti.

Rājā, vinītaḥ, kathayati, «tvaṃ devī, nāgī, yakṣiṇī, gandharvī, kinnarī, mah"|ôragī?» iti.

36.185 Sā kathayati, «na.»

«Atha kā tvam?»

«Bhagavataḥ śrāvikā, Anāgāminī. mayā Bhagavato 'ntika Anagāmi|phalaṃ sākṣāt|kṛtam, ebhiś ca pañcabhiḥ strī|śataiḥ Satyāni dṛṣṭāni» iti.

Rājā, abhiprasannaḥ, kathayati, «varaṃ te 'nuprayacchāmi» iti.

Sā kathayati, «yadi Devo 'bhiprasannaḥ, yadā Devo 'ntaḥ|puraṃ praviśati, tadā mam' ântike Dharm'|ânvayam upasthāpayet» iti.

The king, beside himself with rage, fitted an arrow to his bow and set out. The world is full of friends and foes. A woman told Shyámavati, "His majesty, exceedingly angry and with his bow drawn, is heading this way! Beg his forgiveness!"

Shyámavati addressed her retinue, "Ladies, all of you must enter into the state of boundless amity." They all imbued themselves with boundless amity.

Just then, the king entered, drew the bowstring to his ear and let the arrow fly. In mid-flight, it fell. He loosed a second arrow. It reversed directions and fell near the king. He prepared to shoot a third, when Shyámavati said, "Your majesty, don't shoot! Don't make the next arrow fly back at you all the way!"

The king, now subdued, asked, "Are you a goddess or a divine serpent? Or a demon or a celestial nymph? Or a centaur or a great serpent?"

She replied, "No." 36.185

"Then what are you?"

"A disciple of the Lord Buddha, a Non-Returner. I realized the fruit of a Non-Returner in the Lord's presence while these five hundred women perceived the Truths."

The king, now favorably disposed toward Shyámavati, declared, "I grant you a boon."

Shyámavati replied, "If your majesty is favorably disposed toward me, then whenever he enters the women's apartments may he arrange for me to receive regular instruction in the Dharma."

36.190 Rājā kathayati, «śobhanam! evaṃ bhavatu» iti. so 'nupamāyā Śyāmāvatyā antike Dharm'|ânvayaṃ prasādayati. yāny asya nava|sasyāni nava|phalāni nava'|rtukāni samāpadyante, tāni tat|prathamataḥ Śyāmāvatyāḥ prayacchati.

Īrṣyā | prakṛtir mātṛ | grāmaḥ. Anupamā saṃlakṣayati, «ayaṃ rājā mayā sārdhaṃ rati|krīḍāṃ pratyanubhavati. Śyāmāvatyā navaiḥ phalaiḥ, navaiḥ sasyakaiḥ, nava'|rtukaiḥ kārāṃ karoti. tad|upāya|saṃvidhānaṃ kartavyaṃ yen' âiṣā praghātyata!» iti. sā ca, tasyāḥ praghātanāya, randhr'|ânveṣaṇa|tat|par'|âvasthitā.

Rājñaś c' ânyatamaḥ kārvaṭiko viruddhaḥ. ten' âikaṃ daṇḍa|sthānaṃ preṣitam. tadd hata|prahatam āgatam. evaṃ dvitīyam, tṛtīyam. amātyāḥ kathayanti, «Devasya balaṃ hīyate, kārvaṭikasya balaṃ vardhate. yadi Devaḥ svayam eva na gacchati, sthānam etad vidyate yat sarvath" âsau durdamyo bhaviṣyati.»

Tena Kauśāmbyāṃ ghaṇṭ"|âvaghoṣaṇaṃ kāritam: «yo mama vijite kaś cic chastr'|ôpajīvī prativasati, tena sarveṇa gantavyam» iti. tena saṃprasthitena, Yogāndharāyaṇa uktaḥ, «tvam iha tiṣṭha» iti.

Sa na saṃpratipadyate. sa kathayati, «Deven' âiva sārdhaṃ gacchāmi» iti. Ghoṣilo 'py uktaḥ, evam eva kathayati. rājñā Mākandikaḥ sthāpitaḥ, uktaś ca, «Śyāmāvatyā yog'|ôdvahanaṃ kartavyam» iti. saṃprasthiten' âpy anuvrajan, sa evam ev' ôktaḥ. nivartamānen' âpi tena saṃpratipannam.

Said the king, "Fine! It shall be so." And so the king granted the favor of regular instruction in the Dharma for Anúpama and Shyámavati. And whatever new grains and fruits, the first of the season, were produced from his lands, these he gave first to Shyámavati. 36.190

Womenfolk are jealous by nature. Anúpama reflected, "The king enjoys love-play with me. But it is Shyámavati whom he honors with the new grains and fruits, the new season's harvests. I must devise some means to take her life!" And so Anúpama, in order to kill her, became obsessed with discovering how Shyámavati was vulnerable.

Now, the king had a subject, a village headman, who was leading a rebellion against him. For this reason, the king dispatched a single division of his army. It returned, however, battered and bruised. And so a second and a third time. Udáyana's ministers said, "Your majesty's army grows weaker, the headman's grows stronger. If your majesty does not himself lead the army, what will happen is that this fellow will become exceedingly difficult to tame."

The king had the proclamation bell in Kaushámbi rung: "All those who dwell in my kingdom and who live by the sword are going to war." The king went and told Yogándharáyana, "You remain here."

The minister did not consent. He said, "I am going along with your majesty." Ghóshila, similarly instructed, said the very same thing. So the king had Makándika stay behind, telling him, "Ensure that Shyámavati has whatever she needs." Even as he was departing, he repeated to Makándika, who was walking along with him, the very same

36.195 So 'nupamāyāḥ sakāśaṃ gataḥ. tayā pṛṣṭaḥ, «tāta, ka iha Devena sthāpitaḥ?»

«Aham.»

Sā saṃlakṣayati, «śobhanam! śakyam anena sahāyena vaira|niryātanaṃ kartum» iti viditvā, kathayati, «n' ânujānīṣe Śyāmāvatī kā mama bhavati?» iti.

«Putri, jāne sa|patnī» iti.

«Tāta, satyam evam. n' ânujānīṣe kataro dharmo 'ty|artham bādhate?» iti.

36.200 «Putri, jāna īrṣyā mātsaryaṃ ca.»

«Tāta, yady evam, Śyāmāvatīṃ praghātaya.»

Sa kathayati, «kiṃ me dve śirasī? yāvat trir apy ahaṃ rājñā saṃdiṣṭaḥ, ‹Śyāmāvatyā yog'|ôdvahanaṃ kariṣyasi› iti. bhavatu nām' âpi na gṛhītum!» iti.

Sā kathayati, «īdṛśo 'pi tvaṃ mūrkho 'sti kaś cit pitā duhitur arthe vimukhaḥ, yaḥ sapatnyāḥ sakāśe 'tīva snehaṃ karoti? praghātayasi! ity evaṃ kuśalam. no ced, ahaṃ paurāṇe sthāne sthāpayāmi!» iti.

Sa, bhītaḥ, saṃlakṣayati, «strī|vaśa|gā rājānaḥ. syād evam» iti viditvā, kathayati, «putri, n' âivam eva śakyate praghātayitum! upāya|vidhānaṃ karomi» iti.

36.205 Sā kathayati, «śobhanam! evaṃ kuru!»

Sa Śyāmāvatyāḥ sakāśaṃ gataḥ. sa kathayati, «Devi, kiṃ te karaṇīyam asti?»

instructions. Although he was being left out of the campaign, Makándika assented.

Makándika went to see Anúpama. She asked, "Papa, who 36.195
is the chief minister that the king is having remain in Kaushámbi?"

"I am."

She reflected, "Splendid! It will be possible, with my father as ally, to kill my enemy." And, knowing this, she said, "Do you not know Shyámavati? Who is she to me?"

"Daughter, I know she is your co-wife."

"Papa, that's right. And do you not know the emotion that is most troubling?"

"Daughter, I know about jealousy and spite." 36.200

"Papa, if that is so, have Shyámavati put to death."

Makándika retorted, "Do I have two heads? Three times the king instructed me: 'Ensure that Shyámavati has whatever she needs.' Let that name not even be uttered!"

She replied, "Papa, are you such a fool as that? Does the father exist who turns away from his daughter's welfare, who loves her co-wife more? Have her killed! Then all will be well. If you don't, I'll reduce you to your former condition!"

Makándika, fearful, reflected, "Even kings fall under the power of women." Thinking, "This may be the case," he said, "Daughter, I can't just have Shyámavati put to death! I'd have to devise some workable strategy."

Anúpama replied, "Splendid! Do it!" 36.205

Makándika paid a visit to Shyámavati. He said, "My lady, what can I do for you?"

Sā kathayati, «Mākandika, na kiṃ cit karaṇīyam asti. api tv etā dārikāḥ, rātrau, pradīpena, Buddha|vacanaṃ paṭhanti, atra bhūrjena prayojanam, tailena, masinā, kalamayā, tulena.»

Sa kathayati, «Devi, śobhanam. upāvartayāmi» iti.

Tena, prabhūtam upāvartya, praveśitaṃ dvāra|koṣṭhake rāśir vyavasthāpitaḥ. Śyāmāvatī kathayati, «Mākandika, alaṃ paryāptam!» iti.

36.210 Mākandikaḥ kathayati, «Devi, praveśayāmi. na bhūyo bhūyaḥ praveśitavyam.»

Tena, apaścime bhūrja|bhārake, agniṃ prakṣipya, śaraḥ praveśitaḥ. tena saṃdhukṣitena dvāra|koṣṭhakaḥ prajvālitaḥ. Kauśāmbī|nivāsī jana|kāyaḥ pradhāvito nirvāpayitum. Mākandikaḥ, niṣkoṣam asiṃ kṛtvā, jana|kāyaṃ nirvāsayitum ārabdhaḥ. «tiṣṭhata! kiṃ yūyaṃ rājño 'ntaḥ|puraṃ draṣṭum?»

Kauśāmbyāṃ yantra|kar'|ācāryaḥ kathayati, «aham enaṃ dvāra|koṣṭhakaṃ jvalantaṃ yantreṇ' ânya|sthānaṃ saṅkramayāmi» iti. so 'pi Mākandiken' âivam ev' ôkto nivartitaḥ.

Śyāmāvatī, ṛddhyā, ākāśam utplutya, kathayati, «bhaginyo 'smābhir ev' âitāni karmāṇi kṛtāni, upacitāni, labdha|saṃbhārāṇi, pariṇata|pratyayāni, oghavat pratyupasthitāni, avaśyaṃ|bhāvīni. asmābhir eva kṛtāny upacitāni—ko 'nyaḥ pratyanubhaviṣyati?

She replied, "Makándika, there is nothing at all you need do for me. However, at night, by lamplight, these maidens study the word of the Buddha for which they require birchbark, pen and ink as well as oil and wick for the lamp."

He said, "Fine, my lady. I'll bring some."

And Makándika brought a great supply, which he had carried in and placed in a pile in the gatehouse. Said Shyámavati, "Makándika, you've brought enough!"

He replied, "My lady, I'll have it brought inside. There 36.210
is not much more to be brought in."

Makándika then set the last load of birchbark on fire and brought in some grass. He kindled the flames and set the gatehouse on fire. A crowd of the residents of Kaushámbi rushed forward to extinguish the blaze. Makándika drew his sword and began to drive back the crowd. "Stand back! Are you here to gawk at the king's women?"

A man who was a master-mechanic in Kaushámbi spoke up. "I'll use machinery to move this burning gatehouse to another place." But Makándika addressed him just as he had the crowd and drove him back.

Shyámavati, using her psychic powers, flew up into the air, and declared, "Ladies! It is we alone who have performed and accumulated these deeds, the bases of which have ripened, which exist in a multitude, which are present like a flood, the effects of which are inevitable. We alone have performed and accumulated these deeds—who else could experience their effects?

Uktaṃ ca Bhagavatā:

36.215 N' âiv' ântarīkṣe na samudra|madhye
na parvatānāṃ vivaraṃ praviśya,
na vidyate sa pṛthivī|pradeśo
yatra sthitaṃ na prasaheta karma. iti»

«Tat karma|parāyaṇair vo bhavitavyam» ity uktvā, gāthāṃ bhāṣate:

Dṛṣṭo mayā sa Bhagavān tiryak|prākāra|saṃnibhaḥ;
ājñātāni ca satyāni kṛtaṃ Buddhasya śāsanam. iti

Śyāmāvatī|pramukhāḥ, tāḥ striyaḥ pataṅgā iv' ôtplutya, agnau nipatitāḥ. iti tatra Śyāmāvatī|pramukhāni, pañca strī|śatāni dagdhāni. Kubj'|ôttar" ôdaka|bhrameṇa niṣpalāyitā. Mākandikena teṣāṃ pañcānāṃ strī|śatānāṃ kalevarāṇi śmaśāne choritāni. rāja|kulaṃ s'|ântar|bahiḥ śodhitam. Kauśāmbī|nivāsī jana|kāyo nānā|deś'|âbhyāgataś ca vikrośan nivāritaḥ.

Atha saṃbahulā bhikṣavaḥ, pūrv'|âhṇe nivāsya, pātra|cīvaram ādāya, Kauśāmbīṃ piṇḍāya prāvikṣan. aśrauṣuḥ saṃbahulā bhikṣavaḥ Kauśāmbī|nagara Udayanasya Vatsa|rājasya jana|padān gatasy' ântaḥ|puram agninā dagdhaṃ pañca|mātrāṇi strī|śatāni Śyāmāvatī|pramukhāni. śrutvā ca punaḥ Kauśāmbīṃ piṇḍāya praviśya, caritvā, pratikramya, punar yena Bhagavāṃs ten' ôpasaṃkrāntāḥ, etad ūcuḥ: «aśrauṣma

Indeed, the Lord has declared:

Neither in the heavens nor in mid-ocean, 36.215
Nor by climbing into a mountain cave,
Nor anywhere on earth can one find a place
That karma does not wield power."

Then, having declared, "Therefore you should dedicate yourselves to good deeds," Shyámavati recited this verse:

I beheld the Lord, who was like unto a low rampart;
I understood the truths when I practised the
Buddha's teaching.

Led by Shyámavati, those women rose up into the air and, like moths, cast themselves into the flames. And so, right then, those five hundred women, led by Shyámavati, were consumed in the blaze. Shyámavati's servant Kubjóttara escaped through a drain. As for Makándika, he had the bodies of those five hundred women dumped in the cremation-ground and the royal palace cleaned and purified inside and out. He also had his men ward off a weeping crowd made up of residents of Kaushámbi and of people from various other countries.

The next morning, a large company of monks dressed themselves, took their bowls and outer robes and entered Kaushámbi for alms. In the city of Kaushámbi that company of monks learned that five hundred palace women, led by Shyámavati, had died in a fire in the palace of Udáyana, King of Vatsa, who was travelling in the countryside. After learning that, they again entered Kaushámbi for alms and completed their alms-round. Then they left the city,

vayaṃ, Bhadanta, saṃbahulā bhikṣavaḥ Kauśāmbīṃ piṇḍāya carantaḥ, Udayanasya Vatsa|rājasy' ântaḥ|puram agninā dagdhaṃ pañca|mātrāṇi strī|śatāni Śyāmāvatī|pramukhāni dagdhāni.»

36.220 Bhagavān āha, «bahu, bhikṣavaḥ, tena moha|puruṣeṇ' âpuṇyaṃ prasūtaṃ yen' Ôdayanasya Vatsa|rājasya jana|pada|gatasy' ântaḥ|puram agninā dagdhaṃ pañca|mātrāṇi strī|śatāni Śyāmāvatī|pramukhāni. kiṃ c' âpi, bhikṣavaḥ, tena moha|puruṣeṇa bahv|apuṇyaṃ prasūtam, api tu na tā durgatiṃ gatāḥ. sarvāḥ śuddha|pudgalāḥ kāla|gatāḥ. tat kasya hetoḥ?

Santi, tasminn antaḥ|pure, striyo yāḥ, pañcānām avara|bhāgīyānāṃ saṃyojanānāṃ prahāṇāt, upapādukāḥ. tatra, parinirvāyiṇyo 'nāgāminyo 'nāvṛttika|dharmiṇyaḥ punar imaṃ lokam. evaṃ|rūpās tasminn antaḥ|pure striyaḥ santi.

Santi, tasminn antaḥ|pure, striyo yāḥ, trayāṇāṃ saṃyojanānāṃ prahāṇād rāga|dveṣa|mohānām, kālaṃ kṛtvā, Sakṛd|āgāminyaḥ sakṛd imaṃ lokam āgamya, duḥkhasy' ântaṃ kariṣyanti. evaṃ|rūpās tasminn antaḥ|pure striyaḥ santi.

proceeded to where the Buddha was, and said this: "Venerable sir, we, a large company of monks, while on our alms-round in Kaushámbi, learned that the women's quarters in the palace of Udáyana, King of Vatsa, burned down and that five hundred women, the entire retinue of Queen Shyámavati, died in the blaze."

The Lord said, "Monks, immense is the demerit that de- 36.220
luded man generated as a result of which those five hundred women, led by Shyámavati, died in the fire in the women's quarters of the palace of Udáyana, King of Vatsa, who is travelling in the countryside. Although, O monks, that deluded man has generated much demerit, those women did not suffer rebirth in evil realms. All those who died were pure and virtuous individuals. What is the reason for that?

There were, in the women's apartments, women who, because they had abandoned the five fetters that bind one to rebirth in lower states, have been spontaneously reborn in one of the heavens. There, as Non-Returners, whose nature it is never to be reborn in this world, they will attain final nirvana. Of such a kind were those women in the women's apartments of the royal palace.

There were in the women's quarters of that palace women who, because they had abandoned the three fetters of craving, enmity and delusion, after dying, have become Once-Returners, whose nature it is to be reborn in this world only once more before making an end to suffering. Of such a kind were the women in the women's apartments of the royal palace.

Santi, tasminn antaḥ|pure, striyo yāḥ, trayāṇāṃ saṃyojanānāṃ prahāṇāt, Śrota|āpannā avinipāta|dharmiṇyaḥ, niyata|samādhi|parāyaṇāḥ, sapta|kṛtvo bhava|paramāḥ, sapta|kṛtvo devāṃś ca manuṣyāṃś ca saṃdhāvya, saṃsṛtya duḥkhasy' ântaṃ kariṣyanti. evaṃ|rūpās tasminn antaḥ|pure striyaḥ santi.

Santi, tasminn antaḥ|pure striyo yāḥ, sva|jīvita|hetor api, śikṣāṃ na vyatikrāntāḥ. ity evaṃ|rūpās tasminn antaḥ|pure striyaḥ santi.

36.225 Santi, tasminn antaḥ|pure, striyo yāḥ, mam' ântike prasanna|citt'|âlaṃ|kāraṃ kṛtvā, kāyasya bhedāt su|gatau svarga|loke deveṣ' ûpapannāḥ. evaṃ|rūpās tasminn antaḥ|pure striyaḥ santi.

Āgamayata, bhikṣavaḥ, yena Śyāmāvatī|pramukhānāṃ pañca|strī|śatānāṃ kalevarāṇi.»

«Evaṃ Bhadanta», iti bhikṣavo Bhagavataḥ pratyaśrauṣuḥ.

Atha khalu Bhagavān, saṃbahulair bhikṣubhiḥ sārdhaṃ, yena tāsāṃ pañcānāṃ strī|śatānāṃ kalevarāṇi ten' ôpasaṃkrāntaḥ. upasaṃkramya, bhikṣūn āmantrayate sma, «etāni, bhikṣavaḥ, tāni pañca|śata|kalevarāṇi yatr' Ôdayano Vatsa|rājo raktaḥ, saktaḥ, gṛdhraḥ, grathitaḥ, mūrchito 'dhyavasito 'dhyavasāyam āpannaḥ. tatra n' âiva prājña|dhīḥ pāden' âpi spṛśet.»

There were in the women's quarters of that palace women who, because they abandoned the three fetters, have become Stream-Enterers whose nature it is never again to fall into evil rebirths, who are devoted to constant meditation and who, after seven more worldly births as humans or gods, shall make an end to suffering. Of such a kind were the women in the women's quarters of the royal palace.

There were, in the women's quarters of the royal palace, women who did not transgress the Teaching even to preserve their lives. Of such a kind were the women in the women's quarters of the royal palace.

There were in the women's quarters of the royal palace 36.225
women who ornamented my presence with minds filled with serene faith. They, after the breaking up of their bodies, will take an auspicious rebirth among the gods in a heavenly realm. Of such a kind were the women in the women's quarters of the royal palace.

Betake yourselves, O monks, to the bodies of those five hundred women who were led by Shyámavati."

"Very well, Venerable sir," the monks replied to the Lord.

Then the Lord, accompanied by that large company of monks, approached the place where the bodies of those five hundred women lay. Having approached, the Buddha declared to the monks, "Monks, the bodies of these five hundred women are those by which Udáyana, King of Vatsa, was impassioned, to which he clung, for which he longed, by which he was bound, infatuated, attached, at which he grasped and by which he was afflicted. No wise man would ever touch them, even with his foot."

Gāthāṃ ca bhāṣate:

36.230 Moha|saṃvardhanaḥ, loko bhavya|rūpa iva dṛśyate.*
upadhi|bandhanāḥ, bālās tamasā parivāritāḥ.
asat sad iti paśyanti, paśyatāṃ n' âsti kiṃ cana. iti

Evaṃ c' āha, «tasmāt tarhi, bhikṣavaḥ, evaṃ śikṣitavyam: yad dagdha|sthūṇāyām api cittaṃ na pradūṣayiṣyāmaḥ, prāg eva savijñānake kāye. ity evaṃ vaḥ, bhikṣavaḥ, śikṣitavyam.»

Atha Kauśāmbī|nivāsinaḥ paurāḥ saṃnipatya, saṃjalpitum ārabdhāḥ. «bhavantaḥ, rājña īdṛso 'narthaḥ saṃvṛttaḥ! tat ko nv asmākaṃ rājña ārocayiṣyati» iti.

Tatr' âike kathayanti, «yo 'sāv apriy'|ākhyāyī, s' ārocayiṣyati. taṃ śabdayāma!» iti.

Apare kathayanti, «evaṃ kurmaḥ!»

36.235 Taiḥ, asāv āhūya, uktaḥ, «Devasy' êdam īdṛsam apriyam anupūrvyā nivedaya» iti.

«Vṛttir dīyatām.»

«Kim apriy'|ākhyāyino vṛttir dīyata ity ayaṃ sa kālaḥ?»

«Yūyam eva nivedayata.»

Te kathayanti, «ato 'rtham eva tava vṛttir dattā! kāryaṃ nivedaya» iti.

And he recited this verse:

To those who foster delusion, the world appears as if beautiful. 36.230
Bound by attachment, fools are veiled in the darkness of ignorance.
The unreal they see as real, but there is nothing to what they see.

And he added, "Therefore, then, monks, in this way should you train yourselves: we must not permit our minds to be corrupted even by such burned pillars as these, much less by bodies endowed with consciousness. In this way, monks, should you train yourselves."

The citizens of Kaushámbi gathered together and began to talk. "Gentlemen, such great misfortune has befallen the king! Who among us shall inform him of this?"

At that, some said, "He who is the announcer of ill tidings should inform the king. Let us summon him!"

Others declared, "Yes! Let's do that."

They summoned him and said, "Inform his majesty of 36.235
these ill tidings in the order in which they occurred."

"Then let my wages be paid."

"Why have we been paying you the wages of an announcer of ill tidings all this time?"

"It is you people who should inform the king."

They replied, "It is for this very purpose you have been paid! Tell us what to do."

36.240 «Samayato nivedayāmi—yad ahaṃ bravīmi, tat kurudhvam.»

«Brūhi! kariṣyāmaḥ.»

«Evam anupūrveṇ' âsya nivedayitavyam: ‹pañca|hasti|śatāni prayacchata, pañca|hastinī|śatāni, pañc'|âśva|śatāni, pañca|vaḍavā|śatāni, pañca|kumāra|śatāni, pañca|kumārikā|śatāni, suvarṇa|lakṣam.› Kauśāmby|adhiṣṭhānaṃ paṭe lekhayata Puṣpa|danta|prāsādaṃ yathā Mākandikena bhūrjam, kalamā, tailam, tūlam, asiḥ, apaścime ca bhūrja|bhāge 'gniḥ prakṣiptaḥ. yathā dvāra|koṣṭhakaḥ prajvālitaḥ; yathā Kauśāmbī|nivāsī jana|kāyo nirvāpayituṃ pradhāvitaḥ; yathā Mākandikena niṣkoṣam asiṃ kṛtvā, nivāritaḥ; yathā yantra|kal'|ācārya āgatya, kathayati, ‹dvāra|koṣṭhakaṃ jvalantam anyat sthānaṃ saṃkramayāmi› iti, so 'pi Mākandikena nivāritaḥ; yathā Śyāmāvatī|pramukhāni pañca|strī|śatāny utplutya, nipatitāni.»

Te kathayanti, «evaṃ kurmaḥ.»

Taiḥ pañca|hasti|śatāny upasthāpitāni, pañca|hastinī|śatāni pañc'|âśva|śatāni, pañca|vaḍavā|śatāni, pañca|kumāra|śatāni, pañca|kumārikā|śatāni, suvarṇasya lakṣam. Kauśāmby|adhiṣṭhānaṃ paṭe likhitaṃ Puṣpa|danta|prāsādaḥ; yathā Mākandikena bhūrjam, kalamā, tailam, tūlam, asiḥ, apaścime ca bhūrja|bhārake 'gniḥ prakṣiptaḥ; yathā dvāra|koṣṭhake prajvālitaḥ; yathā Kauśāmbī|nivāsī jana|kāyo nirvāpayituṃ pradhāvitaḥ; yathā Mākandikena niṣkoṣam asiṃ kṛtvā, nivāritaḥ; yathā yantra|kal'|ācārya āgataḥ kathayati «aham enaṃ dvāra|koṣṭhakaṃ jvalantam anyat sthānaṃ

"I'll tell you on one condition—that you do as I say." 36.240

"Tell us! We'll do it."

"Inform the king in the following way: 'Provide me with five hundred bull and five hundred cow elephants, five hundred stallions and five hundred mares, five hundred youths and five hundred maidens, plus one hundred thousand gold coins.' Then, on a cloth, paint the scene in Kaushámbi: the Flower-Bower Palace, the birchbark, reed pens, sesame oil and lampwicks and Makándika setting ablaze the last load of birchbark. In the same way, depict the burning gatehouse, the crowd of Kaushámbians rushing to extinguish the fire and Makándika drawing his sword and driving them back. In the same way, paint the master-mechanic coming and saying, 'I'll move the burning gatehouse elsewhere,' and Makándika driving him back. And, in the same way, show Shyámavati at the head of those five hundred women, rising up and falling into the flames."

The people said, "We'll do it."

And they presented him with five hundred bull and five hundred cow elephants, five hundred stallions and five hundred mares, five hundred youths and five hundred maidens, plus one hundred thousand gold coins. On a cloth they painted the scene in Kaushámbi: the Flower-Bower Palace, the birchbark, reed pens, sesame oil and wicks, and Makándika setting ablaze the last load of birchbark. In the same way, they depicted the burning gatehouse, the crowd of Kaushambians rushing to extinguish the fire and Makándika drawing his sword and driving them back. In the same way, they painted the master-mechanic coming and saying, "I'll move this burning gatehouse elsewhere," and

saṃkramayāmi» iti, so 'pi Mākandikena nivāritaḥ; yathā Śyāmāvatī|pramukhāni pañca|strī|śatāny agnāv utplutya, nipatitāni. tat sarvaṃ paṭe likhitam.

36.245 Tato 'priy'|ākhyāyin" âmātyānāṃ lekho 'nupreṣitaḥ: «rājña īdṛśo 'nartha utpanno 'ham asy' ânen' ôpāyena nivedayiṣyāmi. yuṣmābhiḥ sāhāyyaṃ kalpayitavyam» iti. sa, teṣāṃ lekhāṃ lekhayitvā, catur|aṅga|bala|kāya|yukto 'nyatamasmin pradeśe gatvā, avasthitaḥ. Udayanasya ca lekho 'nupreṣitaḥ: «Deva, aham amuṣmin pradeśe rājā. mama ca putro mṛtyun" âpahṛtaḥ. tad ahaṃ tena sārdhaṃ saṃgrāmaṃ saṃgrāmayiṣyāmi. yadi tāvat tvaṃ śaknoṣi yuddhena niyoktum—ity evaṃ kuśalam—no cet, pañca|hasti|śatāni, pañca|hastinī|śatāni, pañc'|âśva|śatāni, pañca|vaḍavā|śatāni, pañca|kumāra|śatāni, pañca|kumārikā|śatāni, suvarṇasya lakṣaṃ dattvā, tam āneṣyāmi» iti.

Rājña Udayanasya sa kārvaṭiko balavān saṃnāmaṃ na gacchati. so 'mātyānāṃ kathayati, «bhavantaḥ, īdṛśo 'pi rājā mūrkho 'sti kaś cin mṛtyun" âpahṛtaḥ śakyata ānetum? tad gatam!» etat tasy' âivaṃ likhitam: «mam' âivaṃ|nāmā kārvaṭikaḥ saṃnāmaṃ na gacchati. sa tvam asmākaṃ tāvat sāhāyyaṃ kalpaya, paścāt tav' âpi sāhāyyaṃ karomi» iti. so 'mātyais tasy' âivaṃ lekho 'nupreṣitaḥ. sa, lekha|śravaṇād ev' āgatya, kārvaṭikasya n'|âtidūre vyavasthāpitaḥ.

Makándika driving him back. In the same way, they showed Shyámavati at the head of those five hundred women, rising up and descending into the flames. All this they depicted on the cloth.

Then the announcer of ill tidings sent a letter to the king's 36.245
ministers, which said: "That such a calamity has befallen the king I shall inform him by means of this stratagem. But you must provide assistance." Then, having written the letter to them, the announcer of ill tidings, accompanied by an army of the four divisions, proceeded to and took up position in a certain district. Then to Udáyana he sent a letter, which said: "Your majesty, I am ruler in this district. And my son has been carried off by Death. And so I shall engage Death in battle. If perchance you are able to defeat him in battle—well and good—if not, I shall pay Death a ransom of five hundred bull and five hundred cow elephants, five hundred stallions and five hundred mares, five hundred youths and five hundred maidens, plus one hundred thousand gold coins, and thereby recover my son."

Meanwhile, the powerful village chieftain would still not surrender to King Udáyana. Udáyana said to his ministers, "Gentlemen, what sort of fool is this king whose letter you have just read to me? Is it possible that one who has been carried off by death can be brought back? When that happens, it's finished!" Then Udáyana wrote a letter to the announcer of ill tidings: "This so-called village chieftain will not surrender to me. Render us assistance now; afterward I shall do the same for you." Udáyana's ministers dispatched the letter to the announcer of ill tidings, who, once the letter

Kārvaṭikena śrutam. sa saṃlakṣayati, «ekena tāvad ahaṃ rājñā daśa diśo viśrānto 'yaṃ ca dvitīyaḥ. sarvathā, punar api viṣayān, na tu prāṇān nirgacchāmi» iti. sa, kaṇṭhe 'siṃ baddhvā, nirgatya, Rājña Udayanasya pādayor nipatitaḥ. sa Rājñ" Ôdayanena karado vyavasthāpitaḥ.

Ath' âsāv apriy'|ākhyāyī, rāja|līlayā, Rājña Udayanasya sakāśaṃ gatvā, kathayati, «Deva, mama putro mṛtyun" âpahṛtaḥ. tvaṃ mama devaḥ sāhāyyaṃ kalpayatu. ahaṃ tena sārdhaṃ saṃgrāmaṃ saṃgrāmayiṣyām' îti. yadi tāvat tvaṃ śaknoṣi yuddhena nirjetum—ity evaṃ kuśalam—no cet, pañca|hasti|śatāni, pañca|hastinī|śatāni, pañc'|âśva|śatāni, pañca|vaḍavā|śatāni, pañca|kumāra|śatāni, pañca|kumārikā|śatāni, suvarṇasya lakṣaṃ dattvā, tam āneṣyāmi» iti.

Udayano Rājā kathayati, «priya|vayasya, mūrkhas tvam! asti kaś cic chakyate mṛtyoḥ sakāśād ānetum?» iti.

36.250 Sa kathayati, «Deva, na śakyate. yady evam, imaṃ paṭaṃ paśya» iti. tena paṭaḥ prasāritaḥ.

Rājā, paṭaṃ nirīkṣya, marma|vedha|viddha iva ruṣyamāṇaḥ, kathayati, «bhoḥ kim,» kathayati, «bhoḥ puruṣa! kiṃ kathayasi Śyāmāvatī|pramukhāni pañca strī|śatāny agninā dagdhāni?» iti.

was read to him, came and took up position not far from the village chieftain.

When the rebel chieftain learned of this, he reflected, "Until now, by only one king in the ten directions have I been pacified—and this is the second. In any case, once again I shall give up my territories, but not my life." Then he tied his sword around his neck, approached King Udáyana and fell at his feet. King Udáyana appointed him a tribute-bearer.

Then the announcer of ill tidings, playing at being a king, went before King Udáyana and said, "Your majesty, my son has been carried off by Death. Let my lord render me assistance. I am going to engage Death in battle. If perchance you are able to defeat him in battle—well and good—if not, I shall pay Death a ransom of five hundred bull and five hundred cow elephants, five hundred stallions and five hundred mares, five hundred youths and five hundred maidens, plus one hundred thousand gold coins, and thereby recover my son."

King Udáyana declared, "My dear fellow, you are a fool! Can anyone be brought back from the presence of Death?"

The announcer of ill tidings replied, "Lord, that is not 36.250
possible, and since it is not, look at this painting." He then unrolled the scroll.

The king examined the painting and, wounded as if cut to the quick, cried out, "What is this?," and demanded, "Listen, my man, are you telling me that Shyámavati and her retinue of five hundred women died in a fire?"

Sa, paṭṭaṃ mauliṃ c' âpanīya, gāthāṃ bhāṣate:

N' âhaṃ nar'|êndro na nar'|êndra|putraḥ
pād'|ôpajīvī tava, Deva, bhṛtyaḥ.
ath' âpriyasy' êva nivedan'|ârtham
ih' āgato 'haṃ tava pāda|mūlam. iti

Rājā, sutarāṃ nirīkṣya, vicārayati, «iyaṃ Kauśāmbī nagarī; idaṃ rāja|kulam; ayaṃ Mākandika Puṣpa|dantaṃ Prāsādaṃ bhūrj'|ādinā prayogeṇa dahati; imāni Śyāmāvatī|pramukhāni pañca strī|śatāny agninā dahyamānāny utplutya nipatitāni» iti. vicārya, kathayati, «bhoḥ puruṣa! kiṃ kathayasi Śyāmāvatī dagdhā?» iti.

36.255 «Deva, n' âhaṃ kathayāmi, api tu Deva eva kathayati.»

«Bhoḥ puruṣa, upāyena me tvayā niveditam! anyathā, te may" âsinā nikṛntita|mūlaṃ śiraḥ kṛtvā, pṛthivyāṃ nipātitam anvabhaviṣyat.» ity uktvā, mūrchitaḥ pṛthivyāṃ nipatitaḥ.

Tataḥ, jala|pariṣekeṇa pratyāgata|prāṇaḥ, kathayati, «saṃnāhayata, bhavantaḥ, catur|aṅga|bala|kāyam. Kauśāmbīṃ gacchāmaḥ» iti. amātyaiś catur|aṅga|bala|kāyaṃ saṃnāhitam. rājā Kauśāmbīṃ saṃprasthito 'nupūrveṇa saṃprāptaḥ. tena paurāṇāṃ sakāśāt sarvaṃ śrutam. tair amarṣitaṃ tam ārāgitam. tato Yogāndharāyaṇasy' ājñā dattā: «gaccha!

The announcer of ill tidings, pulling off his crown and turban, recited this verse:

No king am I, nor the son of one,
  Your majesty, but a servant living at your feet;
  To inform you this very calamity,
  I have come here to your feet.

The king studied the painting intently, thinking to himself, "This is the city of Kaushámbi; this is the royal palace; this is Makándika using the birchbark and other materials to set the Pushpa·danta Palace on fire; this is Shyámavati and the five hundred women being consumed by the flames after they have risen up and leaped into them." So thinking, he said, "Good fellow, are you telling me that Shyámavati was burned to death?"

"Your majesty, I do not say that! It is your majesty who 36.255
says so."

"Good fellow, by means of a clever strategem you have broken the news to me! Had you done otherwise, I would have cut off your head with my sword and it would have fallen to the earth." So saying, he fainted and himself fell to the ground.

After sprinkling with water had restored him to consciousness, Udáyana said to his ministers, "Gentlemen, have the army of four divisions ready itself. We are returning to Kaushámbi." The ministers ordered the army of four divisions to ready itself. The king set out and in due course reached Kaushámbi. In the presence of the townsfolk, he heard everything. In his wrathful impatience, they sought to placate him. Then the king commanded Yogándharáyana:

Mākandikam Anupamayā saha yantra|gṛhe prakṣipya, dahyatām!» tato Yogāndharāyaṇena su|guptaṃ bhūmi|gṛhe prakṣipya sthāpitaḥ.

Rājñaḥ saptame divase śoko vigataḥ; sa vigata|śokaḥ. sa kathayati, «Yogāndharāyaṇa, kutr' Ânupamā?» iti. tena yathā|vṛttaṃ niveditam.

Rājā kathayati, «śobhanam! Mākandikena Śyāmāvatī praghātitā, tvay" âpy Anupamayā saparivārayā sārdhaṃ mayā pravrajitavyaṃ jātam» iti.

36.260 Yogāndharāyaṇaḥ kathayati, «Deva, ity artham eva may" âsau bhūmi|gṛhe prakṣipya sthāpitā. paśyāmi tāvad yadi jīvati» iti.

Ten' âsau bhūmi|gṛhād ānītā, tad|avasthān'|âkliṣṭ'|âmlāna|śarīrā. rājā, dṛṣṭvā, saṃlakṣayati, «yath" êyam amlānā, n' âiṣā nir|āhārā. nūnam anayā para|puruṣeṇa sārdhaṃ paricāritam.» iti viditvā, kathayati, «Anupame, anyena paricāritam?» iti.

Sā kathayati, «śāntaṃ pāpam! n' âham evaṃ|kāriṇī!»

«Kathaṃ jāne? abhiśraddadhasi tvaṃ Bhagavataḥ?»

«Abhiśraddadhe Gautame.»

36.265 «Tat tadā śramaṇo Gautamaḥ—idānīṃ Bhagavān. api tu kiṃ nava|śavāyā arthe Bhagavantaṃ pravakṣyāmi? Śyāmāvatyā arthe pravakṣyāmi?» iti viditvā, yena Bhagavāṃs ten' ôpasaṃkrāntaḥ. upasaṃkramya, Bhagavataḥ pādau śirasā vanditvā, ek'|ânte niṣaṇṇaḥ. Udayano Vatsa|rājo Bhagavantam idam avocat: «kiṃ, Bhadanta, Śyāmāvatī|pramukhaiḥ

"Go! Cast both Makándika and Anúpama into the torture chamber and torture them!" But Yogándharáyana secretly threw them into a cellar and left them there.

Seven days later, the king's grief had departed; he was free from grief. He said, "Yogándharáyana, where is Anúpama?" He told the king exactly what he had done.

The king said, "Splendid! Makándika caused Shyámavati's death, although you and I should send Anúpama, together with her retinue, into exile."

Replied Yogándharáyana, "Your majesty, it was for this 36.260
very reason that I cast her into a cellar and left her there. I'll see if she is still alive."

When he brought her out of the cellar, Anúpama was in an untroubled state and her body was clear and bright. Looking upon her, the king reflected: "Since her appearance is clear and bright, she has not been without food. Surely she has been enjoying herself with another man!" So thinking, he said, "Anúpama, have you been enjoying yourself with another man?"

She replied, "Heavens no! I would never do that!"

"How do I know? Do you have faith in the Lord?"

"I have faith in Gáutama."

"Then he was the ascetic Gáutama—now he is the Lord. 36.265
But what shall I say to the Lord about that woman who just died? What shall I say to the Lord about Shyámavati?" So thinking, he went to see the Lord. He approached, paid homage with his head at the Lord's feet and sat down to one side. Udáyana, King of the Vatsas, then said this to the Lord: "Venerable sir, what deed did those five hundred women, led by Shyámavati, perform as a result of which

pañcabhiḥ strī|śataiḥ karma kṛtaṃ yen' âgninā dagdhāni? Kubj'|ôttar" ôdaka|bhrameṇa niṣpalāyitā?» iti.

Bhagavān āha, «ābhir eva, mahā|rāṭ, karmāṇi kṛtāny upacitāni, labdha|saṃbhārāṇi, pariṇata|pratyayāni, oghavat pratyupasthitāni, avaśyaṃ|bhāvīni. ābhiḥ karmāṇi kṛtāny upacitāni. ko 'nyaḥ pratyanubhaviṣyati? na, mahā|rāja, karmāṇi kṛtāny upacitāni bāhye pṛthivī|dhātau vipacyante, n' âb|dhātau, na tejo|dhātau, na vāyu|dhātau, api t' ûpātteṣv eva skandha|dhātv|āyataneṣu karmāṇi kṛtāny upacitāni vipacyante, śubhāny aśubhāni ca.

Na pranaśyanti karmāṇi, api kalpa|śatair api:
sāmagrīṃ prāpya kālaṃ ca phalanti khalu dehinām.
iti

Bhūta|pūrvam, mahā|rāja, Vārāṇasyāṃ nagaryām, Brahma|datto Rājā rājyaṃ kārayati, ṛddhaṃ ca, sphītaṃ ca, kṣemaṃ ca, subhikṣaṃ ca, ākīrṇa|bahu|jana|manuṣyaṃ ca, praśānta|kali|kalaha|ḍimba|ḍamaram, taskara|rog'|âpagatam, śāl'|îkṣu|go|mahiṣī|saṃpannam, akhilam, akaṇṭakam. dhārmikaḥ, dharma|rājo dharmeṇa rājyaṃ kārayati.

they perished in that fire? And why did Kubjóttara manage to escape through a drain?"

Replied the Lord, "Those women, great king, performed and accumulated many deeds, the bases of which were about to ripen, which exist in a multitude and the effects of which are inevitable. Those women themselves performed and accumulated those deeds. Who else could experience their effects? Great king, deeds performed and accumulated do not manifest their effects without, in the earth-element or in the water-element, or in the fire-element or in the air-element. Rather, deeds that are performed and accumulated manifest their effects in the five constituents of the personality, in the whole complex of embodied experience of the six senses, where they were performed, and these results may be wholesome or unwholesome.

Deeds are never destroyed, even after hundreds of
aeons:
When conditions and time are right, they inevitably
bear fruit among living beings.

In a previous existence, great king, in the city of Varánasi, King Brahma·datta ruled his kingdom: it was prosperous, thriving, peaceful, provided with abundant food, densely populated, free from riots, fighting, battle and war as well as from thieves and disease; rich in rice, sugarcane, cattle and buffalo; entirely without troubles. Being virtuous, that righteous king ruled the kingdom justly.

Asati Buddhānām utpāde, Pratyeka|buddhā loka utpadyante, hīna|dīn'|ânukampakāḥ, prānta|śayan'|āsana|bhaktāḥ, eka|dakṣiṇīyā lokasya.

36.270 Yāvad anyatamaḥ Pratyeka|buddho jana|pada|cārikāṃ caran, Vārāṇasīm anuprāptaḥ. so 'nyatamasminn udyāne kuṭikāyām avasthitaḥ. Rājā ca Brahma|dattaḥ, s'|ântaḥ|pura|parivāraḥ, tad udyānaṃ nirgataḥ. tā antaḥ|purikāḥ, krīḍā|puṣkiriṇyāṃ snātvā, śīten' ânubaddhāḥ. tato 'gra|mahiṣyā preṣya|dārik" ôktā: ‹dārike, śīten' âtīva bādhyāmahe. gacch' âitasyāṃ kuṭikāyām, agniṃ prajvalaya› iti.

Sā, ulkāṃ prajvalya, gatā. paśyati taṃ Pratyeka|buddham. tayā tasyā niveditam, ‹Devi, pravrajito 'tyāṃ tiṣṭhati› iti.

Sā kathayati, ‹pravrajito vā tiṣṭhatu—agniṃ dattvā, tāṃ prajvalaya!› iti. tayā na dattam. tatas tayā kupitayā svayam eva dattam. sa Pratyeka|buddho nirgataḥ. ābhiḥ sarvābhir antaḥ|purikābhir anumoditam, ‹Devi, śobhanaṃ tvayā yad agnir dattaḥ! sarvā vayaṃ prataptāḥ› iti.

Sa Pratyeka|buddhaḥ saṃlakṣayati, ‹kṣatā etāḥ; tapasvinya upahatāś ca. mā atyanta|kṣatā etā bhaviṣyanti. anugraham āsāṃ karomi› iti. sa, tāsām anukamp'|ârtham, tata ev' ākāśam utplutya, tapana|varṣaṇa|vidyotana|prātihāryāṇi kartum ārabdhaḥ. āśu pṛthag|janasya' rddhir āvarjana|karī.

Now, when no Buddhas have appeared, Solitary Buddhas appear in the world, full of compassion for the wretched and miserable, having their food, seats and beds in remote areas, singularly worthy of the world's veneration.

At that time, a certain Solitary Buddha making his way 36.270
through the countryside arrived at Varánasi. He settled in a hut in a certain park. Meanwhile, King Brahma·datta, accompanied by the palace women and his retainers, went out to that same park. After bathing in a lotus pool, the palace women caught a chill. So the chief consort addressed one of the maidservants: 'Girl, a great chill oppresses us! Go, light a fire in that hut.'

Lighting a torch, off she went, but saw that Solitary Buddha. Returning, she informed the queen, 'My lady, there is a wanderer staying in that hut.'

The chief consort declared, 'Let the wanderer stay there or not—take a torch and set the hut on fire!' But the girl would not. At that, the chief consort became angry and herself set the hut on fire. The Solitary Buddha came out. All the palace women applauded what she had done, saying, 'My lady, it is splendid that you lit the fire! Now we are all warm.'

That Solitary Buddha reflected, 'Ruined are these women; afflicted and stricken are they. May they not be so in perpetuity. I'll come to their aid.' Then, out of compassion for them, he flew up into the air and began to exhibit his psychic powers, emitting from his body fire, water and lightning. A display of psychic powers quickly secures the favor of ordinary people.

Tā mūla|nikṛntita iva drumaḥ, pādayor nipatya, kṣamayitum ārabdhā: ‹avatara, avatara, sad|bhūta|dakṣiṇīya! asmākaṃ kāma|paṅka|nimagnānāṃ hast'|ôddhāram anuprayaccha!› iti.

36.275 Sa, tāsām anukamp'|ârtham, avatīrṇaḥ. tāni tasmin kārān kṛtvā, praṇidhānaṃ kartum ārabdhā: ‹yad asmābhir evaṃ sad|bhūta|dakṣiṇīye 'pakāraḥ kṛtaḥ, mā asya karmaṇo vipākam anubhavema. yat tu kārāḥ kṛtā anena vayam, kuśala|mūlen' âivaṃ|vidhānāṃ dharmāṇāṃ lābhinyo bhavema, prativiśiṣṭa|taraṃ c' âtaḥ śāstāram ārāgayemaḥ› iti.

Kiṃ manyase, mahā|rāja, tadā y" âsau Rājño Brahma|dattasy' âgra|mahiṣī? eṣ" âiva sā Śyāmāvatī, tena kālena, tena samayena. yāni pañca strī|śatāni, etāny eva tāni pañca strī|śatāni, tāni tena kālena, tena samayena. yā sā preṣya|dārikā, eṣ" âiv' âsau Kubj'|ôttarā, tena kālena, tena samayena. yad ābhiḥ Pratyeka|buddhasya kuṭikāṃ dagdhvā, anumoditaṃ, tasya karmaṇo vipākena, bahūni varṣāṇi narakeṣu paktāḥ, yāvad etarhy api dṛṣṭa|satyā agninā dagdhāḥ. Kubj'|ôttar" ânukrameṇa niṣpalāyitā.

Like trees cut off at the roots, those women fell at his feet and begged his forgiveness: 'Come down, come down, O you who are worthy of veneration by the good! To us, who are sunk in the mud of desire, extend your redeeming hand!'

Out of compassion for those women, he descended. After 36.275
venerating him, those women made a solemn religious vow: 'Although we have in this way wronged him who is worthy of the veneration of good people, may we not suffer the karmic consequences of that deed. But since we have offered him veneration, as a result of planting these roots of merit, may we acquire such characteristics as are commensurate with our deed of piety and may we also, as a result of this virtuous deed, honor a teacher even more distinguished than this one.'

Who do you think, great king, was King Brahma·datta's chief consort at that time? She was no other than Shyámavati, at that time, on that occasion. Those five hundred women, the chief consort's retinue, were no other than these five hundred women, Shyámavati's retinue, at that time, on that occasion. She who was that maidservant was no other than this Kubjóttara, at that time, on that occasion. Because those women set the Solitary Buddha's hut on fire and applauded the deed, by the fruit of that deed for many years they broiled in the hells, and even after they had, in this birth, perceived the Truths, they were consumed by fire. As for Kubjóttara, she escaped through a drain.

Yat praṇidhānaṃ kṛtam, tena mam' ântike Satya|darśanaṃ kṛtam. iti hi, mahā|rāja, ‹ek'|ânta|kṛṣṇānāṃ karmāṇām, ek'|ânta|kṛṣṇo vipākaḥ; ek'|ânta|śuklānām karmāṇām, ek'|ânta|śuklo vipākaḥ; vyatimiśrāṇāṃ karmāṇām, vyatimiśro vipākaḥ.› tasmāt tarhi, mahā|rāja, ek'|ânta|kṛṣṇāni karmāṇy apāsya vyatimiśrāṇi ca, ek'|ânta|śukleṣv eva karmasv evam ābhogaḥ karaṇīyaḥ. ity evaṃ te, mahā|rāja, śikṣitavyam.»

Atr' Ôdayano Vatsa|rājo Bhagavato bhāṣitam abhinandy' ânumodya, Bhagavataḥ pādau śirasā vanditvā, Bhagavato 'ntikāt prakrāntaḥ.

Bhikṣavaḥ, saṃśaya|jātāḥ, sarva|saṃśaya|chettāraṃ Buddhaṃ Bhagavantaṃ papracchuḥ. «kim, Bhadanta, Kubj'|ôttarayā karma kṛtaṃ yena kubjā saṃvṛttā?»

36.280 Bhagavān āha, «Kubj'|ôttaray" âiva, bhikṣavaḥ, karmāṇi kṛtāny upacitāni, labdha|saṃbhārāṇi, pariṇata|pratyayāni oghavat pratyupasthitāni, avaśyaṃ|bhāvīni. tayā karmāṇi kṛtāny upacitāni. ko 'nyaḥ pratyanubhaviṣyati? na, mahā|rāja, karmāṇi kṛtāny upacitāni, bāhye pṛthivī|dhātau vipacyante, n' âb|dhātau, na tejo|dhātau, na vāyu|dhātau, api t' ûpātteṣv eva skandha|dhātv|āyataneṣu karmāṇi kṛtāny upacitāni vipacyante, śubhāny aśubhāni ca.

However, because of the solemn vow those women made, they perceived the Truths in my presence. Therefore, great king, it is said, 'The fruit of wholly black deeds is itself wholly black; the fruit of wholly white deeds is itself wholly white; and the fruit of mixed deeds is itself mixed.' Therefore, then, great king, abandon wholly black deeds as well as mixed deeds and direct your own earnest efforts toward wholly white deeds. In this way, great king, should you train yourself."

At that, Udáyana, King of the Vatsas, delighted and gladdened by the Lord's words, honored the Lord's feet with his head, and departed from the presence of the Lord.

The monks, their doubts again aroused, questioned the Lord Buddha, who resolves all doubts. "Venerable sir, what deed did Kubjóttara perform as a result of which she became a hunchback?"

Replied the Lord, "Kubjóttara herself, O monks, per- 36.280
formed and accumulated many deeds, the bases of which are about to ripen, which exist in a multitude and the effects of which are inevitable. She herself performed and accumulated these deeds. Who else could experience their effects? Great king, those deeds performed and accumulated by her did not manifest their effects without, in the earth-element or in the water-element, or in the fire-element or in the air-element. Rather, deeds that are performed and accumulated manifest their effects in the five constituents of the personality, in the whole complex of embodied experience of the six senses, where they were performed, and these results may be wholesome or unwholesome.

Na pranaśyanti karmāṇi, api kalpa|śatair api:
sāmagrīṃ prāpya kālaṃ ca phalanti khalu dehinām.
iti

Bhūta|pūrvaṃ, bhikṣavaḥ, Vārāṇasyāṃ nagaryām, Brahma|datto nāma rājā rājyaṃ kārayati, ṛddhaṃ ca, sphītaṃ ca, kṣemaṃ ca, subhikṣaṃ ca, ākīrṇa|bahu|jana|manuṣyaṃ ca, praśānta|kali|kalaha|ḍimba|ḍamaram, taskara|rog'|âpagatam, śāl'|îkṣu|go|mahiṣī|saṃpannam, akhilam, akaṇṭakam. dhārmikaḥ, dharma|rājo dharmeṇa rājyaṃ kārayati.

Naimittikair dvā|daśa|vārṣikā anāvṛṣṭir ādiṣṭāḥ. rājñā Vārāṇasyām evaṃ ghaṇṭ"|âvaghoṣaṇaṃ kāritam: ‹yasya dvā|daśa|vārṣikaṃ bhaktam asti, tena sthātavyam. yasya n' âsti, ten' ânyatra gantavyam iti, yataḥ kālen' āgantavyam› iti.

Tena khalu samayena, Vārāṇasyāṃ Saṃdhāno nāma gṛha|patiḥ prativasati, āḍhyaḥ, Mahādhanaḥ, mahā|bhogaḥ, vistīrṇa|viśāla|parigraho Vaiśravaṇa|dhana|samudito Vaiśravaṇa|dhana|pratispardhī. tena, koṣṭh'|âgārika āhūy' ôktaḥ, ‹bhoḥ puruṣa, bhaviṣyati, mama sa|parivārasya, dvā|daśa varṣāṇi bhaktam?› iti.

36.285 Sa kathayati, ‹ārya, bhaviṣyati› iti.

Asati Buddhānām utpāde, Pratyeka|buddhā loka utpadyante, hīna|dīn'|ânukampakāḥ, prānta|śayan'|āsana|bhaktāḥ, eka|dakṣiṇīyā lokasya. yāvat Pratyeka|buddha|sahasraṃ

Deeds are never destroyed, even after hundreds of aeons:
When conditions and time are right, they inevitably bear fruit among living beings.

In a previous existence, O monks, in the city of Varánasi, a king named Brahma·datta ruled the kingdom. It was prosperous, thriving, peaceful, endowed with an abundance of food, densely populated, free from riots, fighting, battle and war as well as from thieves and disease, and rich in rice, sugarcane, cattle and water buffalo—entirely without troubles. Being righteous, that righteous king ruled justly.

The soothsayers foretold a twelve-year drought. The king had the proclamation bell in Varánasi rung: 'Those who possess a twelve-year supply of food should remain in Varánasi. Those who do not are to go elsewhere, from where, in time, they may return.'

Now, at that time there lived in Varánasi a householder by the name of Sandhána. He was wealthy, having a great deal of money and possessions. His properties were extensive and he had produced enormous wealth. Indeed, his wealth rivalled that of the God of Wealth, Vaishrávana himself. Sandhána summoned his steward and asked him, 'Well, my man, will there be enough food for twelve years for me and my household?'

The fellow replied, 'Sir, there will.' 36.285

When no Buddhas have appeared, Solitary Buddhas appear in the world, full of compassion for the wretched and miserable, having their food, seats and beds in remote areas, singularly worthy of the world's veneration. Just then, a

jana|pada|cārikāṃ caran, Vārāṇasīm anuprāptam. te 'nyatamasminn udyāne kuṭikāyeṣv avasthitāḥ.

‹Bhoḥ puruṣa, vinyasya pravrajita|sahasrasya mama dvā|daśa varṣāṇi bhaktam› iti.

Sa kathayati, ‹ārya, bhaviṣyati› iti.

Tena teṣāṃ pratijñātam. dāna|śālā māpitāḥ. pūrva|vat tatra dine dine Prayeka|buddha|sahasraṃ bhuṅkte. tatr' âikaḥ Pratyeka|buddho glānaḥ. so 'nyatamasmin dine n' āgacchati. Saṃdhānasya duhitā kathayati, ‹tāta, eko 'dya pravrajito n' āgataḥ› iti.

36.290 Sa kathayati, ‹putri, kīdṛśaḥ?› iti.

Sā, pṛṣṭhaṃ vināmayitvā, kathayati, ‹tāta, īdṛśaḥ› iti. yad anayā Pratyeka|buddho vināditaḥ, tasya karmaṇo vipākena, kubjā saṃvṛttā.»

Punar api, bhikṣavo Buddhaṃ Bhagavantaṃ papracchuḥ: «kim, Bhadanta, Kubj'|ôttarayā karma kṛtaṃ yena śruta|dharā jātā» iti.

Bhagavān āha, «tena kālena, tena samayena, Pratyeka|buddhānāṃ yaḥ saṃgha|sthaviraḥ, sa vāyv|ābādhikaḥ. tasya bhuñjānasya pātraṃ kampate. tasya Saṃdhāna|duhitrā hastāt kaṭān avatārya, sa Pratyeka|buddha uktaḥ, ‹Ārya, tais tat pātraṃ sthāpaya› iti. tena tatra sthāpitam. niṣkampam avasthitam.

thousand Solitary Buddhas who were travelling through the countryside reached Varánasi. They settled down in huts in a certain park.

'Well, my man, now you must supply food to those thousand renunciates and to me and my household for twelve years.'

The steward replied, 'Sir, it will be done.'

And so Sandhána promised the Solitary Buddhas that he would feed them. He had almshouses built and there, as before, every day those thousand Solitary Buddhas took their meals. At that time, a certain Solitary Buddha had fallen ill, and one day did not come to receive alms. Sandhána's daughter said, 'Daddy, today one of the wanderers did not show up.'

He said, 'Daughter, what is he like?' 36.290

Hunching her back forward, she said, 'Daddy, he's like this.' And because she mocked that Solitary Buddha, by the maturing of that deed, in a subsequent birth she became a hunchback."

Again the monks questioned the Lord Buddha: "Venerable sir, what deed did Kubjóttara perform as a result of which she became learned in the Buddha's teachings?"

The Lord replied, "At that time, on that occasion, there was an elder in the community of Solitary Buddhas who suffered from palsy, due to an excess of the wind humor. When he ate, his bowl shook. Sandhána's daughter removed the bangles from her wrist and said to that Solitary Buddha, 'Holy One, steady your bowl with these.' He placed his bowl on the bangles; it stood firm without wobbling.

Tayā, pādayor nipatya, praṇidhānaṃ kṛtam: ‹yath" âiva tat pātraṃ niṣkampam avasthitam, evam eva mam' âpi saṃtāne ye dharmāḥ praviśeyuḥ, te niṣkampaṃ tiṣṭhantu› iti.

36.295 Yat tayā praṇidhānaṃ kṛtam, tasya karmaṇo vipākena śruta|dharā saṃvṛttā.

Punar api, bhikṣavo Bhagavantaṃ papracchuḥ: «kim, Bhadanta, Kubj'|ôttarayā karma kṛtaṃ yena dāsī saṃvṛttā» iti.

Bhagavān āha, «anayā, bhikṣavaḥ, tatr' âiśvarya|mada|mattayā, parijano dāsī|vādena samudācaritaḥ. tasya karmaṇo vipākena, dāsī saṃvṛttā.»

Punar api, bhikṣavo Bhagavantaṃ papracchuḥ: «kim, Bhadanta, Anupamayā karma kṛtaṃ yad eṣā, nir|āhārā bhūmi|gṛhe sthāpitā, amlāna|gātrī c' ôtthitā?»

Bhagavān āha, «Anupamay" âiva, bhikṣavaḥ, karmāṇi kṛtāny upacitāni, labdha|saṃbhārāṇi, pariṇata|pratyayāny ogha|vat pratyupasthitāni, avaśyaṃ|bhāvīni. tayā karmāṇi kṛtāny upacitāni. ko 'nyaḥ pratyanubhaviṣyati? na, bhikṣavaḥ, karmāṇi kṛtāny upacitāni, bāhye pṛthivī|dhātau vipacyante, n' âb|dhātau, na tejo|dhātau, na vāyu|dhātau, api t' ûpātteṣv eva skandha|dhātv|āyataneṣu karmāṇi kṛtāny upacitāni vipacyante, śubhāny aśubhāni ca.

Prostrating herself at that Solitary Buddha's feet, Sandhána's daughter made this solemn religious vow: 'Just as this bowl stands firm without wobbling, even so may the teachings of the Dharma enter into my mind-stream in successive births, and may I retain them unshakably.'

Because she made that solemn religious vow, as a result 36.295 of the maturing of that deed, she became, in a subsequent birth, learned in the Buddha's teachings.

Again the monks questioned the Lord: "What deed did Kubjóttara perform as a result of which she became a slave?"

The Lord replied, "Monks, because she was intoxicated with her position of authority, she addressed one of her attendants with the word 'slave.' By the maturing of that deed, in a subsequent birth she became a slave."

Once again the monks questioned the Lord: "Venerable sir, what deed did Anúpama perform as a result of which, although cast into a cellar without food, when she came out her body had suffered no ill effects?"

Replied the Lord, "Monks, Anúpama herself performed and accumulated many deeds, the bases of which are about to ripen, which exist in a multitude and the effects of which are inevitable. She herself performed and accumulated these deeds. Who else could experience their effects? Great king, those deeds performed and accumulated by her did not manifest their effects without, in the earth-element or in the water-element, or in the fire-element or in the air-element.Rather, deeds that are performed and accumulated manifest their effects in the five constituents of the personality, in the whole complex of embodied experience of the

36.300 Na pranaśyanti karmāṇi, api kalpa|śatair api:
sāmagrīṃ prāpya kālaṃ ca phalanti khalu dehinām.
iti

Bhūta|pūrvam, bhikṣavo 'nyatamasmin karvaṭake, dve dārike anyonya|saṃstutike, kṣatriya|dārikā brāhmaṇa|dārikā ca.

Asati Buddhānām utpāde, Pratyeka|buddhā loka utpadyante, hīna|dīn'|ânukampakāḥ, prānta|śayan'|āsana|bhaktāḥ, eka|dakṣiṇīyā lokasya.

Yāvad anyatamaḥ Pratyeka|buddho 'nyatamasmiñ śānte pradeśe rātriṃ vāsam upagataḥ. aparasmin divase, pūrv'|âhṇe, nivāsya, piṇḍ'|ârthī pracalitaḥ. taṃ dṛṣṭvā, te dārike, prasādite, asmai praṇīt'|ânna|pūrṇaṃ pātraṃ prayacchataḥ. tat|karmaṇo vipākena, Anupamā jāt" âikā, Ghoṣilasya gṛha|pater duhitā jātā, mahā|sundarī Śrīmatī nāma.»

Ekasmin samaye, rājñā dṛṣṭā, pṛṣṭā ca, «kasy' êyaṃ kanyā?»

36.305 Mantribhiḥ kathitam, «Ghoṣilasya gṛha|pateḥ.»

Tato Ghoṣilo gṛha|patiḥ, samāhūya, uktaḥ, «gṛha|pate, tava duhit" êyaṃ kanyā?»

six senses, where they were performed, and these results may be wholesome or unwholesome.

> Deeds are never destroyed, even after hundreds of aeons: 36.300
> When conditions and time are right, they inevitably bear fruit among living beings.

In a previous existence, monks, in a certain mountain village, lived two girls who were close friends, a nobleman's daughter and a priest's.

When no Buddhas have appeared, Solitary Buddhas appear in the world, full of compassion for the wretched and miserable, having their food, seats and beds in remote areas, singularly worthy of the world's veneration.

At that time, a certain Solitary Buddha was passing the night in a quiet spot in the countryside. The following day, in the morning, he dressed and went out to obtain alms. The two girls saw him, and, filled with serene faith, presented to him a bowlful of fine food. By the maturing of that deed, one of them was reborn as Anúpama, the other as the daughter of the householder Ghóshila, an exceedingly beautiful girl whom he named Shrímati, 'Gloria.'"

On one occasion, King Udáyana saw Shrímati and asked, "Whose daughter is she?"

His ministers told him, "She is the daughter of the house- 36.305
holder Ghóshila."

Then the householder Ghóshila was summoned and asked, "Householder, this girl is your daughter?"

Sa prāha, «mama, Deva.»

«Kasmān mama na dīyate? dīyatāṃ mahyam!»

Sa prāha, «Deva, dattā bhavatu.» Ghoṣilena gṛha|patinā dattā. Udayanena Vatsa|rājen' ântaḥ|puraṃ praveśya, mahatā śrī|samudayena pariṇītā.

36.310 Apareṇa samayena, rāj" ôktaḥ, «Deva, bhikṣu|darśanam abhikāṅkṣāmi» iti.

Sa kathayati, «ākāṅkṣase, kiṃ tu bhikṣavo rāja|kulaṃ praviśanti?»

«Deva, ahaṃ nāma dārakaṃ praveśitā. sarvathā, yadi bhikṣu|darśanaṃ na labhe, ady' âgreṇa na bhokṣye, na pāsye» iti. s" ân|āhāra|tāṃ pratipannā.

Rājñā Ghoṣilo gṛha|patir uktaḥ, «gṛha|pate, na tvaṃ duhitaraṃ pratyavekṣase?»

«Deva, kim?»

36.315 «An|āhāra|tāṃ pratipannā.»

«Kim|artham?»

«Bhikṣu|darśanam ākāṅkṣate. tad" ātmano gṛhe bhaktaṃ sādhitvā, kakṣāyāṃ Bhikṣu|saṃgham upanimantrya, bhojaya, antareṇa ca dvāraṃ chedaya» iti.

Rājño Ghoṣilasya ca saṃsakta|sīmaṃ gṛham. Ghoṣilena gṛha|patinā dvāraṃ chinnam. tato bhūri karma kārayitvā, yena Bhagavān ten' ôpasaṃkrāntaḥ. upasaṃkramya, Bhagavataḥ pādau śirasā vanditvā, ek'|ânte niṣaṇṇaḥ. ek'|ânta|niṣaṇṇaṃ Ghoṣilaṃ gṛha|patiṃ Bhagavān dharmyayā

He replied, "She is, your majesty."

"Is there any reason she can't be given to me? Indeed, let her be given to me!"

He replied, "Your majesty, let her be so given." And so the householder Ghóshila gave her in marriage to the king. Udáyana, King of the Vatsas, brought her into the women's apartments of the palace and married her with great pomp and ceremony.

Some time after that, Shrímati said to the king, "Your 36.310
majesty, I long to see the monks."

Udáyana replied, "You long to see them, but what about the prohibition against monks entering the royal palace?"

"Your majesty, I am in truth with child, a son. In any case, if I don't get to see the monks, starting today I shall neither eat nor drink." And she began to fast.

The king spoke to the householder Ghóshila, "Householder, will you not look after your daughter?"

"What do you mean, your majesty?"

"She has begun a fast." 36.315

"For what reason?"

"She longs to see the monks. Therefore, prepare food at your own house, invite the community of monks into a private courtyard, feed them and bore a hole in the door from the inside."

Now, the king and Ghóshila had adjoining houses. The householder Ghóshila bored a hole in the door to his courtyard. He had a lot of other work done, then went to see the Lord. Having approached, he honored the Lord's feet with his head and sat down to one side. Then the householder Ghóshila, who was seated to one side, the Lord illuminated,

kathayā saṃdarśayati, samādāpayati, samuttejayati, saṃpraharṣayati. aneka|paryāyeṇa dharmyayā kathayā saṃdarśya, samādāpya, samuttejya, saṃpraharṣya, tūṣṇīm.

Atha Ghoṣilo gṛha|patiḥ, utthāy' āsanāt, yena Bhagavāṃs ten' âñjaliṃ praṇamya, Bhagavantam idam avocat: «adhivāsayatu me, Bhagavāñ śvo 'ntar|gṛhe bhaktena mama nimantritaṃ sārdhaṃ Bhikṣu|saṃghena.»

36.320 Atha Ghoṣilo gṛha|patiḥ śuci praṇītaṃ, khādanīyaṃ bhojanīyaṃ, samudānīy' āsanāni prajñapya, Bhagavato dūtena kālam ārocayati: «samayaḥ, Bhadanta, sajjaṃ bhaktaṃ yasy' êdānīṃ Bhagavān kālaṃ manyate» iti.

Bhagavān aupadhike sthitaḥ.* Śāriputra|pramukho Bhikṣu|saṃghaḥ saṃprasthitaḥ.

Pañcabhiḥ kāraṇair Buddhā Bhagavanta aupadhike tiṣṭhanti, abhinirhṛta|piṇḍa|pātaḥ. caturṇām āyuṣmanta ājñ" âkopyā: Tathāgatasya, Arhataḥ samyak|saṃbuddhasy' ârhato bhikṣoḥ; kṣīṇ'|āśravasy' ôpadhi|vārakasya; rājñaś ca kṣatriyasya mūrdhn" âbhiṣiktasya.

Smṛtim upasthāpayati. «praviśāmaḥ» iti. sa, praviśya, purastād Bhikṣu|saṃghasya, prajñapta ev' āsane niṣaṇṇaḥ.

inspired, roused and delighted with a discourse on Dharma. After having illuminated, inspired, roused and delighted him in numerous ways with a discourse on Dharma, the Lord fell silent.

Then the householder Ghóshila rose from his seat, venerated the Lord with raised hands joined and said this to the Lord: "May the Lord, accompanied by the community of monks, consent to receive alms tomorrow in my home."

The next morning, the householder Ghóshila had the 36.320
finest pure foods prepared, both hard and soft, arranged for the required seating and then informed the Lord by messenger that it was time for the meal: "It is time, Venerable sir. The food is ready if the Lord thinks now is the right time."

The Lord refrained from partaking of the material gift.* Instead, Shari·putra, at the head of the community of monks, set out for Ghóshila's home.

Five are the circumstances in which the Lord Buddhas refrain from accepting material gifts, that is, almsfood that has been prepared. And four are those whose command is inviolable: a Tathágata, an Arhat, a Fully Awakened One; a monk who is an Arhat; a supervisor of monks who has destroyed the defilements; and a consecrated king of noble lineage.

Shari·putra established himself in full mindfulness. "Let us go in." Then he entered Ghóshila's house and sat down before the community of monks on the seat provided.

Atha Śrīmatī Devī sukh'|ôpaniṣaṇṇaṃ Śāriputra|pramukhaṃ Bhikṣu|saṃghaṃ viditvā, śucinā praṇītena khādanīyena bhojanīyena sva|hastaṃ saṃtarpya, saṃpravārya, Śāriputraṃ bhuktavantaṃ viditvā, dhauta|hastam apanīta|pātram, nīca|taram āsanaṃ gṛhītvā, Śāriputrasya purastān niṣaṇṇā dharma|śravaṇāya.

36.325 Ath' Āyuṣmāñ Śāriputraḥ Śrīmatīṃ Devīṃ dharmyayā kathayā saṃdarśayati, samādāpayati, samuttejayati, saṃpraharṣayati. sā Satyāni na paśyati. Āyuṣmāñ Śāriputraḥ saṃlakṣayati, «kim asyāḥ santi kāni cit kuśala|mūlāni?» na sant' îti paśyati. «santi kasy' ântike pratibaddhāni?» paśyaty ātmanaḥ.

Tasya Dharmaṃ deśayato vicārayataś ca sūry'|âstaṃ|gamana|samayo jātaḥ. bhikṣavaḥ, utthāy' āsanāt, prakrāntāḥ. Āyuṣmāñ Śāriputraḥ saṃlakṣayati, «kiṃ c' âpi Bhagavatā n' ânujñātam. sthānam etad vidyate, yad etad eva pratyakṣaṃ kṛtvā, anujñāsyati» iti.

Sa, viney"|âpekṣayā, tatr' âiv' âvasthitaḥ. tena tasyā āśay'|ânuśayaṃ dhātuṃ ca prakṛtiṃ ca jñātvā, tādṛśī Dharma|deśanā kṛtā, yāṃ śrutvā, Śrīmatyā viṃśati|śikhara|samudgataṃ sat|kāya|dṛṣṭi|śailaṃ jñāna|vajreṇa bhittvā, Srota|āpatti|phalaṃ sākṣāt|kṛtam. sā, dṛṣṭa|satyāḥ, trir udānam udānayati:

Then, when Queen Shrímati knew that the community of monks , led by Shari·putra, were comfortably seated, with her own hands she served and satisfied them with the finest pure foods, both hard and soft. And when she saw that Shari·putra had finished eating, had washed his hands and had set aside his bowl, she took a stool and sat down in front of Shari·putra in order to listen to the Dharma.

The Venerable Shari·putra then illuminated, inspired, 36.325
roused and delighted Queen Shrímati with a discourse on Dharma. But she did not perceive the Truths. The Venerable Shari·putra reflected, "Does this woman have any bases of skillfulness at all?" He saw that she did not. "Due to whose presence are there obstructions?" He saw that it was due to himself.

While he was expounding and discussing the Dharma, the hour of sunset came. The other monks rose from their seats and departed. The Venerable Shari·putra reflected, "Now, this present situation the Lord has not authorized, but what will happen is that he will clarify it and give his authorization."

And out of regard for her who required spiritual training, Shari·putra remained right there. Knowing Shrímati's mental disposition, her character and circumstances, Shari·putra imparted to her such instruction in the Dharma that, listening to it, Shrímati shattered with the thunderbolt of insight the twenty-peaked mountain that is the erroneous belief in a permanently existent self, and attained the fruit of Entrance into the Stream. Realizing the truth, she thrice proclaimed this joyous utterance:

«Idaṃ mama, Bhadanta, na mātrā kṛtam, na pitrā kṛtam, na rājñā, n' êṣṭa|sva|jana|bandhu|vargeṇa, na devatābhiḥ, na pūrva|pretaiḥ, na śramaṇa|brāhmaṇaiḥ, yad Bhagavatā me tat kṛtam. ucchoṣitā rudhir'|âśru|samudrā! laṅghitā asthi|parvatāḥ! pihitāny apāya|dvārāṇi! pratiṣṭhāpit" âhaṃ deva|manuṣyeṣu.» āha ca:

Tav' ânubhāvāt pihitaḥ sughoro
hy apāya|mārgo bahu|doṣa|duṣṭaḥ,
apāvṛtā svarga|gatiḥ supuṇyā
nirvāṇa|mārgaṃ ca may" ôpalabdham.

36.330 Tvad|āśrayāc c' āptam apeta|doṣaṃ
mam' âdya śuddhaṃ suviśuddha|cakṣuḥ,
prāptaṃ ca kāntaṃ padam Ārya|kāntaṃ
tīrṇā ca duḥkh'|ârṇava|pāram asmi.

Jagati daitya|nar'|âmara|pūjita,
vigata|janma|jarā|maraṇ'|āmaya,
bhava|sahasra|su|durlabha|darśana
sa|phalam adya, mune, tava darśanam!

"Such a kind favor as you have done for me, Venerable sir, was never done by my mother or father, nor by the king nor by any of my relatives or immediate family, nor by the gods or by my ancestors, nor by any priest or ascetic. The oceans of blood and tears are dried up! The mountains of bones have been surmounted! The gates of misery are shut fast! I am established among the most excellent among gods and humans!" And then she declaimed these verses:

Through your spiritual power, closed is the path to
evil rebirths,
So frightful, so filled with sin and wickedness;
Opened for me is the meritorious way to heaven
And gained for me the path to nirvana.

Through taking refuge in you, I have this day attained 36.330
freedom from sin,
Acquired the faultless, wholly purified vision,
And have attained that longed-for goal sought by
the Holy Ones—
I have crossed to the further shore of the ocean of
suffering.

O you who in this world are honored by gods, men
and demons,
Who are freed from birth, old age, disease and death,
The sight of whom is so exceedingly difficult to gain
even in a thousand births—
O Sage, seeing you this day has borne great fruit!

Atikrānt" âham, Bhadanta, atikrāntā! eṣ" âhaṃ Bhagavantaṃ śaraṇaṃ gacchāmi, Dharmaṃ ca, Bhikṣu|saṃghaṃ ca. upāsikāṃ ca māṃ dhāray' âdy' âgreṇa yāvaj|jīvam—prāṇ'|ôpetāṃ śaraṇaṃ gatām abhiprasannām» iti.

Ath' Āyuṣmāñ Śāriputraḥ Śrīmatīṃ Satyeṣu pratiṣṭhāpya, prakrānto yena Bhagavāṃs ten' ôpasaṃkrāntaḥ. upasaṃkramya, Bhagavataḥ pādau śirasā vanditv" âik'|ânte niṣaṇṇaḥ. ek'|ânte niṣaṇṇaḥ, Āyuṣmāñ Śāriputra etat prakaraṇaṃ bhikṣavo Bhagavate vistareṇ' ārocayati.

Bhagavān āha, «sādhu! sādhu, Śāriputra! saptānām ājñā akopyā: Tathāgatasya, Arhataḥ samyak|saṃbuddhasya; arhato bhikṣoḥ kṣīṇ'|āśravasya; rājñaḥ kṣatriyasya mūrdhn" âbhiṣiktasya; Saṃgha|sthavirasya; upadhi|vārikasya; ācāryasya; upādhyāyasya.»

36.335 Atha Bhagavān, śikṣā|kāmatayā, varṇaṃ bhāṣitvā ... pūrvavad yāvat* ... pūrvikā prajñaptiḥ. «iyaṃ c' âbhyanujñāt" âivaṃ ca me śrāvakair Vinaya|śikṣā|padam upadeṣṭavyam.

Yaḥ punar bhikṣuḥ, anirgatāyāṃ rajanyām, anudgate 'ruṇe, anirhṛteṣu ratneṣu, ratna|saṃmateṣu vā, rajñaḥ kṣatriyasya mūrdhn" âbhiṣiktasy' êndra|kīlaṃ vā, indra|kīla|sāmantaṃ vā, samatikrāmed anyatra, tad|rūpāt pratyayāt, pāyantik" êti.

I have gone beyond the cycle of birth-and-death, Venerable sir, I have gone beyond! I, this very person, go for refuge to the Lord, to the Dharma and to the Monastic Community. Please accept me as a lay disciple from this day forth for as long as I shall live—in faith I have gone for refuge as long as I breathe."

Having thus established Shrímati in the Truths, the Venerable Shari·putra departed and went to see the Lord. He approached, honored the Lord's feet with his head and sat down to one side. Seated thus to one side, the Venerable Shari·putra explained the situation in detail to the Lord and to the monks.

The Lord said, "Well done! Well done, Shari·putra! Seven are the persons whose command is inviolable: a Tathágata, an Arhat, a Fully Awakened One; a monk who is an Arhat and who has destroyed the defilements; a consecrated king of noble lineage; an elder in the community of monks; a monastic administrator; a monk who is an eminent teacher; and a monk who is a spiritual preceptor."

Then, out of a desire to teach, the Lord, having spoken 36.335
praise . . . as before,* up to . . . the previous regulation. And this regulation he certified as valid, saying, "And in this way should my disciples impart instruction in the Rules of Training of our Discipline.

Again, when night has not yet departed and when dawn has not yet arisen, when the treasures or those things regarded as treasures have not yet been put away, a monk who steps across the threshold, or its environs, of a consecrated king of noble lineage, in circumstances other than Shari·putra's, commits a transgression* of the monastic code.

Yaḥ punaḥ ‹bhikṣuḥ› iti ‹Udāyī› iti–sa vā punar anyo 'py evaṃ|jātīyaḥ. ‹anirgatāyāṃ rajanyām› ity ‹aprabhātāyām›. ‹anudgate› iti ‹anudite›. ‹aruṇe› iti ‹aruṇaḥ: nīl'|âruṇaḥ, pīt'|âruṇaḥ, tāmr'|âruṇaḥ›. tatra, ‹nīl'|âruṇo› nīl'|ābhāsaḥ, ‹pīt'|âruṇaḥ› pīt'|ābhāsaḥ, ‹tāmr'|âruṇas› tāmr'|ābhāsaḥ. iha tu, ‹tāmr'|âruṇo 'bhipretaḥ.

‹Ratneṣu vā› iti ratnāny ucyante ‹maṇayaḥ, muktā, vaiḍūryam, śaṅkha|śilā, pravāḍam, rajatam, jāta|rūpam, aśma|garbhaḥ, musāra|galvaḥ, lohitikā dakṣiṇāvartāḥ›. ‹ratna|saṃ|mateṣu vā› iti ‹ratna|saṃ|matam ucyate sarvaṃ saṃgrām'|âvacara|śastraṃ, sarvaṃ ca gandharv'|âvacaraṃ bhāṇḍam›.

‹Rājñaḥ kṣatriyasya mūrdh'|âbhiṣiktasya› iti vā ‹rājye stry api rājy'|âbhiṣekeṇ' âbhiṣiktā bhavati, rājā sa kṣatriyo mūrdhn" âbhiṣiktaḥ›. kṣatriyo 'pi, brāhmaṇo 'pi, vaiśyo 'pi, śūdro 'pi, rājy'|âbhiṣekeṇ' âbhiṣikto bhavati, ‹rājā kṣatriyo mūrdhn" âbhiṣiktaḥ.›

36.340 ‹Indrakīlaṃ vā› iti traya Indra|kīlā: nagare Indra|kīlaḥ, rāja|kule Indra|kīlo 'ntaḥ|pura Indra|kīlaś ca. ‹indra|kīla|sāmantaṃ vā› iti tat|samīpam. ‹samatikramet› api, ‹vigacchet›. ‹anyatra, tad|rūpāt pratyayāt› iti ‹tad|rūpaṃ pratyayaṃ sthāpayitvā›. ‹pāyantikā› iti ‹dahati, pacati, yātayati›, pūrvavat.*

Again, 'a monk' here means 'Udáyin*'—he, or again, another of the same character. 'When night has not yet departed' means 'before dawn.' 'Not arisen' means 'not appeared.' 'At dawn' means 'the successive phases of dawn: blue-black dawn, yellow dawn, red dawn.' In this sense, 'blue-black dawn' is characterized by blue-black light, 'yellow dawn' by yellowish light, 'red dawn' by reddish light. But here 'red dawn' is intended.

In the phrase 'when the treasures or . . . ,' the treasures indicated are 'gemstones, pearls, lapis lazuli, mother-of-pearl, coral, silver, gold, emerald, tiger's-eye, ruby and conch-shells with their spirals curving to the right.' 'Or those things regarded as treasures' indicates 'all types of armaments used in battle as well as all musical instruments.'

'Of a consecrated king of noble lineage' indicates a kingdom in which even the women of the royal family are consecrated by the royal consecration and in which the king, who is of noble lineage, has undergone the proper consecration ceremony. So long as he has undergone the proper royal consecration ceremony, 'a consecrated king of noble lineage' can be from the nobility, or from the priestly, mercantile or servant classes.

'Threshold' refers to three different thresholds: the thresh- 36.340
old of the city, the threshold of the royal palace and the threshold of the apartments of the palace women. 'Or the environs of the threshold' refers to the immediate vicinity of those three. As for 'if a monk steps across,' it means 'if he goes astray.' 'In other circumstances, as a result of

Tatr' āpattiḥ kathaṃ bhavati? bhikṣuḥ, aprabhāte, prabhāta|saṃjñī, nagar'|êndra|kīlaṃ samatikrāmati, āpadyate duṣ|kṛtām. aprabhāte vaimatikaḥ, āpadyate duṣ|kṛtām. prabhāte, aprabhāta|saṃjñī, āpadyate duṣ|kṛtām. prabhāte vaimatikaḥ, āpadyate duṣ|kṛtām. bhikṣuḥ, aprabhāte, aprabhāta|saṃjñī, antaḥ|pur'|êndrakīlaṃ samatikrāmati, āpadyate pāyantikām. prabhāte, aprabhātasaṃjñī, āpadyate duṣ|kṛtām. prabhāte vaimatikaḥ, āpadyate duṣ|kṛtām. anāpattī rājā śabdayati, ‹devyaḥ! kumārāḥ! amātyāḥ! aṣṭānām antarāyāṇām anyatam'|ânyatamam upasthitaṃ bhavati, rājā caura|manuṣy'|âmanuṣya|vyāḍ'|âgny|udakānām.› anāpattir ādikarmikasy' êti pūrvavat.»

iti Śrī|divy'|âvadāne
Mākandik'|âvadānaṃ samāptam.

such a deed' means 'committing such a deed would constitute.' 'Transgression' means 'that the karmic consequences of which burn, torment, punish,' as previously discussed.*

In such circumstances, then, how is an offense incurred? A monk who, at the time before dawn, yet aware that dawn is nigh, steps across the threshold of a city, commits a misdeed. If he is in doubt that it is before dawn, he commits a misdeed. If it is dawn, but he thinks that it is not yet dawn, he commits a misdeed. If he is uncertain whether it is dawn, he commits a misdeed. If, before dawn, a monk who is aware it is before dawn steps across the threshold of the palace women's apartments, he commits an offense. If, at dawn, he thinks it is still before dawn, he commits misdeed. If he is uncertain whether it is dawn, he commits a misdeed. But there is no offense when the king calls, 'Queens! Princes! Ministers! One or other of the eight who have entered the women's apartments is a king of thieves, or of humans or non-humans or beasts, or of fire or of water.' For a beginner, this, as mentioned previously, is not an offense."

Thus ends, in the Glorious Heavenly Exploits,
"The Story of Makándika."

NOTES

Bold *references are to the English text;* ***bold italic*** *references are to the Sanskrit text. An asterisk (*) in the body of the text marks the word or passage being annotated.*

1.3 **Three conditions:** The following theory of conception is found in the Buddhist Canon and is peculiar to Buddhists.

1.8 *Adhar imāṃ*, "**lowest**"; see EDGERTON BHSD p. 12.

1.12 **Shrona Koti·karna:** ("Shrona with ten million in his ears") In the language used by Buddhists before they began to use Sanskrit, Shrona is the equivalent of Sanskrit *Śravaṇā*. It was common in ancient India to name a child after the constellation under which it was born.

1.15 **Expert in the evaluation of these eight:** Here the manuscripts list only *vāstu/parīkṣā* and *ratna/parīkṣā;* I supply the other six *parīkṣā*s from CN 58.17–18, 100.3–4, 441.29–442.1; V 35.25, 63.6, 287.11–12.

1.16 This common Buddhist motif goes back to the Canon. It came to be applied to the early life of Siddhártha, the Buddha himself. According to tradition, he left home one night when bored with the ladies' orchestra.

1.45 **Mode of rebirth:** Buddhists believe in six realms of rebirth: in heaven as a god, on earth as a human, on earth as an animal, just under the earth as an anti-god, as a hungry ghost who haunts the earth, or in a hell. It is from being a hungry ghost that the meritorious acts of those left on earth can sometimes save one.

1.47 This blessing on the donkeys echoes a canonical passage, *Aṅguttara Nikāya* IV.46, which in turn echoes the Vedic blessing (*Ṛg Veda* X.169.1) on cows as they are let out to graze, a text also used in brahminical rituals.

1.76 *āsī:* A Buddhist Hybrid Sanskrit alternative for the Classical Sanskrit 1st sg. *āsam.* (cf. EDGERTON BHSG § 32.20 and p. 205 for *āsī* used as 1st, 2nd and 3rd sg. and for 3rd pl.)

1.144 **Entry into the Stream:** Spiritual progress is classified into four stages: stream-entry, once-returner, non-returner, Arhat. The stream-enterer will be reborn on earth *at most* seven more times, the once-returner only once, the non-returner not at all. The Arhat has realised nirvana, i.e. is enlightend.

1.148 **Pupils:** The text uses the technical terms for monastic pupillage.

1.149 **Three Knowledges:** Knowledge of his former birth, knowledge of the rebirths of others, knowledge that his moral defilemenst had passed away. The last is tantamount to enlightenment.

1.151 **Tathágata:** a term for the Buddha.

1.153 By implication, the following message requests modifications to the monastic code of discipline.

1.154 ***Jandurako*, silk:** See Edgerton BHSD, s.vv. *eraka, janduraka, syandaraka.*

1.167 **Varánasi:** The ancient name for Benares. **Káshyapa** was the Buddha who preceded Gáutama Buddha ("our" Buddha). ***Stūpa*** is a synonym for *caitya* ("relic-mound"), which occurs just before in the same passage. BHSD takes *caitya* generally as any "object of veneration," while it translates *stūpa* as "relic-mound." However, in this passage, it's clear that *caitya* and *stūpa* refer to the same monument.

2.200 **Lord of Shaci** = Indra. **Hari** = Vishnu. **Shánkara** = Shiva.

2.237 **Insight**: According to an early Buddhist tradition (which however probably does not go back to the Buddha himself), Enlightenment may be attained by two different kinds of meditation. The more intellectual path, unlike the other, does not necessarily entail developing supernormal powers, such as flight.

2.243 **Foremost**: In the Canon, the Buddha declares various individuals to be foremost in some virtue or spiritual quality; This however is evidently a joke. What is here meant be *caitya (=stūpa)* is not clear.

2.250 **Most senior monks**: Evidently these were capable of simply materializing in the city.

2.311 Or: "made her a present of it." The text does not state the recipient.

2.320 **Perfect Awakening**: Maudgalyáyana is enlightened, an Arhat, and indeed in the Thera·vada tradition is considered one of the Buddha's two chief disciples. But here he regrets that he did not aspire to become a Buddha.

30.39 **Gáruda**: A huge, mythical bird of prey which is eternally at enmity with divine serpents *(nāga).*

30.42 *Sarvasaṃmataḥ*: Conjectural emendation GOMBRICH, *sarva/ santaḥ* MS.

30.45 **Three conditions:** This theory of conception is found in the Buddhist Canon and is peculiar to Buddhists.

30.58 The phrase ***pañca/sthāneṣu kṛtāvī saṃvṛttaḥ*** suggests that Súdhana masters five categories of skills, but it is unclear how one derives five categories from the list.

30.97 *Yakṣa:* Name of a class of "demigods," attendants of Kubéra (= Vaishrávana), the god of wealth, who guard his gardens and treasures. The term is also applied to Vaishrávana himself. Compare this scene to Purna's encounter with *yaksha*s in the second story in this volume.

30.105 These are the "treasures" that distinguish a universal monarch (cakra·vartin): wheel, elephant, horse, gem, woman, householder (or treasurer) and counsellor. See the *Pāli Mahāpadānasuttanta*, ed. T. W. RHYS DAVIDS & J. E. CARPENTER, Dīghanikāya, 3 vols., London: Pali Text Society, 1890-1910, vol. II, pp. 173-178; tr. M. Walshe, *Thus Have I Heard: The Long Discourses of the Buddha*, London: Wisdom Publications, 1987, pp. 280-283.

30.157 Before seeking out the sage at his ashram, Súdhana returns to Hástina·pura.

30.199 An **ádhaka** *(āḍhaka)* is a measure of grain equivalent to 7 lbs., 11 oz., or about 3.7 kg.

36.97 The Tibetan and Chinese recensions of the *Mūlasarvāstivāda-vinaya* give the full text of this episode. For purposes of narrative continuity, I give below an English rendition of HUBER's (1906:23) summary translation of the Chinese. "The helmsman warned the merchants of the perils of the ocean. They provided themselves with planks and inflatable leather sacks in order to be able to escape any shipwreck. A sea monster *(makara)* smashed up the ship; those merchants who were destined not to die yet were carried by the waves to *Tāmra·dvīpa* (Ceylon), to the city of the demons *(rākṣasī)*. On the highest tower of that city were planted two magic flagstaffs: the movement of one flag announced to the demons good fortune, the other misfortune. On that day the former began flapping and fluttering and from this the sirens concluded that shipwrecked men from India were about to reach the shore. There the sirens welcomed the men. Each merchant married one of them and lived with her in joy and luxurious comfort. To each man was born a son and a daughter. The sirens, however, forbade their husbands access to the road that led to the southern part of the city. Símhala, suspicious, proceeded there one night while the women were sleeping and arrived at a city enclosed by high iron walls that had no door or gate. From the interior of this city issued the sound of plaintive voices: 'Alas, India! Alas, our parents!' Símhala clambered up a *śirīṣa* tree and spoke with the prisoners. They also were shipwrecked Indians; they had been imprisoned since the day Símhala's company had landed on the island. From time to time their former wives came to devour one of them and the same fate awaited Símhala and his companions the day that a new group of shipwrecked men were cast onto the island. The fifteenth day of each month, *upoṣadha* day, the gods gathered in the air above that sorrowful city to lament the fate of the unfortunates whom the iron walls prevented from returning to the north of the city—because on that day of the month, Bálaha, the divine horse, waited in the north of the city to offer transport to whomever wished to cross to the other shore of the ocean, which was India. Símhala explained to his companions what he had learned and on the fifteenth day of the lunar month they all betook themselves to the north of the city where they found Bálaha, who promised to save them, so long as they did not allow themselves to be bewitched by the sirens at the last moment, for if that were to happen, he would not be able to carry them. The horse then rose up into the air and the flag of misfortune which was driven into the ground above the city began to flutter. The sirens, more beautiful than ever, hurried to the seashore and entreated the departing men to remain or at least not to leave without their children. All except Símhala were filled with regret; they fell from the horse and were devoured by the *rākṣasīs*. . . " For other versions of this story, see *Kāraṇḍavyūha* (ed. VAIDYA) 281, 284–288; *Guṇakāraṇḍavyūha* (ed. CHANDRA) 139–145, 158–203.

36.140 **Flag**: HUBER (1906: 24 fn. 1) points out that an earlier passage in I-TSING's Chinese translation of the *Mūlasarvāstivāda-vinaya* describes two flags in the demon's city. For details, see the note to 7.94 on page 309.

36.230 Recite this hypermetrical *anuṣṭubh* verse as if it read *°rūpeva dṛśyate*.

36.321 On this passage (***bhagavān aupadhike sthitaḥ,*** etc.), see BHSD, s.v. *aupadhika* (2) and the citations therein. See also the closely parallel passage in the *Mūlasarvāstivāda-vinayavastu* (ed. BAGCHI, i.236.24–237.2): "The topic [of monastic discipline] connected with *Śrāvastī:* At that time a certain householder invited the community of monks, led by the Buddha, to a meal at his house. The community of monks entered. The Lord refrained from partaking of that material gift, the food that had been prepared. Five are the circumstances in which the Lord Buddhas refrain from partaking of material gifts, that is, almsfood that has been prepared. What are these five? When they wish to withdraw into privacy; when they wish to expound the Dharma to deities; when they wish to engage in deep reflection; when they wish to look after [a monk] who is ill; and when they wish to instruct their disciples in the Rules of Training of the Vinaya. In this case, however, there were two reasons that the Lord Buddha refrained from partaking of the material gift, the almsfood that had been prepared." Comparable passage at MSV i.262.18–21.

36.335 Of the dozens of places in these stories where ***pūrvavad yāvat***, inserted in the text, signals that a passage has been abbreviated, this was one of the very few I have been unable to fill in.

36.336 **Transgression:** More specifically, a transgression that, if not confessed and expiated, would cause him to fall into an evil rebirth.

36.337 **Udáyin** is generally portrayed as foremost of all the Buddha's disciples in his knowledge of—and, by implication, adherence to—the Vinaya (monastic code).

36.340 **As before** *(pūrvavat)* refers to an earlier section of the Vinaya, which I have thus far not identified.

INDEX

INDEX

Sanskrit words are given according to the accented CSL pronuncuation aid in the English alphabetical order. They are followed by the conventional diacritics in brackets.

Permitted finals: (*Except* āḥ/aḥ)

k	ṭ	t	p	ṅ	n	m	ḥ/r	āḥ	aḥ	*Initial letters:*
k	ṭ	t	p	ṅ	n	ṃ	ḥ	āḥ	aḥ	k/kh
g	ḍ	d	b	ṅ	n	ṃ	r	ā	o	g/gh
k	ṭ	c	p	ṅ	ṃś	ṃ	ś	āś	aś	c/ch
g	ḍ	j	b	ṅ	ñ	ṃ	r	ā	o	j/jh
k	ṭ	ṭ	p	ṅ	ṃṣ	ṃ	ṣ	āṣ	aṣ	ṭ/ṭh
g	ḍ	ḍ	b	ṅ	ṇ	ṃ	r	ā	o	ḍ/ḍh
k	ṭ	t	p	ṅ	ṃs	ṃ	s	ās	as	t/th
g	ḍ	d	b	ṅ	n	ṃ	r	ā	o	d/dh
k	ṭ	t	p	ṅ	n	ṃ	ḥ	ā	aḥ	p/ph
g	ḍ	d	b	ṅ	n	ṃ	r	ā	o	b/bh
ṅ	ṇ	n	m	ṅ	n	ṃ	r	ā	o	*nasals* (n/m)
g	ḍ	d	b	ṅ	n	ṃ	r	ā	o	y/v
g	ḍ	d	b	ṅ	n	ṃ	*zero*[1]	ā	o	r
g	ḍ	l	b	ṅ	l̃[2]	ṃ	r	ā	o	l
k	ṭ	c ch	p	ṅ	ñ ś/ch	ṃ	ḥ	āḥ	aḥ	ś
k	ṭ	t	p	ṅ	n	ṃ	ḥ	āḥ	aḥ	ṣ/s
gg h	ḍḍ h	dd h	bb h	ṅ	n	ṃ	r	ā	o	h
g	ḍ	d	b	ṅ/ṅṅ[3]	n/nn[3]	m	r	ā	a[4]	*vowels*
k	ṭ	t	p	ṅ	n	m	ḥ	āḥ	āḥ	*zero*

[1]ḥ or r disappears, and if a/i/u precedes, this lengthens to ā/ī/ū. [2]e.g. tān+lokān=tāl̃ lokān.
[3]The doubling occurs if the preceding vowel is short. [4]Except: aḥ+a=o '.